DEEP COMEDY

CURATED BY DAN GRAHAM WITH SYLVIA CHIVARATANOND

JOHN BALDESSARI   FISCHLI & WEISS
ISA GENZKEN   JEF GEYS   RODNEY GRAHAM
CHRISTIAN JANKOWSKI   JULIA SCHER
ROMAN SIGNER   MICHAEL SMITH & JOSHUA WHITE
WILLIAM WEGMAN   JOHN WESLEY
AND OTHERS

JUNE 25 — JULY 30

MARIAN GOODMAN GALLERY

24 WEST 57TH STREET NEW YORK, NY 10019
TEL: 212-977-7160 FAX: 212-581-5187 WWW.MARIANGOODMAN.COM

Louise Bourgeois (signature)

HAUSER & WIRTH ZÜRICH

LOUISE BOURGEOIS
LA RIVIÈRE GENTILLE

1 JUNE — 26 JULY 2008

LIMMATSTRASSE 270
8005 ZÜRICH
+41 (0) 44 446 80 50

HAUSER & WIRTH LONDON

Hans Josephsohn

28 MAY — 26 JULY 2008

196A PICCADILLY
LONDON W1J 9DY
+44 (0) 20 7287 2300

IT'S NOT YOUR FAULT

Art from Iceland

June 28 – August 8, 2008

Birgir Andrésson
Hrafnhildur Arnardóttir
Ásmundur Ásmundsson
Ásdís Sif Gunnarsdóttir
Unnar Örn Audarason Jónasson
Haraldur Jónsson

Ragnar Kjartansson
Katrín Sigurdardóttir
Magnús Sigurdarson

CURATED BY

Markus Thor Andresson
and Ragnar Kjartansson

LUHRING AUGUSTINE   531 WEST 24TH STREET I NEW YORK, NY 10011 TEL 212 206 9100 I LUHRINGAUGUSTINE.COM

Richard Prince
Four Blue Cowboys

June 20 – August 8, 2008

Gagosian Gallery, 16 Via Francesco Crispi, Rome 00187
T. 39 06 4208 6498, www.gagosian.com

MODERN ART OXFORD

30 Pembroke Street, Oxford OX1 1BP
Tel +44 (0)1865 722733

www.modernartoxford.org.uk

FREE ADMISSION

14 June – 31 August 2008

GARY HUME: DOOR PAINTINGS
encounters VICTOR ALIMPIEV

marlene dumas measuring your own grave

JUNE 22–SEPT 22, 2008 | MOCA GRAND AVENUE

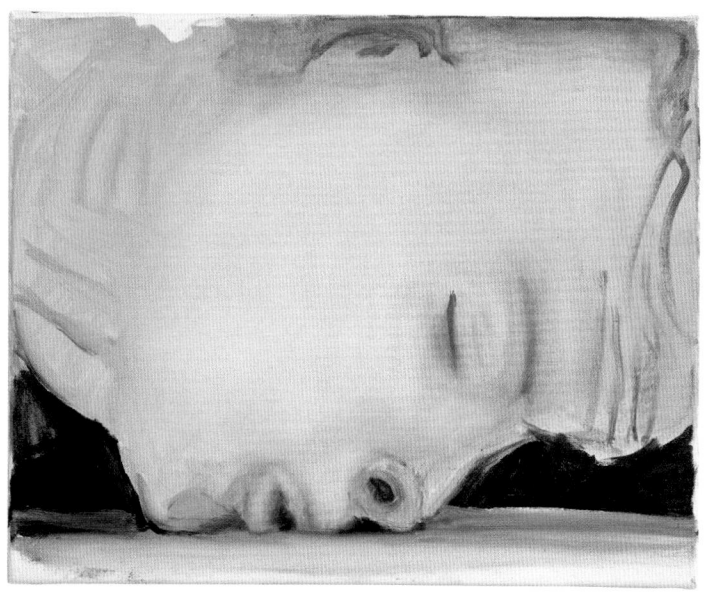

The Kiss, 2003, oil on canvas, 15 ¾ x 19 ¹¹/₁₆ in., © 2008 Marlene Dumas

THIRTY YEARS OF DRAWINGS AND PAINTINGS

Marlene Dumas: Measuring Your Own Grave is organized by The Museum of Contemporary Art, Los Angeles (MOCA) in association with The Museum of Modern Art, New York (MoMA). The exhibition debuts at MOCA (June 22–September 22, 2008) and travels to MoMA (December 14, 2008–February 16, 2009) and The Menil Collection, Houston (March 26–June 21, 2009).

MOCA's presentation is made possible by generous support from Brenda R. Potter and Michael C. Sandler; Mondriaan Foundation, Amsterdam; Blake Byrne; Mark Fisch; Steve Martin; The MOCA Contemporaries; the Barbara Lee Family Foundation; the Robert Lehman Foundation; the Pasadena Art Alliance; Elizabeth A. Sackler, JCF, Museum Educational Trust; Jack and Connie Tilton; Netherland-America Foundation; Linda and Jerry Janger; Dr. S. Sanford Kornblum and Mrs. Charlene S. Kornblum; B. J. Russell Mylne; and Jerome and Ellen Stern.

Ovation TV is the Official Network Partner of MOCA.

Marlene Dumas is represented by Galerie Paul Andriesse, Amsterdam; Frith Street Gallery, London; Gallery Koyanagi, Tokyo; Zeno X Gallery, Antwerp; and David Zwirner, New York.

MOCA
250 SOUTH GRAND AVENUE, LOS ANGELES, CA 90012
THE MUSEUM OF CONTEMPORARY ART, LOS ANGELES

moca.org

Roy Arden
Mike Disfarmer
Mari Eastman
Thomas Eggerer
Kirsten Everberg
Paul Graham
Rodney Graham

Curated by Russell Ferguson   26 JUNE – 15 AUGUST 2008

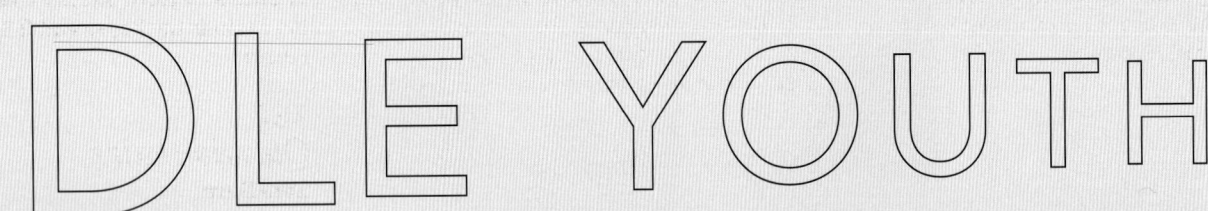

IDLE YOUTH

Jonathan Hernandez
Larry Johnson
Nathan Mabry
Catherine Opie
Michael Queenland
George Shaw
Kerry Tribe
Martin Wong

GLADSTONE GALLERY

515 West 24 Street New York NY 10001

212 206 9300 gladstonegallery.com

Summer 2008

Courtesy: Galerie Urs Meile, Beijing/Lucerne

Ai Weiwei and Serge Spitzer
Ghost Gu Coming Down the Mountain
(detail)
2005
Porcelain
Dimensions variable

Chantal Joffe

24 June - 2 August 2008

Victoria Miro 16

www.victoria-miro.com

Front

Back

Front cover:
Ryan Gander
Didactease Expanded
2006
Offset print
42×30 cm
Courtesy: STORE, London, Annet
Gelink Gallery, Amsterdam, and
Tanya Bonakdar, New York

frieze.com

Current Issue
Find out more online about features
in this issue:
American Beauty music videos by Madonna
Fever Pitch excerpts from *Substitute* (2006)
and *Fußball wie noch nie* (1971)
Music MP3 from *Black Stars*
Events audio recording of *Stifter's Dinge*
Life in Film excerpts from Raqs Media
Collective's favourite films
Time and Space Monika Sosnowska's
Schaulager exhibition
Doors of Perception Loris Gréaud's video
Bucky (2007)
Travels with an artist exclusive video for
frieze by Danh Vo

Current Shows
More exhibition reviews from London, Paris, Berlin,
Los Angeles, Lisbon, Glasgow, Bangkok, New York,
Tokyo, Oslo and Auckland, including:
Boris Groys by Dan Kidner
Amy Granat & Emily Sundblad by Joanna Fiduccia
Dan Attoe by Jörn Ebner
Sigalit Landau by Katie Kitamura
Paul Winstanley by Louise Menzies
Armen Eloyan & Roman Wolgin by Burkhard
Meltzer

Comment
Join in the discussion with the latest opinion and
debate from *frieze* editors and regular writers.
Ronald Jones explores the controversy of Guillermo
Vargas' dead dog
Mark Fisher looks at hauntology
Jennifer Kabat on the history of the recycling logo
Nick Currie on the 1980s TV series *Shock of the New*

Olafur Eliasson

THE
NEW YORK CITY
WATERFALLS

SUMMER 2008

PRESENTED BY
Public Art Fund

IN COLLABORATION WITH
**THE CITY OF
NEW YORK**

IN PARTNERSHIP WITH

TISHMAN

CIRCLE LINE
DOWNTOWN

MADE POSSIBLE IN PART BY

LMDC
Lower Manhattan
Development Corporation

U.S. DEPARTMENT OF HOUSING
AND URBAN DEVELOPMENT

www.nycwaterfalls.org

What is missing? What has eluded us? If we are to believe that Noah was the first obsessive collector (he wanted *two* of everything), are we also to swallow the idea that there were no gaps in the living archive of what was important and what wasn't? In the rush to collect the world in order to save it, what wonders were lost to indifference?

The recent 'Archive Fever' exhibition at the International Center for Photography in New York, curated by Okwui Enwezor, included Zoe Leonard's *Fae Richards Photo Archive* (1993–6), a collection of sepia-toned photographs, dog-eared publicity shots and film stills chronicling the life of an African-American Hollywood actress who sank into oblivion and, as it turns out, never actually existed. Why are we so willing to believe the account of her disappearance from our collective cultural memory even after this fabricated fiction is revealed? Perhaps in the American story of celebrity, race and artistic self-invention she is considered an acceptable loss either way. In the same exhibition Hans-Peter Feldmann's collection of front pages from newspapers on 12 September 2001, displayed without comment, reveals how the seemingly transparent process of recording can eclipse actual experience and draw a veil across personal memory. What remain are our vivid recollections, out-sourced to the mass media, dulled by repetition and the collateral damage of subsequent events.

I recently made a pilgrimage to Upper Manhattan, to the all but forgotten Hispanic Society of America at the Beaux-Arts Audubon Terrace, the most important cultural complex in New York that remains invisible to most Gothamites. Appropriately it was in this splendid eddy of once majestic institutions that the currently homeless Dia Art Foundation squirrelled away a contemporary art installation that contained no contemporary art: Francis Alÿs' collection of over 300 portraits of the obscure fourth-century saint Fabiola. Here Alÿs proffered the devotional fruits of a little-known pictorial cult, culled from flea markets, attics and junk shops in Europe and Mexico over a period of 15 years, hung salon-style in the dark interior. The images, mostly anonymous and produced by amateurs, are copies of copies of copies of copies, based on a 19th-century painting by a French academician that was itself a replica of some lost 'original'. Talent and technical skill have little to do with these pictures, which tell us next to nothing about their long-gone subject but which – executed in a range of media, from oils and watercolours to embroidery, beads, beans, rice, glass and mosaic tiles – speak volumes about the people who felt compelled to make them.

Alÿs couldn't have found a better setting for his treasury of the anonymous paying homage to the ignored. Audubon Terrace was built in 1906 in semi-rural uptown Manhattan as a sweeping acropolis of museums and cultural institutions in anticipation of a *belle époque* City Beautiful that never arrived. It was to be the Lincoln Center of its day, built for the edification of generations of New Yorkers, but after the subway lines were laid under Broadway, the area became an outlying district for tides of immigrant population. In the 1980s it was known for its crack-dealing and gangland gun-play. Today it's a culturally diverse working-class neighbourhood, home to Dominicans, Puerto Ricans, Mexicans and others with roots across Latin America.

Of the original five institutions, only two remain. The American Academy of Arts and Letters began with dreams of fostering a new Athens on the Hudson, with high-minded rhetoric holding up its lintels, friezes and architraves, and quotations from John Milton and Ralph Waldo Emerson on every available surface; but as a centre of artistic vanguardism it sank into inconsequence. The other main institution, the Hispanic Society – a gem of a museum with its prized Goyas, Velázquezes and El Grecos – also gently withdrew into itself for the long, lingering twilight.

One by one all the other institutions either moved or vanished – the American Geographical Society pulled up stakes, soon followed by the Museum of the American Indian. The old brass plaque listing the resident museums is a study in erasure, the name of each deserter sequentially blotted out with different shades of black paint. The entire decaying complex of buildings is a set of lists that no one consults or questions, texts accruing meanings unforeseen by those who carved them. No one knew in 1906 that one hundred years hence, descendents of both the conquerors and conquered of Latin America would daily pass these wrap-around rosters of cultural subjugation and genocide on their way to the subway: the Zapotec, Carib, Arawak, Tupi, Yahgan, Aymara and others blithely immortalized alongside those who participated in their wholesale extirpation, Coronado, De Soto, Balboa, Da Gama.

Just south is the overgrown expanse of Trinity Church Cemetery, built on the site of John James Audubon's family estate. Here the famed artist-naturalist retired to spend his final years maintaining a menagerie of creatures that he would observe and, on occasion, throttle and drag back to his study to dissect, index and illustrate. Now on the same ground generations of New Yorkers resident six feet under are similarly indexed, a pot-pourri of once happy-go-lucky nabobs and notables (a prostitute-turned-socialite, a scandal-plagued mayor, an Astor who gallantly went down with the *Titanic*) alongside mill workers, clerks, shopkeepers – all mouldering away democratically neglected and unvisited. These grounds seem unusually devoted to the oblivion of collecting and naming, to dreaming and forgetting, to grand gestures and the fading away of aspirations: *sic transit gloria mundi*.

Audubon, who moved to New York to study its prodigious variety of rats, is buried here too, under a cenotaph festooned with taxonomical reliefs of birds and mammals – zoology as epitaph. In almost Whitmanesque fashion the man is revealed through the tools of his trade (depicted in stone around the base are a flintlock rifle, a powder horn, specimen basket, palette, brush and pens) and by what small part of the world he managed to save from oblivion. As the economy slumps and previously certain values are questioned, take a minute to consider the overlooked, the irrelevant and underappreciated, to reconcile yourself to everything that is already falling through the cracks, to overreaching dreams, to plans half-baked and glorious futures unrealized. Here's to the obscure lacks we'll never know: to the missing, the lost, the forgotten, the dead.

James Trainor is US editor of frieze.

Finding Time

A celebration of the over-looked, the under-appreciated and the disappeared
by James Trainor

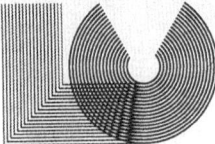

Luton University
MA Curating Liminal Art Practices

Monty Panesar Centre for
Contemporary Art, Stopsley

PRESS RELEASE

The Best Lack All Conviction, While The Worst Are Full Of Passionate Intensity.

Annika A. Annika; Bruce Douche; Joos Jonckheere; Reece Peer; Daley Rowner.

10.06.08 – 11.07.08

The graduating class of Luton University's MA in Curating Liminal Art Practices are proud to present 'The Best Lack All Conviction, While The Worst Are Full Of Passionate Intensity', their end of course exhibition.

Purposefully spurning the conservative curatorial convention of adopting a 'theme', the 16 students have instead employed an acephalous methodology to bring together a group of emerging and historically neglected artists to pre- and re-contextualise their latent potentiality. Dialoguing the local and the global, the exhibition might be imagined as a set of nomadic subject positions in search of (temporary) refugee status. Following its opening at Luton University's Monty Panesar Centre for Contemporary Art, 'The Best Lack All Conviction…' will travel to Rough Beast Projects - an artist-run space in Bethlehem, Israel.

Entering the exhibition, visitors pass through a proscenium arch erected by the British artist **Reece Peer** (b.1976). Built from MDF and coated in the contents of the last surviving tin of Dulux Paints' discontinued 1987 shade 'Docklands Sunrise (Gloss)', its curvature apes the precise angle at which, in the opening credits of the BBC sitcom *Brush Strokes* (1986-91), the wise-cracking house painter protagonist, Jacko, swoops down to steal a crisp from a packet belonging to a pretty girl as she passes him in the street. Peer has said that 'For me, Jacko is a essentially a yBa, and this is my monument to him. Not that *I'm* a yBA, of course, or even one of that lot that came afterwards. Did I mention that I hadn't even started shaving when that 'Modern Medicine' show was on?'. During the exhibition's private view, the artist will read from his archive of early 1950s ration books, accompanied by his band, *Arise!*

An 'author function' created by an anonymous Quebecois collective in 2003, **Daley Rowner** is named after a popular brand of artists' sketchbook. While Rowner's contribution to the exhibition, a poster entitled *OUTLAW THE POLICE* (2003-8), appears to call for political action, closer inspection reveals that the work also bears the tiny, biro-ed inscription 'Are you sure? Personally, I quite like *Roxanne*, and that one where Sting mentions Nabokov isn't bad, either', creating a palimpsest in which agitprop is overwritten, but never entirely erased, by a mild interest in reggae-influenced pop.

In 1972, Swedish artist **Annika A. Annika** (b. 1946) announced that she was abandoning art to become a nit nurse for the Malmö area's primary schools - a role that she still occupies today. Recognizing Annika's practice as a vital precursor to much contemporary 'relational' or 'participatory' art, the curators of 'The Best Lack All Conviction…' traveled to Malmö to clandestinely film her working during a recent outbreak of head-lice. In addition to its presentation in the exhibition, this footage – which has been overdubbed with a soundtrack by the Swedish Black Metal group *Fear Hose* – will also be posted on the Department of Curating Liminal Art Practices' Facebook page.

Every day for the last two decades, Belgian artist **Joos Jonckheere** (b. 1958) has made a painting of a concrete step in front of a Bureau de Change in his native Ostend. A meditation on the implacable march of time, each of his rectangular, almost monochromatic canvases are also haunted by the ghost of a particular set of political events, and their impact on global money markets. Speaking in a recent interview about his most famous work, *11.09* (2001), Jonckheere recalled: 'That day, I found a candy wrapper on the step. No problem. I picked it up, and got on with the job'.

A key figure in Williamsburg art circles, **Bruce Douche** (b. 1981) has appeared over 20 times in artforum.com's social diary, 'Scene and Herd'. Known for his candid photographs of hip young artists at work and play, in 'The Best Lack All Conviction…' he presents his series *Dude, wake up! Seriously, wake the fuck up!* (2007), in which we see Douche and his friends score poor quality drugs, wrestle a homeless man for coins, and plan a 'panty raid' on a dinner in honour of Barbara Kruger.

'The Best Lack All Conviction, While The Worst Are Full Of Passionate Intensity' is accompanied by an exhibition catalogue, with an essay by Tom Morton.

For more information / images, please contact: press@luton.ac.uk

frieze

Publishing Directors
Matthew Slotover
Amanda Sharp

Editors
Jennifer Higgie *jennifer@frieze.com*
Jörg Heiser *joerg@frieze.com*

Associate Editor
Dan Fox *dan@frieze.com*

US Editor
James Trainor *james.trainor@frieze.com*

Publisher
Anna Starling

Design Consultant
Paul Barnes

Art Direction
Claudia Schenk

Design
Simon Josebury

Assistant Editors
Christy Lange
Jonathan Griffin

Website Editor
Sam Thorne

Editor at Large
Polly Staple

Contributing Editors
Dominic Eichler
Tom Morton
Jan Verwoert

Design Editor
Eugenia Bell

Subeditors
Matthew Taylor
Rosalind Furness

Picture Researcher
Faye Dowling

Head of Communications
Camilla Nicholls

Senior Marketing & Circulation Manager
Claire Hewitt

Communications & Distribution Assistant
Nicola Harvey

Advertising & Subscriptions Administrator
Sarah Hillier

Accounts *accounts@frieze.com*
Ravinder Gill
Josh O'Connor
Marsha Temple

London Intern
Sascha Hurrell

Advertising Representatives
Marisa Futernick (London office)
(UK, Ireland, Australasia, Greece, Italy,
Portugal and Spain)
tel +44 20 7833 7272 *marisa@frieze.com*

Mareike Dittmer (Berlin office)
(Rest of Europe, Middle East and Africa)
tel +49 30 2362 6504 *mareike@frieze.com*

Molly McIver (New York office)
(US, Canada, Central and South America)
tel +1 718 965 1755 *molly@frieze.com*

frieze
3-4 Hardwick Street, London EC1R 4RB, UK
tel +44 20 7833 7270
fax +44 20 7833 7271
editors@frieze.com
www.frieze.com

US office
P.O. Box 231448, New York, NY 10023, USA
tel +1 718 965 1755
fax +1 646 328 3181

Berlin office
Fehrbelliner Str. 32, 10119 Berlin, Germany
tel +49 30 2809 2760
fax +49 30 2362 6505
berlin@frieze.com

frieze magazine is printed in England and published eight times a year by Durian Publications Ltd. Unsolicited material cannot be returned, though all correspondence receives attention. The views expressed in *frieze* are not necessarily those of the publishers.

© 2008 ISSN No. 0962 0672. Unauthorised reproduction of any material strictly a no-no.

Subscriptions:
Please call +44 (0) 870 458 4403
or subscribe online at www.frieze.com

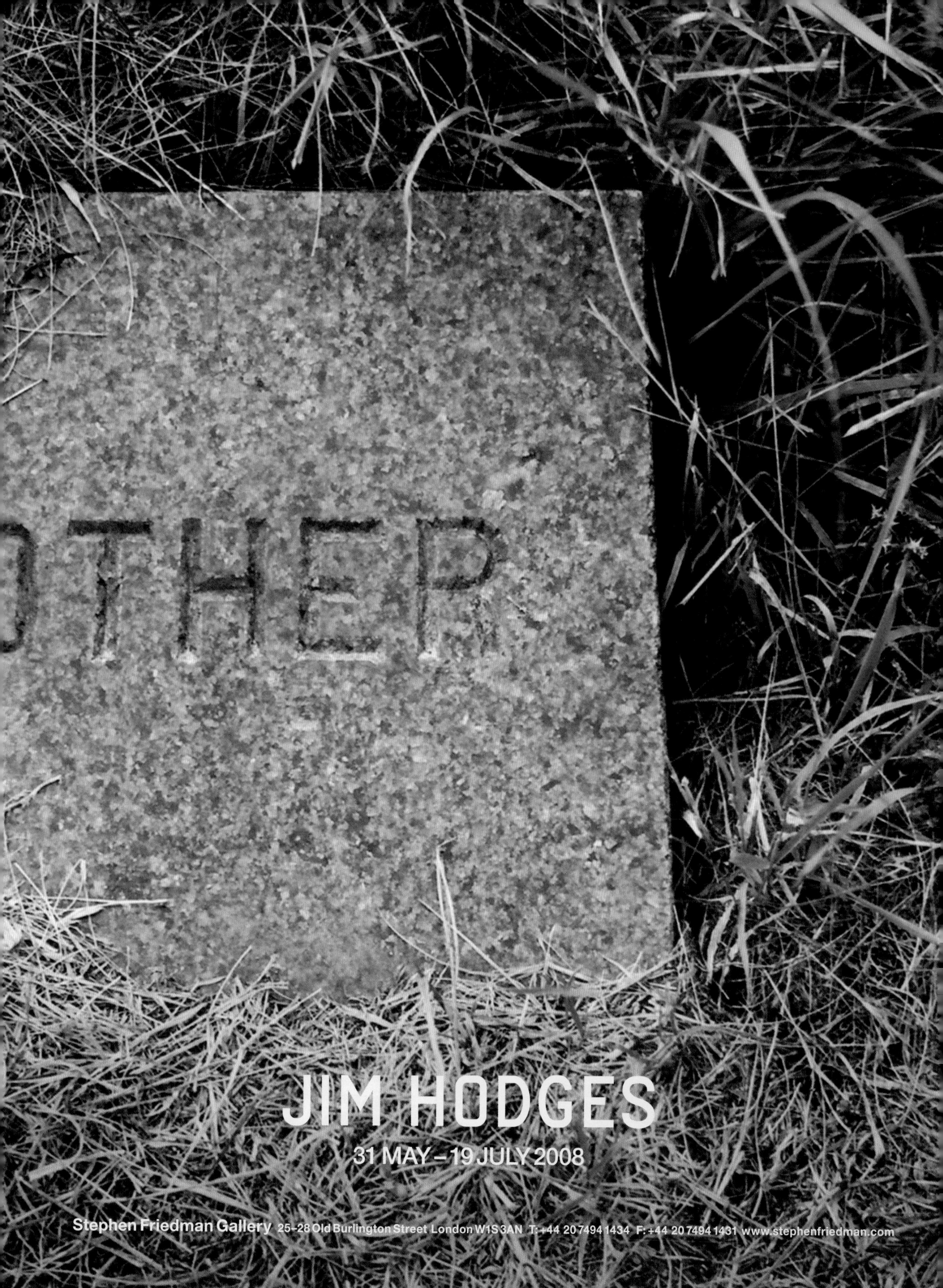

JIM HODGES

31 MAY – 19 JULY 2008

Stephen Friedman Gallery 25–28 Old Burlington Street London W1S 3AN T: +44 20 7494 1434 F: +44 20 7494 1431 www.stephenfriedman.com

CREAM

Milton Keynes Th...
Registered Charity No. ...

Flora & Fauna
28 June – 21 September 2008

Keynes Gallery

English Partnerships
The National Regeneration Agency

Admission Free
900 Midsummer Blvd
Central Milton Keynes, MK8 3QA
01908 676 900 www.mk-g.org

ARTS COUNCIL ENGLAND

Milton Keynes Gallery

English Partnersh...
The National Regeneration Agenc...

& Fauna
September 2008

Richard Woods

Flora & Fauna
28 June – 21 September 2008

MILTON KEYNES
COUNCIL

Flora & F
28 June – 21 Septe

Phase 1 of a complementary collaborative
project for Fermynwoods Contemporary Art is
available to view from 19 June – 7 September
2008. Phase 2 from October 2008. Visit
www.fermynwoods.co.uk for further details.

Milton Keynes Theatre & Gallery
Registered Charity No. 1059678

UNIVERSITY OF W...

Milton Keynes

fermynwoods
more than a gallery

Admission Free
900 Midsummer Blvd
Central Milton Keynes, MK8 3QA
01908 676 900 www.mk-g.org

Richar

THE MILTON KEYNES GALLERY IS SUPPORTED BY ARTS COUNCIL ENGLAND,
...LTON KEYNES THEATRE GROUP COMPANY, ENGLISH PARTNERSHIPS
...D THE MILTON KEYNES COUNCIL
...TERIOR COMMISSION SUPPORTED BY THE ABBEY HARRIS MURAL FUND

...LTON KEYNES

ARTS COUNCIL ENGLAND

CATHY WILKES

June 21–July 19, 2008
Preview June 20, 7–9pm

The Modern Institute · Floor 1 Suite 6, 73 Robertson Street, Glasgow G2 8QD, United Kingdom · Tel +44 141 248 3711 / Fax +44 141 2483 3280
www.themoderninstitute.com / mail@themoderninstitute.com · Gallery hours Monday–Friday 10am–5pm, Saturday 12 noon–5pm

THE MODERN INSTITUTE

WHOLE LOTTA LOVE

YOU'RE JUST TOO GOOD TO BE TRUE

JUNE 21 – AUGUST 16, 2008

CONTEMPORARY FINE ARTS

WWW.CFA-BERLIN.COM

Let's just call it misconceptualism. You know it when you see it, and you see it everywhere in art exhibitions, at art fairs and – first alert! – in art academies, where it incubates like a low-grade infection in the hidden recesses of seminar rooms, nourishing itself on inarticulate obscurities fostered by the 'strong' misreading and/or helpless misunderstanding of critical discourse. It is idea art without an idea, identity art without an identity, the 'Oh wow!' school of 1960s' philosophy and politics updated for the 2000s, the spawn of bone-headedness and the *bon mot*. Misconceptualism is the zone where narrow minds go to escape self-induced claustrophobia only to find the abyss. It is a 'counterculture' of deeply insecure, often resentful, all too often petulant scholastics, and, as a result of an ever-growing labour force of underemployed or 'lumpen' theorists, its apologists and enablers outnumber its practitioners.

But this column will not be devoted to a general complaint. Rather, my purpose in making it at the outset is to set the stage for celebrating in inverse proportion two artists who vindicate Conceptualism and its offshoots at a time when that tradition is widely travestied or trivialized by wannabes: two artists whose work shows how far the ramifications of having a substantial but protean idea and a hard-won but mutable identity can go, as well as how far work thus grounded can take a thoughtful and observant public.

As it happened, their retrospectives were simultaneously on view at the Whitney Museum last winter, neatly drawing the comparison for elevator-riding museum-goers who made their way up or down the building floor by floor. (Who says the psycho-geographic equivalence between our cultural institutions and department stores is all bad?) Of the two, Lawrence Weiner was

the old master. And of the two his exhibition rates as one of the most beautiful New York has seen in recent years, owing to its combined openness, spareness and fullness. For Weiner, text is image in a double sense; his elliptical phrasings and shifting punctuation gently nudge propositional prose towards matter-of-fact poetry even as exquisitely plain but visually arresting typography converts word into graphic pictures that concretize thought while transcending logic. Example: 'LAID OUT FLAT/BENT [NOW] THIS WAY/TURNED [NOW] THAT WAY/in effect LOOPED OVER.' This is language as relational sculpture. Example: 'MANY COLORED OBJECTS PLACED SIDE BY SIDE TO FORM A ROW OF MANY COLORED OBJECTS.' This is language as still life, with the subtle ambiguity of whether 'many' modifies 'colored' or 'objects' triggering multiple variants in the mind's eye. Weiner, of course, was a founding father of Conceptual art, and these slippages are characteristic of its cryptic phases – one finds them in Bruce Nauman too – but nowhere outside Weiner's work does one experience the emancipation of sound, sense and sight more fully. To look back on his career is thus to reread the fragments that set language free – free to notice, to wonder, to marvel at its own plasticity and polyvalence.

The younger half of the Whitney pair was Kara Walker. She too has sought to liberate signs and symbols from bondage, but in her case, as has been typical of her historically sceptical Postmodern generation, linguistic play involves etymological back-checking and cross-referencing as much as it does semantic inversion and formal reversal. While text is image for Weiner, for Walker images are texts – texts waiting to be reconfigured and rewritten or commented on by other texts. Of course, the chains that bind them to their

Lawrence Weiner: 'As Far as the Eye can See' (left) and Kara Walker: 'My Complement, My Enemy, My Oppressor, My Love' (right) at the Whitney Museum of American Art, New York 2007

original meanings are the unspoken attitudes that readers bring to Walker's narratives, attitudes she explodes in the face of the viewer/reader like the firecracker cigar that explodes in the minstrel show comic's cork-carboned visage. In this sardonic vein Walker's silhouetted tableaux are burlesque pantomimes of American racism that mock those who mock the 'Other'. Meanwhile her verbal vignettes seethe with bitter ironies that destabilize conventional thinking just as thoroughly as, but far more jarringly than, Weiner's laconic koans. Like him, she conjugates colours and objects but with 'a difference'. Unlike him, she conjures with coloured-ness and objectification. Example: 'MANY BLACK WOMEN ARE PHYSICALLY STRONG/MANY BLACK WOMEN HAVE ACTIVE, HEALTHY SEX DRIVES/MANY BLACK WOMEN ARE THE SOLE PROVIDERS IN THEIR FAMILIES/MANY BLACK WOMEN FACE DISCRIMINATION IN THE WORKPLACE.' Thus Walker blackens the white page of literary Modernism and marbles its white cube.

At the close of a long, contentious season one looks back with heightened appreciation at moments of intellectual and artistic clarity. In a period when the 'interrogation of the subject' so often descends into essentialism and solipsism one is grateful when questions addressed to the viewer acknowledge that both the viewer and the questioner are possessed of a complex consciousness. And in a context where 'misconceptualism' grabs headlines, causing the talkers to talk *ad nauseam*, one seeks dialogue that lends existential substance to weightless ideas. On all counts Weiner's and Walker's exhibitions were highlights of a murky year.

Robert Storr is a critic, curator and Dean of the Yale School of Art.

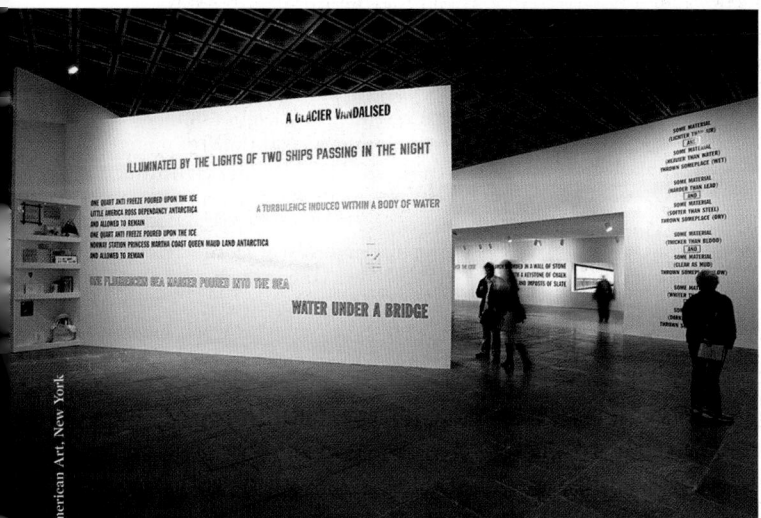

Courtesy: Whitney Museum of American Art, New York

Art and Text
Two vindications of Conceptualism and its offshoots
by Robert Storr

Power Play

When so much art is trumpeted as being 'political' why do so few artists enter politics? **by George Pendle**

'Are you involved in politics now? Leave that to the writers and to the ugly girls.'
Albert Camus, *Jonas, ou l'artiste au travail*, (Jonas, or The Artist at Work), 1957

The home page of Fiber Artists for Obama welcomes 'all Barack Obama supporters who quilt, sew, craft, crochet, knit or otherwise express themselves thru the fiber arts'. One of the many groups that can currently be found under the aegis of 'Artists for Obama', this is the latest attempt to attract artistic support for a political campaign. Traditionally such attempts have not been particularly successful. While musicians and actors are happy to endorse a presidential candidate, contemporary artists are generally notable by their absence from the political fray. So far the best-known name to be coaxed onto Obama's artist pages is Shepard Fairey, who is responsible for the 'OBEY Giant' campaign, which saw the monochrome portrait of the wrestler Andre the Giant spread unstoppably around the world. The picture's omnipresence, not to mention its obscurity, was a remarkably successful example of propaganda without a point. Now, however, Fairey has harnessed his skills to a different but no less strident imperative – 'change'. Incorporating Obama's much-used tagline into his work, he has produced a series of Federal Art Project-style prints that

portray the candidate in the colours of the American flag. Yet why is the final image somewhat uncomfortable? Is it the unfortunate lexical similarity between 'OBEY' and 'Obama'? Is it the recognition that political propaganda can be just as unappetizing when it is for the underdog as when it is for the overlord? Or is there something profoundly unnatural about an artist's unabashed involvement with politics?

It is 40 years since the fabled May demonstrations in Paris, the student sit-in at New York's Columbia University, the Tlatelolco Massacre in Mexico City and the brutal quashing of the Prague Spring by the Soviet Union. But while artists are quite happy to reference and romanticize these events in their work, it is hard to find an artist who has actually been driven to enter politics because of them. Why is it that, when so much art is trumpeted as being 'political', so few artists are interested in engaging directly in politics? Other creative fields have always contributed to the political ranks. Benjamin Disraeli was a popular novelist before he was Prime Minister of Great Britain, Ignacy Jan Paderewski was a renowned composer before he became Prime Minister of Poland, Thomas Jefferson an admired architect before becoming President of the USA. And it is not just in the distant past: the novelist Norman Mailer ran for mayor of New York in 1969, and the Brazilian singer–songwriter Gilberto Gil has been his

Shepard Fairey's *Progress* poster featuring Barack Obama 2008

country's culture minister since 2003. In India being a Bollywood star is a well-established stepping-stone to public office. Yet the visual arts have provided fewer politicians of national standing than either wrestling (which can boast Jesse 'The Body' Ventura, Governor of Minnesota) or pornography (Ilona 'La Cicciolina' Staller, parliamentary representative for Lazio). Are artists too unruly a breed to be trusted with the flame of civic authority? Or is it that they are aware that the gross egotism of art production could cause untold trouble if given free rein? The precedent of Adolf Hitler – twice refused entry to the Academy of Fine Arts in Vienna – may have permanently discouraged artists from seeking positions of power, not simply because of ethical concerns but because of the scale of his political (and aesthetic) successes. As Frederic Spotts states in his book *Hitler and the Power of Aesthetics* (2003): 'His dream was to create a culture state in which Germans were to listen to music he liked, attend operas he loved, see paintings and sculptures he collected, and admire the buildings he constructed.' What artist today could possibly succeed in such a multi-disciplinary task?

In 1978 the dissident playwright and future President of the Czech Republic, Václav Havel, wrote an essay entitled 'The Power of the Powerless', in which he stated that artists' desire to live 'within the truth' would forever thrust them into an involvement in politics. In 2006 Orhan Pamuk, the Turkish writer and Nobel laureate, who was arrested for 'insulting' the Turkish government, seemed to refute this dictum. He declared that artists are inherently bad politicians because they are unable to acquiesce in public opinion. 'Art and citizenship are not necessarily compatible. Good citizens do not make good artists most of the time. Bad citizens produce good artists; artists tend to be egoists and are more successful when they care only about their art and ignore the other citizens.'

Yet these two seemingly opposite viewpoints are perhaps more similar than one would think. In Albert Camus' short story 'Jonas, ou l'artiste au travail' (Jonas, or The Artist at Work, 1957) a young painter becomes the subject of vast popular and critical acclaim. His studio overflows with visitors, and demands on his time begin to pile up. The more life intrudes upon his work, however, the less accomplished he becomes, and in an attempt to recapture his former brilliance he builds a dark loft in his house and locks himself in it. When he eventually falls ill after months of seclusion, a friend climbs up into the loft to see what he has been working on. The only sign of any work is a blank canvas with one word scrawled in its middle. However, the friend cannot tell whether it reads *'solitaire'* or *'solidaire'*.

George Pendle's official biography of death, Death: A Life, *will be published by Three Rivers Press in October 2008.*

WOLFGANG TILLMANS 28 May – 13 July 2008
MAUREEN PALEY. 21 Herald Street, London E2 6JT *telephone:* + 44 (0)20 7729 4112 *fax:* + 44 (0)20 7729 4113 www.maureenpaley.com

JUNE 1 TO AUGUST 2, 2008

UGO RONDINONE

JUNE 1 TO AUGUST 2, 2008

DOUG AITKEN

GALERIE EVA PRESENHUBER

WWW.PRESENHUBER.COM
TEL: +41 (0) 43 444 70 50 / FAX: +41 (0) 43 444 70 60
LIMMATSTRASSE 270, P.O.BOX 1517, CH–8031 ZURICH
GALLERY HOURS: TUE-FR 12-6, SA 11-5

DOUG AITKEN, EMMANUELLE ANTILLE, MONIKA BAER, MARTIN BOYCE, ANGELA BULLOCH, VALENTIN CARRON, VERNE DAWSON, TRISHA DONNELLY, MARIA EICHHORN, URS FISCHER, PETER FISCHLI/DAVID WEISS, SYLVIE FLEURY, LIAM GILLICK, DOUGLAS GORDON, MARK HANDFORTH, CANDIDA HÖFER, KAREN KILIMNIK, ANDREW LORD, HUGO MARKL, RICHARD PRINCE, GERWALD ROCKENSCHAUB, TIM ROLLINS AND K.O.S., UGO RONDINONE, DIETER ROTH, EVA ROTHSCHILD, JEAN-FRÉDÉRIC SCHNYDER, STEVEN SHEARER, JOSH SMITH, BEAT STREULI, FRANZ WEST, SUE WILLIAMS

At the 5th Berlin Biennial, I could hear more than a few snickers in the audience watching Lars Laumann's *Berlinmuren* (Berlin Wall, 2008), a documentary about a Swedish woman's love affair with the Berlin Wall. It is amusing to imagine a woman falling in love with 156 kilometres of brick and reinforced concrete. She describes herself as 'objectum-sexual': emotionally and sexually attracted to objects. She was so infatuated, in fact, that in a semi-public ceremony in 1979 she 'married' the wall and became Mrs Eija-Riitta Berliner-Mauer, adopting the German name of her new 'husband'; she was devastated when he was fatally assaulted in November 1989. Goethe would have sympathized. 'To see an inanimate object being punished is in and of itself something truly terrible,' wrote the young poet, after witnessing a public book-burning in Frankfurt.

Apart from the snickers, there were also some serious faces illuminated by the glowing screen. After all, doesn't Mrs Berlin-Wall reflect some part of us? Aren't we all art lovers, and thus object lovers? Don't try to avoid the question with some argument about the 'dematerialization of the art object' because we are encouraged to love all art – and as much art as possible. Museums are always asking us to become 'Friends' with their collections; you know what comes next: adopting an art work. Beyond the institutions, there are the individual symptoms: buying a postcard of a favourite work or getting the catalogue to take home. That's more commitment than a one-night stand! Inevitably, you can't help but get all your friends involved: have you seen X? What do you think about X? What are other people saying about X? Next thing you know, you are flying across continents to see X again, maybe acquire X and then put X in your house forever!

Of course, that's not love, that's just … object co-habitation / fixation / obsession / commodity fetishism / animism / state-sponsored polygamy? Most art lovers go further than Mrs Berlin-Wall, since she never relocated to Germany from her Swedish hometown, being content to love her husband from afar; nor did she commission architects to build a foundation, let alone appeal for money to fund it (though she does run a little private museum of miniature models of walls, fences, bridges and guillotines). Many would like to believe that they love art works because they are extensions of their human creators, as if the two were interchangeable. But that's not true either. 'We knew we were serious collectors', Erika Hoffmann and her husband, the late Rolf Hoffmann, once told me, 'when we were no longer interested in meeting artists.'

Yet devotion to art has long been purged of sexuality and religiosity, as if a passion for objects might be objective and secular. As far back as 1688, French essayist Jean de la Bruyère ridiculed curious collectors for their

Objects of Desire

The devotional aspects of looking at art **by Jennifer Allen**

excessive attachments. A century later in Germany, *Kunstkenner* (art knowers) opposed their knowledge to the emotional swoons of *Kunstliebhaber* (art lovers). Yet another century later, the Stendhal syndrome effectively defined art loving as a pathology. If loving art didn't make you sick, it would make you inept. Consider the degradation of 'amateur' – from the Latin verb 'to love' – from a compliment to a slight.

In light of such tyranny, thank goodness for Mrs Berlin-Wall. Finally, I, too, can reveal the biggest love of my life: Wim Delvoye's *Cloaca* (2000). When I read about the machine that ate food and produced shit, I thought: 'That's extreme.' But something more extreme happened when I came face to face with *Cloaca*, shortly before the opening of the group show 'A Baroque Party' at the Vienna Kunsthalle in 2001. Delvoye and I sauntered into the exhibition hall, which was devoid of visitors except for a bacteria expert, a computer man and a technician fussing with *Cloaca*. (Caretakers, followers or handlers?) Right away, I knew *Cloaca* was important.

Taking a closer look, I could see why. The glass jars, connected to one another like robotic intestines, made the whole process of digestion visible, from nutrition to waste. You've got to admire someone who lets it all hang out like that. The shit, delivered on a rotating conveyor

Jennifer Allen feeding Wim Delvoye's *Cloaca* (2000)
2001

belt, didn't really smell, although Delvoye told me that live bacteria made *Cloaca* an official public health hazard. Suddenly, a guard appeared with lunch: salad and spaghetti, fresh from the museum restaurant. Climbing up *Cloaca*'s staircase with the food and a jug of water, we slowly fed the art work's steely mouth: a garborator, placed on a high platform to exploit gravity, just as the mouth does to swallow. I've never had so much fun on a double date. *Cloaca* was as precise as a machine yet as unrefined as a klutz. Echoing the fragility of life, if *Cloaca* didn't get fed every four hours, it would die, drowning in its own bacteria.

Today – seven years later – I recognize that gooey gaze of love on my face in the snapshots that Delvoye made of the feeding session: I look stupid and happy. I had found my object: a combination of smart shit, needy child, official culture and outsider. Indeed, I've been with lots of people but never with a museum piece *and* a health hazard rolled into one. Since then, the work and its offspring have been exhibited several times, but I could never bring myself to visit. The idea of seeing *Cloaca* without getting close, without eating together, was like catching a glimpse of an old lover across a dance hall without going for a spin on the floor.

Jennifer Allen is a writer living in Berlin.

MONIKA SPRÜTH PHILOMENE MAGERS LONDON

7A GRAFTON STREET · LONDON W1S 4EJ · UK
TEL +44.(0)207.4081613 · FAX +44.(0)207.4994531
LONDON@SPRUETHMAGERS.COM · WWW.SPRUETHMAGERS.COM

ROBERT ELFGEN

ANTRIEBSWELLE
MAY 13 – JUNE 19, 2008

ROBERT MORRIS

MORNING STAR EVENING STAR
JUNE 26 – AUGUST, 2008

MONIKA SPRÜTH PHILOMENE MAGERS COLOGNE

WORMSER STRASSE 23 · D-50677 COLOGNE
TEL +49.(0)221.380415/16 · FAX +49.(0)221.380417
ART@SPRUETHMAGERS.COM · WWW.SPRUETHMAGERS.COM

ROBERT ELFGEN

DES BIEN ICH
APRIL 16 – JULY 26, 2008

MONIKA SPRÜTH PHILOMENE MAGERS MUNICH

SCHELLINGSTRASSE 48 · D-80799 MUNICH
TEL +49.(0)89.33040600 · FAX +49.(0)89.397302
CONTACT@SPRUETHMAGERS.COM · WWW.SPRUETHMAGERS.COM

AXEL KASSEBÖHMER

NEUE ARBEITEN
MAY 29 – JULY 26, 2008

SPRÜTH MAGERS PROJEKTE

LUDWIGSTRASSE 7 · D-80539 MUNICH
TEL +49.(0)89.28890760 · FAX +49.(0)89.28890761
PROJEKTE@SPRUETHMAGERS.COM · WWW.SPRUETHMAGERSPROJEKTE.COM

MARTIN WÖHRL

BLANKO
JUNE 18 – JULY 26, 2008

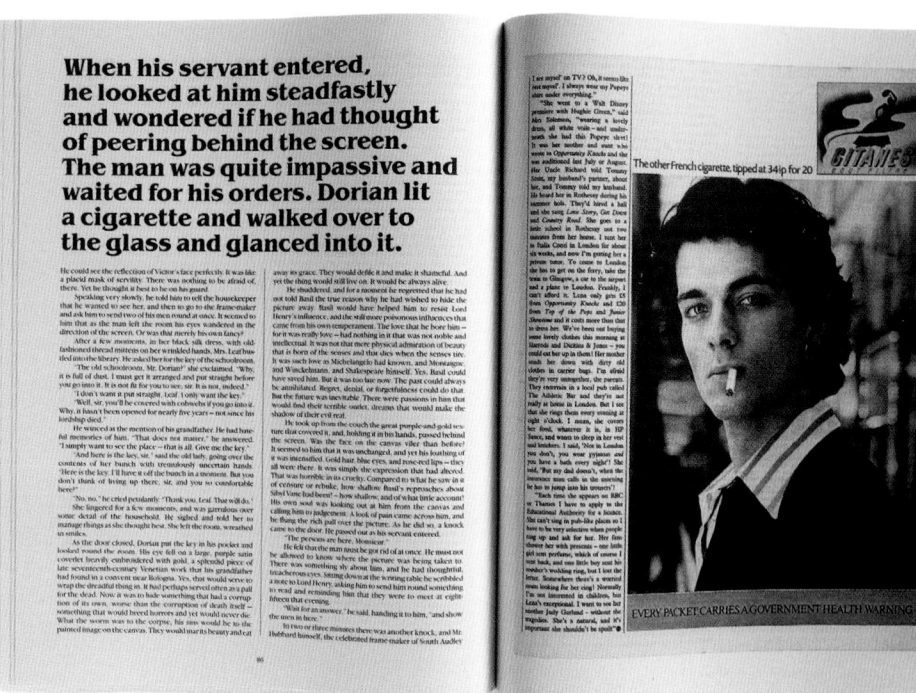

As evidenced by such recent ventures in artist-led publishing as the 'Familiars' list from Elinor Jansz and Richard Embray's Four Corners Books and Book Works' 'Fabrications' series, there is a developing interest in the idea that classic texts, 'lost' books or previously hard-to-find publications can be simultaneously revived, reassessed and repositioned as new editions created by artists. In this, a book or text is both being made newly available and, equally importantly, being entered into what might be described as a process of print re-enactment: a renewed engagement with the history of a work, in which the processes of publishing as much as the text itself – its authorship, context and editorial ancestry – become both media for new art-making and venues for cultural historical inquiry.

The 'Familiars' series, which commenced last autumn with an acclaimed new edition of Oscar Wilde's *The Picture of Dorian Gray* (1890), designed by John Morgan to a concept and art work by Gareth Jones, is a bravura example of how an iconic book might be re-enacted. Returning, on the one hand, to the publishing history of Wilde's novel, which first appeared in print on 20 June 1890, as pages 3–100 of *Lippincott's Monthly Magazine*, the 'Familiars' edition restored the book to its physical form as a large-format, magazine-style publication. The pages turn over with languid ease, as though to the neat flick of a doubtlessly yellow-gloved hand. The phrase 'A young man of extraordinary personal beauty' is printed on the pale blue cover in dense black letters. Wilde's famous preface to his novel, in the form of a succession of aphorisms (concluding 'All art is quite useless'), is printed in large italics, with entire pages and double-page spreads luxuriously given over to the rolling flow of each maxim and paradox. The effect is to refresh and dramatize one's reading of the text, while also reminding the reader of the complexities of Wilde's cultural enshrinement. And yet this is only one half of the artistic formula at work in *The Picture of Dorian Gray* as reconceived by Jones. By way of design, motif, typography and, most

The Picture of Dorian Gray (1890) by Oscar Wilde, conceived and illustrated by Gareth Jones and designed by John Morgan 2008

importantly, the inclusion within the text (as illustration) of advertisements for Gitanes cigarettes – originally made in the 1970s by the Hipgnosis advertising agency for UK print media and featuring suave, Gallically handsome male models – Jones re-routes the novel to both concepts of masculine beauty and the reclamation of Art Nouveau and Wildean foppishness within the subcultural pop styling and fashions of the early 1970s. Other new publications in the 'Familars' series include an edition of Bram Stoker's *Dracula* (1897), conceived and illustrated by the artist James Pyman, and Franz Kafka's disturbing short story 'Blumfeld, An Elderly Bachelor' (1915), with images by David Musgrave. In both cases, more formally, the texts reinterpret themselves by way of the artist's intervention: Pyman's soft, ghostly illustrations to *Dracula*, in the form of exquisitely poised and shaded drawings, work to highly dramatic effect, seeming to combine the peculiar inscrutability of illustrations to a child's first reading book with a tense, poetic and obsessive timbre, reminiscent of David Lynch's eye for particular detail. Likewise, Musgrave's illustrations to the Kafka story have an other-worldly, ethnographical air; miniatures, pictorially untethered to the occurrences within Kafka's tale, they seem to suggest prehistoric, occult or extraterrestrial presences – thus adding a new gloss, all the more chilling for being intentionally indistinct, to this account of a man haunted by two tirelessly bouncing rubber balls. →

Editions of You

A revival in independent publishing has seen a boom in new imprints, often designed by artists, of classic novels and 'lost' books
by Michael Bracewell

Dracula (1897), by
Bram Stoker,
conceived and
illustrated by James
Pyman and designed
by John Morgan
2008

Books are being made newly available and, equally importantly, being entered into a process of renewed engagement with the history of a text.

In a separate venture, yet linked in Gothic sensibility, the artist Pablo Bronstein conceived and published in 2005 a new edition of Horace Walpole's *The Castle of Otranto* (1765). Such affiliation to the Gothic as fable and futurology is matched in the Book Works 'Fabrications' series, edited by Gerrie van Noord, and the reclamation of Gustave Affeulpin's quasi-science-fictional satire on state-sponsored culture, *The So-called Utopia of the Centre Beaubourg – An Interpretation* first published in 1976. Affeulpin being the pseudonym adopted by Albert Meister, this oddly Punkish/Situationist fable, re-envisaged and redesigned by Luca Frei, describes a subterranean (hence literally underground) venue for radical creativity that has been established directly beneath the flamboyantly iconoclastic new centre for the visual arts in Paris. Co-published by Book Works and CASCO Office for Art, Theory and Design, Utrecht, the re-enacted book also adheres to a trend that stretches back in the history of British publishing to the Virago and Picador lists of the 1970s, through which hitherto hard-to-find Beat, Surrealist, feminist, fabular and New Journalistic titles were republished in new editions and their political, gender-political, countercultural or avant-garde pronouncements reassessed.

This relationship between lost or occluded texts, appropriation,

re-enactment and history as subject matter, particularly in relation to countercultural bibliography, is well summarized by the statement of intent from the Amsterdam venture (Missingbooks), whose re-publication in 2005 of the Argentinian New Journalist Rodolfo Walsh's *A Dark Day of Justice* (1973) was accompanied by the making of a film reconstruction, *In The Last Twenty Minutes* (2005), of Walsh's assassination in 1977. As proposed by (Missingbooks), their intention is 'to bring what has disappeared back into view', in such a manner that 'the background of the disappearance is contextualized […] intervening in the canon of cultural heritage'. This might also be a perfect description of another of the 'Fabrications' series, *Today in History/Tarihte Bugün* (2007), by Ahmet Öğüt, in which drawings and paraphrased stories taken from Turkish newspapers over the last four decades are reprinted, removed from their context. Likewise (also from Book Works) Maria Fusco's new series of publications 'The Happy Hypocrite' (2007–ongoing), which aims to investigate and survey radical and experimental methods of writing about art by, among other means, incorporating found texts and parodic writing.

The notion of publication and republication as a venue for creativity and polemical, 'secret' history is also well documented at Metronome Press,

Paris (founded in 2005 by Clémentine Deliss and Thomas Boutoux), whose forthcoming *Unhouse – The Architecture of Dwelling Portably*, created by artist Oscar Tuazon (with an epilogue by the novelist and former *nest* magazine literary editor Matthew Stadler) provides an astonishing account of Bert and Holly Davis' nomadic existence in the forests of Oregon, including facsimile reproductions from their 'zine *Dwelling Portably* – 'written by and for a close community of hardcore hippie survivalists'. As mainstream literary publishers begin to explore, by way of new, digital reprint and print-on-demand technologies, economically viable means of bringing unfairly lost and out-of-print titles back to availability, so it would seem that these artist-driven ventures into print re-enactment are not alone in their desire to escape subordination to the extended and homogenizing processes of cultural globalization. The world wants more than celebrity chefs. And as Patti Smith so memorably remarked, at the conclusion of her winter 1975 performance in Cleveland, Ohio of The Who's 'My Generation' (1965): 'We created it – let's take it over.'

Michael Bracewell's latest book Re-make/Re-model: Art, Pop, Fashion and the Making of Roxy Music, 1953–1972 *(2007) is published by Faber & Faber.*

GILLIAN WEARING
July 12–August 23, 2008

REGEN PROJECTS II
9016 Santa Monica Boulevard
at Almont Drive

REGEN PROJECTS
633 North Almont Drive
Los Angeles, CA 90069
310 276 5424 t 310 276 7430 f
www.regenprojects.com

Andrea Rosen Gallery

Tetsumi Kudo

June 20 - August 8

Curated in collaboration with Joshua Mack
In cooperation with Hiroko Kudo and the estate of the artist

The Walker Art Center will present *Tetsumi Kudo: Garden of Metamorphosis*,
the late artist's first U.S. retrospective, in October 2008

image
Pollution -- Cultivation -- Nouvelle Écologie
1971-72

Courtesy of Albert Benamou

525 West 24th Street New York NY 10011 telephone 212 627 6000 fax 212 627 5450 www.andrearosengallery.com

Juergen Teller filmed himself watching the 2002 World Cup final (Germany lost 2–0 to Brazil). Eyes on the television set, he twists and shouts, stewing with bullish rage. He later said that this film was 'the most disturbing thing' he'd ever seen.[1]

'Zidane's melancholy is my melancholy,' explains the narrator of a story by Jean-Philippe Toussaint. Watching the infamous 2006 World Cup final during which Zidane was sent off for headbutting Italian defender Marco Materazzi, he becomes absorbed by the player's weariness, by 'the intoxication of fatigue and nervous tension. I know it,' he confesses, 'I have nourished it and I feel it.'[2]

Harun Farocki's 12-channel video projection *Deep Play* (2007) unpacks the visual archive of the Fédération Internationale de Football Association (FIFA) for the same match. Farocki's spectators have to tear themselves away from his installation – even knowing the outcome, gallery-goers drop their masks of cool sophistication in their compulsion to watch this two-hour drama unfold again and again, from impossible angles and in overwhelming statistical detail.

Douglas Gordon and Philippe Parreno's *Zidane: A 21st Century Portrait* (2006) pushes that geometry to a new level by training 17 cameras on Zidane for the duration of a Real Madrid match. Isolated from the game by the camera's focus, we wait with Zidane for the pass, for the attack. The soundtrack layers Scottish band Mogwai and crowd noise, the slap of foot against ball and the scratch of Zidane's boot against the pitch. Over 90 minutes he smiles and laughs once in an exchange with a teammate. The singularity of this moment tells us he is at work. The film reveals nothing so well as Zidane's expert control over his face.

Unlike that of 20-year-old football stars, lithe from running around and fond of diamond studs and long, flowing hair (Dimitar Berbatov or Lionel Messi), Zidane's is a hard, menacing beauty. Gordon and Parreno's film would have had an entirely different tone had they chosen an exuberant or openly flirtatious subject. Ronaldinho smiles every minute he is on the field, no matter how badly things are going. David Beckham's audience is packed with fewer Marxist art critics (who prefer their subjects miserable) and with more women and gay men – as was the case for Sam Taylor-Wood's video *David* (2004), a film of the footballer sleeping which functions as a homage to Andy Warhol's *Sleep* (1963).

Gordon and Parreno cite Andy Warhol's films as an inspiration, but it is hard to see the connection: *Zidane ...* is too beautiful, too controlled, too glossy. You can buy the DVD in supermarkets in France – a sign of →

Fever Pitch
The art of football **by Jennifer Doyle**

Above:
Douglas Gordon and
Philippe Parreno
*Zidane: A 21st Century
Portrait*
2006

Top:
Juergen Teller
*World Cup Final,
Germany 0, Brazil 2,
London 2002*
2002

Below:
Hellmuth Costard
Fußball wie noch nie
(Football as Never
Before)
1971

Below middle:
Yrsa Roca Fannberg
Icon (Didier Drogba)
2007

Bottom:
Fred Poulet
Substitute
2006

The real Warholian moment of football cinema is Hellmuth Costard's 1971 portrait of the famously charming George Best, *Fußball wie noch nie* (Football as Never Before), which is due for a DVD re-release this summer.

how deeply the film co-operates with and expands Zidane's celebrity. It has much more in common with Warhol's portraits.

The real Warholian moment of football cinema is Hellmuth Costard's film *Fußball wie noch nie* (Football as Never Before, 1971). A point of reference for *Zidane* .... and due for a European DVD re-release this summer, the film takes the famously charming George Best as its subject and edits multiple camera views to produce a real-time portrait of the player singled out during the course of an entire match. Lest we miss the homoerotic subtext of football art (and football culture), the half-time interval features a cruisey bit of filmmaking as we follow Best through a narrow hall-way and into what looks like the boot room. Best turns and faces the camera for nearly three minutes. He holds our gaze as long as he can, pursing his lips, looking away and then back in a seem-ingly overt homage to the Warholian screen test. Best strikes a deal here with the camera, inviting us to look at him when he takes the field again; shots of his socks, his shoulders and his crotch seem to go on for ever.

In her ongoing watercolour diary Yrsa Roca Fannberg sneaks onto Barcelona's pitch. These small, moody paintings are close cousins to Costard's film and an important counterpoint to work such as *Deep Play* and *Zidane* .... Costard and Fannberg give the lie to the game's open secret. Football is a deeply sentimental space of male intimacy. Players explode in ecstasy, but they also love each other in more ordinary ways. They collapse in frustration, they cry. They are lost and wounded. They wrap their arms around each other and talk.

Eduardo Galeano (the Roland Barthes of football writing) describes 'the history of soccer' as 'a sad voy-age from beauty to duty'. That 'duty' is paid to the sports 'telecracy', in which 'functionaries specialize in avoiding defeat'.[3] Artists respond to this aspect of the game with melancholy and nostalgia – and often both. In 'big' art such as Farocki's installation and Gordon and Parreno's film, both of which were made in collaboration with that telecracy, the game itself is a receding horizon of pure experience in which the player dissolves

with a pivot and a swing of the foot. His body – how it feels to be him – is beyond the reach of any representation. Technology and telecracy unite in the erasure of the player's body, and his pleasure, from the picture. Roca Fan-nberg counters that theft by choosing as her medium a very simple dissolve of water on paper to capture how our moods, our thoughts, our legs get entangled with theirs. If the player dis-solves, it is with us, and in tears.

The game is excised from the less romantic experimental film *Substitute* (2006) but not out of any formal trick. Fred Poulet gave his friend Vikash Dhorasoo a Super-8 camera so that the latter might keep a cinematic diary of his summer performances for the French national team during their 2006 World Cup run. The project was a disas-ter. Dhorasoo's teammates refused to be filmed. Some, such as Zidane and Thi-erry Henry, are global brands; their im-ages are trademarked. In spite of having featured in qualifying matches, Dhora-soo scarcely left the bench – many think the film project was to blame. Filming training is off limits, and the telecracy owns the game. The camera isolated Dhorasoo; we hardly ever leave his ho-tel room. His footage is grainy, often out of focus, while the narrative is sparse and grim. We track Dhorasoo's struggle to keep his alienation and bitterness in check. Poulet and Dhorasoo replace the macho heroics of wounded masculin-ity with a far more compelling truth of exile, desire and resentment. The film ends not with a defiant *geste* but with Dhorasoo climbing the stairs to his apartment and sitting down at a table to open a large stack of mail.

Jennifer Doyle is the author of Sex Objects: Art and the Dialectics of Desire (2006) *and blogs about football at* From a Left Wing (*http://fromaleftwing. blogspot.com*).

⦾ Find out more at frieze.com

1 Cited by Liz Hoggard in 'This is for You, Dad', *The Observer*, Sunday 14 September 2003
2 Jean-Philippe Toussaint, 'Zidane's Melancholy', in *New Formations: A Journal of Culture/Theory/Politics*, 62, 2007, pp. 12–14
3 Eduardo Galeano, *Soccer in Sun and Shadow*, Verso, London, 1998

JAMES LEE BYARS, "THE MOON BOOKS", 1989, GILDED MARBLE AND GILDED WOOD, 40 ½ X 197 INCHES; "EROS (15 MOONS)", 1993, SHAPED JAPANESE PAPER, DIMENSIONS VARIABLE

Glasgow museums

Culture & Sport ᴳˡᵃˢᵍᵒʷ

GALLERY OF MODERN ART (GoMA)

Untitled, 2007 © Jim Lambie,
courtesy of the artist and The Modern Institute/Toby Webster Ltd, Glasgow.
Photo by Ruth Clark

FREE
Entry

Forever Changes
Jim Lambie

11 April–29 September 2008

Gallery Of Modern Art I Royal Exchange Square I Glasgow G1 3AH I Phone: 0141 229 1996 I
Fax: 0141 204 5316 I Text phone: 0141 248 2891 I www.glasgowmuseums.com I

Glasgow
CITY COUNCIL

Forever Changes is commissioned by Glasgow Museums in association
with the Gi Festival 2008

American Beauty

Elvis Presley died on Madonna's 19th birthday. As the queen of pop approaches 50, the two stars can be seen as complex and contradictory emblems of their shared homeland **by Sarah Khan**

Right: Madonna onstage during her 'Confessions' tour 2006

Far right: Elvis Presley onstage in Las Vegas 1975

Both images courtesy: Getty Images

Cologne-based collector and former gallerist Rolf Ricke recently told me about a phenomenon he experienced in the late 1960s: brilliant young American artists suddenly abandoning art-making to become organic farmers. They gave up art as their abilities peaked for the first time, often before reaching the age of 30. Lewis Stein, for example, told Ricke: 'I've made my contribution to the art of the 20th century, now I'm through.' Or Harriet Korman. Or Peter Young, who went to Arizona to farm vegetables and run a hotel for poor people. Or Lee Lozano, who told Ricke as she left New York never to return: 'My new name is Lee Free, I feel totally free.' Just like that? For no particular reason? Misogyny in the art world, existential worries and the rise of a new alternative culture are sure to have played a part in such decisions. But there is another theme that emerges here: ambition as an aesthetic problem.

A recent example are television talent shows; many of the contestants are the children of immigrants. These shows have provoked disgust among many middle-class viewers – disgust at unbridled ambition. Likewise, middle-class offspring lament the demise of pop, and the lack of a suitable arena for their own ambition, which, according to the conventions of cool, should be disguised as effortlessness. If an open display of ambition is aesthetically displeasing, then it follows that some overtly sensitive artists might find it so repugnant that they can no longer bring themselves to live through the arduousness of making art. In such cases, vegetable gardens, with their seasonal regularity, may be more attractive – the biblical humility of working in the fields, bent over, head down.

Madonna is one pop star who has climbed the ladder of success without letting any concerns over the ugliness of ambition get in her way. Madonna *is* ambition.

Ambition has a dead mother.
Ambition has a cold father.
Ambition has an immigrant grandpa.
Ambition has a growing fat-phobia.
Ambition erects altars.
Ambition feels unloved.
Ambition gives interviews gladly at first, later only rarely.
Ambition knows it is ensnared by fate.

Madonna embodies America the way Elvis Presley once embodied America, and as she has recalled on several occasions with proprietorial pride, Elvis died on her 19th birthday. It might seem odd for the singer to

believe herself mystically linked to Elvis in some way. They are, after all, totally diverse cultural icons. To some degree Elvis still embodies America, although the America he embodies today is that of the old, the overweight, the sad and the ill. These are the unfit people who lack the proverbial 'healthy dose of ambition'. It is the members of this group who need Elvis the most and who therefore venerate him. With their love of Elvis, ill and broken Americans can love themselves a little.

In the beginning, everything was easy. Elvis Presley's warm chuckle (later mimicked by Bill Clinton) instantly made the audience forget the sweaty workouts of his dances. But later in his life, it became clear that he had lost something essential – his ambition. He expected his countrymen to say it didn't matter, but this was asking too much of a nation whose white, male population had been suffering from an impotence trauma since the Great Depression, a trauma only aggravated by the war in Vietnam and the civil rights and women's movements.

This is not impotence in the sense of an individual, sexual disorder, but that of the distressed male who seeks solace through violence and subjugation. This, as a fantasy, is articulated in American culture in the pulp aesthetic, ranging from detective stories through to the films of Quentin Tarantino. Classic pulp operates with two main types of women: the innocent country girl, whose vulnerability does not rule out blatant erotic display (plunging necklines, bulging breasts), and the vamp who is unwilling to sacrifice herself for

love. Both archetypes put the lonely, male hero – always dressed in a trench coat, all the better to conceal his big, big gun – in a position where he must react.

Square jaw, ooo, such a handsome face, why do you have to save the human race?
Madonna 'He's A Man' (1990)

Madonna has often borrowed looks and attitudes from pulp. Thanks to the pulp aesthetic, fetish gear and other sexual stimulation aids acquired a major role in American culture. They made not entirely serious appearances in the fun bondage photos of Bettie Page. Today, the breast tape of old has been replaced by the Wonderbra, and the whips, gags and stilettos have been chemically transformed into Viagra. Pulp speaks of a culture of the prosthetic, in which the orthopaedic side of male self-assertion is concealed by an elaborate show.

Towards the end of his life, Elvis began to make a show of illness. This was met not with understanding, but with scorn and derision. It probably was a little too much to ask of those who once saw Elvis' lithe hips as the greatest symbolic incentive not to abandon the cultural, economic and military battlefields to 'others' (women, Native Americans, Afro-Americans, Vietnamese, Koreans) but to keep them in the hands of the white man. And those unfit people and losers who did understand the wonderful human turn taken by the ailing Elvis now wallow drowsily in memories of youth instead of fighting for their right to fail, to get fat, to grow old or sick with any degree of cultural visibility. Where was their outcry when

Mourners at Elvis Presley's funeral, Memphis
1977

Bill and Hillary Clinton were prevented from introducing universal health care in the USA in the mid-1990s, thus depriving the American struggle for life of its cruellest barb?

In 1972, Elvis recorded his version of 'Always on my Mind' – an ode to things left undone, and ultimately his own requiem:

Maybe I didn't treat you Quite as good as I should have Maybe I didn't love you Quite as often as I could have.

One cannot love Madonna with the same despairing passion required to love a broken, unhappy person such as Elvis. Once one has learned to embrace an icon's descent into the gutter, to love in the hope of curing the blind, the crippled and the impotent – all things of which fans are capable – then one knows what addiction is and that ultimately there is no consolation. (Although it's still a great joy, right?)

And yet Madonna is right when she points to their shared fate. Elvis' death was a sign of sorts. On 16 August 1977, when this monarch who had lost his ambition, this king of pill-poppers and super-sized people, finally left the building named USA, he made way for someone who replaced rather than perpetuated him. (Today he apparently lives on a vegetable farm in Mexico with Ricke's former artists, where Thomas Pynchon and J.D. Salinger drop in to help with the harvest.)

How amazed Madonna must have been on her 19th birthday when she looked into all the tearstained faces

Madonna on stage,
Maidstone, England
2008

around her. No one was laughing; no one ate the birthday cake made by her detested stepmother; everyone dissolved into self-pity and pain. No one understood what only she sensed on this magical day. Although ruined by the death of Elvis, this birthday nonetheless gave her a great gift: the realization that Elvis was an ailing, impotent guy who did nothing but spoil the party you'd been looking forward to for so long.

She also realized that this kind of misery was no good for the country in the long run, that the USA needed something strong, something healthy, something that doesn't spoil your well-deserved special day. She sang about this in her first hit 'Holiday' (1983) – a hymn to a happy, healthy day that brings everyone together, a day that's different to everyday life, which for many people will never come. Of course, though, she doesn't say that in so many words, the clever woman.

> It's time for the good times
> Forget about the bad times, oh yeah
> One day to come together
> To release the pressure

Pop music was once an ideal way of expressing ambition. It could be worked through physically without being identified as a form of labour, without killing the mood. Madonna's ambition and her oft-cited 'will to power' have even been able to mask her main technical shortcoming, her notoriously petite voice, which in pathos-driven musical genres – such as opera or country – would have been indefensible.

Madonna blends pop and sport at the level of military drill, further emphasizing this aspect of her performances through her choice of costumes. In her work, effort is always noble, and any thought of refusal, decay or illness, of boundaries, misfortune or existential alienation is absolutely banned. This is the root of the relentless humourlessness for which Madonna has always been famous for. Slipping up on the banana skin of life is not something we can expect to see her doing, nor emitting an infectious giggle as consolation.

Emblematic, above all, of the USA of the 1980s, Madonna provided a visual definition of sex for her nation that worked wonderfully even under the shadow of AIDS: libido channelled through a Catholic fixation ('Like A Virgin', 1984; 'Papa Don't Preach', 1986) and a focus on giving, but above all taking ('Pretender', 1984; 'Material Girl', 1985; 'Hollywood', 2003). Madonna stands for the USA that confidently and stubbornly denies death – despite huge swaths of the population having no health insurance – driven by the conviction that the dynamism and virility of a free society can only be maintained if that society's members have good reason to push themselves. She is the goddess of this American brand of existential gymnastics. The fact that she sees herself as an opponent of the Bush administration is not a contradiction; nor is the fact that she has become a figurehead for feminist, homosexual and even, to some extent, African-American and Hispanic self-assurance and idealization: Madonna is presumably just as mistaken about herself as her

For Madonna, unlike for Elvis, effort is always noble, and any thought of refusal, decay, illness, misfortune or existential alienation is absolutely banned.

followers have always been. Members of discriminated minorities that once derived joy and strength from her music now find themselves on the stage of the neo-liberal dance floor asking, along with everyone else, is this all there is?

Madonna has her merits, in the wonderful way she has taught marginalized groups with an affinity for pop that anyone wishing to gain access to the mainstream and its riches must, above all, get their act together. But the practical life lessons emanating from the singer and her music don't make her a saint. If you take a look at her slightly more discrete side-products – her Kabbalah propaganda, her children's books – you're assailed, absurdly enough, by Madonna the desperate moralist. This, if not the rest, must be rejected as metaphysical kidnapping. It also sheds some light on her lack of cheerfulness. Madonna is healthy, beautiful, dominant, self-determined and as heroic as an ancient statue.

Sarah Khan is a freelance writer and novelist based in Berlin.
Translated by Nicholas Grindell

🌀 Find out more at frieze.com

Courtesy: Getty Images

Stephen Prina
Galerie Gisela Capitain

Ideal Syllabus: Adrian Piper

In an ongoing series *frieze* asks curators, artists and writers to list the books that have influenced them

Adrian Piper is a first-generation Conceptual artist and philosopher who lives and works in Berlin, where she runs the Adrian Piper Research Archive. Both volumes of her project in Kantian metaethics, Rationality and the Structure of the Self: The Humean Conception *and* Rationality and The Structure of the Self: A Kantian Conception *are forthcoming from Cambridge University Press.*

I really liked *frieze*'s original 1998 publication *An Ideal Syllabus* (ed. Jerry Saltz) and so was delighted to be invited to contribute my own. I've listed the following 13 books in the chronological order in which I discovered them: I read (1) through (3) during my first decade; (4) through (7) during my second decade; (8) through (12) during my third decade; and (13) during my sixth decade (I spent my fourth and fifth decades absorbing the lessons of the first three).

(1) Ruth Krauss

I Can Fly (Little Golden Books, New York, 1950)

For ages four and up. A first reader, and my first reader in English, with clear and simple poems and beautiful, eye-catching illustrations. It started me thinking about lifting off, and how to do it, right away.

(2) Lewis Carroll

Alice's Adventures in Wonderland (Macmillan, Cambridge, 1865) and *Through the Looking-Glass* (Macmillan, Cambridge, 1871), with original illustrations by John Tenniel

An invaluable primer to social reality, better than Kafka. Purports to be for children, but don't be fooled. My life experience has been exactly as these two books predicted it would be.

(3) Booth Tarkington

Penrod (Grosset & Dunlap, New York, 1914)

A forgotten and greatly underestimated early-20th-century novelist, who became an embarrassment in retrospect because of his explicit, naive racism and fascism. Get over them and enjoy his distantly amused but affectionate rendering of turn-of-the-century middle America, seen from the perspective of a ten-year-old boy, the ten-year-old boy in all of us.

(4) Bhagavad Gita: Song of God

Translated by Christopher Isherwood & Swami Prabhavananda (Marcel Rodd, Los Angeles, 1944)

There is too much in this beautiful translation that goes too deeply to describe quickly. It's a short book. You'll find in it what you're ready to find. At the very least, you'll find the first succinct statement of the fundamental questions of Western philosophy.

(5) How to Know God: The Yoga Sutras of Patanjali

Translated with a commentary by Christopher Isherwood & Swami Prabhavananda (Allen & Unwin, London, 1953)

When you start thinking that this can't possibly be all there is (whatever 'this' is for you), then you're ready to start reading this text. This particular translation is not the most precise, but the commentary is beautiful, and perfect for Westerners who are feeling the first stirrings of serious dissatisfaction with the version of reality even the most sophisticated amongst us take for granted.

(6) Swami Vivekananda

Karma Yoga (Ramakrishna-Vivekananda Center, New York, 1955; first published 1896)

A no-holds-barred introduction to Vedanta ethics and epistemology, a useful and bracing corrective to Postmodernist abstraction by a highly educated and very eloquent avatar who practised what he preached.

John Tenniel
Illustration for
Alice's Adventures in Wonderland
1865

Swami Vivekananda
1893

(7) Plato

Apology (c. 399 BC)

This dialogue introduces us to Socrates the person and personality (wise and deep, but bitchy, a real nag, always ready to publicly humiliate the dim-witted) and offers us a model of how to live in such a way that, when confronted with the imminence of death, we are able to rise to the occasion with honour and dignity. Socrates' bad attitude is: bring it on and fuck you! Personally, I have found this early dialogue deeply inspiring.

(8) Immanuel Kant

Critique of Pure Reason, translated by Allen Wood and Paul Guyer (Cambridge University Press, Cambridge, 1998; first published 1781)

This is the only book in Western philosophy you need to read. Once you get through it, everything else – both precursors and successors, including Hegel – will seem easy, and also familiar.

(9) Immanuel Kant

Groundwork of the Metaphysics of Morals, translated by H.J. Paton (1948, Hutchinson's University Library, London, 1948; first published 1785)

Many women philosophers have found this terse, profound treatise on the ethics of autonomy, freedom and rationality to be particularly important, and for good reason.

(10) George Kubler

The Shape of Time: Remarks on the History of Things (Yale University Press, New Haven, 1962)

This feverishly brilliant and highly condensed theory of originality in art history was published the same year as Thomas Kuhn's *The Structure of Scientific Revolutions* (1962). Kubler never mentions Kuhn, but the two works have so much in common that it's inconceivable to me that there was no mutual influence. However, Kubler is more of a big picture thinker whereas Kuhn is more case-oriented. This book should be required reading for artists who have not yet had their 15 minutes, and also for those who have.

(11) Thomas Kuhn

The Structure of Scientific Revolutions (University of Chicago Press, Chicago, 1962, 2nd Edition)

The only really convincing defence of qualified subjectivism there is, and probably the most revolutionary and influential book since Charles Darwin's *On the Origin of Species* (1859).

(12) John Rawls

A Theory of Justice (Belknap Press, Cambridge, Massachusetts, 1971)

Rawls is now generally recognized as being to the 20th century what John Stuart Mill was to the 19th century. A few of the reasons: (1) In response to the upheavals of the 1960s, *A Theory of Justice* returned the field of moral and political philosophy from the esoteric abstractions of linguistic analysis to the urgent practical questions of how to live. (2) It formulated a conception of the good society that refuted Karl Marx's criticism that traditional Social Contract Theory lacked a theory of economic, i.e. distributive, justice. (3) It offered the first serious modern philosophical competitor to Utilitarianism, by incorporating decision theory and game theory into its foundations.

(13) Thomas McEvilley

The Shape of Ancient Thought: Comparative Studies in Greek and Indian Philosophy (Allworth Press, New York, 2001)

McEvilley is best known in the art world as an art critic; but in reality he is a very learned classical philologist, philosopher and Sanskritist. This big yet clear and beautifully written book is his masterpiece, on which he worked in isolation for 30 years. It traces and documents the mutual influences of ancient Greek on Indian philosophy and of Indian on ancient Greek philosophy – a topic most of the documentary evidence for which was lost with the burning of the library at Alexandria; and which virtually no other scholar is competent to address or evaluate because it requires both fluency in ancient Greek plus deep familiarity with the classical Greek philosophical texts, and also fluency in classical Sanskrit plus deep familiarity with the ancient Indian philosophical texts. It's going to take the rest of us a long time to catch up with the brilliant cultural and intellectual synthesis contained in this work.

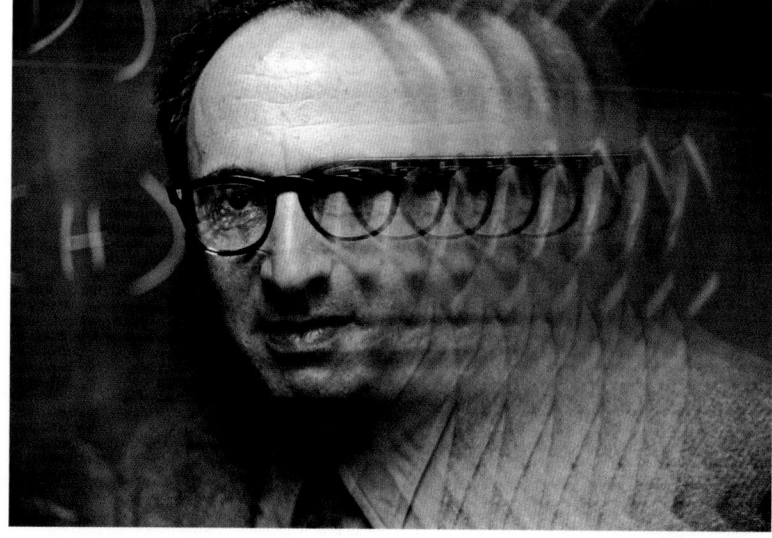

Thomas Kuhn
1973

Thomas McEvilley
c. 2001

Kuhn courtesy: Time & Life Pictures/Getty Images • McEvilley courtesy: Allworth Press

Cartier

FRIEZE FILM

 An open invitation:

Make your own movie
Make someone else's movie
Make it your mission to
read 'The Road'
Make a small part of a bigger whole
Make it on YouTube
Make it into Frieze Art Fair

Be a part of an experiment
in movie-making
www.friezefoundation.org/film

4

Life in Film: Raqs Media Collective

In an ongoing series, *frieze* asks artists and filmmakers to list the movies that have influenced their practice.

The members of Raqs Media Collective (Jeebesh Bagchi, Monica Narula and Shuddhabrata Sengupta) have been described as artists, media practitioners, curators, researchers and editors. Their work, which has been exhibited widely in local and international venues, locates them squarely along the intersections of contemporary art, historical enquiry, philosophical speculation, research and theory – often taking the form of installations, online and offline media objects, performances and encounters. They live in Delhi, and are based at Sarai, Centre for the Study of Developing Societies, an initiative they co-founded in 2000. They are members of the editorial collective of the 'Sarai Reader' series, and are co-curating Manifesta 7 in northern Italy for the summer of 2008.

Films are like landmarks. Memories of watching films together, watching them again after many years on the tiny screen on the back of an airplane seat, downloading them from a film-sharing website, sharing them, arguing about them, learning from them, becoming enamoured of them or indifferent to them: these are all signposts in a continuing journey. Here is one makeshift and eclectic itinerary, not just of films

but of things learnt from films. There could be many others, but this one seemed to suggest itself during a few days spent building a lighthouse inside an abandoned cinema.

Asked to shoot his first film at the age of 21, Subrata Mitra found the lighting of interiors in the world cinema of the day (the 1950s) artificial. To give the rooms, corridors and inner courtyards of his own films a feeling of light as he experienced it, the feel and texture of the 'shadowless' interiors of a Calcutta tropical summer, he innovated his own light-boxes and diffusion and reflection materials. Mitra, who shot Satyajit Ray's early films, including the ***Apu Trilogy*** (1955–60) and ***Charulata*** (The Lonely Wife, 1964), was a solitary maverick. He had a deep love of cinema, light meters, bad Indo–Chinese food and endless conversation. We learnt about him during the five years we researched the history and practice of cinematography in India.

Allied to Mitra's liberation of cinematography from a dependence on heavy industrial lighting fixtures was K.K. Mahajan's decision to improvise and experiment with film stock, lighting and handheld camera shooting,

Ki-duk Kim
Bin-jip
(3 Iron)
2004
A film about the consolations of invisibility.

Harun Farocki
Aufschub
(Respite)
2007
Haunting in its absence of violence.

notwithstanding limited budgets and severe shortages of film stock and equipment. In film after film – ***Sara Akash*** (The Big Sky, 1969), ***Uski Roti*** (Our Daily Bread, 1970), ***Calcutta 71*** (1971), ***Maya Darpan*** (Mirror of Illusion, 1972), ***Chorus*** (1974) – he achieved remarkable results that helped inaugurate a new attitude to image-making in the late 1960s and early '70s in Mumbai and Calcutta. The legacy of Mitra and Mahajan is a confidence about making art with very spare means. The intelligence of an image is not necessarily coincident with its carbon footprint.

The understated élan of two comedians and character actors, Robi Ghosh and Johnny Walker (Badruddin Kazi), demonstrated that the throwaway performances about the adventures of the little man can have a more enduring place in history than the histrionics of a star. Their separate careers – Ghosh's in Bengali and Walker's in Hindi cinema – saw them perform a robust, quizzical, subaltern urbanity on the screen. Their on-screen personae (which they could deploy as character actors) were whimsical and sceptical annotations to the more earnest contours of the narratives they found themselves in. They brought to life the middle-men, charmers, fixers, hustlers and flunkeys of post-independence urban India in a way that could help undo the grandiose and sentimental aspiring towards a heroic national self.

Ajantrik (The Unmechanical, 1958) by Ritwik Ghatak refused to believe that an ageing automobile is a thing without a soul. *Ajantrik* is a film about a solitary taxicab driver in a remote provincial town in the middle of Bengal, and his relationship with his run-down car. An amalgam of automobile fetishism and technological hubris, it serves as an ironic, sentimental but bittersweet obituary for early modernity and its eccentric inner world.

A viewing many years ago at the Goethe-Institut in New Delhi of Hartmut Bitomsky's essay film *Reichsautobahn* (1986) brought home the relationship between infrastructure, motorways, cars, the will to power and capitalism's ability to conjure up euphoric participation. As the image-building of the emerging economies currently goes into hyperbolic overdrive, and big dreams are sold on the back of millions of nano-mobiles, Bitomsky's car-chase through history seems fresh, like recent roadkill.

Tengiz Abuladze's fabulist critique of the pettiness of totalitarianism in *Monanieba* (Repentance, 1984) remains as a caution, in cinematic shorthand, about the intoxication and lethal euphoria of power and progress.

Das Leben der Anderen (The Lives of Others, 2006) by Florian Henckel von Donnersmarck makes us pay attention to what it means to listen. It marks the tracks left by the casual and accidental intimacies of surveillance. We might like to think that those who watch what we do and listen to what we say will become philosophical rather than unkind. We know this does not happen, and that secret policemen do not become gentle saints. But cinema can occasionally help us privilege what could be, in the face of what so brutally is.

Buster Keaton's performance about a man who runs away from his own face, and indeed anything remotely resembling a face, in a strange little film written by Samuel Beckett called *Film* (1965), talks about the terror of perception, recognition and visibility.

Obversely, Ki-duk Kim's film *Bin-jip* (3 Iron, 2004) brought home to us the consolations of invisibility. The film features a protagonist whose reticence borders on perceived insignificance.

He becomes a silent and compassionate witness to the lives of others by breaking into their homes (without intent to commit violence, robbery or damage). Eventually, he is transformed from being virtually to actually invisible – training himself to remain outside the peripheral vision of people, who, in any case, hardly even see when they look – to all but those who look out for him. The film portrays self-effacement and imperceptibility as acts of choice rather than of compulsion.

Harun Farocki's silent film *Aufschub* (Respite, 2007) presents archival footage of a Nazi transit camp in the Netherlands, where Jews are shown

Mrinal Sen
Chorus
1974
Cinematographer K.K. Mahajan helped inaugurate a new attitude to image-making in the late 1960s and early '70s in Mumbai and Calcutta.

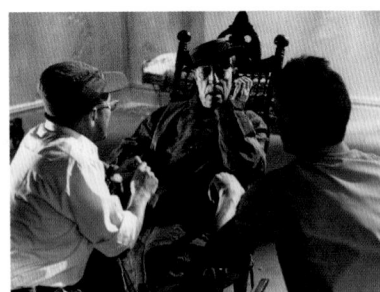

Alan Schneider
Film
1965
A strange little film written by Samuel Beckett.

Below:
Florian Henckel von Donnersmarck
Das Leben der Anderen **(The Lives of Others)**
2006
It makes us pay attention to what it means to listen.

dancing, smiling and harvesting grain. The film examines this footage in relentless detail for the things it does not reveal. It shows how fine the line between the reading and misreading of images can be. The exercise is haunting not because it shows violence, but because it exhibits the absence of violence in a context that can be comprehended only through a prior understanding of terror.

Finally, the breathless whisper of Richard Attenborough in countless natural history documentaries seen on television, when he holds his face close to some momentarily still specimen of exotic fauna, perhaps a geriatric Galapagos tortoise. For no other reason than to say that sometimes, watching moving images is all about being outside and/or beside yourself, switching constantly between being the object and subject of attention, between being the whispering, observant, attentive naturalist and the oblivious, observed, indulgent tortoise.

⊛ Find out more at frieze.com

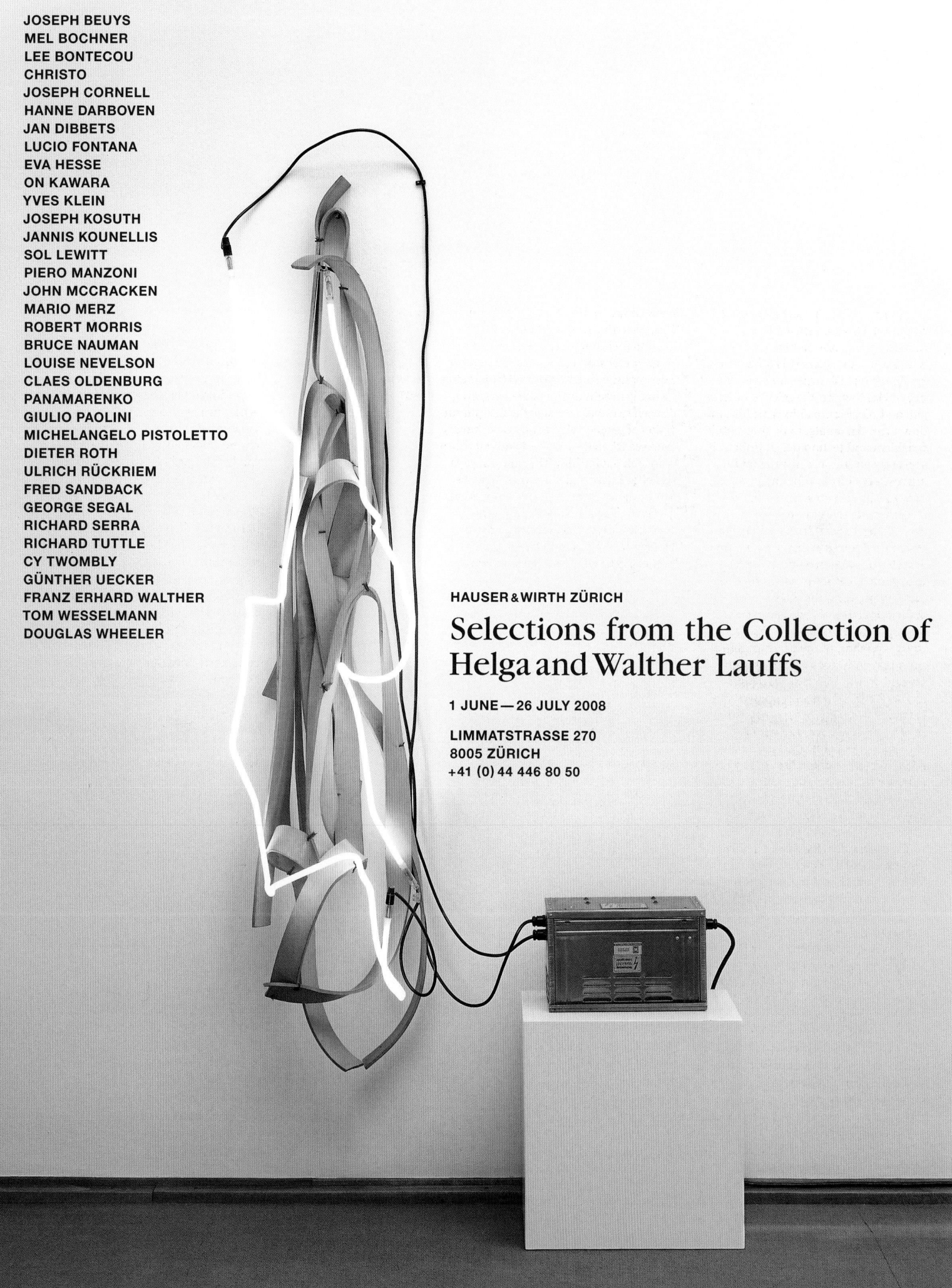

JOSEPH BEUYS
MEL BOCHNER
LEE BONTECOU
CHRISTO
JOSEPH CORNELL
HANNE DARBOVEN
JAN DIBBETS
LUCIO FONTANA
EVA HESSE
ON KAWARA
YVES KLEIN
JOSEPH KOSUTH
JANNIS KOUNELLIS
SOL LEWITT
PIERO MANZONI
JOHN MCCRACKEN
MARIO MERZ
ROBERT MORRIS
BRUCE NAUMAN
LOUISE NEVELSON
CLAES OLDENBURG
PANAMARENKO
GIULIO PAOLINI
MICHELANGELO PISTOLETTO
DIETER ROTH
ULRICH RÜCKRIEM
FRED SANDBACK
GEORGE SEGAL
RICHARD SERRA
RICHARD TUTTLE
CY TWOMBLY
GÜNTHER UECKER
FRANZ ERHARD WALTHER
TOM WESSELMANN
DOUGLAS WHEELER

HAUSER & WIRTH ZÜRICH

Selections from the Collection of Helga and Walther Lauffs

1 JUNE — 26 JULY 2008

LIMMATSTRASSE 270
8005 ZÜRICH
+41 (0) 44 446 80 50

RICHARD SERRA, WHITE NEON BELT PIECE, VULCANIZED RUBBER, NEON TUBES, CABLE, IRON CLIPS, TRANSFORMER, 1967, 74 3/4 x 19 5/8 x 11 3/4 INCHES, 190 x 50 x 30 CM

frieze Writer's Prize 2008

frieze magazine writer's prize is an annual international award to discover and promote new art critics. The award will be judged in 2008 by Tate Triennial curator Nicolas Bourriaud, *frieze* co-editor Jennifer Higgie and Guardian critic Adrian Searle.

- Entrants must submit one previously unpublished 700 word review of a recent contemporary art exhibition.
- Entries must be submitted in English, but it may be a translation (this must be acknowledged).
- Entrants must be over 18 years old.
- To qualify, entrants may only previously have had a maximum of three pieces published in any national or regional newspaper or magazine. Publication online does not prohibit entry.
- The winning entrant will be commissioned to write a review for the October issue of frieze and be awarded £2000.
- Two further awards of £500 will be made for outstanding entries.
- Closing date is: 23rd June 2008
- Entries should be emailed as a word attachment to writersprize@frieze.com

Books

One Break, A Thousand Blows!

Maxi Kim (Book Works, London, 2008)

Index

Bridget Penney (Book Works, London, 2008)

The original *Semina* was a hand-produced journal published by the American artist Wallace Berman between 1955 and 1964, featuring Berman's own photography and collages alongside images and texts by both canonical and overlooked artists and writers. Berman was at the centre of a group that extended from his West Coast peers to the Beat poets, Black Mountain College and Andy Warhol's Factory, among others – a continuation of a trajectory that, for him, included such avant-gardists as Charles Baudelaire and Antonin Artaud. So Stuart Home's adoption of the title 'Semina' for a series of commissioned novels could be seen as a somewhat self-mythologizing gesture, or, less cynically, as signalling a continued need for a community supportive of producers of non-commercial and 'difficult' genres.

The ongoing call for open submissions for the series reads like a style sheet for motifs and Gestalts: 'Think of the ways in which time and space died yesterday, how acceleration exceeds accumulation, the dead city and the perpetual twilight of technology: Georges Bataille, Henri Michaux, Alexander Trocchi, William Burroughs, Ann Quin, Clarence Cooper Jr, Claude Cahun etc.' Evaluating open submissions is a tiresome process, and any method for stemming the flood of drivel is a sensible undertaking, but editing at the level of taste seems at odds with the liberal openness associated with public funding – and it's particularly, and pleasingly, ribald that the selection process is overseen by the author of such titles as *Cunt* (1999).

Curator Michael Duncan has written that the original *Semina* publications were pretty hermetic: 'Inside

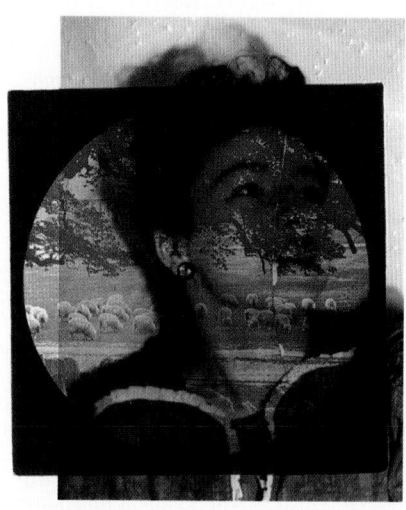

Semina No. 1

jokes, wilful obfuscation, and hermetic systems abound, giving an air of insular impenetrability to the uninitiated.' One of the first books in Home's 'Semina' series, Maxi Kim's novel *One Break, A Thousand Blows!* (2008) is an infuriating continuation of this tendency. Kim's use of language, and proper nouns in particular, as a mule for meaning often makes passages rather business-like, quashing the potential for linguistic play. Throughout the book a rash of artists', writers' and academics' names prick the prose until it's almost unbearable, as Kim ham-fistedly stakes a claim to a patch of cultural territory. For instance, in a moment of reverie one of the characters evokes the particularities of a former lover with the grace of an inventory clerk: 'The way Miju's small fingers snaked around his cock. Miju's restless description of the ontological similarities between Eileen Myles and Slavoj Zizek.'

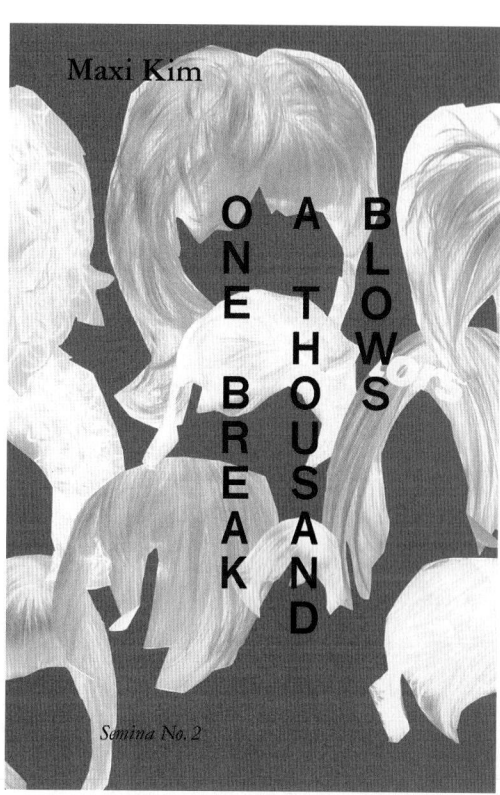

Semina No. 2

At a structural level Kim's fragmentary tactic is more lithe, interweaving characters, geographies and time-frames so that we are often unsure where we are or in whose voice we are reading. Bridget Penney's *Index* (2007) also demonstrates this anti-literary strategy. Here the orthodox narrative arc is utterly splintered and reconfigured, and lyrically wrought vignettes of historical and fictional episodes are held enigmatically apart rather than enmeshed. Much of the historical material relates to 18th-century sources and the unknowable interiority of figures and events in an age of reason and revolution. The inference of an ultimately scrambled and therefore failed index emphasizes the hubris of taxonomy and genre, which, while fulfilling the series' intention to 'demonstrate total disregard for the conventions that structure received ideas about fiction, may frustrate others who require causality in their novels.
Sally O'Reilly

Digital Culture, Play, and Identity

eds. Hilde G. Corneliussen and Jill Walker Rettberg (MIT Press, Cambridge, 2008)

Exodus to the Virtual World

Edward Castronova (Palgrave Macmillan, Basingstoke, 2007)

Do virtual worlds reflect the real world, or does the real world reflect the virtual one? This was a favourite question of Philip K. Dick, whose illusory novels constantly challenged the reader's situational expectations, and it is a question that is rapidly forcing its way into the real world. It is at the heart of two new books on online gaming: Edward Castronova's *Exodus to the Virtual World: How Online Fun Is Changing Reality* and the collection of essays *Digital Culture, Play, and Identity: A World of Warcraft® Reader*.

Castronova believes that the fun had in virtual worlds will end up changing the real world. Virtual worlds, such as those created in 'massively multiplayer online role-playing games' (MMOR-PGs), for example World of Warcraft and Everquest, have been designed for the maximum entertainment value. Why, asks Castronova, can't these same designs be used in the real world?

Given that these games are played by around 30 million players whose average age is 33 (a figure that goes up by one every year), Castronova wants us to stop thinking of them as toys, as well as bad influences. He writes that 'violence is only the tip of the iceberg of social effects' that games can produce. With human-to-human interaction within these games comparable to that in the real world, Castronova wants us to start using them as policy laboratories.

Take, for example, employment. In virtual worlds players control their own economic lives. They work with others and build teams voluntarily in order to gain new powers and enter new lands. Castronova suggests that this could encourage workers in the real world to step beyond their isolation and start collaborating in a happier, more collegial fashion.

The authors of *Digital Culture* ... prefer to focus solely on World of Warcraft (WoW), the world's most popular MMORPG. Within it they see not so much a world of fun and fantasy as one subsumed within corporate ideology, sexist ideals and colonialist rhetoric. To them WoW offers its players 'a capitalist fairytale in which anyone who works hard enough can rise through society's ranks and acquire great wealth'. One of the first quests whereby a character can earn money in WoW involves clubbing lazy Orcs into working. Even combat is suffused with market forces, being 'a form of production, through which the avatar generates experience, currency and reputation'. 'Fun' has just become another term for 'work'.

What's more, female characters are shown as being bizarrely sexualized, and the ethno-cultural schema follows traditional lines, with Trolls and Orcs resembling black Africans, Night Elves resembling Asians and humans, of course, being white and Western. If we are to take lessons from the digital world, as Castronova proposes, the authors of *Digital Culture* ... suggest that we will just be getting the same old world reflected back at us.

George Pendle

Celebration at Persepolis

Michael Stevenson (JRP Ringier, Zurich, 2008)

Celebration at Persepolis, the latest in the Christoph Keller Editions series, is a scintillating publication by the

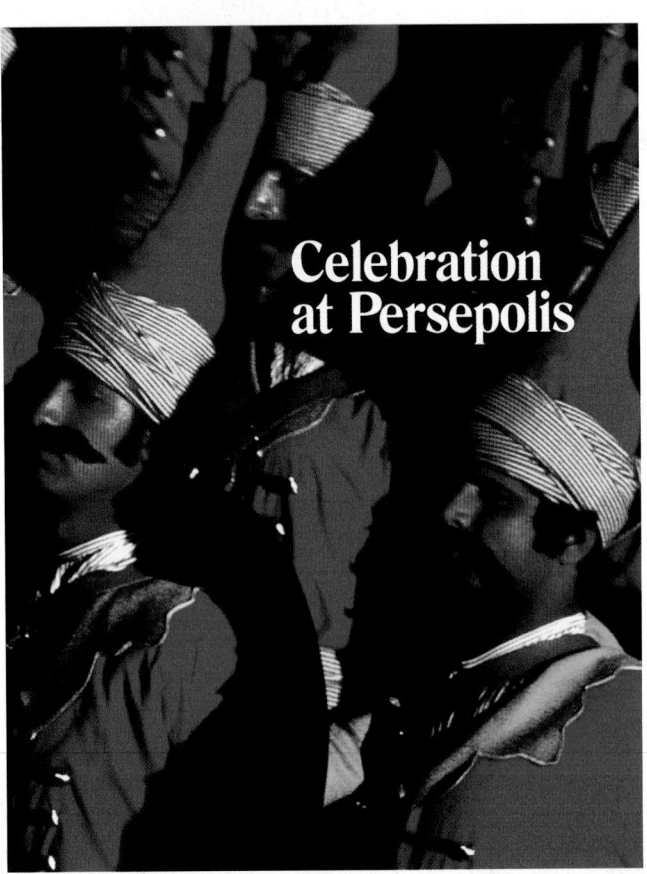

Berlin-based New Zealand artist Michael Stevenson. The small, cleanly designed, black and white book details a gripping tale of cloak-and-briefcase art dealings, a revolution, the dissolution of a monarchy and an opulent party beyond compare. The eponymous week-long celebration was held in 1971 on the site of the ancient city of Persepolis, and was intended to illustrate the grandeur of the 2,500-year-old Persian empire. The list of invitees who travelled to the Iranian desert for the event included kings, princesses, presidents, oil barons and all manner of hangers-on. The book is both the recounting of this mythologized event and an insight into Stevenson's research process, usually borne out in his complex installations and sculptures.

Celebration at Persepolis is more than a document of the legendary party. It is, in part, about art, political propaganda and dictatorial regimes, which have made amicable bedfellows throughout the 20th century. During the oil price boom of the 1970s the Shah of Iran, His Imperial Majesty Mohammad Reza Pahlavi, while amassing one the world's most powerful military forces, simultaneously spent much of his seemingly unlimited funds collecting and sponsoring contemporary art. His choice of artists (or rather that of his third wife, Her Imperial Majesty Shahbanou Farah Pahlavi, who steered his taste) perhaps surprisingly included such avant-gardists as Merce Cunningham, Iannis Xenakis and Andy Warhol. The Shahbanou was herself closely advised by the infamous art dealer Tony Shafrazi, who amassed on her and her husband's behalf one of the most comprehensive collections of postwar Modernist art in the world. Following the revolution in 1979, in which the Shah and his wife were ousted by Ayatollah Khomeini, the collection was locked away in the basement of the Tehran Museum of Contemporary Art, where it has since been viewed by only a privileged few, its precise contents the subject of speculation.

While Stevenson's disjointed paragraphs give an anecdotal insight into this moment in Persian history, the book also depicts another layer of the artist's research: an installation, shown as part of 'Art Unlimited' at Art Basel 2007, which consisted of a 1:1 scale replica of a decaying structure that was one of the many purpose-built tents constructed for the celebration at Persepolis. The original, still in the Iranian desert, is now a skeleton, only a whisper of its former ostentation remaining. By exhibiting this installation at an art fair (and by elaborating on the process of its production in the book), Stevenson pulls the fable of the Shah and Shahbanou into a contemporary context. He stops short, however, of concluding that the fate of the Persian monarch awaits the currently heady art market. Instead, with a skilful knack for storytelling, he prods the reader to uncover clues as though in an old-fashioned murder mystery, dangling the suggestion, like the cluster of Warhol's *Silver Clouds* (1966) which once bounced across the stage at Persepolis, that all great things must come to an end.

Nicola Harvey

PERPLEXED
—IN PUBLIC—

FIVE LOCATIONS ACROSS LONDON JUNE/JULY 2008

**ALLORA & CALZADILLA • CLAIRE FONTAINE
LARA FAVARETTO • SHARON HAYES
SANTIAGO SIERRA**

www.lissongallery.com   LISSON GALLERY

Kilgour

Art of Field Recording

*Volume I: 50 Years of Traditional
American Music Documented by Art
Rosenbaum (Dust-to-Digital, 2007)*

Made over the last half a century, *Art of Field Recording*, the life's work of Art Rosenbaum, a genial professor at the University of Georgia, brings together hundreds of recordings of virtually unknown American folk music. Issued as a three-part series of box sets and accompanied by drawings and paintings of many performers, weighty texts and contributions from Rosenbaum's family, the monumental release is a testament to how the practice of recording in the field can preserve oral narrative traditions. Apart from the mid-1950s' releases of John and Alan Lomax's two collections of early commercial reissues and Harry Smith's *Anthology of American Folk Music* (1952) (which was an influence on the young Bob Dylan, who stole the six-LP set from a friend), there has been little that rivals the scale of Rosenbaum's project.

The first volume of *Art of Field Recording* runs across four discs, whose categories – Survey, Religious, Blues, Instrumental & Dance – nod to those of Smith's *Anthology* (although the latter was less wide-ranging, recorded exclusively in the South during the late 1920s and early '30s). Neither of the collections, which should be considered equals, makes claims to academic methodology or comprehensiveness: their forms are dictated only by the compilers' good judgement and the limitations of portable recording equipment. Although the 1930s saw the introduction of wide aluminium discs (as used by the Lomaxes), early collectors, such as the Englishman Cecil Sharp, had to make do with just pencil and paper to notate songs. It was not until magnetic tape came into general use during the 1950s that recordings could tip the three-minute mark.

Starkly different from studio sessions, these recordings are of musicians playing music passed down by railroad workers, preachers and pioneers in the environment in which

ART OF FIELD RECORDING
VOLUME I

FIFTY YEARS OF TRADITIONAL AMERICAN MUSIC DOCUMENTED BY ART ROSENBAUM

the songs were written – homes, churches, front porches and at festivals. Only one-fifth of the recordings have been previously issued, and the anthology includes many forms (prison songs, sea shanties and unaccompanied ballads) that were ignored by mid-century record labels because they were deemed to have insufficient commercial appeal.

Gathering his examples 'shotgun-style' by arriving in a community and asking around for old-time fiddlers and banjo pickers, Rosenbaum recorded non-professionals playing outside the commercial context, performing songs that have been learnt from the family or the community. (Frank Walker, a pioneering A&R man from the 1920s, categorized his own findings as 'heart songs' and 'event songs'.) Rosenbaum's close relationship with the performers

is clear: many of them explain when and how they learnt the song. ('Me daddy learnt me how to play the organ, way-ay back in tens – he was an awful good singer.') While some of the songs are centuries old, the weirdly out-of-time renditions from such a vast cast of performers focus the collection on individuals. Some songs, such as the seven-year-old Ray Rhodes' tale of a hanging in Missouri and Margaret Kimmet's unabashed bar-room ditties (with the clicking of pool balls audible in the background), I've wanted to play over and over. Others, such as the Sacred Harp Singing Group's raucous antiphonals, a righteous hymn of demons and angels, put the fear of God in me. And I'm not religious.

Sam Thorne

Black Stars: Ghana's Hiplife Generation

Various artists (Out There, 2008)

Despite hundreds of thousands of fund-raising dollars and a small fleet, in 1921 Marcus Garvey's Black Star Line never made its intended repatriation run from the New World to Africa. Ships vanished. Cash escaped into mysterious pockets (W.E.B. DuBois blamed Garvey – leader of the Universal Negro Improvement Association and African Communities League – and Garvey blamed J. Edgar Hoover). In the years that followed, the Black Star's mighty symbolism – as an icon of homeland

and of black emancipation – went viral with gleeful homelessness: you can find it in the centre of Ghana's flag, in the name of their national soccer team (not to mention shipping line) and, with hip-hop's omnivorous logic, in the title of an excellent new CD presenting contemporary Ghanaian pop: *Black Stars: Ghana's Hiplife Generation*.

Take highlife – an upbeat, optimistic genre whose sweet guitars and jazz horn play exploded to become one of West Africa's most popular 20th-century sounds. Add an underlying love of reggae, hip-hop and R&B; wrap it up with melodic vocals in Twi, Fanti, Ga, Ewe, Hausa and that other one, English; put special emphasis on luscious sung choruses – and you've got hiplife.

'Combination-combine-combine' is how Nigerian breakdancer-turned-hip-life vocalist Tony Harmony describes his sound. Stylistic formulas mutate from hit to hit – hiplife is more an attitude than a genre. Here he gets remixed by a German producer (changes in immigration laws made cities such as Hamburg attractive to Ghanaian migrants); the key, constant undertone in this compilation is musical fluidity. Hiplife reinvigorates its history using relatively inexpensive digital tools, and that history includes Busta Rhymes (revered and ripped off: listen for Tic Tac's verbal allusions to Busta's woo-ha phraseology in 'Kangaroo') and the flamboyant Nigerian highlife trickster Sir Victor Uwaifo.

Listening to *Black Stars*' effortless polyglot switch-ups can make a multilingual European feel parochial. In 'Edua Neb U' – to pick a juicy example – after Nkasei's Twi singing, Reggie Rockstone drops verses in English, using media

apparitions of the Dark Continent as a starting-point ('I'm trying to see an African 20th Century Fox') to address you, *outsider* – then suddenly Twi lyrics return, the discussion shifts away from your understanding and you go from centre audience to incidental. But it's too late: the music pulled you in while you were following the words, and now you're moving. Inside/outside metaphors look cheap against such richness. The beat on 'Edua Neb U', and on two other tracks on *Black Stars*, comes from the Ghanaian super-producer Jay Que. He layers catchy arrangements around intricate sampled beats without making either seem dense.

In the brave new world of African music repackaged for Western audiences, *Black Stars* stands out for its populism. The music here is not only contemporary: it's hot in Ghana, now. Plus we get stuff like Tic Tac's dance craze 'Kangaroo' or the Pidgen All Stars' 'Toto Mechanic', a blatant pro-sex electro anthem that sparked a catchphrase despite a ban. The bigger artists here sell tens of thousands of copies locally, yet their music still works when flung into audiences who cannot locate Ghana on a map, let alone distinguish Twi from Hausa. But who needs maps when we've got URLs? *Black Stars*' MySpace contains YouTube videos – hiplife is music for dancing. Faster than you can say 'Kwame Nkrumah', the digital plugs back into the sweat and rhythm feedback of now. Hits aimed square at the Accra dance-floor ring in cosmopolitan ears. *Black Stars* ships in all directions.
Jace Clayton

⊛ Find out more at frieze.com

Fanal II

Fanal (Sonig, 2008)

It's often the case that music made by a renowned visual artist is appraised in relation to the more familiar side of his or her practice. Not that this should necessarily be an issue, but the novelty of an abrupt transfer of medium can divert attention away from the possible shortcomings of the actual music. By any standards Kai Althoff's second solo LP under his pseudonym Fanal, *Fanal II*, is an accomplished project. Althoff's musical output has been prolific over a number of years: his band Workshop (in collaboration with Stephan Abry) has produced a total of seven albums, the last of which, *Yog Sothoth* (2004), gave their own brand of demented homespun pop a further twist. The second Fanal album appropriates styles from across Cologne's heritage of alternative music, from Krautrock to some of the more contemporary techno and electro-acoustic productions.

Offering German lyrics that are fiercely brutal and coarse, *Fanal II* provides accounts of issues such as sexual obsession, eviction, deportation and

even the occult. Althoff uses the formal effects of his voice in unconventional styles that are regularly intended to sit with a certain discomfort alongside the consummate structure of the music compositions. On many of the tracks his words are smothered by heavy distortion, creating the sense of a person involuntarily positioned as an outsider. Each of the eleven tracks emphasizes the impossibility of any coherent narrative for the types of persona that Althoff adopts, tending towards more corporeal, pre-verbal evocations.

The pulsating electronica of the opening track, 'Hure der Geschichte' (Whore of History), constitute an abrasive and brooding elegy. Embedded within an atmospheric soundscape, its ramblings are offered directly from a disturbed unconscious that appears to be anticipating some inevitable reckoning. The nature of Althoff's musical *oeuvre* is patently violent and existential, heightened by the contrast between the voice and with his deeply textural, sometimes even melodious, electronics. 'Die Tage, Nun' (The Days, Now), one of the album's highlights, offers another morose and other-worldly perspective. Possessing a minimal

framework with simple repetitions of synth and voice, it creates an affecting dirge that is in some ways a requiem for the wretched. But *Fanal II* is not just dependent on the presence of the artist's voice – some of the tracks consisting of raw acoustics and synth, such as the uncomplicated 'Mit den Hunden' (With the Dogs), are reminders that an opus can be formed though effortless gestures.

Krautrock, as the musician Julian Cope has elucidated, was ultimately a British phenomenon in the sense that the definition was mainly based on the reception of the music in the UK, rather than the German scene from which it emerged. It was almost as though some of the appeal of the genre was down to the desired perception of a Germanic essence. The international success of Althoff as a contemporary artist is in part related to this 'essence'. While *Fanal II* as a musical endeavour is certainly born of Cologne's legacy, it is not necessary to contextualize it in this way – the last thing Althoff's Fanal guise is ever likely to claim is a birthright. Through its utterly stark ingenuity it deserves to reverberate widely.
Nav Haq

Stifter's Dinge

Heiner Goebbels, P3, London, UK

Apparently random sounds from earth float through the universe, eternally detached from their source or original time. I remembered this when I attended the performance of Heiner Goebbels' thrilling new work, *Stifter's Dinge* (Stifter's Things, 2008), which suggests, in the most imaginative ways possible, that time may not be as linear as conventional thinking might imply, that meaning can be elusive (and no less meaningful for it) and that atmosphere and evocation can be as illuminating as explanation. (All of which recalls performances by Pina Bausch, who explores similar ideas through dance.) The title is a reference to Adalbert Stifter, a 19th-century Austrian writer, poet and occasional painter best known for his vivid descriptions of the natural world. Goebbels describes his homage thus: 'The contemporary and radical aspects of Stifter's work show through the deliberate slowing down of time and are of particular significance to today's reader […] the performance/installation takes his *oeuvre* as a confrontation with the unknown: with the forces that man cannot master. It is a plea for readiness to adopt judgments other than our own.' It took place in P3, the vast former construction hall for the University of Westminster's school of engineering.

It's hard to pin down what exactly this work – co-commissioned by Artangel and Théâtre Vidy-Lausanne – is. I, for one, have never seen five pianos play themselves in a largely un-peopled environment that, at various moments, evoked snow and the ocean, Romantic and Renaissance landscape painting, forests and cancer cells, all to the accompaniment of recordings of Johann Sebastian Bach's Italian Concerto (1735), incantations for the south-westerly winds recorded in Papua New Guinea in 1905, an extract of interviews with Claude Lévi-Strauss, Malcolm X and William Burroughs, antiphonal singing by Colombian Indians and a traditional Greek song in chromatic scale sung by Ekaterini Mangoulia in 1930 to 'welcome immigrants and offer good luck to the fishermen arriving from the Barbary Coast'.

Stifter's Dinge opened with a low electronic rumbling that sounded like a huge heart beating quietly in a German nightclub. The pianos, like disembowelled bouncers, perched at the edge of three pools of water that two men – the only people visible – sprinkled with what looked like icing sugar from a giant sieve. What followed was like an elaborate hallucination that veered wildly between politics and poetry, centuries and moods: from the achingly melancholic (Bach played tentatively to raindrops) to a bleak misanthropy (Lévi-Strauss declaring: 'I don't believe there is any reason' to have faith in humankind) to an almost upbeat Malcolm X declaring that times have changed and, finally, to dark intimations of ecological disaster. (References abounded to threatening and threatened forests and polluted water.) The out of tune pianos performed a range of pieces – from atonal mutterings to swßeet melodies – by themselves, like wildly gifted children who occasionally throw expressive tantrums. A recording of an excerpt from Stifter's book *Die Mappe meines Urgroßvaters* (My Great Grandfather's Portfolio, 1864) was read by Bill Paterson, a man with a mesmerizing delivery, mellifluous tone and Scottish accent. As he read, a projection of a 19th-century landscape painting with trees – Jacob van Ruisdael's *Marsh* (c. 1600s) – seemed to dream itself into view; it was later superimposed with Paolo Uccello's *Hunt in the Forest* (c. 1465–70), which drifted over the floor like an electronic carpet. Stifter's words, which describe the experience of ice crashing from a tree in a snow forest, were alternately gorgeous and chilling: 'We saw in front of us a delicate spruce fir bent into an arch over our path, like a triumphal arch of the kind offered to the returning emperors […] If something amongst the trees gained only an ounce of weight, it could fall, the tips of the pine cones fall like wedged slivers to the ground and bore holes right through us … '. The night ended with the pianos, a little ominously, gliding towards the audience to the accompaniment of ferocious, gloom-laden sounds before retreating, once again, to where they first began.
Jennifer Higgie

Find out more at frieze.com

Impressionism is Feminine

Schirn Kunsthalle, Frankfurt am Main, Germany

Linda Nochlin's 1971 essay 'Why Have There Been No Great Women Artists?' (*ARTnews*, issue 69) examined how the art-historical canon had been entirely constructed from a male viewpoint and paved the way for re-adjusting that perspective. Thirty-seven years later, you'd think that a seminar covering similar ground, with Nochlin – now a Professor at New York University's Institute of Fine Arts – as the keynote speaker, might be unwarranted. You'd be wrong.

As co-panellist and Mary Cassatt expert Griselda Pollock noted, as recently as 2006 the BBC produced a three-part drama on *The Impressionists* – the first major art group to include women at

Berthe Morisot
Les Soeurs
(The Sisters)
1869

its founding core – that still ignored all of the movement's female figures. Accompanying the exhibition 'Women Impressionists', curated by Ingrid Pfeiffer, this symposium explored why and how they were quite purposefully excluded from and categorically denied entry into the canon. Nochlin, Pollock and Tamar Garb – author of *Sisters of the Brush: Women's Artistic Culture in Late-Nineteenth Century Paris* (1994) – all gave critical papers that summarized and continued their research. These analyzed how images made by women changed the way we looked at the world (and at women themselves) and revealed the discrepancies between the historical evidence – which clearly shows how women artists were esteemed by their male colleagues and contemporary critics – and the present-day perspective, which has either written them out, turned them into students or lovers of 'the Masters', or demoted them to such positions as 'a painter of mothers and babies'. Anna Havemann, a curator and a lecturer at the University of Potsdam, gave a more factual talk, comparing the progressive attitude of the Pennsylvania Academy of the Fine Arts to the European art academies of the period. A more recent Penn alumnus, artist Bill Scott – a close friend of Berthe Morisot's descendants – gave what started as an interesting glimpse into the painter's world through intimate snapshots of her home, studio and private collection, but descended into a rather long exposition on how she influenced his own work.

It might have been the late hour and the hard seats, but the crowd was close to rioting at the irony of a man using Morisot's work to advance his own while posing as her apologist.

Before attending the symposium, I wondered how all this might still be relevant in 2008. As Garb noted, however, 'misogyny is an endemic part of modernity' and we live in the modern age, the transition into which Impressionism documented along with all its attendant social changes. The most stunning of these was the increasing inclusion of women in the workforce and their growing independence, without which there would have evolved no need for men to 'keep them in their place'. I realized that my own present-day freedom – which my mother, a student at Vassar together with Nochlin in the 1950s, fought for – cannot be taken for granted while the Louvre still refuses to hang any of its Morisots and while, as recently as 2002, the Palais des Beaux-Arts in Lille chose to continue undermining the artist's significant contribution by advertising her retrospective not with one of her *own* works, which would highlight her staggeringly inventive and revolutionary brushwork, but with a Manet painting that portrays Morisot as a languid sexpot rather than an independent working woman. Just as racism still exists despite a black man running for president in the USA, this symposium showed we must remain ever-vigilant toward the prejudices in the annals of art history.
Amanda Coulson

Home Works IV

Beirut, Lebanon

Since its inception in 2002 'Homeworks: A Forum on Cultural Practices' has been unique in its context and its breadth. Conceived and organized by Ashkal Alwan, the Lebanese Association for Plastic Arts, under the formidable leadership of curator Christine Tohme, 'Home Works' is an eight-day programme of performances, film screenings, talks, discussions, publications and exhibitions – a discursive platform for artists, writers and thinkers working both in and outside the Middle East. Its original geographical, cultural and political focus has expanded over the past six years in terms of both content and participation.

The short, influential history of 'Home Works' runs parallel to a tumultuous flow of events: the Second Intifada, the invasion of Iraq, the assassination of Prime Minister Rafiq Hariri. 'Home Works IV', which took place this April in the Masrah al-Madina theatre in Hamra and other locations around Beirut, was an on-again off-again affair owing to the political instability in Lebanon since the war with Israel in 2006.

The line-up of contributors in the past has included Walid Raad and

The Atlas Group, Emily Jacir, Elias Suleiman, Bilal Khbeiz, Walid Sadek, Jalal Toufic, The Otolith Group, Catherine David and Jacques Rancière, on subjects ranging from identity and trauma, religion and sexuality to human rights and living with terror. While individual works and presentations stand out, it is the cumulative effect of its strands and the contacts established over the packed days and nights of the programme that give it its indelible impact.

Among the highlights of 'Home Works IV' were: Vahid Zara Zade's beautiful video *POW 57187* (2007), about an Iraqi political prisoner in Iran who has created his own museum of the prison and its past prisoners; Julia Meltzer and David Thorne's stunning documentary shot in Damascus, *We Will Live to See These Things* (2007) about 'competing visions of an uncertain future'; and Akram Zaatari's provocative video programme on the body and sex. Artists' talks by Michael Rakowitz and Mireille Astore, lectures by Tom Keenan and keynote speaker Brian Holmes and Mounira Al Solh's first issue of *NOA* ('Not Only in Arabic') provided further layers of critical reflection, as did the elegant performances of Jérôme Bel's *Pichet Klunchun and Myself* (2006) and Rabih Mroué's, *How Nancy Wished*

It Was All an April Fool's Joke (2007), an absurdist roller-coaster ride across Lebanon's history since 1975 as a series of 'reincarnations' that chart the shifting allegiances of conflicting factions.

As with earlier works by Mroué and other artists from Beirut, the image and the archive as a repository for collective memory were appropriated into a polyphonic narrative of competing histories. The posters that inspire the changing visual backdrop in Mroué's work are from the archive of Zeina Masri and were presented in a stunning exhibition in downtown Beirut.

While the energy and urgency of 'Home Works' reflect the fraught and disputed context of Beirut and the Middle East region in general, the event's uniqueness as an arena for different forms of expression and the exchange of ideas has also made it a vital space outside the market-led environment of the contemporary art world. For all those who contribute to the forum's realization, it is a space in which viewpoints are made visible, speakers made audible and individuals recognized. For those who are privileged to attend this event, it is a horizon-shifting and exhilarating experience, for its multiplicity and its liberating spirit of permission.
Suzanne Cotter

HAUNCH OF VENISON   ZÜRICH

Lessingstrasse 5
8002 Zürich
Switzerland

Universal Recipient
(detail), 2008
Acrylic on canvas, bronze
249 x 173 cm

Catalogue available

T +41 (0) 43 422 8888
F +41 (0) 43 422 8889
zurich@haunchofvenison.com
www.haunchofvenison.com

JITISH KALLAT
UNIVERSAL RECIPIENT
31.05 — 02.08.08

team

dawn

mellor

team
(gallery, inc.)
josé freire
83 grand street   nyc 10013 usa
+1 212 279 9219   teamgal.com

Contemporary
Art from South Africa
—
David Goldblatt
Nicholas Hlobo
William Kentridge
Vivienne Koorland
Santu Mofokeng
Berni Searle
Guy Tillim
—
Curated by Tamar Garb

HOME LANDS
LAND MARKS
31 MAY–5 JULY 2008

HAUNCH OF VENISON LONDON

6 Haunch of Venison Yard
off Brook Street
London W1K 5ES
United Kingdom

T+ 44 (0) 20 7495 5050
F+ 44 (0) 20 7495 4050
london@haunchofvenison.com
www.haunchofvenison.com

Catalogue available

Lower Gallery: 4 July to 10 August 2008

MATTHEW HIGGS
ART IS TO ENJOY

Upper Gallery and Project Space: 4 July to 10 August 2008

UNRELATED

Curated by Matthew Higgs

DAN ASHER
PAUL BLOODGOOD
SAM GORDON
JANICE GUY
JUDY LINN

WILKINSON

50 to 58 Vyner Street, London E2 9DQ
Tel. 020 8980 2662 / Fax. 020 8980 0028
www.wilkinsongallery.com

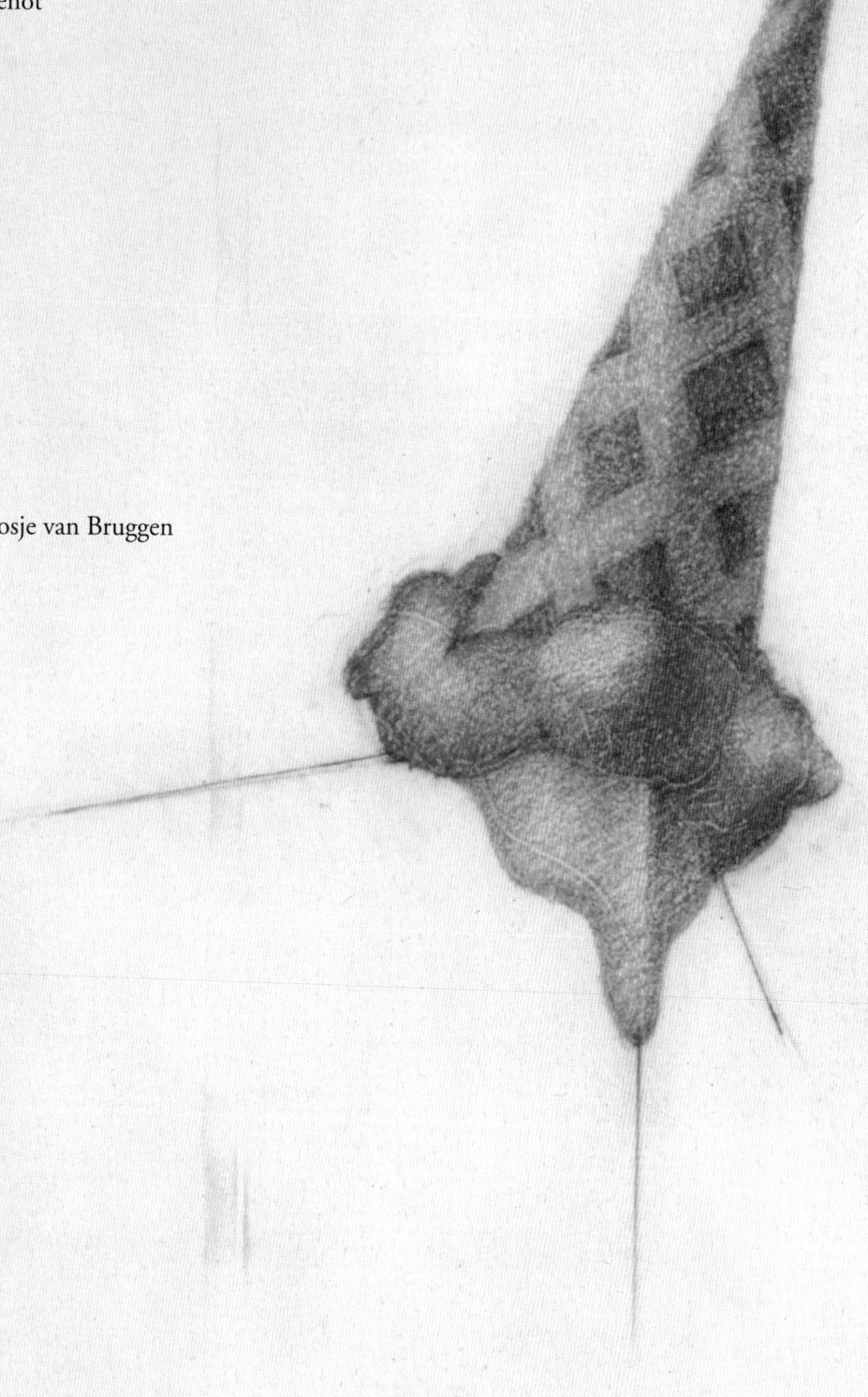

ARTISTS

Carl Andre

Jonathan Borofsky

Céleste Boursier-Mougenot

Sophie Calle

Mark di Suvero

Sam Durant

Wayne Gonzales

Robert Grosvenor

Hans Haacke

Donald Judd

Julian Lethbridge

Sherrie Levine

Sol Lewitt

Christian Marclay

Claes Oldenburg & Coosje van Bruggen

Walid Raad

Rudolf Stingel

Atsuko Tanaka

John Tremblay

Kelley Walker

Dan Walsh

Meg Webster

Robert Wilson

Jackie Winsor

Bing Wright

Carey Young

WORKS BY

Jo Baer

Jennifer Bartlett

Dan Flavin

Michael Hurson

Akira Kanayama

Yayoi Kusama

Zoe Leonard

Joel Shapiro

PAULA COOPER GALLERY

534 WEST 21ST STREET NEW YORK NY 10011 212 255 1105 WWW.PAULACOOPERGALLERY.COM

Claes Oldenburg & Coosje van Bruggen *Proposal for a Sculpture in the Form of a Dropped Cone, for Neumarkt Galerie, Cologne* 1998

Liam Gillick
Three perspectives
and a short scenario*
Work 1988 – 2008

19.1.2008 - 24.3.2008
Witte de With, Rotterdam

26.1.2008 - 30.3.2008
Kunsthalle Zürich

26.9.2008 - 2.11.2008
Kunstverein München*

3.10.2009 - 3.1.2010
Museum of Contemporary Art, Chicago

Sam Lewitt
Printer, Scriptor: Folios

20 June – 29 August

Galerie Daniel Buchholz
Neven-DuMont-Str. 17 · 50667 Köln
Tel +49–221–257 49 46   Fax +49–221–25 33 51
post@galeriebuchholz.de · www.galeriebuchholz.de

Cheyney Thompson

20 June – 29 August

Galerie Daniel Buchholz · Elisenstraße 4-6 · 50667 Köln

JOHN M ARMLEDER

25 JUNE . 29 AUGUST 2008

SIMON LEE

12 BERKELEY STREET
LONDON W1J 8DT
T +44 (0) 20 7491 0100
F +44 (0) 20 7491 0200

SIMONLEEGALLERY.COM

Galpão Fortes Vilaça

Rua James Holland, 71 | Barra Funda | 01138-000 São Paulo Brasil

T + 11 3392 3942 | F + 11 3392 5969

www.fortesvilaca.com.br | galpao@fortesvilaca.com.br

Cerith Wyn Evans
Carlos Bevilacqua

14.06.08 - 12.07.08

Los Carpinteros
Marina Rheingantz

26.07.08 - 23.08.08

Arturo Herrera

14.06.08 - 12.07.08

Gerben Mulder

26.07.08 - 23.08.08

Galeria Fortes Vilaça

Rua Fradique Coutinho 1500 | 05416-001 São Paulo Brasil

T +55 11 3032 7066 | F +55 11 3097 0384

www.fortesvilaca.com.br | galeria@fortesvilaca.com.br

JULESde**BALINCOURT**
MALPAIS

JUNE – JULY 2008

GALERIE THADDAEUS ROPAC
PARIS   FRANCE   7 RUE DEBELLEYME   TEL: 331 4272 9900   FAX: 331 4272 6166   WWW.ROPAC.NET

Kunstmuseum St. Gallen

DR. FOURQUET 12, 28012 MADRID. TEL:(34) 91 468 05 06 FAX:(34) 91 467 51 34
e-mail:galeria@helgadealvear.com   www.helgadealvear.com

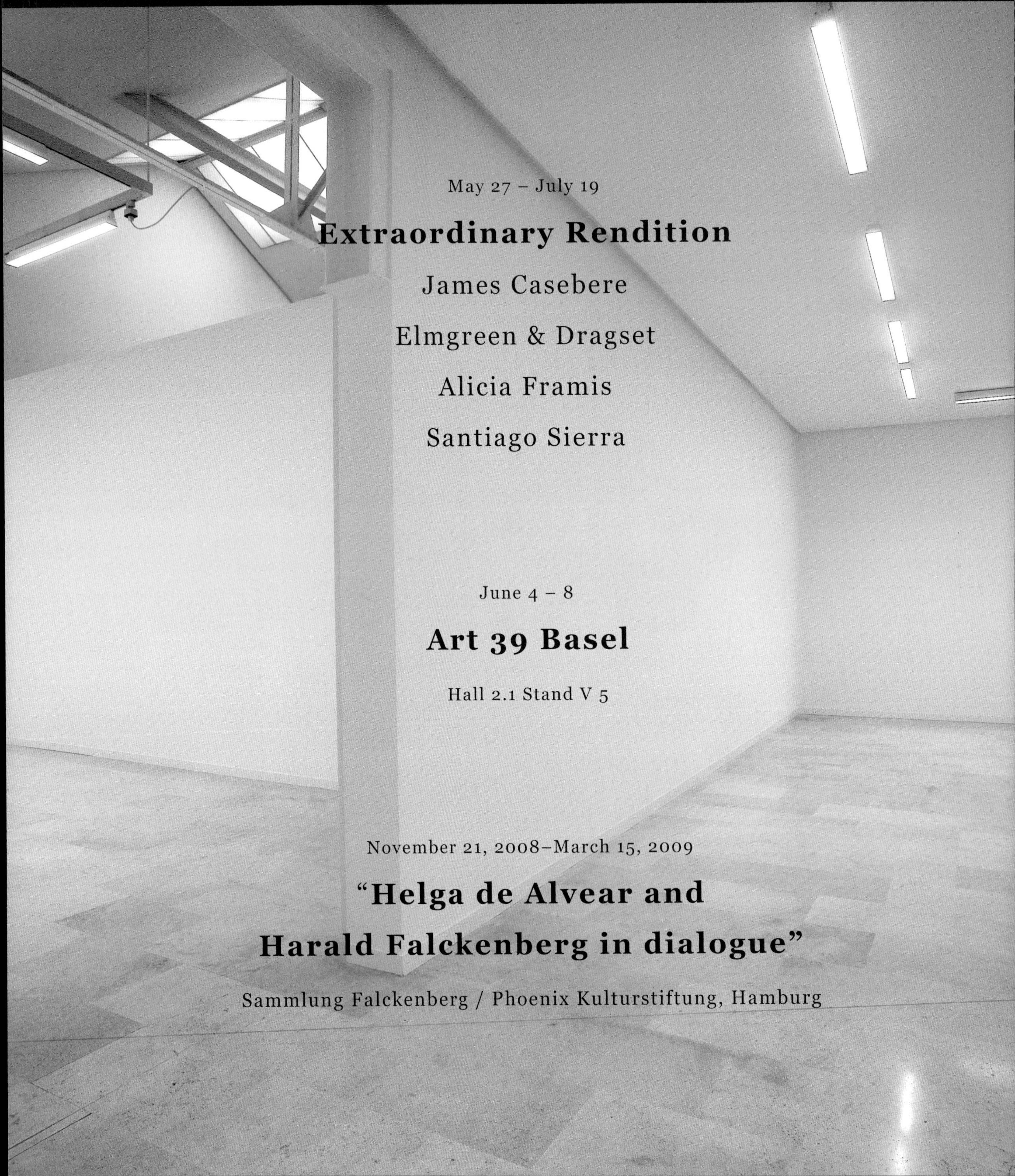

May 27 – July 19

Extraordinary Rendition

James Casebere

Elmgreen & Dragset

Alicia Framis

Santiago Sierra

June 4 – 8

Art 39 Basel

Hall 2.1 Stand V 5

November 21, 2008–March 15, 2009

"Helga de Alvear and Harald Falckenberg in dialogue"

Sammlung Falckenberg / Phoenix Kulturstiftung, Hamburg

MARLENE DUMAS
For Whom The Bell Tolls

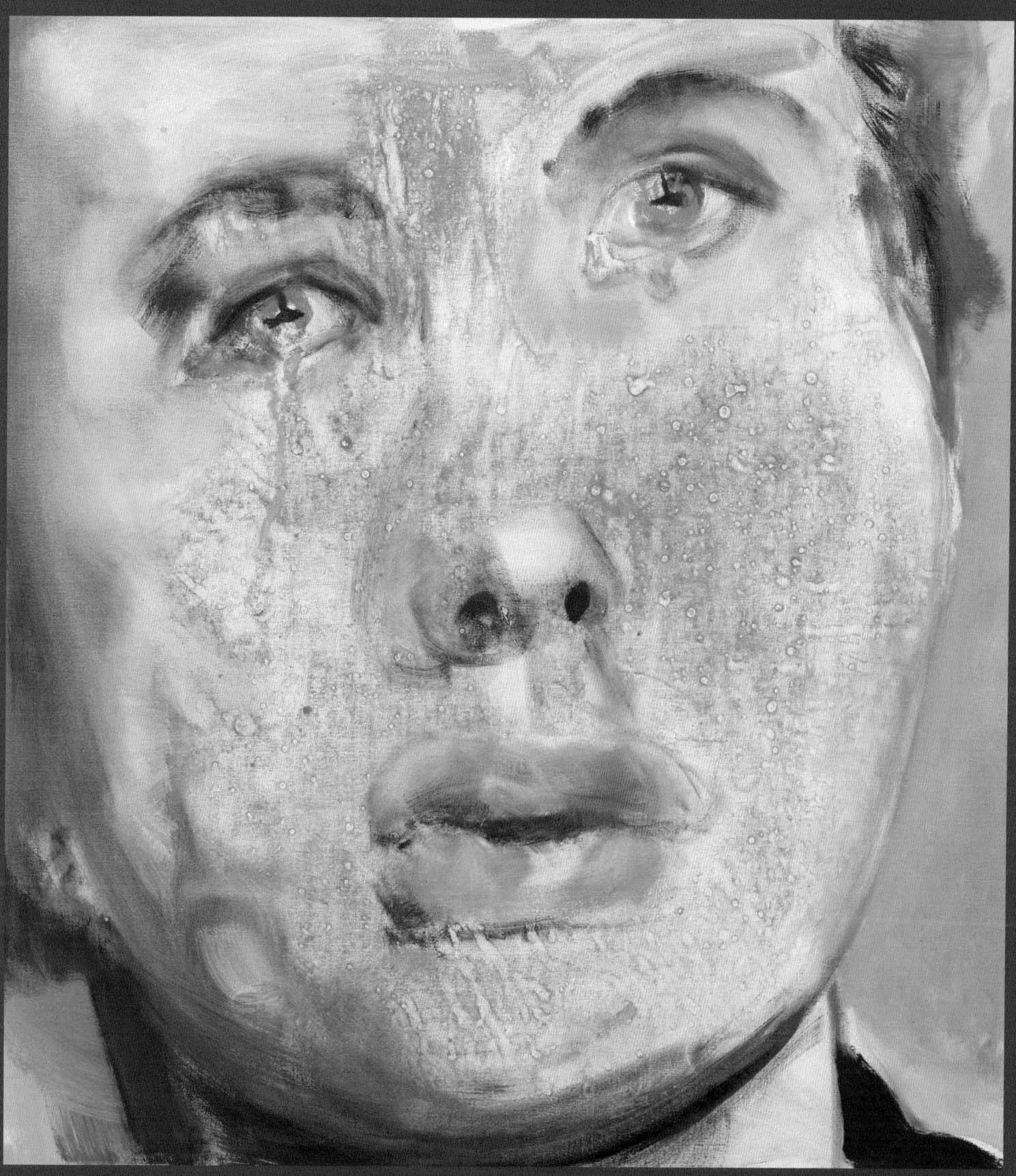

ZENO X GALLERY
September 6 - October 11, 2008

Leopold De Waelplaats 16, 2000 Antwerp, Belgium
www.zeno-x.com   info@zeno-x.com   +32 3 216 16 26

MICHAEL STEVENSON Ground floor Buchanan Building 160 Sir Lowry Road Woodstock 7925 Cape Town T +27 (0)21 462 1500 info@michaelstevenson.com www.michaelstevenson.com

10 JULY –
23 AUGUST 2008

GUY TILLIM
AVENUE PATRICE LUMUMBA

ÂNGELA FERREIRA
FOR MOZAMBIQUE

MANTHIA DIAWARA
MAISON TROPICALE

Guy Tillim *Avenue Samora Machel, Quelimane, Mozambique, 2008*

Fiona Rae

23 May – 28 June 2008

Timothy Taylor Gallery

15 Carlos Place, London W1K 2EX
Tel +44 (0)20 7409 3344 Fax +44 (0)20 7409 1316
mail@timothytaylorgallery.com

we go in search of our dream, 2007, oil and acrylic on canvas, 84 × 69 in (213 × 175 cm) (detail)

LONG MARCH SPACE, BEIJING

林天苗 LIN TIANMIAO

MOTHER'S !!!

JULY 26 - AUGUST 27, 2008

ALSO SHOWING AT

HALF LIFE OF A DREAM: CONTEMPORARY CHINESE ART FROM THE LOGAN COLLECTION
JULY 10 – OCTOBER 5
SFMOMA

SHCONTEMPORARY ART FAIR
SEPTEMBER 10 – 13
林天苗 LIN TIANMIAO   展望 ZHAN WANG

FRIEZE ART FAIR
OCTOBER 16 – 19
林天苗 LIN TIANMIAO   郭凤怡 GUO FENGYI

长征空间   4 Jiuxianqiao Rd, Chaoyang District, Beijing, P.R.China 100015
Long March Space   T +86 (0)10 6438 7107   F   +86 (0)10 6432 3834   lm@longmarchspace.com   www.longmarchspace.com

ANSELM KIEFER

AUGUST 2008
CATALOGUE

GALERIE THADDAEUS ROPAC
SALZBURG AUSTRIA MIRABELLPLATZ 2 TEL: 43 662 881 393 FAX: 43 662 881 3939 WWW.ROPAC.NET

MIKE PARR

MILK

A photographic survey of performance
works from 1971 – 2008

June 2008

CarriageWorks
245 Wilson Street Darlington 2008
Telephone +612 8580 7002
mail@annaschwartzgallery.com
www.annaschwartzgallery.com

ANNA
SCHWARTZ
GALLERY
—
SYDNEY

detail: *The Emetics (Primary Vomit) I am Sick of Art (Red, Yellow and Blue)*, 1977

MICHAEL BROWN
The People's Playground
June 19 - July 31, 2008

MARTIN CREED
29 MAY - SEPTEMBER 2008

GALLERIA LORCAN O'NEILL ROMA

1E VIA ORTI D'ALIBERT · ROMA 00165 · ITALY   TEL +39 06 6889-2980 · LORCANONEILL.COM

LEHMANN MAUPIN

540 West 26th Street
New York NY 10001
Telephone 212 255 2923
Fax 212 255 2924

201 Chrystie Street
New York NY 10002
Telephone 212 254 0054
Fax 212 254 0055

lehmannmaupin.com

SUMMER 2008

8 May – 14 June 26th Street	Lee Bul
10 May – 7 June Chrystie Street	Stefano Arienti
26 June – 8 August 26th Street	Rei Sato
24 June – 8 August Chrystie Street	Mario Ybarra Jr.
4 June – 8 June Booth F2	Art Basel

That's The Way It Is

June 21 – August 2, 2008

GALERIE GUIDO W. BAUDACH

Oudenarder Straße 16-20   13347 Berlin   T +49 30 280 477 27   F +49 30 450 244 81   guidowbaudach.com

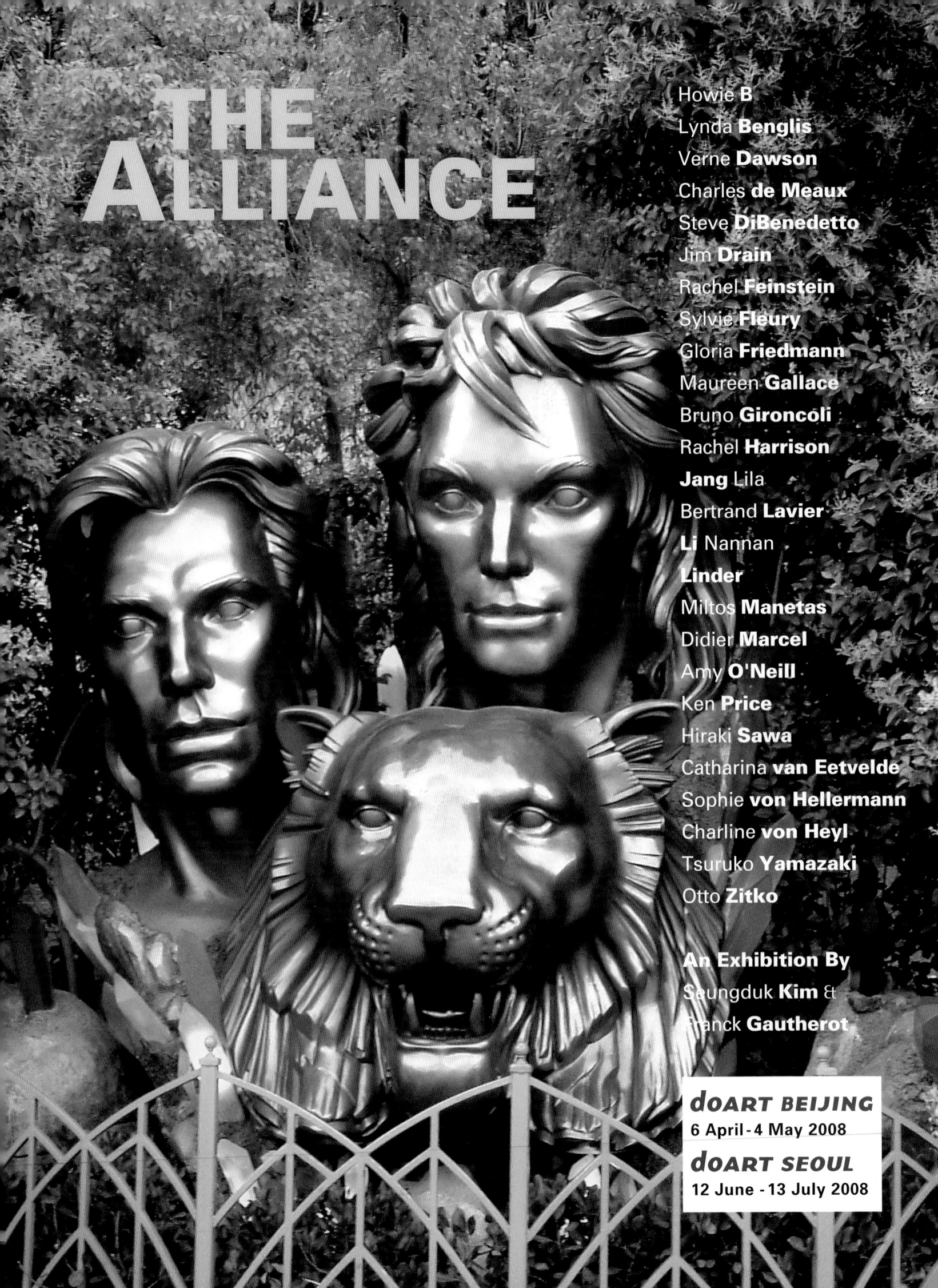

THE ALLIANCE

Howie **B**
Lynda **Benglis**
Verne **Dawson**
Charles **de Meaux**
Steve **DiBenedetto**
Jim **Drain**
Rachel **Feinstein**
Sylvie **Fleury**
Gloria **Friedmann**
Maureen **Gallace**
Bruno **Gironcoli**
Rachel **Harrison**
Jang Lila
Bertrand **Lavier**
Li Nannan
Linder
Miltos **Manetas**
Didier **Marcel**
Amy **O'Neill**
Ken **Price**
Hiraki **Sawa**
Catharina **van Eetvelde**
Sophie **von Hellermann**
Charline **von Heyl**
Tsuruko **Yamazaki**
Otto **Zitko**

An Exhibition By
Seungduk **Kim** &
Franck **Gautherot**

doART *BEIJING*
6 April - 4 May 2008
doART *SEOUL*
12 June - 13 July 2008

*do*ART BEIJING

OLIVIER MOSSET

June 14 - July 13, 2008

DOUGLAS GORDON

August 2 - 31, 2008

*do*ART SEOUL

ON KAWARA

I MET / I WENT / I GOT UP / ONE MILLION YEARS / PURE CONSCIOUSNESS
Curated by Michèle Didier

July 23 - August 24, 2008

GALLERY HYUNDAI COMPANY
*do*ART BEIJING / SEOUL

BEIJING 261 Caochangdi, Airport Service Rd.,
Chaoyang District, Beijing 100015, China
www.doartbeijing.com

SEOUL 80 Sagan-dong Jongro-gu
Seoul 110-190 Korea
www.doartseoul.com

(T) +44(0)20 7168 2566   (F) +44(0)20 7613 0009   (E) MAIL@HERALDST.COM

PETER COFFIN
&
DJORDJE OZBOLT

JUNE

HERALD ST 2 HERALD STREET LONDON E2 6JT ENGLAND WWW.HERALDST.COM

(T) +44(0)20 7168 2566   (F) +44(0)20 7613 0009   (E) MAIL@HERALDST.COM

JOSH BRAND
&
BRIAN MORAN

LISTE 08, BASEL
3RD - 8TH JUNE

HERALD ST 2 HERALD STREET LONDON E2 6JT ENGLAND WWW.HERALDST.COM

doggerfisher

Alexander Heim

31 July - 13 September 2008

doggerfisher / susanna beaumont
11 gayfield square edinburgh eh1 3nt
t + 44 (0) 131 558 7110 f + 44 (0) 131 558 7179
mail@doggerfisher.com www.doggerfisher.com

Tues - Fri 10 am - 6 pm, Sat 12 - 5 pm or by appointment

RICHARD LONG

14.06.08
—
16.09.08

HAUNCH OF VENISON   BERLIN

Heidestrasse 46
10557 Berlin
Germany

T+ 49 (0) 30 39 74 39 63
F+ 49 (0) 30 39 74 39 64
berlin@haunchofvenison.com
www.haunchofvenison.com

Richard Long installing
One Circle Leads
To Another,
Melbourne, 2008
Photo: Naomi Milgrom

MEREDYTH SPARKS
MIKA TAJIMA

LISTE 08
THE YOUNG ART FAIR IN BASEL

Elizabeth Dee
545 West 20th Street New York NY 10011   www.elizabethdeegallery.com   t +1 212 924 7545   f +1 212 924 7671

Frith Street Gallery
GOLDEN SQUARE

4 July – 15 August 2008

Interlude – A series of curated summer exhibitions

BAGHDAD/SPACE COG/ANALYST
Eugenio Dittborn, Diango Hernández,
Gabriel Kuri, João Onofre

CURATED BY ANDREW RENTON

17–18 Golden Square, London W1F 9JJ   T +44 (0)20 7494 1550
F +44 (0)20 7287 3733 www.frithstreetgallery.com info@frithstreetgallery.com

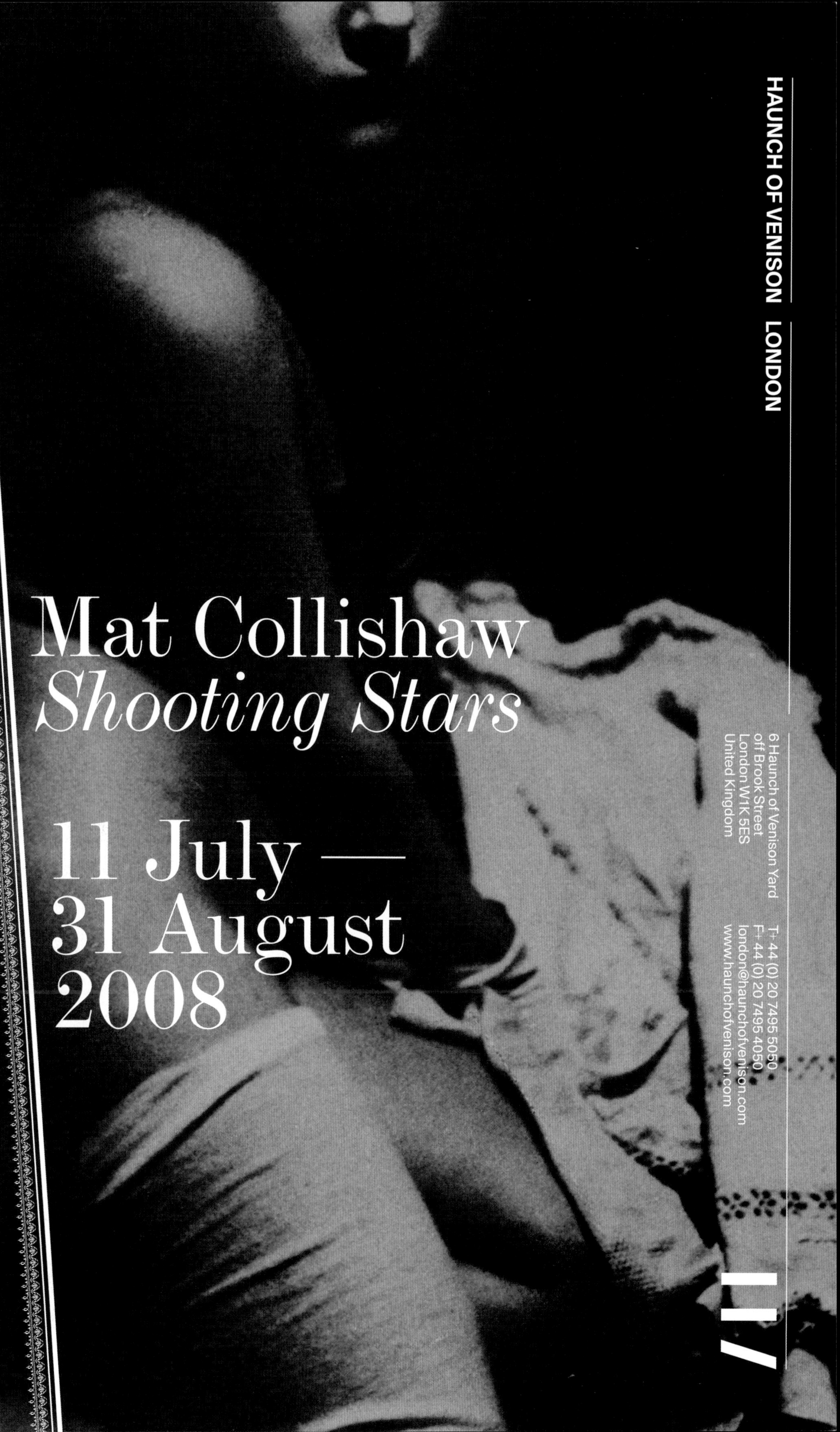

Mat Collishaw
Shooting Stars

11 July —
31 August
2008

HAUNCH OF VENISON   LONDON

6 Haunch of Venison Yard
off Brook Street
London W1K 5ES
United Kingdom

T+ 44 (0) 20 7495 5050
F+ 44 (0) 20 7495 4050
london@haunchofvenison.com
www.haunchofvenison.com

SCHAULAGER ®

MONIKA SOSNOWSKA

ANDREA ZITTEL

1:1

26.04. – 21.09.08

Tue – Fri, noon – 6 p.m.; Thu, noon – 7 p.m.; Sat/Sun, 10 a.m. – 5 p.m.
During Art Basel: 2 – 3 and 5 – 8 June, 10 a.m. – 6 p.m.; 4 June, noon – 6 p.m.
Open on 1 August

Schaulager, Ruchfeldstrasse 19, CH-4142 Münchenstein/Basel
www.schaulager.org

LAURENZ FOUNDATION

Joe Colombo
Design and the
Invention of the Future

Kunsthaus Graz
June 7 to
August 31, 2008

An exhibition by the
Vitra Design Museum
and La Triennale di
Milano in cooperation
with the Studio
Joe Colombo, Milano

Kunsthaus Graz am
Landesmuseum Joanneum
Lendkai 1, A-8020 Graz
Tue–Sun 10am–6pm
info@kunsthausgraz.at
www.kunsthausgraz.at

A1

Sophie von Hellermann

ACCIDENTAL PORTRAITS

16 May to 15 June 2008

VILMA GOLD
6 Minerva Street
London E2 9EH

www.vilmagold.com
Phone: +44 2077299888
Fax: +44 2077299898

RINKO KAWAUCHI

Utatane

GALERÍA PEPE COBO

C/Fortuny 39, 28010 MADRID - Tel.: +34 91 319 0683 - Fax.: +34 91 308 3190 - www.pepecobo.com

NINA RIKE SPRINGER

MAY – JUNE 2008

FIAT LUXX

JENNY HOLZER

BRIGITTE KOWANZ

FRANCOIS MORELLET

MAURIZIO NANNUCCI

KEITH SONNIER

JAMES TURRELL

RICHARD LONG

JULY – AUGUST 2008

AES+F

JULY – AUGUST 2008

ALESSANDRO RAHO

AUGUST – SEPTEMBER 2008

GALERIE NIKOLAUS RUZICSKA
FAISTAUERGASSE 12   5020 SALZBURG   AUSTRIA
T +43 662 630 360   F +43 662 630 360 60
SALZBURG@RUZICSKA.COM   WWW.RUZICSKA.COM

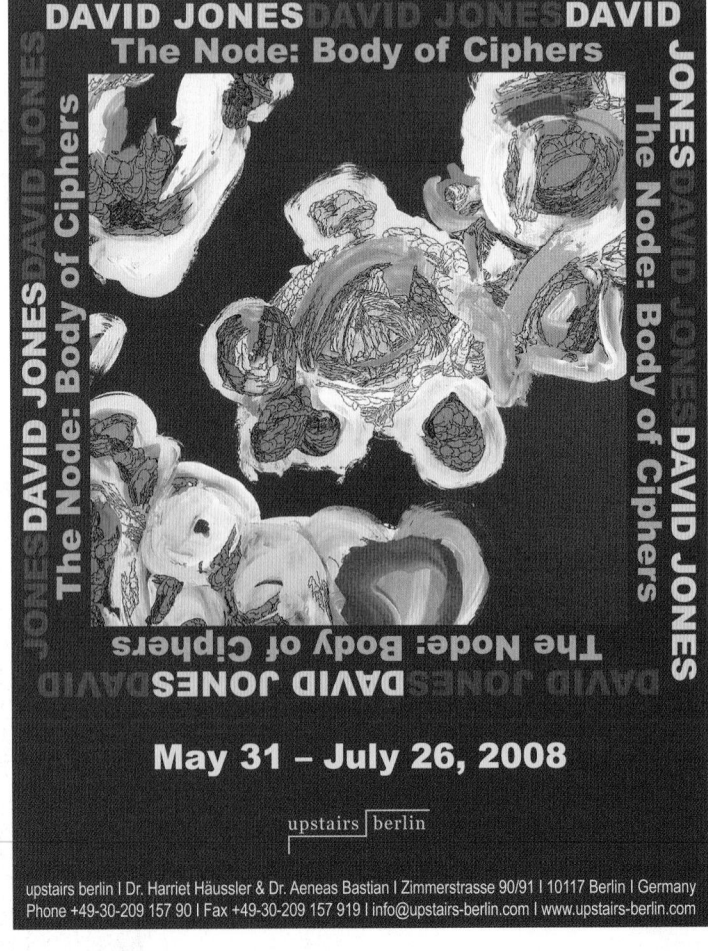

Anne-Mie Van Kerckhoven

Nothing More Natural

Kunstmuseum Luzern
16 August–23 November 2008
www.kunstmuseumluzern.ch

Wiels Centre for Contemporary

Kunsthalle Nürnberg
March–May 2009
www.kunsthalle.nuernberg.de

FRAC Pays de la Loire

Catalogue with texts by Susanne Neubauer,
Gertrud Sandqvist, Dirk Snauwaert,
Anne-Mie Van Kerckhoven

Organised with the support of
Zeno X Gallery

DOUGLAS GORDON &
PHILIPPE PARRENO

daadgalerie

Zimmerstraße 90/91
10117 Berlin
16. Juni – 9. August 2008
täglich 11.00–18.00 Uhr

Zidane:
A 21st Century Portrait

2005, Filminstallation, 93 min.

DEUTSCHE BANK & THE SOLOMON R. GUGGENHEIM FOUNDATION

ON VIEW 2008/2009

26.04. – 22.06.2008
FREISTELLER · VILLA ROMANA FELLOWS 2008
DANI GAL, JULIA SCHMIDT, ASLI SUNGU, CLEMENS VON WEDEMEYER

05.07. – 21.09.2008
FREEWAY BALCONIES
CURATED BY COLLIER SCHORR

30.10.2008 – 25.01.2009
ANISH KAPOOR · COMMISSIONED WORK

Deutsche Guggenheim

Unter den Linden 13/15 · 10117 Berlin · Phone + 49 30 20 20 93 - 0 · Fax + 49 30 20 20 93 - 20
www.deutsche-guggenheim.de · berlin.guggenheim@db.com
Open daily 10 a.m. to 8 p.m. · Thursday to 10 p.m. · Mondays admission free

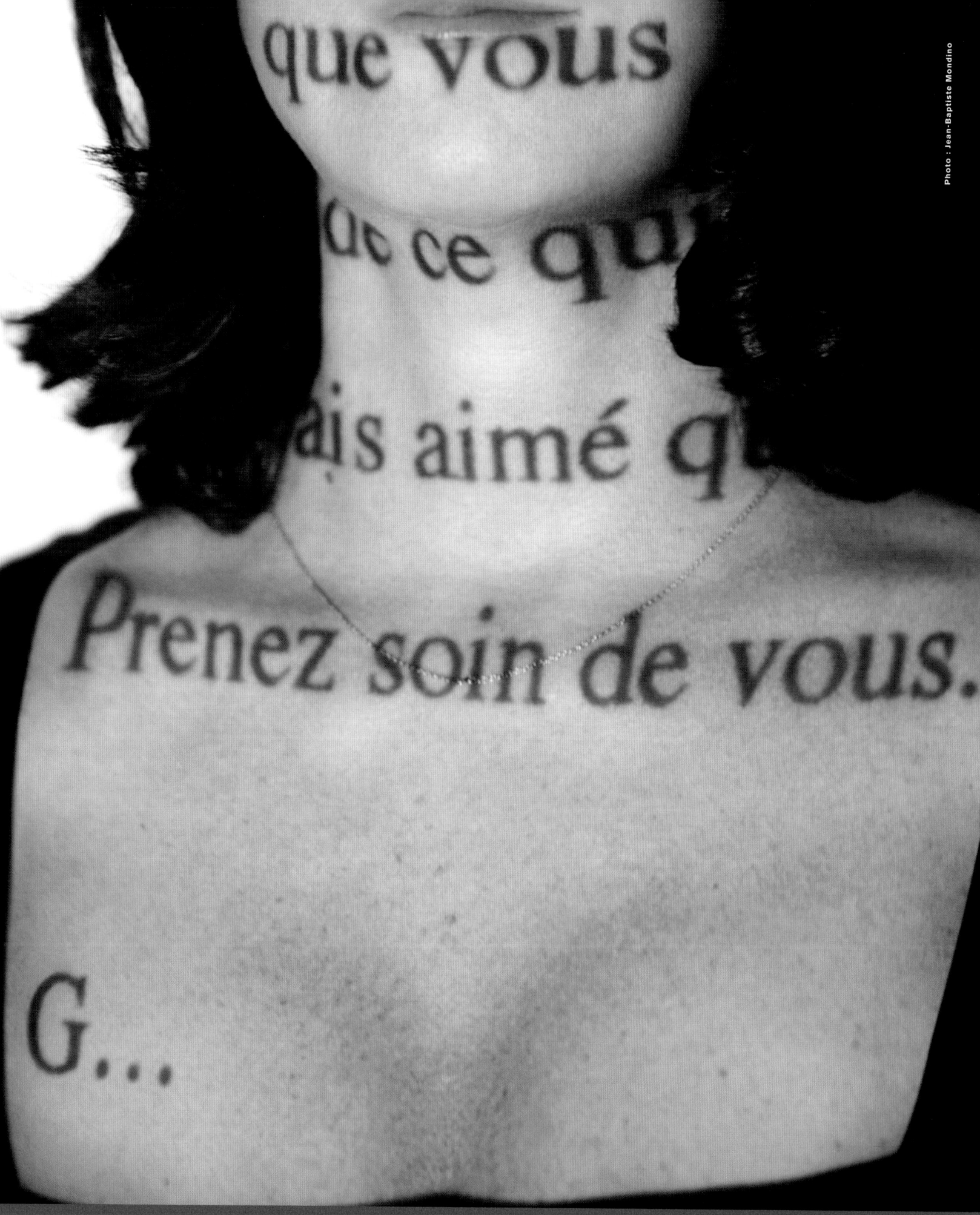

Sophie Calle

July 2008 — October 2008

dhc■art

DHC/ART Fondation pour l'art contemporain / Foundation for Contemporary Art
451, St-Jean street, Montréal (QC) • 514 849-3742 • www.dhc-art.org

MASSIMO VITALI

A PORTFOLIO OF
LANDSCAPES WITH FIGURES

Fiftytwo Plates, in a Limited Edition of 120 and 20 a.p.
Printed by Steidl

BRANCOLINIGRIMALDI
ARTECONTEMPORANEA

Via dei Tre Orologi, 6/A 00197 ROMA
Tel +39 06 80693100 info@brancolinigrimaldi.com

HALES GALLERY

Interior
20 June – 26 July

Beth Campbell, Laura Letinsky,
Laura Oldfield-Ford, Courtney Smith,
Jessica Stockholder, Amy Yoes

Hales Gallery
Tea Building
7 Bethnal Green Road
London E1 6LA
E info@halesgallery.com
T +44 (0)20 7033 1938
www.halesgallery.com

Laura Oldfield-Ford, *Threshold of the Arcades (London 2013)*, 2008

Juneau Projects
Trappenkamp

7 June – 26 October 2008
at Tate Britain

⊖ Pimlico, Free admission
www.tate.org.uk/britain

BRITAIN
TATE

ART NOW

Image courtesy of Juneau Projects

9 SCRIPTS FROM A NATION AT WAR

DAVID THORNE
KATYA SANDER
ASHLEY HUNT
SHARON HAYES
ANDREA GEYER

Level 2 Gallery

13 June – 25 August   Tate Modern   ⊖ Southwark   Free admission   www.tate.org.uk/modern

MODERN
TATE

SPECIAL EXHIBITION
Luisa Rabbia: Travels with Isabella,
Travel Scrapbooks 1883/2008
June 26 - Sept 28

ISABELLA
SEWART GARDNER
MUSEUM

280 THE FENWAY BOSTON MASSACHUSETTS   WWW.GARDNERMUSEUM.ORG

SOUTHBANK CENTRE

Specially commissioned artwork transforming The Hayward into a 'Psycho Building' © Atelier Bow-Wow

ARTISTS AND ARCHITECTURE

ATELIER BOW-WOW
MICHAEL BEUTLER
LOS CARPINTEROS
GELITIN
MIKE NELSON
ERNESTO NETO
TOBIAS PUTRIH
TOMAS SARACENO
DO-HO SUH
RACHEL WHITEREAD

THE HAYWARD
28 MAY–25 AUGUST

sponsored by Bloomberg

TICKETS 0871 663 2519
WWW.SOUTHBANKCENTRE.CO.UK

PSYCHO BUILDINGS

The Henry Moore Foundation   outset.   **40**

Susan Hiller
Outlaw Cowgirl
and Other Works

BAWAG FOUNDATION
9.5.–17.8.2008
Foundationsquartier
Wiedner Hauptstraße 15, 1040 Wien

Di–So und feiertags 11–18 Uhr, Do 11–20 Uhr
Führungen jeweils Do 18 Uhr und Sa 15 Uhr
Eintritt frei, Tel. +43-1-504 98 80-38
www.bawag-foundation.at

BAWAG

Susan Hiller, OUTLAW COWGIRL, 2005
Courtesy Galerie Volker Diehl Berlin, Foto: © Marcus Schneider

barbican do something different

**curve
art
Huang Yong Ping
25.06.08–21.09.08
Rafael
Lozano-Hemmer
09.10.08–18.01.09**

barbican artgallery

Curve Art is a series of new
commissions created for The Curve
by contemporary artists

Admission Free
www.barbican.org.uk

For his first UK solo show, *Frolic*, Huang
Yong Ping, creates a new installation
exploring the complex imperial history
between Britain and China in the 19th
century, focusing on the Opium Wars.

Julian Opie
Recent Works

11.6.–21.9.2008

MAK EXHIBITION HALL Weiskirchnerstraße 3, Vienna 1. Tue MAK NITE[c] 10 a.m.–12 p.m., Wed–Sun 10 a.m.–6 p.m., Mon closed www.MAK.at

FREE ADMISSION ON SATURDAYS[c]
POWERED BY
Verbund

M A K

Applied Arts | Contemporary Art

ABOVE THE FOLD

Museum für Gegenwartskunst Basel
June 1 to October 12, 2008   www.kunstmuseumbasel.ch

AYŞE ERKMEN
CEAL FLOYER
DAVID LAMELAS
&
COLLECTION SELECTION

Sponsor: Fonds für künstlerische Aktivitäten im Museum für Gegenwartskunst
der Emanuel Hoffmann-Stiftung und der Christoph Merian Stiftung

Lucy Skaer
17 May – 9 July 2008

Janet Cardiff and George Bures Miller
31 July – 28 September 2008

A collaboration between The Fruitmarket Gallery, Edinburgh and Modern Art Oxford

Market Street, Edinburgh
Mon–Sat 11am–6pm, Sun 12–5pm

Always free

The
Fruitmarket
Gallery

www.fruitmarket.co.uk

Scottish
Arts Council

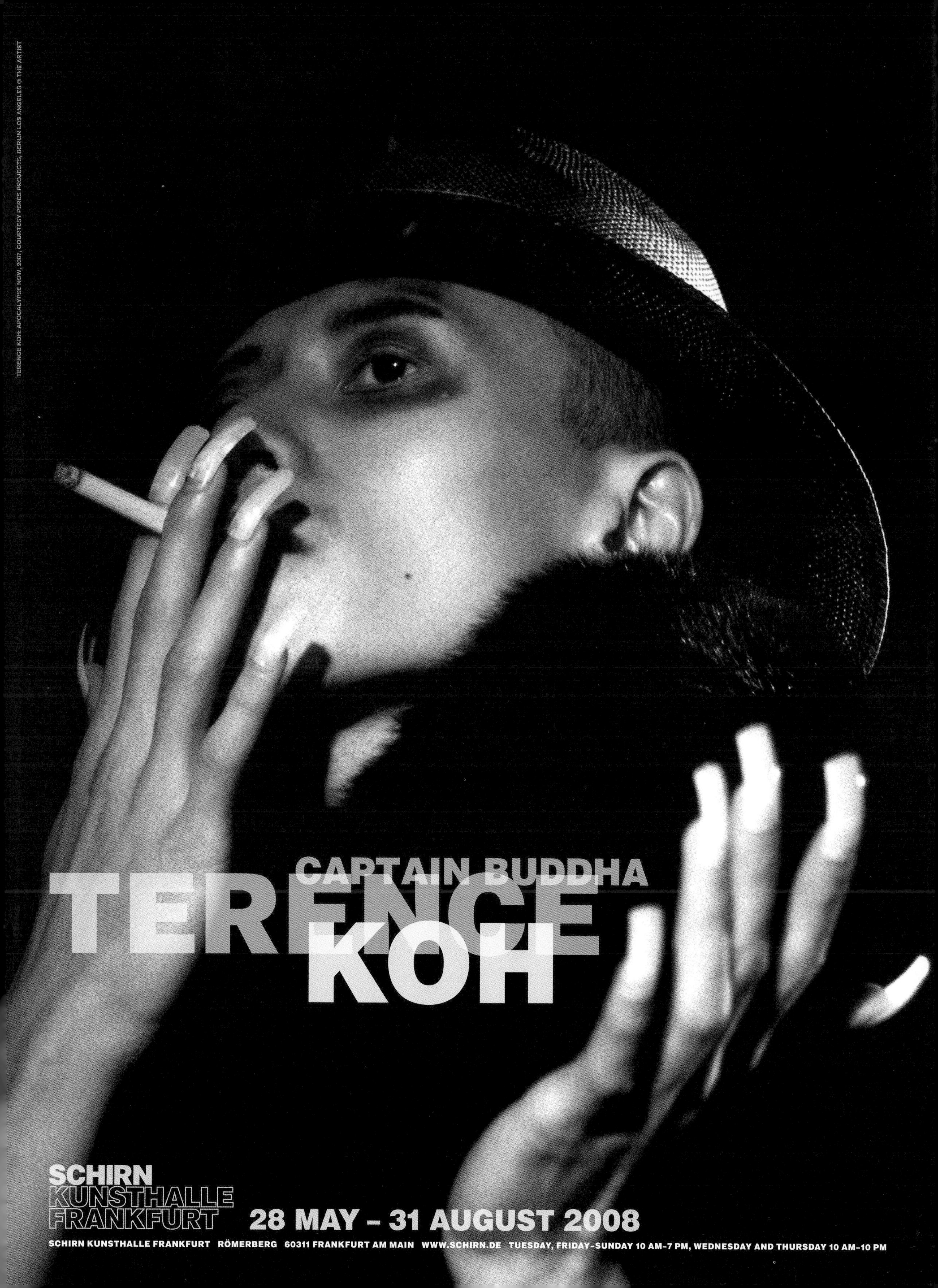

TERENCE KOH: APOCALYPSE NOW, 2007, COURTESY PERES PROJECTS, BERLIN LOS ANGELES © THE ARTIST
CAPTAIN BUDDHA
TERENCE KOH
SCHIRN KUNSTHALLE FRANKFURT
28 MAY – 31 AUGUST 2008
SCHIRN KUNSTHALLE FRANKFURT RÖMERBERG 60311 FRANKFURT AM MAIN WWW.SCHIRN.DE TUESDAY, FRIDAY–SUNDAY 10 AM–7 PM, WEDNESDAY AND THURSDAY 10 AM–10 PM

TRAMWAY

Kenny Hunter
A Shout in the Street
Sunday 13 July – Sunday 24 August
Tramway 5

OPENING TIMES
Closed Mondays
Tue – Fri 10am – 5pm
Sat & Sun 12 – 5pm
Admission free

25 Albert Drive
Glasgow
G41 2PE
www.tramway.org
0845 330 3501

ARTIST TALK:
Saturday 19 July, 2pm
Free all welcome

88 TWENTY 08

Culture & Sport Glasgow   Scottish Arts Council

NAIRY BAGHRAMIAN The Walker's Day Off
17.05. – 06.07.2008
Eröffnung: 16.05.2008, 19 Uhr

Staatliche Kunsthalle Baden-Baden
Lichtentaler Allee 8a, 76530 Baden-Baden
Telefon 07221-30076-3, Fax 07221-30076-500
www.kunsthalle-baden-baden.de

CENTRE OF CONTEMPORARY ART
ZNAKI CZASU
TORUŃ / POLAND
OFFICIAL INAUGURATION
JUNE 13TH – 14TH 2008

OPENING EXHIBITIONS

FLOWERS OF OUR LIVES

Jesper Alvaer / Kutlug Ataman / Walerian Borowczyk
Anetta Mona Chisa & Lucia Tkáčová / Oskar Dawicki
Wojtek Doroszuk / Lilla Khoór & Will Potter
Robert Kuśmirowski / Goshka Macuga / Łukasz Skąpski
Janina Turek / Andrzej Urbanowicz
Curator: Joanna Zielińska

THE WAY THINGS ARE...
WORKS FROM
THE THYSSEN–BORNEMISZA
ART CONTEMPORARY COLLECTION

Los Carpinteros / Anetta Mona Chisa & Lucia Tkáčová
Julian Rosefeldt / Allan Sekula / Andreas Siekmann
True [Hi]stories of Work – Film Program

ICEBERG
Angelika Markul

13 Wały gen. Sikorskiego Street
87-100 Toruń / Poland
www.csw.torun.pl

ANTHEA HAMILTON
GYMNASIUM

29 MAY – 13 JULY 2008

CHISENHALE GALLERY

64 CHISENHALE ROAD LONDON E3 5QZ UK
T +44(0)20 8981 4518 WWW.CHISENHALE.ORG.UK

THIS EXHIBITION IS A JOINT COMMISSION BETWEEN CHISENHALE GALLERY
AND KUNSTVEREIN FREIBURG, GERMANY AND WILL BE PRESENTED AT
KUNSTVEREIN FREIBURG FROM 23 JANUARY TO 15 MARCH 2009
WITH THANKS TO IBID PROJECTS, LONDON

ALTERED STATES OF PAINT

5 July–7 September

Jutta Koether
Till Gerhard
Andreas Dobler
Angela de la Cruz
Neil Clements
Rabiya Choudry

DCA

Dundee Contemporary Arts

Exhibition open
Tues to Sat 10.30am-5.30pm
Sun 12 noon-5.30pm
Open late Thurs until 8.30pm
Admission Free

152 Nethergate,
Dundee DD1 4DY
01382 909900 www.dca.org.uk
Image: Angela de la Cruz *Super Clutter XXL
(Pink and Brown), 2006* Oil and acrylic on
canvas 210 x 142 x 85 cm Courtesy of the
artist and Lisson Gallery

Dundee Contemporary Arts is supported by

   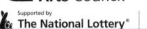

Registered Charity no. SC026631

INGLEBY GALLERY

NEW SPACE OPENING:
1 AUGUST 2008

15 CALTON ROAD
EDINBURGH   EH8 8DL
SCOTLAND

WWW.INGLEBYGALLERY.COM
INFO@INGLEBYGALLERY.COM
TEL N° +44 (0) 131 556 4441

INGLEBY GALLERY

NEW SPACE OPENING:
1 AUGUST 2008

15 CALTON ROAD
EDINBURGH   EH8 8DL
SCOTLAND

WWW.INGLEBYGALLERY.COM

PHOTO: PETER LIVERSIDGE

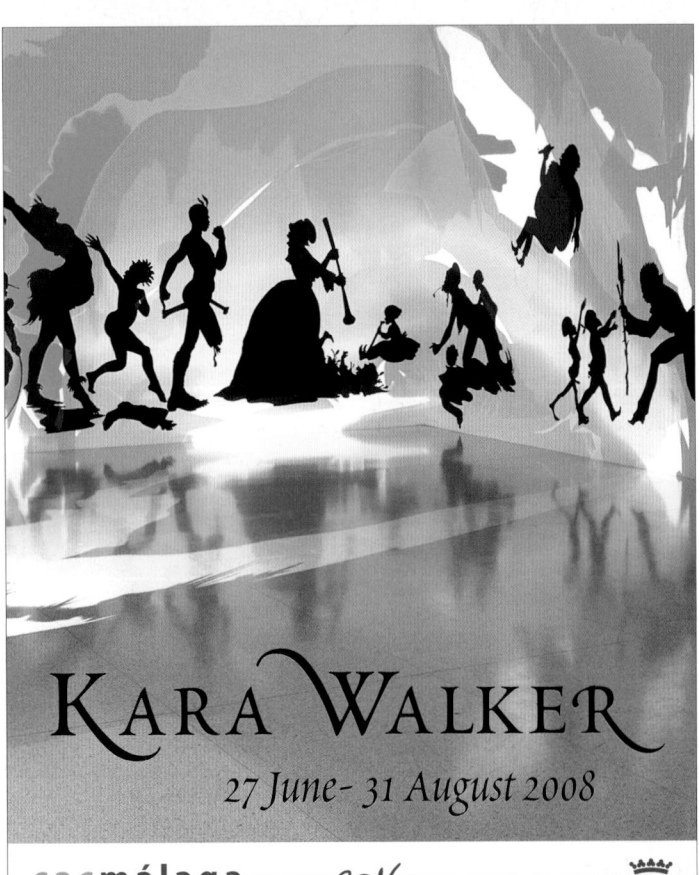

KARA WALKER

27 June– 31 August 2008

International KEBAB
国际快餐

Wang Du 王度

Aug 2-28, 2008

Tang Contemporary Art - Beijing
798 Art District, No.2 Jiuxianqiao Road, Chaoyang District, Beijing 100015, China
T: +86-10-64363518/64363658   F: +86-10-64363018
info@tangcontemporary.com   www.tangcontemporary.com

当代唐人艺术中心
Tang Contemporary Art

Design by ricebowldesign

lustwarande 08
Wanderland

28.06-28.09.08 park de oude warande tilburg nl

David Altmejd [CDN/USA]
David Bade [NL]
Mirosław Bałka [PL]
Caroline Coolen [B]
José Damasceno [BR]
Bart van Dijck [B]
Laura Ford [GB]
Brian Griffiths [GB]
Subodh Gupta [IND]

Jeppe Hein [DK/D]
Lothar Hempel [D]
John Isaacs [GB/D]
Ham Jin [ROK]
Maartje Korstanje [NL]
Gereon Krebber [D]
Skafte Kuhn [D]
Paul McCarthy [USA] *
Jonathan Meese [D]

Renato Nicolodi [B]
Michael Nitsche [D]
Vincent Olinet [F/B]
Jens Pfeifer [E/NL]
André Pielage [NL]
Jon Pylypchuk [CDN/USA]
Ryan Trecartin &
Lizzie Fitch [USA]
Erwin Wurm [A]

entrance: warandelaan tilburg
(parking space auberge du bonheur)
open daily 11.00-17.30
opening sat june 28 at 14.30

* under restriction

extra venue: Museum De Pont
wilhelminapark 1 tilburg
David Altmejd 28.06-31.08.08
open tue-sun 11.00-17.00

www.fundamentfoundation.nl

Jerwood Artists Platform

Jerwood Artists Platform seeks to identify and promote
emerging and talented visual artists, providing them with a major
London solo exhibition at a pivotal time in their career.

Stephen Sutcliffe

21 June-27 July 2008

cell
PROJECT SPACE

Open Fri-Sun 12-6pm
258 Cambridge Heath Road
London E2 9DA
T 020 7241 3600
www.cell.org.uk

ARTS COUNCIL ENGLAND

JERWOOD
CHARITABLE FOUNDATION

GALERIE URS MEILE
BEIJING · LUCERNE

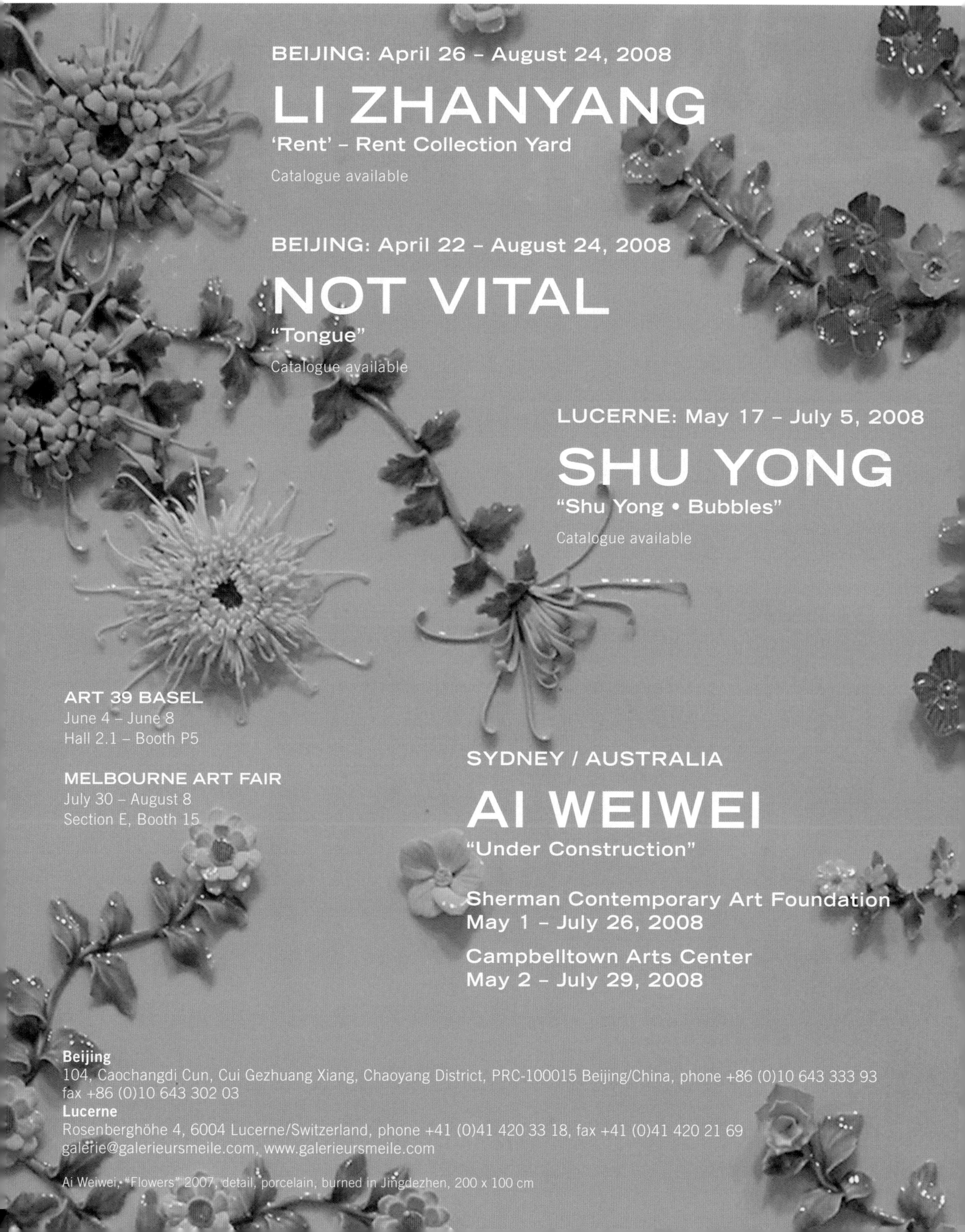

BEIJING: April 26 – August 24, 2008

LI ZHANYANG
'Rent' – Rent Collection Yard

Catalogue available

BEIJING: April 22 – August 24, 2008

NOT VITAL
"Tongue"

Catalogue available

LUCERNE: May 17 – July 5, 2008

SHU YONG
"Shu Yong • Bubbles"

Catalogue available

ART 39 BASEL
June 4 – June 8
Hall 2.1 – Booth P5

MELBOURNE ART FAIR
July 30 – August 8
Section E, Booth 15

SYDNEY / AUSTRALIA

AI WEIWEI
"Under Construction"

Sherman Contemporary Art Foundation
May 1 – July 26, 2008

Campbelltown Arts Center
May 2 – July 29, 2008

Beijing
104, Caochangdi Cun, Cui Gezhuang Xiang, Chaoyang District, PRC-100015 Beijing/China, phone +86 (0)10 643 333 93
fax +86 (0)10 643 302 03
Lucerne
Rosenberghöhe 4, 6004 Lucerne/Switzerland, phone +41 (0)41 420 33 18, fax +41 (0)41 420 21 69
galerie@galerieursmeile.com, www.galerieursmeile.com

Ai Weiwei, "Flowers" 2007, detail, porcelain, burned in Jingdezhen, 200 x 100 cm

Matt's Gallery, London

Paul Rooney
Until 15 June

Susan Hiller
12, 13, 19, 20, 26 & 27 July

Roy Voss
10 September – 2 November

2009
Lindsay Seers
Richard Grayson

www.mattsgallery.org

Twenty Six
Things

A film by Marion Coutts
29 MAY–29 JUNE

Twenty Six Things explored
THURSDAY 19 JUNE, 19.00–20.30

www.wellcomecollection.org

**wellcome
collection**

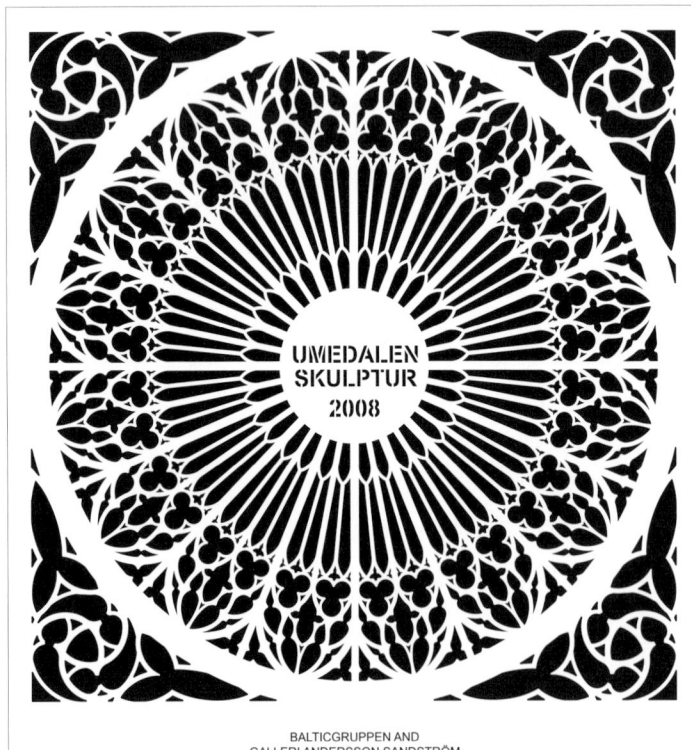

UMEDALEN
SKULPTUR
2008

BALTICGRUPPEN AND
GALLERI ANDERSSON SANDSTRÖM

7 June – 23 August

KLITSA ANTONIOU, ERNST BILLGREN,
KARI CAVÉN, SHIH CHIEH HUANG,
WIM DELVOYE, LENNART GREBELIUS,
CRISTINA IGLESIAS, JULIUS POPP, GUNILLA
SAMBERG, ANNA STAKE & MAARIA WIRKKALA

GALLERI ANDERSSON SANDSTRÖM, Aktrisgränd 34, 903 64 Umeå, +46 90 14 49 90, www.gsa.se

NOWHEREISƎЯƎH

AXEL ANTAS
NOGAH ENGLER
FRANZISKA FURTER
REECE JONES
DAMIEN ROACH

12 JUNE – 20 JULY 2008
WED – SUN 12.00 – 18.00

Tues 17 June 19.00 Melissa Gronlund in conversation with
the artists. Admission free. Booking essential.
exhibition touring to **fruehsorge contemporary drawings**,
Berlin, 20 September – 25 October 2008

The Drawing Room
Tannery Arts
Brunswick Wharf
55 Laburnum Street
London E2 8BD
+44 (0)20 7729 5333
mail@drawingroom.org.uk
www.drawingroom.org.uk

Directions: Old Street then buses 55 or 243 or Liverpool Street station
then buses 149, 26 or 242

Tannery Arts Ltd., Industrial & Provident Society, Reg. No. 29034R
Inland Revenue Charity Title Ref. No. XR40641

KONNEKT
COLOUR
John Jones

A LISTENING ROOM

IÑIGO CABO   MATTHIEU CLAINCHARD   TAL HADAD   FRANCK LEIBOVICI   BETTINA SAMSON   VITTORIO SANTORO   ERIC STEPHANY

CURATED BY MANUEL CIRAUQUI

21 May – 19 July 2008

ANNE+
ART PROJECTS

OPENING : 21 May 2008 7pm-10pm   PERFORMANCE BY FRANCK LEIBOVICI 8:30pm
85 RUE VICTOR HUGO 94200 IVRY-SUR-SEINE TEL (+33) 01 49 60 20 10 www.anneplus.com

---

Adam Chodzko *Pattern for a Procession with Two Masks* 2007 © The artist

Adam Chodzko
Proxigean Tide
24 May —
21 September 2008

St IVES

TATE

Supported by
Tate St Ives Members
and Tate Members

LOTTERY FUNDED

Porthmeor Beach, St Ives
Cornwall TR26 1TG
Call 01736 796226
www.tate.org.uk/stives

NOTES OF CONCEPTION:
A LOCAL NARRATIVE OF CHINESE CONTEMPORARY PAINTING

A B C D E
观 念 的 笔 记
F G H I J K
中 国 当 代
L M N O P
绘 画 的
Q R S T U
局 部 叙 述
V W X Y Z

Opening: 4:00 pm, July 12, 2008

Exhibition Dates: July 12 — August 15, 2008

Address: 798 Art District, No.4 Jiuxianqiao Road,

Chaoyang District, Beijing,China

Curators: Bao Dong, Sun Dongdong

Presented by: Iberia Center for Contemporary Art

Director: Xia Jifeng

Art Director: Zuo Jing

iberia
Iberia Center for Contemporary Art
伊比利亚当代艺术中心

www.iberiart.org

微觀敘事: 張小濤 +李一凡的社會圖像

Microscopic Narration
Social Images by
Zhang Xiaotao and Li Yifan

Main Hall

Picture Politics
April 24 – July 6, 2008

Main Hall

MARKUS SCHERER
WELTCUPARENA
APRIL 24 – JULY 6, 2008

Main Hall

Gülsün Karamustafa
July 17 – Sept. 14, 2008

SALZBURGER
KUNSTVEREIN

Künstlerhaus
Hellbrunner Strasse 3
5020 Salzburg

T +43 662/84 22 94
www.salzburger-
kunstverein.at

MEUSER

The
Woman
Rides
and
the
Horse
Goes
on
Foot

10.5. – 20.7.2008

Kunsthalle Düsseldorf
www.kunsthalle-duesseldorf.de

The exhibition is supported by SAMMLUNG RHEINGOLD   *The Kunsthalle Düsseldorf is funded by* Landeshauptstadt Düsseldorf

DOMAINE DEPARTEMENTAL DE CHAMARANDE
Contemporary art center

BIENVENUE
Cham
ara
nde
CHEZ VOUS

D. ALTMEJD
D. ATTOE
M. BITZER
S. BOOL
U. v. BRANDENBURG
P. COFFIN
A. COLLIER
W. DANIELS
A. DOBLER
M. EICHWALD
D. FERRIS
A. FROMENT
G. GABELLONE
E. GRONEMEYER
U. HENNEKEN
R. HIORNS
B. HIPP
K. HOLMQVIST
D. JURCZAK
J. KLECKNER
A. KRAMER
B. KRAUSS
K. KRISTALOVA
S. KUHN
R. KUNOY
P. LEE,
C. LIPOMI
F. MARTI
J. MEADOWS
A. MICHAEL
M. MOTI
C. MULL
D. MUSGRAVE
P. MRZYK &
J-F. MORICEAU
P. NEWCOMBE
O. PLENDER
K. RUGGABER
M. SCHINWALD
G. SIBONY
M. SMITH
T. SUZUKI
N. TSUJI
E. VERZUTTI
L. VICENTE
P. WHITE
J. WOLFSON
L. YUSKAVAGE

CONTEMPORARY
ART EXHIBITION

from **may 25th**
until
september 28th
2008

Exhibition open
every day
from 12 am to 19 pm
Free admission

Peter Coffin,
"Tree Pants"
Chamarande, 2008
Courtesy galerie
Emmanuel Perrotin,
Paris/Miami
© Marc Domage

Guest curator:
Alexis Vaillant

Essonne
LE CONSEIL GÉNÉRAL

Chamarande - France
+ 33 (0)1 60 82 52 01
www.legende.essonne.fr

Airport
Kunsthaus
Zürich
6. 6. – 31. 8. 2008

Heimplatz, CH–8001 Zürich
Sat / Sun / Tue 10 a.m. – 6 p.m., Wed / Thu / Fri 10 a.m. – 8 p.m.
www.shifting-identities.ch

Shifting
Identities
(Swiss) **Art Now**

Supported by
Swiss Re

Shirana Shahbazi, [Frau-01-2003] aus der Serie FLOWERS, F...
Adrian Paci, CENTRO DI PERMANENZA TEMPO...

SHILPA GUPTA

GALERIE VOLKER DIEHL

BODHIBERLIN

2008
14.6.

GALERIE VOLKER DIEHL
LINDENSTRASSE 35 10969 BERLIN
DEUTSCHLAND/GERMANY
+49 (0)30-22 48 79 22
INFO@GALERIEVOLKERDIEHL.COM
WWW.GALERIEVOLKERDIEHL.COM

CURATED BY SHAHEEN MERALI —
ASSISTANT CURATOR MARC WELLMANN

OPENING: JUNE 13TH

BODHIBERLIN
HALLE AM WASSER
INVALIDENSTRASSE 50–51
10557 BERLIN
DEUTSCHLAND/GERMANY
+49 (0)30-39 88 72 00
BERLIN@BODHIART.IN
WWW.BODHIART.IN

02.8.

The Fall
Stefan Brüggemann
and Dr Atl
30 May - 12 July 2008

Bloomberg
SPACE

Open
Monday - Saturday 11am - 6pm
Thursday 5 June till 9pm
Thursday 3 July till 9pm

Bloomberg SPACE
50 Finsbury Square
London EC2A 1HD
+44 20 7330 7959
gallery@bloomberg.net
www.bloombergspace.com

Stefan Brüggemann, *List* (detail), unique digital print on canvas, 2005, work obliterated, aluminium paint, 2007

susan pui san lok
Faster, Higher

30 May – 31 Aug 2008

BFI Southbank Gallery
BFI Southbank
Belvedere Road
London SE1

www.bfi.org.uk/lok

Commissioned by BFI and Film and Video Umbrella.
Supported by Arts Council England.

film and video umbrella

ARTS COUNCIL
ENGLAND

PIPPY
HOULDSWORTH

Rag and Bone with Bin, bronze, 2007, commissioned by Turner Contemporary, Margate

LAURA FORD

AESTHETICS OF SIMILARITY,
PRAGUE TRIENNALE
2 June - 16 September

SCULPTURE AT PILANE,
SWEDEN
14 June - 31 August

LUSTWARANDE 08,
FUNDAMENT FOUNDATION,
THE NETHERLANDS
28 June - 28 September

Pippy Houldsworth, 50 Pall Mall Deposit, 124 – 128 Barlby Road, London W10 6BL
t: 020 8969 6166 f: 020 8969 6209 e: gallery@houldsworth.co.uk w: www.houldsworth.co.uk

SITE GALLERY
Centre for Contemporary Art

08X

Celebrating 30 years

<u>Presenting a programme of UK premieres
to celebrate 30 years of international
exhibitions, commissions, residencies & events.</u>

3 May –14 June
Marie Cool
& Fabio Balducci

26 June – 9 August
Mohammed
Bourouissa

15 November – 31 January
Paul Etienne
Lincoln

Site Gallery
1 Brown Street,
Sheffield S1 2BS
T +44 (0)114 281 2077
F +44 (0)114 281 2078

<u>Full Programme
& Information</u>
info@sitegallery.org
www.sitegallery.org

John Hansard Gallery

Juan Bolivar
Geometry Wars
1 July - 30 August 2008

University of Southampton
Southampton, SO17 1BJ, UK
FREE Tue to Fri 11-5 / Sat 11-4
www.hansardgallery.org.uk

Juan Bolivar, *Silver*, 2007. Courtesy the artist.

UNIVERSITY OF
Southampton

ARTPROJX SPACE
ARTISTS PROJECTS | ARTISTS FILM CLUB

ZATORSKI + ZATORSKI
4 JUNE - 30 JUNE
FILM, SCULPTURE, PHOTOGRAPHY AND TEXT

AURA SATZ
8 JULY - 31 JULY
AUTOMAMUSIC
FILM, SOUND, PHOTOGRAPHY, DRAWING, MUSICAL INTRUMENTS

DAVID BLANDY
10 SEPT - 30 SEPT
ARTPROJX DOJO
FILM, SOUND, POSTERS, COMICS, PHOTOGRAPHY, KUNG FU ARTEFACTS

ARTPROJX SPACE
53 BEAUCHAMP PLACE LONDON SW3 1NY
WWW.ARTPROJXSPACE.COM
INFO@ARTPROJXSPACE.COM
TEL: +44 (0)20 7584 0717

Compton Verney Summer exhibition

The Fabric of Myth

21 June – 7 September 2008

Compton Verney, Warwickshire CV35 9HZ
Open Tues – Sun & Bank Holiday Mons,
11am – 5pm
T. 01926 645 500
www.comptonverney.org.uk

Registered charity no. 1032478

Supported by
PETER MOORES FOUNDATION

Detail from Three Fates, 1983-84. Woven at West Dean College, West Sussex by Pat Taylor and Fiona Abercromby from a drawing of 1943 (HMF 1537). Cotton warp; linen and wool weft. © The Henry Moore Foundation: acquired 1984.

Celestial Radio
A Visionary Journey
Zoë Walker and Neil Bromwich's off-site
project Celestial Radio tours the Kent coast
during the exhibition, broadcasting light
and sound via FM radio:

Whitstable Harbour
Saturday 21 and Sunday 22 June
During the Whitstable Biennale

Margate Harbour
Saturday 5 – Tuesday 8 July

Folkestone Harbour
Saturday 19 and Sunday 20 July
During the Folkestone Triennial

www.turnercontemporary.org
Tel: 01843 280261

Turner Contemporary, Margate
On the Threshold of a Dream
Zoë Walker and Neil Bromwich

13 June – 14 September 2008
Turner Contemporary Project Space
53-57 High Street, Margate, CT9 1DX

Open Tuesday – Sunday, 10am – 5pm
Admission free

 Kent County Council WHITSTABLE 2008 BIENNALE Folkestone Triennial

Image credits:
Friendly Frontier, Adrian Hunt © the artists
Celestial Radio, L R Phipps©

ANTONY GORMLEY
LOT

CASTLE CORNET, GUERNSEY
1 MAY – 26 OCTOBER 2008

INTERNATIONAL ARTIST IN RESIDENCE PROGRAMME
www.iairp.com

SPONSORED BY HSBC Private Bank

barbican do something different

Photograph: Anuschka Blommers/Neils Schumm

barbican
artgallery
18 Jun–21 Sep/08
www.barbican.org.uk

The House of
Viktor & Rolf

Partners

CITY
LONDON

premsela
.org/

MS
Mondriaan Stichting
(Mondriaan Foundation)

Associate partner

VandenEnde
FOUNDATION

FOLKE KÖBBERLING & MARTIN KALTWASSER: AMPHIS

19 May – 31 August: Wysing's Gallery as a repository and archive of found and unwanted material

16 July – 31 August: Outdoor construction of Amphis takes place

W

WYSING ARTS CENTRE Fox Road, Bourn, CB23 2TX
T +44 (0)1954 718 881 www.wysingartscentre.org

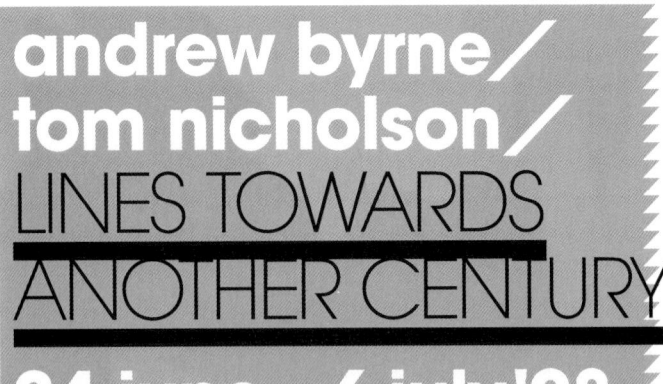

andrew byrne/
tom nicholson/
LINES TOWARDS
ANOTHER CENTURY

24 june – 6 july '08

Performance with The Elysian Quartet
Sunday 22 June/ 16.30 hrs

Media Art Bath at The Holburne Museum

Media Art Bath
+44 (0)1225 442 591
www.mediaartbath.org.uk

Media Art Bath is an Arts Council England South West and Bath & North East Somerset Council Regularly Funded Organisation. Media Art Bath champions bold new contemporary art and ideas, and develops challenging work with artists in Bath, the South West and beyond.

Media Art ^Bath

BROADCAST YOURSELF

Artists' interventions into television and strategies for self-broadcasting from the 1960s to today, co-curated by Sarah Cook and Kathy Rae Huffman.

Cornerhouse, Manchester Fri 13 June – Sun 10 August

www.broadcastyourself.net

Broadcast Yourself is a touring exhibition produced by AV Festival 08 and Cornerhouse in collaboration with the Hatton Gallery.
www.avfestival.co.uk · www.cornerhouse.org · www.ncl.ac.uk/hatton

Doug Hall, Chip Lord, and Jody Procter
The Amarillo News Tapes, 1980

70 Oxford Street, Manchester M1 5NH

CORNERHOUSE
ARTFILMBOOKSFOODDRINK

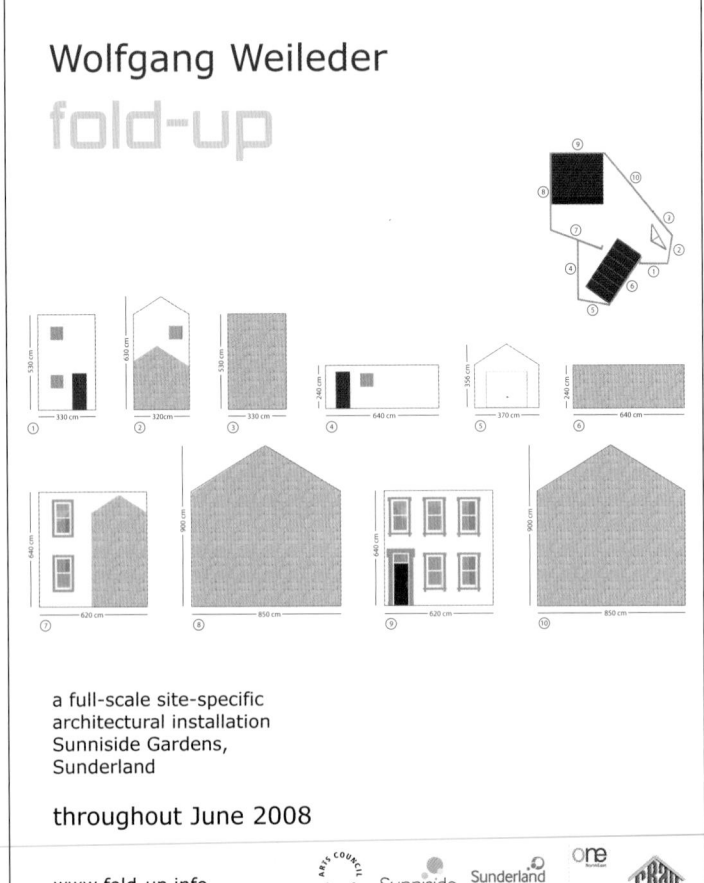

Wolfgang Weileder
fold-up

a full-scale site-specific architectural installation
Sunniside Gardens, Sunderland

throughout June 2008

www.fold-up.info

CAI GUO-QIANG

LONG

CHILLIDA

TUTTLE

RUSCHA

BASELITZ

GIACOMETTI

PICASSO

BOURGEOIS

BEUYS

NOGUCHI

VITAL

V&A

KIEFER

HIRST

PARR

KAPOOR

BLOOD
ON
PAPER

CARO

ILIAZD

LICHTENSTEIN

KOONS

BUREN

MATISSE

LEWITT

CLEMENTE

LECUIRE

MOTHERWELL

McCARTHY

BACON

REGO

DUBUFFET

ROTH

RAUSCHENBERG

TÀPIES

The art of
the book

PHILLIPS

BUSTAMANTE

BALTHUS

MIRÓ

FRANCIS

APRIL–
JUNE
08

FREE ADMISSION
WWW.VAM.AC.UK
⊖ SOUTH KENSINGTON

ILLUSTRATION BY DAMIEN POULAIN

15 APRIL–
29 JUNE
2008

SPONSORED BY

Deutsche Bank

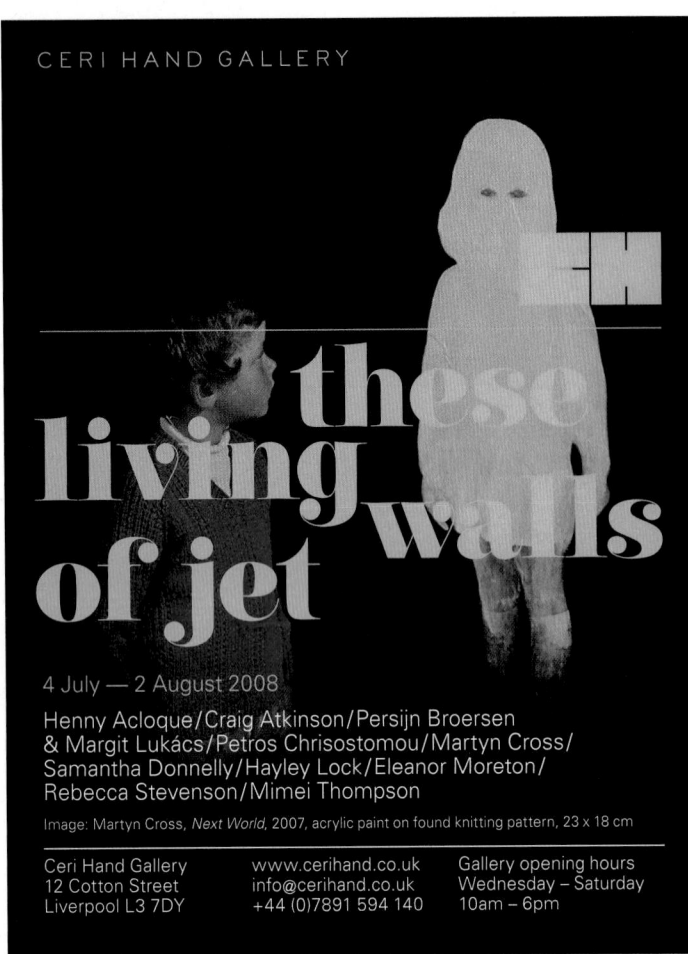

CERI HAND GALLERY

these
living walls
of jet

4 July — 2 August 2008

Henny Acloque/Craig Atkinson/Persijn Broersen
& Margit Lukács/Petros Chrisostomou/Martyn Cross/
Samantha Donnelly/Hayley Lock/Eleanor Moreton/
Rebecca Stevenson/Mimei Thompson

Image: Martyn Cross, *Next World*, 2007, acrylic paint on found knitting pattern, 23 x 18 cm

Ceri Hand Gallery	www.cerihand.co.uk	Gallery opening hours
12 Cotton Street	info@cerihand.co.uk	Wednesday – Saturday
Liverpool L3 7DY	+44 (0)7891 594 140	10am – 6pm

Recursive Shadows

Alan Charlton
Ulrich Rückriem
Ragna Róbertsdóttir

3 May - 5 July
Bury Art Gallery
Museum+Archives
Moss Street
Bury, BL9 0DR
T: 0161 253 5878

Berwick Gymnasium Art Gallery

Data Sculpted Trees
Simon Blackmore
May 17th – June 29th 2008

Elevated Pastoral
Urban Art
Anne Peschken and Marek Pisarsky
July 5th – August 10th 2008
Funded by the Arts Council of England's International Fellowship Programme

As Old As The Industry, As Modern As The Hour
Laura Napier
September 20th – October 31st 2008

FREE admission
Wed-Sun, April – September 11am-5pm, October – December 12-4pm
For information telephone 01289 304 535

Gymnasium Gallery, Berwick Barracks, Berwick-upon-Tweed, TD15 1DG

The Berwick Gymnasium
Art Fellowships are funded by

northern rock foundation   ENGLISH HERITAGE   ARTS COUNCIL ENGLAND

Sanford Wurmfeld E-Cyclorama

EDINBURGH COLLEGE OF ART

24 July to 5 September 2008
Open daily 10–6
Free

Supported by Dunard Fund

eca   EDINBURGH ART FESTIVAL

KENDELL GEERS

OPENING SATURDAY MAY 31 5 – 7 PM

POSTPUNKPAGANPOP POSTPUNKPAGANPOP

de PURY & LUXEMBOURG

LIMMATSTRASSE 264   8005 ZÜRICH   DEPURYLUXEMBOURG.COM   TEL +41 44 276 80 20   FAX +41 44 276 80 21

FONDAZIONE MORRA • Vico lungo Pontecorvo 29/D
80135 Napoli • Italy • Tel. 0814420923 • Fax 081454064
info@fondazionemorra.org • www.fondazionemorra.org

Museo Archivio Laboratorio per le Arti Contemporanee Napoli • Opening September 13th, 2008 in Naples • Italy

HERMANN NITSCH MUSEUMS Naples Mistelbach

Museum Mistelbach • Open since May 2007 • New Exhibition - 20th Painting Action at the „Wiener Secession" 1987

HERMANN NITSCH MUSEUM   HNM MISTELBACH

Opening May 10th, 2008 in Mistelbach • Austria

MZM Museumszentrum Mistelbach • Waldstrasse 44-46 • 2130 Mistelbach • Austria • Tel. +432572-207 19 • Fax +432572-207 19-20
office@mzmistelbach.at • www.mzmistelbach.at

artnet®
ONLINE ART AUCTIONS

CARL FISCHER
Andy Warhol Drowning in a Campbell's Soup Can, 1969
Estimate: $8,000-10,000

PHOTOGRAPHS

Berenice Abbott
Lee Friedlander
Nan Goldin
Gordon Parks
Cindy Sherman
and many others

PRINTS

Wang Guangyi
Robert Indiana
Donald Judd
Takashi Murakami
Andy Warhol
and many others

SCULPTURE

Arman
Anthony Caro
Fritz Koenig
Claes Oldenberg
Victor Vasarely
and many others

WORKS ON PAPER

Jean Dubuffet
Robert Nickle
Irene Rice Pereira
Rolph Scarlett
Jean Xceron
and many others

PAINTINGS

Sonia Delaunay-Terk
Jörg Immendorff
Richard Pettibone
Joseph Solman
Joseph Stella
and many others

VISIT ARTNETONLINEAUCTIONS.COM

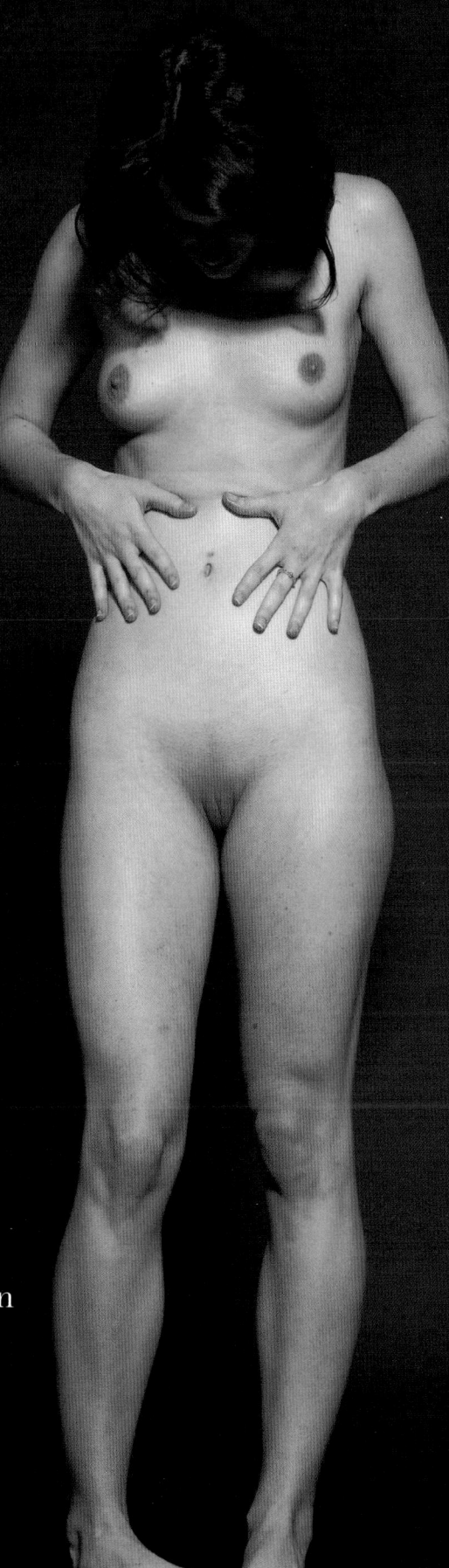

Constance
Jonathan Ellery

A performance
29th May 2008

The Wapping Project, London
T +44 (0)20 7680 2080
thewappingproject.com

Accompanied by a limited
edition publication

WAPPING

Photography by John Ross

a crime against art

Director: Hila Peleg
Madrid/Berlin, 2007, 100 min, original footage DV

Cast

Defendants:	Anton Vidokle and Tirdad Zolgdhar
Prosecutors:	Vasif Kortun and Chus Martinez
Defense attorney:	Charles Esche
Judge:	Jan Verwoert
Expert witnesses:	Maria Lind and Anselm Franke
Artist:	Setareh Shabazi
Public:	Keti Chukrov and Barnaby Drabble

With special contribution by Liam Gillick.

Producer: unitednationpslaza

A Crime Against Art is based
on The Trial in Madrid,
February 2007
Organised by Anton Vidokle
and Tirdad Zolghadr.

Distributed by:

arsenal experimental • Freunde der Deutschen Kinemathek e.V. -- http://fdk-berlin.de
BDV • DVD NTSC, 100 minutes, 25 € Available at: http://www.bureaudesvideos.com

Limited-Edition Photographs

Books

aperture Magazine, Books, Exhibitions, Limited-Edition Photographs, and Special Events   www.aperture.org

Limited-edition photographs (clockwise from top left): Thomas Allen, *Suspended*, 2008; Michal Chelbin, *Alicia in a Golden Dress*, Ukraine, 2005; Edgar Martins, *Untitled*, from the series Hidden, 2005
Books (left to right): Michal Chelbin, *Strangely Familiar*; Jonas Bendiksen, *The Places We Live*; Luigi Ghirri, *It's Beautiful Here, Isn't It. . .*; *Edgar Martins: Topologies*; *Takashi Homma: Tokyo*

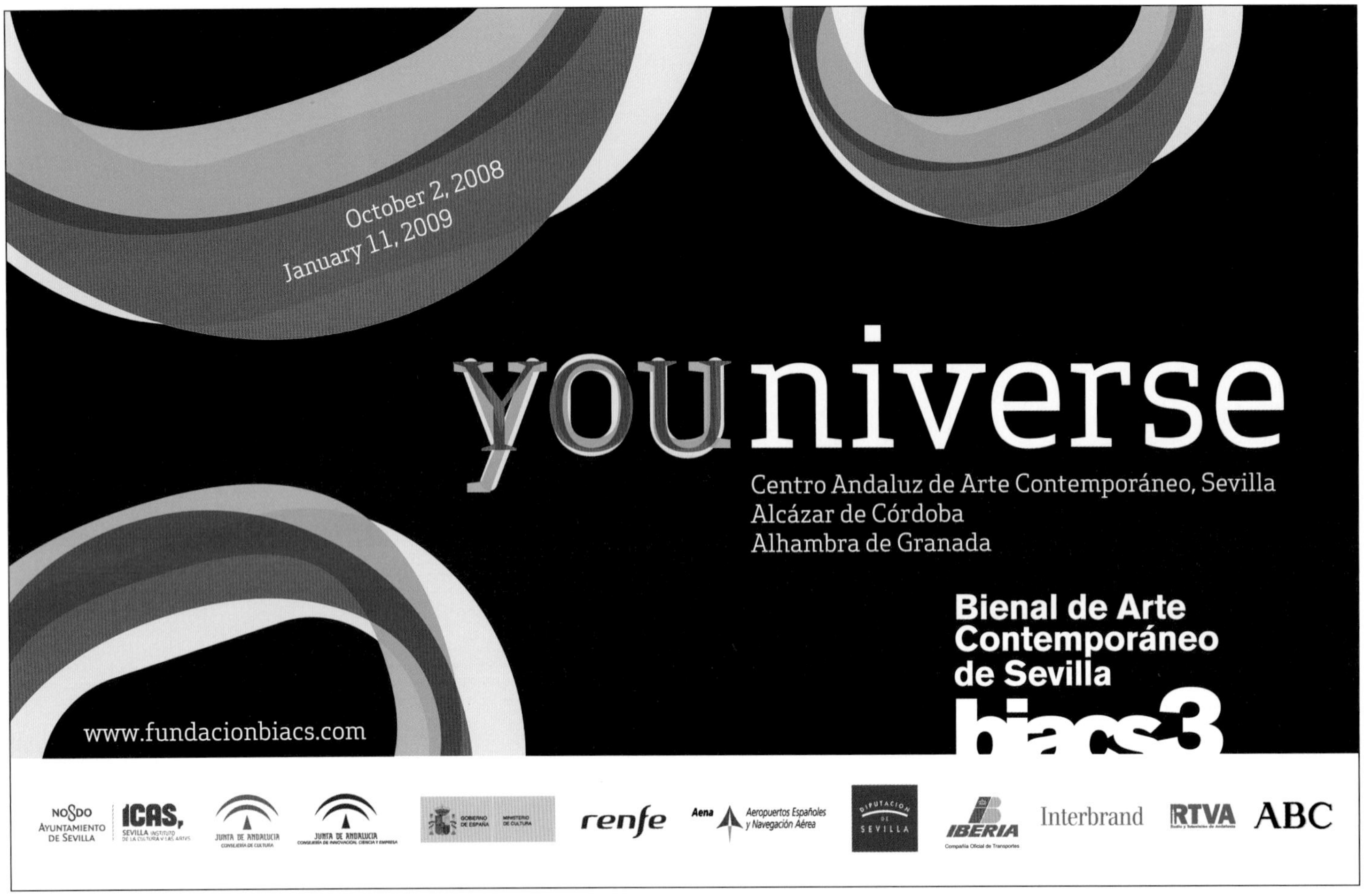

October 2, 2008
January 11, 2009
youniverse
Centro Andaluz de Arte Contemporáneo, Sevilla
Alcázar de Córdoba
Alhambra de Granada
Bienal de Arte
Contemporáneo
de Sevilla
biacs3
www.fundacionbiacs.com
NO8DO Ayuntamiento de Sevilla
ICAS, Sevilla
Junta de Andalucia
Junta de Andalucia
renfe
Aena Aeropuertos Españoles y Navegación Aérea
Diputación de Sevilla
IBERIA
Interbrand
RTVA
ABC

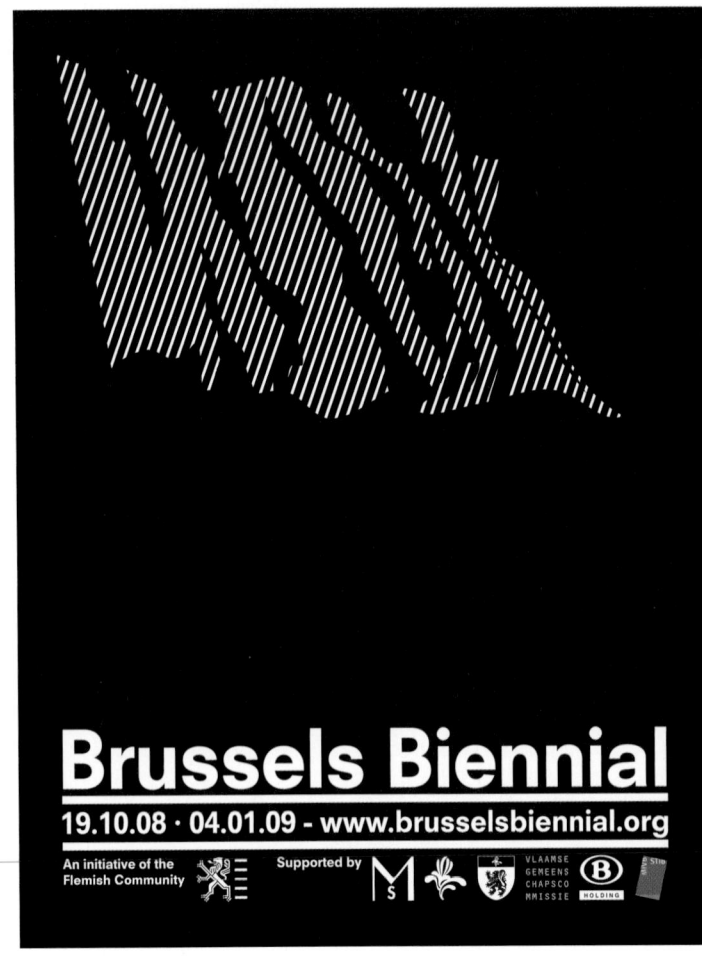

Brussels Biennial
19.10.08 · 04.01.09 - www.brusselsbiennial.org
An initiative of the Flemish Community
Supported by

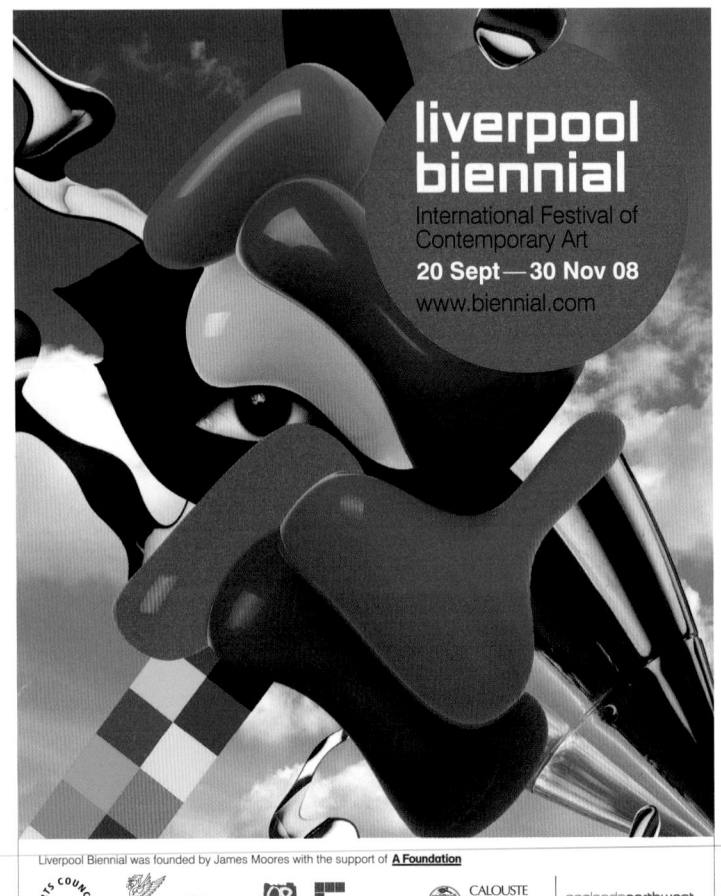

liverpool
biennial
International Festival of
Contemporary Art
20 Sept — 30 Nov 08
www.biennial.com
Liverpool Biennial was founded by James Moores with the support of A Foundation
Arts Council England
The City of Liverpool
Liverpool 08
Northwest
Calouste Gulbenkian Foundation
englandsnorthwest BE INSPIRED

YOKOHAMA TRIENNALE 2008 TIME CREVASSE

SEP 13 – NOV 30 2008
WWW.YOKOHAMATRIENNALE.JP

Artistic Director : Tsutomu Mizusawa (Chief Curator, The Museum of Modern Art, Kamakura & Hayama)
Curators: Daniel Birnbaum (Rector of the Städelschule Art Academy and Director of the Portikus, Frankfurt am Main) / Hu Fang (Artistic Director of the Vitamin Creative Space) / Akiko Miyake (Program Director, Center for Contemporary Art (CCA) Kitakyushu) / Hans Ulrich Obrist (Co-Director of Exhibitions and Programmes and Director of International Projects, the Serpentine Gallery) / Beatrix Ruf (Director, Kunsthalle Zürich)
Venue: Central and Waterfront Sites in Yokohama (New Exhibition Hall for the Yokohama Triennale 2008 at the Shinko Pier, Red Brick Warehouse No.1, NYK Waterfront Warehouse "BankART Studio NYK")

 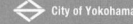 NHK The Asahi Shimbun The Organizing Committee for the Yokohama Triennale

ALLGARVE'08

HOLIDAYS IN THE SUN
Cildo Meireles, Claude Lévêque, Fernanda Fragateiro, João Tabarra, Miguel Palma, Rogelio López Cuenca, Thomas Hirschhorn, Tobias Rehberger, Xana

ALBUFEIRA Santa Eulália and São Rafael beaches FARO Faro Airport LOULÉ Quarteira beach
PORTIMÃO Rocha beach/ Old Fish Market 22 June - 7 September

LOCAL WORDS: SPACES, VISIBILITIES AND TRANSCULTURAL FLOWS
Ângela Ferreira, António Ole, Beatrice Catanzaro, Cláudia Cristóvão, Cláudia Lopes Costa, Eduardo Matos, Eduardo Padilha, Faisal Abdullah, Francisco Vidal, Gustavo Sumpta, Inês Amado, Jorge Pereira, Melanie Jackson, Mónica de Miranda, Paul Goodwin, Psychological Art Circus, Renée Green, Ricardo Valentim, Susana Guardado, Susana de Medeiros, Tiago Cutileiro, Ynaiê Dawson

LAGOS Centro Cultural de Lagos/Forte Pau da Bandeira 14 June - 7 September

William Kentridge - SEVEN FRAGMENTS FOR GEORGE MÉLIÈS/ DAY FOR NIGHT/JOURNEY TO THE MOON (2003)
With the collaboration of Ellipse Foundation Contemporary Art Collection
LAGOA Convento de São José 14 June - 7 September

Ignasi Aballí - NO ACTIVITY
Official Section PHOTOESPAÑA 08
PORTIMÃO Museu de Portimão 15 June - 7 September

CHAIN REACTION: TRANSFORMATIONS IN THE HOTEL ARCHITECTURE
A project by Luís Tavares Pereira with the collaboration of two architects Paula Santos and Paulo Martins Barata, the writer Jorge Gomes Miranda and the photographer Paulo Catrica
LOULÉ Lagar das Portas do Céu/Quinta da Fonte da Pipa 21 June - 7 September

CONTEMPORARY ART

Bill Viola - II VAPORE (1975)
James Turrell - FARGO, BLUE (1967)
With the collaboration of Museu Colecção Berardo
FARO Museu Municipal de Faro 21 June - 7 September

ARTICULATIONS
André Carvalho, Ângelo de Sousa, António Bolota, António Poppe, Carlos Garaicoa, Dan Perjovschi, Diango Hernández, Fernanda Gomes, Francisco Janes, Francisco Tropa, Hugo Canoilas, Ian Kiaer, Ion Grigorescu, João Queiroz, João Maria Gusmão and Pedro Paiva, Leonor Antunes, Nelson Félix, Phill Niblock, Raimond Chaves and Gilda Mantilla, Ricardo Jacinto, Sancho Silva, Sérgio Taborda, Thierry Simões, Rui Moreira/Rui Sanches
FARO Fábrica da Cerveja LOULÉ Mina Campina de Cima/Convento de Santo António
21 June - 7 September

☎ 08453551212

Fábrica da Cerveja ©Fernando Guerra

TURISMO DE PORTUGAL algarve   FUNDAÇÃOSERRALVES   LIFETIME EXPERIENCES **ALLGARVE**

07

연례
보고
Annual
Report

일년동안의
전시
A Year in
Exhibitions

On the Road
길 위에서

Position Papers
제안

Insertions
끼워넣기

Programs
Global Institute 글로벌 인스티튜트
Plenary Sessions 국제학술회의

Artistic Director
Okwui Enwezor

Co-Curators
Hyunjin Kim, Ranjit Hoskote

Position Papers Curators
Claire Tancons, Jang Un Kim, Abdellah Karroum,
Patrick Flores, Sung Hyen Park

08

9.5–11.9.2008
THE 7TH GWANGJU BIENNALE
2008 광주비엔날레
WWW.GB.OR.KR

GWANGJU BIENNALE
광주비엔날레

CENTRAL SAINT MARTINS
DEGREE SHOWS 2008

11 June – 5 July
for details
visit www.csm.arts.ac.uk

University of the Arts London
Central Saint Martins

REGISTERED MUSEUM

Samsonite
BLACK LABEL

---

a new space for contemporary art

+44 (0)113 202 8000
exhibitions@leeds-art.ac.uk
www.leeds-art.ac.uk

LEEDS COLLEGE OF ART & DESIGN

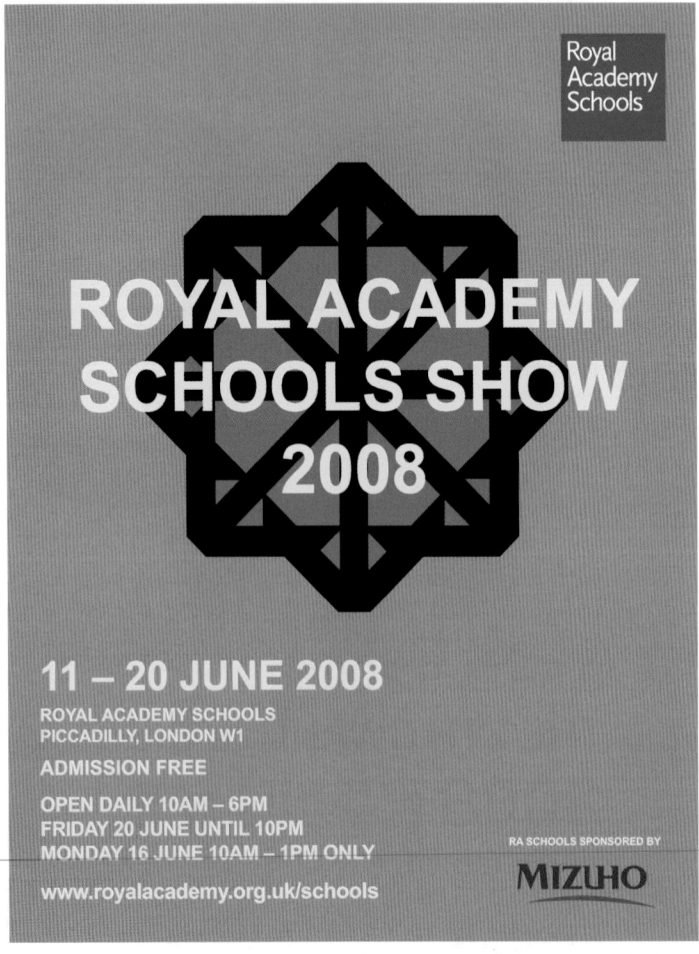

Royal
Academy
Schools

ROYAL ACADEMY SCHOOLS SHOW 2008

11 – 20 JUNE 2008

ROYAL ACADEMY SCHOOLS
PICCADILLY, LONDON W1

ADMISSION FREE

OPEN DAILY 10AM – 6PM
FRIDAY 20 JUNE UNTIL 10PM
MONDAY 16 JUNE 10AM – 1PM ONLY

www.royalacademy.org.uk/schools

RA SCHOOLS SPONSORED BY
MIZUHO

KINGSTON UNIVERSITY
OUT THERE

FACULTY OF ART, DESIGN & ARCHITECTURE
UNDERGRADUATE DEGREE SHOW 2008

LAUNCH
07.06.08 | 1.00PM – 8.30PM

OPENING
08.06.08 | 1.00PM – 4.00PM
9-13.06.08 | 10.00AM – 9.00PM
EXCEPT 10.06.08 | 10.00AM – 5.00PM

KINGSTON UNIVERSITY
KNIGHTS PARK
KINGSTON UPON THAMES
SURREY KT1 2QJ

FREE ADMISSION

OUTTHERE@KINGSTON.AC.UK | WWW.KINGSTON.AC.UK/OUTTHERE

THE INAUGURAL
FOLKESTONE TRIENNIAL
TALES OF TIME AND SPACE
14 JUNE—
14 SEPTEMBER 2008

DAVID BATCHELOR
CHRISTIAN BOLTANSKI
ADAM CHODZKO
NATHAN COLEY
TACITA DEAN
JEREMY DELLER
MARK DION
TRACEY EMIN
AYSE ERKMEN
SEJLA KAMERIC
ROBERT KUSMIROWSKI
LANGLANDS & BELL
KAFFE MATTHEWS
HEATHER & IVAN MORISON
NILS NORMAN
    WITH GAVIN WADE
    MIT SIMON & TOM BLOOR
SUSAN PHILIPSZ
PUBLIC WORKS
PATRICK TUTTOFUOCO
MARK WALLINGER
RICHARD WENTWORTH
PAE WHITE
RICHARD WILSON

CURATOR
ANDREA SCHLIEKER

WWW.FOLKESTONETRIENNIAL.ORG.UK

Folkestone Triennial

creative foundation
The Henry Moore Foundation
Kent County Council
skyARTS Channel 267

The Folkestone Estate
GOETHE-INSTITUT LONDON
ARTS COUNCIL ENGLAND — LOTTERY FUNDED

BERNARD SUNLEY CHARITABLE TRUST
Folkestone Hythe & Romney Marsh Shepway District Council
outset.

southeastern.
CALOUSTE GULBENKIAN FOUNDATION

THE ROGER DE HAAN CHARITABLE TRUST
UBS
SEEDA Working for England's World Class Region — SOUTH EAST ENGLAND DEVELOPMENT AGENCY

MALL GALLERIES

THREADNEEDLE FIGURATIVE PRIZE

20 August - 6 September 2008

Figure it out. Visit the exhibition. Vote online.
www.threadneedlefigurativeprize.com
Mall Galleries, The Mall, London SW1

Voting closes at noon, 3 September 2008

A&B
Arts & Business *working together*

threadneedle.

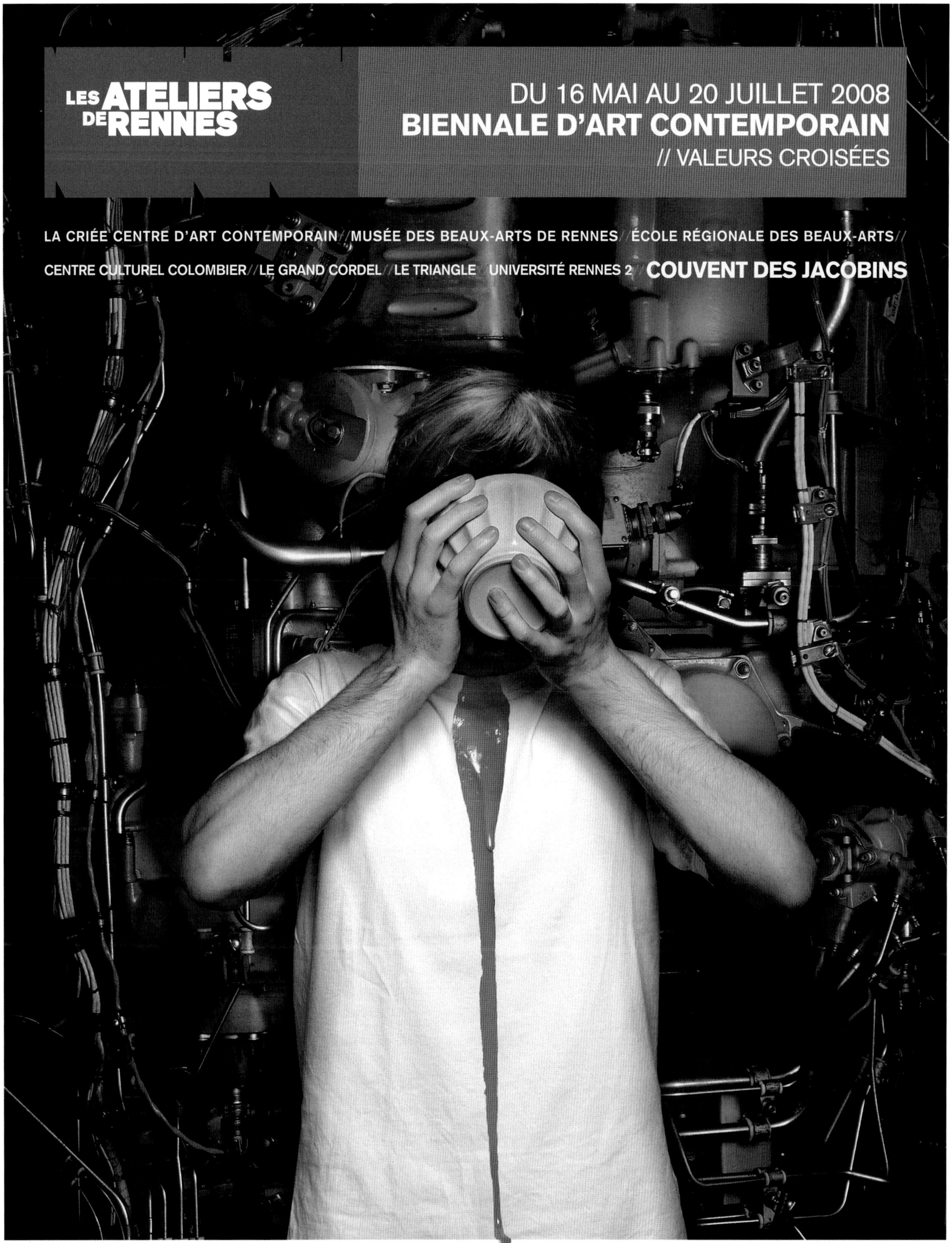

LES **ATELIERS** DE **RENNES**

DU 16 MAI AU 20 JUILLET 2008
BIENNALE D'ART CONTEMPORAIN
// VALEURS CROISÉES

LA CRIÉE CENTRE D'ART CONTEMPORAIN // MUSÉE DES BEAUX-ARTS DE RENNES / ÉCOLE RÉGIONALE DES BEAUX-ARTS //
CENTRE CULTUREL COLOMBIER // LE GRAND CORDEL / LE TRIANGLE UNIVERSITÉ RENNES 2 / **COUVENT DES JACOBINS**

ORGANISATION
ART NORAC

www.lesateliersderennes.fr

MÉCÈNES // CENTRE DE RELATIONS CLIENTS DU GROUPE CANAL+ // DIANA INGRÉDIENTS // GERINTER INTÉRIM //
GROUPE NORAC // INRIA // KEOLIS RÉSEAU STAR // LAMOTTE IMMOBILIER // LE GOUÉS & ASSOCIÉS // LES CHARPENTES RIS //
LOC MARIA // ORANGE LABS // S.A.S. CHRISTIAN FAURE // SOREAL // SULKY-BUREL // THERMOFORMES
CONCEPTION / RÉALISATION // ART TO BE

* COMPAGNIE 360 EURO RSCG - RCS NANTERRE 780 143 707 - RCS NANTERRE 780 14 707 - Photo Alcide Roche - Remerciements à Sabena technics

Frieze Art Fair
Regent's Park, London
16 – 19 October 2008
www.frieze.com

Tickets available from:
+44 (0)870 890 0514
www.seetickets.com

FRIEZE ART FAIR

ACME., Los Angeles
Juana de Aizpuru, Madrid
Helga de Alvear, Madrid
Andersen_s contemporary,
Copenhagen
Paul Andriesse, Amsterdam
The Approach, London
Arndt & Partner, Berlin
Art : Concept, Paris
Catherine Bastide, Brussels
Guido W. Baudach, Berlin
Marianne Boesky, New York
Tanya Bonakdar, New York
Isabella Bortolozzi, Berlin
BQ, Cologne
The Breeder, Athens
Broadway 1602, New York
Gavin Brown's enterprise,
New York
Daniel Buchholz, Cologne
Cabinet, London
Luis Campaña, Cologne
Gisela Capitain, Cologne
Massimo De Carlo, Milan
Casa Triângulo, Sao Paulo
China Art Objects, Los Angeles
Pepe Cobo, Madrid
Sadie Coles HQ, London
Contemporary Fine Arts,
Berlin
Corvi-Mora, London
CRG, New York
Chantal Crousel, Paris
Sorcha Dallas, Glasgow
Thomas Dane, London
Dicksmith, London
doggerfisher, Edinburgh
Eigen + Art, Berlin
The Fair Gallery, London
Fortes Vilaça, Sao Paulo

Marc Foxx, Los Angeles
Carl Freedman, London
Stephen Friedman, London
Frith Street, London
Gagosian, London
GallerySke, Bangalore
Annet Gelink, Amsterdam
A Gentil Carioca, Rio de
Janeiro
Gladstone, New York
Marian Goodman, New York
Bärbel Grässlin,
Frankfurt/Main
Greene Naftali, New York
greengrassi, London
Karin Guenther, Hamburg
Studio Guenzani, Milan
Jack Hanley, San Francisco
Hauser & Wirth, London
Herald St, London
Hotel, London
Taka Ishii, Tokyo
Jablonka, Cologne
Alison Jacques, London
Martin Janda, Vienna
Johnen, Berlin
Juliètte Jongma, Amsterdam
Annely Juda Fine Art, London
Casey Kaplan, New York
Georg Kargl, Vienna
Magnus Karlsson, Stockholm
Paul Kasmin, New York
francesca kaufmann, Milan
Kerlin, Dublin
Anton Kern, New York
Peter Kilchmann, Zurich
Nicole Klagsbrun, New York

Johann König, Berlin
David Kordansky, Los Angeles
Tomio Koyama, Tokyo
Andrew Kreps, New York
Krinzinger, Vienna
Krobath Wimmer, Vienna
Yvon Lambert, Paris
Simon Lee, London
Lehmann Maupin, New York
Lisson, London
Long March Space, Beijing
Kate MacGarry, London
magical Artroom, Tokyo
Mai 36, Zurich
Giò Marconi, Milan
Matthew Marks, New York
Metro Pictures, New York
Meyer Kainer, Vienna
Meyer Riegger, Karlsruhe
Massimo Minini, Brescia
Victoria Miro, London
The Modern Institute/
Toby Webster, Glasgow
Christian Nagel, Cologne
Neu, Berlin
Franco Noero, Turin
Giti Nourbakhsch, Berlin
Patrick Painter, Inc.,
Santa Monica
Maureen Paley, London
Peres Projects, Berlin
Emmanuel Perrotin, Paris
Friedrich Petzel, New York
Francesca Pia, Zurich
Gregor Podnar, Ljubljana
Eva Presenhuber, Zurich
Produzentengalerie,
Hamburg
Raucci/Santamaria, Naples
Almine Rech, Paris
Regina, Moscow
Anthony Reynolds, London
Rivington Arms, New York

Thaddaeus Ropac, Salzburg
Sonia Rosso, Turin
Salon 94, New York
Aurel Scheibler, Berlin
Rüdiger Schöttle, Munich
Gabriele Senn, Vienna
Sfeir-Semler, Beirut
Stuart Shave/Modern Art,
London
Sies + Höke, Dusseldorf
Filomena Soares, Lisbon
Sommer Contemporary Art,
Tel-Aviv
Reena Spaulings Fine Art,
New York
Monika Sprüth Philomene
Magers, Cologne
Standard (Oslo), Oslo
Store, London
Galeria Luisa Strina, Sao Paulo
Sutton Lane, London
Micheline Szwajcer, Antwerp
Timothy Taylor, London
Team, New York
Vermelho, Sao Paulo
Vilma Gold, London
Vitamin Creative Space,
Guangzhou
Waddington, London
Nicolai Wallner, Copenhagen
Barbara Weiss, Berlin
White Cube, London
Max Wigram, London
Wilkinson, London
Christina Wilson, Copenhagen
XL, Moscow
Zeno X, Antwerp
Zero, Milan
David Zwirner, New York

SCOPE Basel
June 3-8 08

International
Contemporary
Art Fairs
Uferstrasse 80
CH- 4057 Basel
Switzerland
SCOPE-ART.COM

Madrid February 12-18 09

Miami December 3-7 08

London October 15-19 08

Hamptons July 24-27 08

Basel June 3-8 08

New York March 26-30 08

Miami December 5-9 07

LISTE 08
THE YOUNG ART FAIR IN BASEL

June 3–8, 2008

Open Hours Tuesday to Saturday 1 p.m. to 9 p.m., Sunday 1 p.m. to 7 p.m.
Opening Reception Monday, June 2, 5 p.m. to 10 p.m.
Burgweg 15, CH-4058 Basel, T +41 61 692 20 21, info@liste.ch, www.liste.ch
A project in the workshop community Warteck pp

64 Galleries from 22 Countries *new at LISTE

Austria: Andreas Huber, Vienna. *Layr Wuestenhagen, Vienna. Mezzanin, Vienna. **Belgium:** dépendance, Brussels. **Chile:** *Traschi, Santiago. **Czech Republic:** hunt kastner, Prague. **Denmark:** kirkhoff, Copenhagen. Christina Wilson, Copenhagen. **France:** Chez Valentin, Paris. Cortex Athletico, Bordeaux. Cosmic, Paris. schleicher + lange, Paris. Jocelyn Wolff, Paris. **Germany:** *Sandra Bürgel, Berlin. Iris Kadel, Karlsruhe. Johann König, Berlin. Linn Lühn, Cologne. Neue Alte Brücke, Frankfurt. Peres Projects, Berlin/Los Angeles. *schnittraum/lutz becker, Cologne. Micky Schubert, Berlin. Van Horn, Dusseldorf. **Great Britain:** *Ancient & Modern, London. Laura Bartlett, London. Sorcha Dallas, Glasgow. Dicksmith, London. Herald St, London. IBID Projects, London/Vilnius. Mary Mary, Glasgow. Jonathan Viner/Fortescue Avenue, London. **Greece:** The Breeder, Athens. **Holland:** Juliette Jongma, Amsterdam. Upstream, Amsterdam. martin van zomeren, Amsterdam. Zinger, Amsterdam. **Italy:** Fonti, Napoli. Francesca Kaufmann, Milano. *Klerkx, Milano. *Francesca Minini, Milano. Monitor, Rome. Raucci/Santamaria, Napoli. **Japan:** Yamamoto Gendai, Tokyo. **Mexico:** *Proyectos Monclova, Mexico. Myto, Mexico. **Norway:** Standard (Oslo), Oslo. **New Zealand:** Michael Lett, Auckland. **Poland:** lokal 30, Warsaw. Raster, Warsaw. **Romania:** Plan B, Cluj. **Spain:** *ProjecteSD, Barcelona. **Sweden:** Elastic, Malmö. **Switzerland:** Evergreene, Geneva. Freymond-Guth, Zurich. Groeflin Maag, Zurich. Laurin, Zurich. **Turkey:** *Rodeo, Istanbul. **USA:** Broadway 1602, New York. *Elizabeth Dee, New York. Zach Feuer, New York. Foxy Production, New York. Daniel Hug, Los Angeles. David Kordansky, Los Angeles. *Overduin and Kite, Los Angeles. Wallspace, New York.

Main Sponsor: **E.GUTZWILLER & CIE, BANQUIERS, Basel**

艺术北京

ART BEIJING 2008
CONTEMPORARY ART FAIR | PHOTO BEIJING
2008|09|06-09|09

ART Breakthrough — Contemporary Water Ink

Asia Art Forum   Art & Economy   Art & Education

Visitor service & VIP special program ASIA ART TOUR : carol@artbeijing.net
www.artbeijing.net

PULSE MIAMI
Contemporary Art Fair

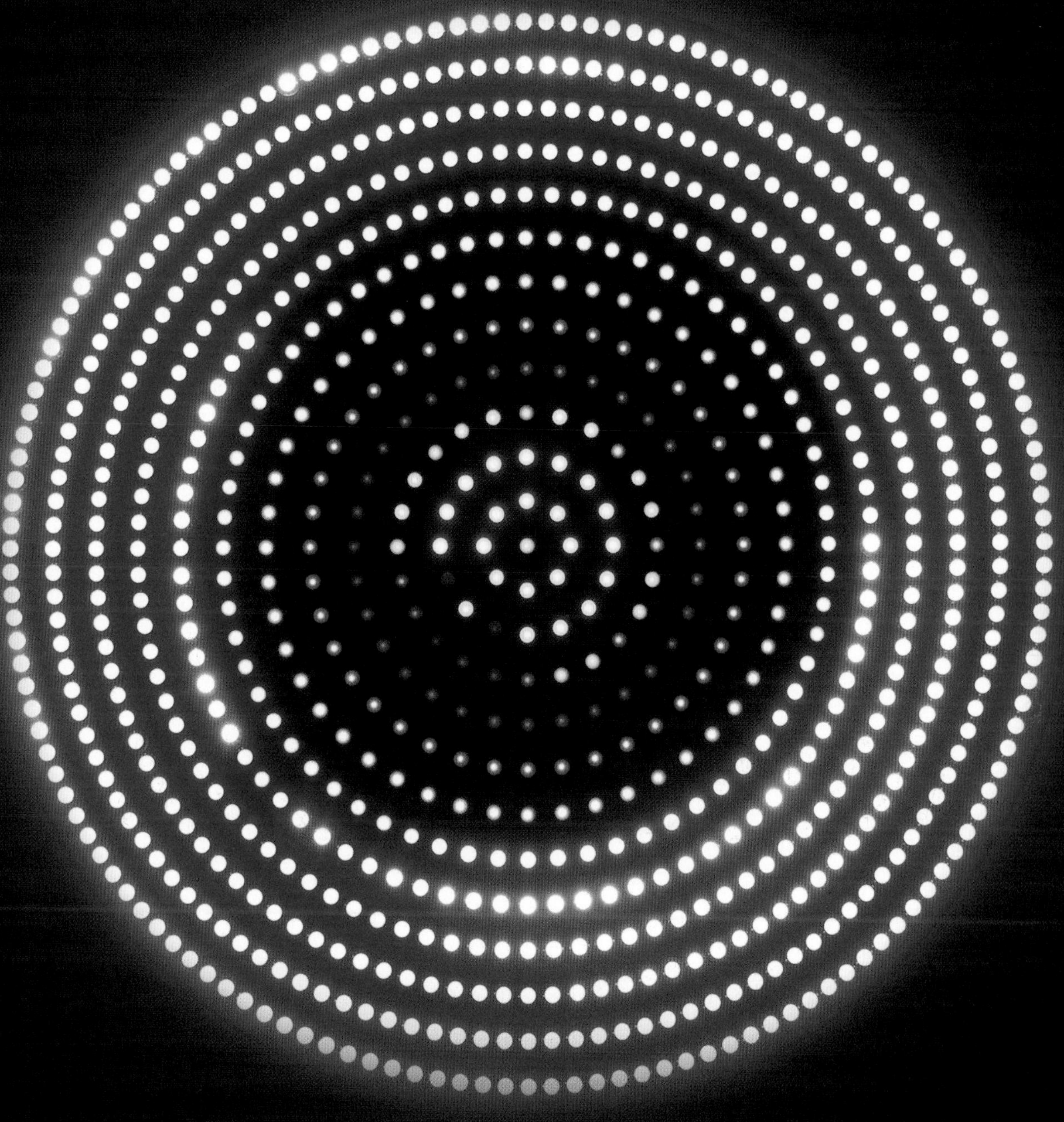

Dec 4 - 7

Soho Studios
Wynwood District

www.pulse-art.com

ART TAIPEI 2008

8.29 - 9.2

Art Taipei 2008 Executive Committee
No.1, Sec.1, Brad Rd., Taipei City 10058, Taiwan   Tel:886-2-2321-4808   Fax:886-2-2321-9300
E-mail:art-taipei@artsdealer.net

Organized by

A FAIR EXPERIENCE ARTISSIMA 15 THE INTERNATIONAL FAIR OF CONTEMPORARY ART IN TURIN NOVEMBER 7 – 9, 2008 LINGOTTO FIERE, TURIN

FONDAZIONE TORINO MUSEI

Regione Piemonte
Provincia di Torino
Città di Torino

Camera di commercio di Torino
Compagnia di San Paolo
Fondazione CRT

info@artissima.it
www.artissima.it

sh ShContemporary

contemporary 上海艺术博览会
国际当代艺术展

08 Sept. 10-13, 2008

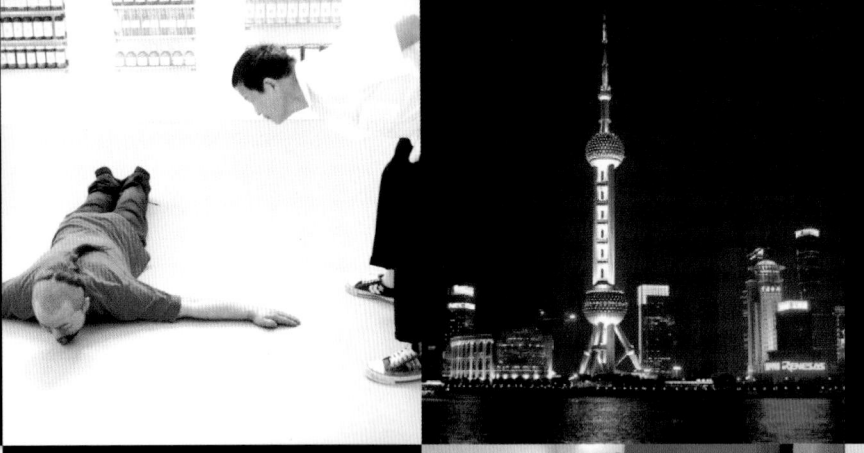

SHANGHAI
IN ART

THE
Asia Pacific
Art Fair

An exciting overview of the best of Asia Pacific
contemporary art
Intriguing dialogue between Orient and Occident
The best galleries from the East juxtaposed with top
galleries from the West
New artist discoveries presented by 10 specialized
curators from all Asia Pacific regions

Opening ShContemporary
Sept. 9, 2008
Opening Shanghai Biennale
Sept. 8, 2008

Travel Partners:
www.turontravel.com
www.italcamel.com

www.shcontemporary.info

BF China Fairs S.r.l.
BolognaFiere group

ART
COLOGNE

43. INTERNATIONALER KUNSTMARKT
22 – 26 APRIL 2009

RED DOT
ART FAIR
LONDON

Art Fair *at the* Radisson Edwardian Grafton Hotel
130 Tottenham Court Road, London
At The Warren Street Tube Station

October 16 - 19, 2008

U.S. Contact
917.273.8621
REDDOTFAIR@YAHOO.COM

U.K. Contact
+44 (0) 208 683 3658
REDDOTLONDON@YAHOO.COM

WWW.REDDOTFAIR.COM

Join us at Red Dot Miami · December 4 - 7, 2008

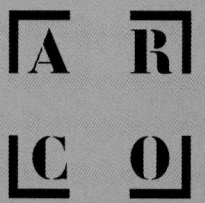

ARCO9

28 INTERNATIONAL CONTEMPORARY ART FAIR
11 - 16 FEBRUARY 2009 | FERIA DE MADRID

GENERAL PUBLIC FROM FRIDAY 13

Organized by:

IFEMA
Feria de
Madrid

www.arco.ifema.es

LINEA IFEMA / *IFEMA CALL CENTRE*

LLAMADAS DESDE ESPAÑA / *CALLS FROM SPAIN*	
INFOIFEMA	902 22 15 15
EXPOSITORES / *EXHIBITORS*	902 22 16 16
LLAMADAS INTERNACIONALES (34) 91 722 30 00 *INTERNATIONAL CALLS*	
FAX	(34) 91 722 57 98
IFEMA	Feria de Madrid 28042 Madrid España / *Spain*

arco@ifema.es

Athens

AD Gallery
3 Pallados Street, 105 54
tel +30 210 3228785
www.adgallery.gr

ANDREAS DEVETZIS
Paintings
through 28 June

GROUP SHOW
July
Please contact the gallery for further summer programme information.

The gallery is closed in August.

Loraini Alimantiri/ gazonrouge
15 Victor Hugo, 104 37
tel +30 210 5248077
www.gazonrouge.com

YORGOS SAPOUNTZIS
'After Electricity'
through 28 June

The gallery is open by appointment only in July and August.

a. antonopoulou.art
20 Aristofanous Street, 105 54
tel +30 210 3214994
www.aaart.gr

EM KEI
'Wake Me Up Before You Go Go, I Wasn't Planning On Going Solo'
through 21 June

The Breeder
6 Evmorfopoulou Street, 105 53
tel +30 210 3317527
www.thebreedersystem.com

STELIOS FAITAKIS
'What a Great Day'
through 30 June

DESTE Foundation for Contemporary Art
11 Filellinon & Em. Pappa Street, 142 34
tel +30 210 2758490
www.deste.gr
'FRACTURED FIGURE: WORKS FROM THE DAKIS JOANNOU COLLECTION'
Curated by Jeffrey Deitch, with Althamer, Altmejd, Antoni, assume vivid astro focus, Basquiat, Bickerton, Bock, Cattelan, Chan, Colen, Condo, Cooke, Cuoghi, De Jong, Djurberg, Douka, Epaminonda, Fischer, Furnas, Gober, Greene, Hawkinson, Helms, Hundley, Johanson, Kippenberger, Koh, Koons, Lowman, Manders, Monahan, et al. through 31 July
The foundation is closed in August.

Kalfayan Galleries
11 Haritos Street, 106 75
tel +30 210 7217679
www.kalfayangalleries.com

APOSTOLOS GEORGIOU
through 14 June

PANOS TSAGARIS
'I am the Sun in His Rising'
19 June – 25 July

Eleni Koroneou Gallery
5–7 Mitseon Street, 117 42
tel +30 210 9244271
www.koroneougallery.com

THOMAS HELBIG
'Complete Birth'
through 15 July

Qbox Gallery
10, Armodiou Street, 105 52
tel +30 211 1199991
www.qbox.gr

LILLIAN LYKIARDOPOULOU
'Loop Ahead'
Installation
through 28 June

Ileana Tounta Contemporary Art Center
48 Armatolon & Klefton Street, 114 71
tel +30 210 6439466
www.art-tounta.gr

KATERINA CHRISTIDI
'Charcoal Overload!'
Drawings on canvas
through 21 June

ZOE XATZIGIANNAKI
Photographs
26 June – 12 July

vamiali's
1 Samou, 104 38
tel +30 210 5228968
www.vamiali.net

SAM HERBERT, JANICE KERBEL, MARIA KONTI, GROUP MEL-AIR, JONATHAN MONK, RUBY OSORIO, RICHARD WOODS ET AL.
Off-site project
through June

The gallery is open by appointment only in July and August.

Australia

Nellie Castan Gallery
Melbourne
Level 1, 12 River Street, South Yarra, 3141
tel +613 9804 7366
www.nelliecastangallery.com

PENELOPE METCALF 'City of Immigrants'
PENELOPE LONG 'Zoom'
2–21 June
CHRIS BOND 'White'
ANNA HOYLE 'Power Moai Buns 'n' Thighs'
26 June – 19 July
CLINTON NAIN 24 July – 2 August
TONY LLOYD 7–30 August

Melbourne Art Fair, 30 July – 3 August
Gordon Hookey 'A Ready Made Joke'

William Mora Galleries
Melbourne
60 Tanner Street, Richmond, 3121
tel +613 9429 1199
www.moragalleries.com.au

STEPHEN EASTAUGH
'Finding Yourself Lost in Melbourne'
24 June – 18 July

NYARRAPYI GILES
'Recent Paintings'
22 July – 15 August

Niagara Galleries
Melbourne
245 Punt Road, Richmond, 3121
tel +613 9429 3666
www.niagara-galleries.com.au

SEAN MEILAK
NEIL TAYLOR
3–28 June

GUNTER CHRISTMANN
MALALUBA GUMANA
1–26 July

EUAN HENG
ROSELLA NAMOK
29 July – 30 August

Gallery Gabrielle Pizzi
Melbourne
Level 3, 75–77 Flinders Lane, 3000
tel +613 9654 2944
www.gabriellepizzi.com.au

'BALGO FAMILY EXHIBITION'
In association with Warlayirti Artists
'EMERGING ARTISTS'
Including Debra Wurrkidj
In association with Maningrida Arts & Culture
10 June – 5 July

RUBY WILLIAMSON
In association with Tjala Arts
8 July – 9 August

Anna Schwartz Gallery
Melbourne
185 Flinders Lane, 3000
tel +613 9654 6131
www.annaschwartzgallery.com

LYNDAL JONES 'the bridge of no return'
7 June – 5 July

MIKALA DWYER
10 July – 9 August

New gallery space:
Sydney
245 Wilson Street, 2008:
MIKE PARR 'Milk'
17 June – 16 August

Tolarno Galleries
Melbourne
Level 4, 104 Exhibition Street, 3000
tel +613 9654 6000
www.tolarnogalleries.com

CAROLINE ROTHWELL
through 14 June

DAVID WADELTON
26 June – 19 July

PETER HENNESEY
24 July – 23 August

Über Gallery
Melbourne
52 Fitzroy Street, St Kilda, 3182
tel +613 8598 9915
www.ubergallery.com

HAMAD KHALAF
'Acts of War II'
Sculpture and painting
4 June – 6 July

MATT COYLE
'Night Stills'
Ink on paper
1–26 August

LISTINGS

Boutwell Draper Gallery
Sydney
82-84 George Street, Redfern, 2016
tel +612 9310 5662
www.boutwelldrapergallery.com.au

'MULTIPLEX'
David Stephenson, eX de Medici,
Ingo Kleinert, Murray Fredericks,
Ken Unsworth, Kirsty Bruce
11 June – 19 July

'STREET ART'
23 July – 28 August
Banksy, Faile, Dface, Anthony Lister

Conny Dietzschold Gallery
Sydney
2 Danks Street, Waterloo, 2017
tel +612 9690 0215
www.connydietzscholdgallery.com

POLLYXENIA JOANNOU
through 9 July

KUNO GONSCHIOR
12 July – 27 August

Multiple Box:
RICHARD TIPPING
through 9 July
FRANZ EHMANN
12 July – 27 August

Gallery Barry Keldoulis
Sydney
New space:
285 Young Street, Waterloo, 2017
tel +612 8399 1240
www.gbk.com.au

SARAH SMUTS-KENNEDY 'Cliffhanger'
through 14 June
JOHN CITIZEN
(AKA GORDON BENNETT)
'Interiors and Coloured People'
20 June – 12 July
FIONA LOWRY 'I Act as the Tongue of You'
16 July – 16 August
HAYDEN FOWLER from 20 August
Melbourne Art Fair, 30 July – 3 August

Darren Knight Gallery
Sydney
840 Elizabeth Street, Waterloo, 2017
tel +612 9699 5353
www.darrenknightgallery.com

ROB MCHAFFIE 'Small Triumph'
RICKY SWALLOW
through 7 June
JAMES MORRISON
14 June – 12 July
CHARLIE SOFO
EUAN MACDONALD
19 July – 16 August
NOEL MCKENNA 'The Weekly Bus-Rail
Ticket: The Return Journey'
23 August – 20 September

MOP Projects
Sydney
2/39 Abercrombie Street,
Chippendale, 2008
tel +612 9699 3955
www.mop.org.au
Galleries 1 and 2: 'SAFARI 08'
12 June – 29 June
Gallery 1: MITCH CAIRNS
Gallery 2: LEO COYTE
3 – 20 July
Gallery 1: HOLLY WILLIAMS 'Curated'
Gallery 2: KIRSTEN FARRELL
24 July – 10 August
Gallery 1: CRAIG BENDER
Gallery 2: PADRAIG SWANN
14 – 31 August

Roslyn Oxley9 Gallery
Sydney
8 Soudan Lane (off Hampden Street),
Paddington, 2021
tel: +612 9331 1919
www.roslynoxley9.com.au

BILL HENSON
through 21 June

DALE FRANK
26 June – 12 July

IMANTS TILLERS
17 July – 9 August

Sherman Contemporary Art Foundation
Sydney
16-20 Goodhope Street, Paddington, 2021
tel +612 9331 1112
www.sherman-scaf.org.au

'AI WEIWEI: UNDER CONSTRUCTION'
Curated by Dr. Charles Merewether
In conjunction with Campbelltown Arts
Centre
through 26 July

JONATHAN JONES
15 August – 11 October

Austria

Grazer Kunstverein
Graz
Im Palais Thinnfeld
Mariahilferstraße 2, 8020
tel +43 316 83 41 41
www.grazerkunstverein.org

VOJIN BAKIC
curated by WHW
4 June – 24 August

LUCA FREI
MARINE HUGONNIER
SEAN SNYDER
20 June – 24 August

Kunsthaus Graz am Landesmuseum Joanneum
Graz
Lendkai 1, 8020
tel +43 316 8017 9200
www.kunsthausgraz.at

'THYSSEN-BORNEMISZA
ART CONTEMPORARY
COLLECTION AS ALEPH'
through 26 October

'JOE COLOMBO
DESIGN AND THE INVENTION OF THE
FUTURE'
7 June – 31 August

Galerie im Taxipalais
Innsbruck
Maria-Theresien-Straße 45, 6020
tel +43 512 508 3171
www.galerieimtaxispalais.at

'VOICE & VOID'
R. Berwick, J. Beuys/U. Klophaus, J. Cage,
J. Cardiff and G. Bures Miller, V. Export,
A. Gaskell, A. Gröting, C. Marclay,
M. Ohanian, H. Schabus, N. Solakov,
J. Swartz, C. Wyn Evans
through 8 June

GETA BRĂTESCU
ANA LUPAŞ
28 June – 24 August

Galerie Christian Hosp
Nassereith
Ingenieur Kastnerstraße 173, 6465
tel +43 650 235 5500
www.kala-gallery.com

Please contact the gallery for information.

Galerie Heike Curtze
Vienna
Seilerstätte 15/16, 1010
tel +43 1 512 9375
www.heikecurtze.com

BRACO DIMITRIJEVIC
through 3 June

Salzburg
Wiener Philharmonikergasse 2, 5020
tel +43 664 112 6026:
'SONNENGOLD'
26 July – 31 August

Engholm Engelhorn Galerie
Vienna
Schleifmühlgasse 3, 1040
tel +43 1 585 7337
www.engholmengelhorn.com

Please contact the gallery for information.

Galerie Ernst Hilger
Vienna
Dorotheergasse 5, 1010
tel +43 1 512 5315
www.hilger.at

ERRÓ
through 19 June

RAINER WÖLZL
26 June through July

Hilger Contemporary
Vienna
Dorotheergasse 5, 1010
tel +43 1 512 5315
www.hilger.at

MIHA STRUKELJ
through 19 June

PAUL KRANZLER
26 June through July

Georg Kargl
Vienna
Schleifmühlgasse 5, 1040
tel +43 1 585 4199
www.georgkargl.com

Georg Kargl Fine Arts:
ROSEMARIE TROCKEL
Georg Kargl BOX:
'KICKEN IN WIEN – DIE WELTMEISTER'
through 25 June

Permanent (Schleifmühlgasse 17):
JO JACKSON
'The Bowl and Time'

Christine König Galerie
Vienna
Schleifmühlgasse 1A, 1040
tel +43 1 585 7474
www.christinekoeniggalerie.com

ADEL ABDESSEMED
'Orient for Global Bordelo'
through 28 June
MICHA PAYER & MARTIN GABRIEL
2 July – 2 August
Third Room:
SISLEJ XHAFA 'Sadnesssurge'
through 28 June
SAMI AL TURKI 'Lifts'
2 July – 2 August
Art Basel, 4 – 8 June

Galerie Krinzinger
Vienna
Seilerstätte 16, 1010
tel +43 1 513 3006
www.galerie-krinzinger.at

Please contact the gallery for information.

**MUMOK – Museum Moderner
Kunst Stiftung Ludwig Wien**
Vienna
Museumsplatz 1, 1070
Tel: +43 1 525 00
www.mumok.at

RUNA ISLAM
through 13 July

**'BAD PAINTING –
MALEREI GEGEN DIE MALEREI'**
6 June – 12 October

**'FOKUS 4 –
RÄUME. AKTIONEN. UTOPIEN'**
25 July – June 2009

**Galerie nächst St. Stephan
Rosemarie Schwarzwälder**
Vienna
Grünangergasse 1/2, 1010
tel +43 1 512 1266
www.schwarzwaelder.at

JOËLLE TUERLINCKX
'Le présent absolument'
through 28 June

The gallery is open by appointment only in
July and August.

Secession
Vienna
Friedrichstraße 12, 1010
tel +43 1 587 5307
www.secession.at

**FRANCES STARK
DAVE ALLEN
JO BAER**
through 22 June
**THOMAS HIRSCHHORN
ISA ROSENBERGER
MIKLÓS ERHARDT**
4 July – 7 September
Secession Display Case:
MIKLÓS ERHARDT
through 7 September

Gabriele Senn Galerie
Vienna
Schleifmühlgasse 1A, 1040
tel +43 1 585 2580
www.galeriesenn.at

AMELIE VON WULFFEN
through 28 June

ABEL AUER
4 July – 2 August

Siemens_artLab
Vienna
Dorotheergasse 12, 1010
tel +43 1 513 4032
www.artlab.at

'P.a.A.'
26 June through July

Galerie Hubert Winter
Vienna
Breite Gasse 17, 1070
tel +43 1 524 0976
www.galeriewinter.at

FRED SANDBACK
through 29 June

**DORIS DRESCHER
FRANZ VANA**
3 July – 6 September

The gallery is closed from 23 July – 17 August.

Belgium

Dagmar De Pooter Gallery
Antwerp
Pourbusstraat 14, 2000
tel +32 3 290 85 74
www.dagmardepootergallery.com

Groundspace:
FRIE J. JACOBS
'Onverzameld, Althans'
Basementspace:
CHRIS GILLIS
'Inside, Into the Frame'
through 22 June

The gallery is closed in July and August.

Galerie Annie Gentils
Antwerp
Peter Benoitstraat 40, 2018
tel +32 3 216 30 28
www.anniegentilsgallery.com

CHARLOTTE SCHLEIFFERT
'Berlin Works'
through 28 June

'ARTISTS OF THE GALLERY'
July–August, by appointment only

Scope, Basel
3 – 8 June, Booth 113

Koraalberg
Antwerp
Pourbusstraat 5, 2000
tel +32 3 226 06 30
www.koraalberg.be

NICK ERVINCK
'GNI – RI May 2008'
through 21 June

Balelatina/Hot Art, Basel
Carla Arocha, Stephane Schraenen
Installation
In collaboration with
Monique Meloche Gallery, Chicago
2 – 8 June

Stella Lohaus Gallery
Antwerp
Vlaamse Kaai 47, 2000
tel +32 3 248 08 71
www.stellalohausgallery.com

DENNIS TYFUS
'I Never Liked Neon Until I Met You'
through 28 June

The gallery is open by appointment only in
July and closed in August.

Art Basel: Art Premiere:
Joëlle Tuerlinckx and Angel Vergara
4 – 8 June

Galerie van der Mieden
Antwerp
Pourbusstraat 15, 2000
tel +32 3 231 77 42
www.vandermieden.com

JASPER KRABBÉ
through 21 June

The gallery is closed 22 June – 3 September.

Aeroplastics
Brussels
32, rue Blanche, 1060
tel +32 2 537 22 02
www.aeroplastics.net

Please contact the gallery for information.

aliceday
Brussels
Fabriekstraat 1B, 1000
2nd floor
tel +32 2 646 3153
www.aliceday.be

Charlotte Beaudry invites
**AGNÈS GEOFFRAY, ANNICK LIZEIN,
MICHAEL DANS, BENOÎT PLATÉUS** and
ERIK OLOFSEN
through 12 July

LISTINGS

Galerie Catherine Bastide
Brussels
62, Chaussée de Forest, 1060
tel +32 2 646 2971
www.catherinebastide.com

T. KELLY MASON
'Who are the Intellectual Luminaries of Our Time'
20 June – 26 July

Project Room:
MARIO DELLAVEDOVA
New work
20 June – 26 July

Erna Hecey
Brussels
Fabrieksstraat 1C, 1000
tel +32 2 502 0024
www.ernahecey.com

KLAUS SCHERÜBEL
'Reconsidering Jack Torrance's All Work and No Play'
through 14 June

SUZANNE LAFONT
'Index'
12 June – 26 July

Rodolphe Janssen
Brussels
35, rue de Livourne, 1050
tel +32 2 538 0818
www.galerierodolphejanssen.com

'FAMOUS ALIENS OF FILMLAND AND AMERICAN FOLK FURNITURE ORIGINALS BY JUSTIN LIEBERMAN'
opening 22 May
continues through 19 July

Sorry We're Closed:
JANSSON STEIGNER
June – August

Art Basel, 4 – 8 June

Deweer Art Gallery
Otegem
Tiegemstraat 6A, 8553
tel +32 56 644 893
www.deweerartgallery.com

JAN FABRE
'Is the Brain the Most Sexy Part of the Body?'
through 22 June and by appointment only through 11 July

Canada

Museum of Contemporary Canadian Art
Toronto
952 Queen Street West, M6J 1G8
tel +416 395 0067
www.mocca.toronto.ca

'BETWEEN MEMORY AND HISTORY: FROM THE EPIC TO THE EVERYDAY'
Raymonde April, Robert Burley, Martin Parr, Chi Peng, Thomas Ruff, Alessandra Sanguinetti, Bert Teunissen et al.
through 1 June

Agnes Etherington Art Centre
Kingston
Queen's University
University Avenue at Bader Lane, K7L 3N6
tel +613 533 2190
www.aeac.ca

CAROLE CONDÉ and KARL BEVERIDGE
'Working Culture'
through 8 June

EDWARD BURTYNSKY
'Material World'
28 June – 19 October

Monte Clark Gallery
Vancouver
2339 Granville Street, V6H 3G4
tel +604 730 5000
www.monteclarkgallery.com

Vancouver:
GREG GIRARD
through 21 June

Toronto:
EVAN LEE
through 8 June
STEPHEN WADDELL
12 June – 20 July
ROY ARDEN
24 July – 7 September

Pierre-François Ouellette art contemporain
Montréal
372 Ste-Catherine West, #216, H3B 1A2
pfoac2: 372 Ste-Catherine West, #423
tel +514 395 6032
www.pfoac.com

ADAD HANNAH
through 5 July

ISABELLE HAYEUR and CHIH-CHIEN WANG
19 July – 23 August

Contemporary Art Gallery
Vancouver
555 Nelson Street, V6B 6R5
tel +604 681 2700
www.contemporaryartgallery.ca

STEPHEN WADDELL
through 1 June

MAX DEAN
'Robotic Chair'
SAMUEL ROY-BOIS
13 June – 24 August

Susan Hobbs
Toronto
137 Tecumseth Street, M6J 2H2
tel +416 504 3699
www.susanhobbs.com

ARNAUD MAGGS
'Contamination'
through 14 June

Charles H. Scott Gallery
Vancouver
1399 Johnston Street, V6H 3R9
tel +604 844 3809
http://chscott.eciad.ca/

Please contact the gallery for information.

Mercer Union, A Centre for Contemporary Art
Toronto
37 Lisgar Street, M6J 3T3
tel +416 536 1519
www.mercerunion.org

Please contact the gallery for information.

Germany

Galerie Thomas Zander
Cologne
Schönhauser Straße 8, 50968
tel +49 221 934 88 56
www.galeriezander.com

ANDREA GEYER
'Spiral Lands / Chapter 1'
through 21 June

HENRY WESSEL
'Standard'
28 June through September

Sprüth Magers Projekte
Munich
Ludwigstraße 7, 80530
tel +49 89 2889 0760
www.spruethmagersprojekte.com

MARTIN WÖHRL
June–July

Künstlerhaus Bethanien GmbH
Berlin
Mariannenplatz 2, 10997
tel +49 30 616 90 30
www.bethanien.de

MING WONG
HARIS EPAMINONDA
6–22 June
MARKUS DEGERMAN
11–27 July
OPEN STUDIOS
14 August, 7–10pm
LIBIA CASTRO / OLAFUR OLAFSSON
DANIEL BARROCA
15–31 August

Galerie Heike Curtze
Berlin
Friedrichstraße 210 (1st floor)/Checkpoint
Charlie, 10969
tel +49 30 3759 1996
www.heikecurtze.com

MICHAEL VENEZIA
'Recent Works – Spray Paintings'
through 5 July

The gallery is closed in August.

Bugdahn und Kaimer
Dusseldorf
Mutter-Ey-Straße 5, 40213
tel +49 211 32 91 40
www.bugdahnundkaimer.com

INGOLF TIMPNER
'Portraiture'
through 8 June

CLAIRE COREY
20 June–2 August

'SUMMER INTERVAL 08'
12 August–6 September

Galerie Tanit
Munich
Maximilianstraße 45, 80538
tel +49 89 29 22 33
www.galerietanit.com

BERNHARD EDMAIER
5 June–12 July

'SUMMER SHOW 2008'
17 July–mid-August

Haus am Waldsee
Berlin
Argentinische Allee 30, 14163
tel +49 30 801 89 35
www.hausamwaldsee.de

OLAV CHRISTOPHER JENSSEN
'At Times'
through 8 June

PETER ABLINGER
'Listen to Listening'
21 June–3 August

Galerie Nordenhake
Berlin
Lindenstraße 34, 10969
tel +49 30 206 14 83
www.nordenhake.com

HREINN FRIDFINNSSON
through June 14

GUNILLA KLINGBERG
opening Wednesday 18 June
continues through 26 July

The gallery is closed in August.

Galerie Voss
Dusseldorf
Mühlengasse 3, 40213
tel +49 211 13 49 82
www.galerievoss.de

MAIA NAVERIANI
'At Home with Good Ideas'
through 7 June

SILKE REHBERG
13 June–12 July

'ARTISTS OF THE GALLERY'
15 July through end of August

Galerie Reinhard Hauff
Stuttgart
Paulinenstraße 47, 70178
tel +49 711 60 97 70
www.reinhardhauff.de

FRANK AHLGRIMM
14 June–26 July

NGBK Neue Gesellschaft für Bildende Kunst
Berlin
Oranienstraße 25, 10999
tel +49 30 616 51 30
www.ngbk.de
'EIN LEBEN LANG...ALL YOUR LIFE...'
B. Brenner, B. Burwitz, L. Clayton/J. Price,
D. Cumming, M. Esterhazy, R. von Felten,
M. Geerlinks, P. Granser, F. Kersten,
A. Soltau, M. Yanagi et al.
26 July–31 August
Realismus Studio:
KLAUS METTIG
'Don't Be Left Behind: Photographic Work
and Projections 1978–2007'
through 13 July

Galerie Michael Schultz
Berlin
Mommsenstraße 34, 10629
tel +49 30 319 91 30
www.galerie-schultz.de

RÖMER + RÖMER
14 June–26 July
'MEISTERSCHÜLERPREISTRÄGER DER
UNIVERSITÄT DER KÜNSTE, BERLIN'
16 August–7 September
Schultz Contemporary:
JAN MUCHE
'Alles kann, nichts muss'
through 7 June
STEFANIE GUTHEIL
14 June–26 July

Bernhard Knaus Fine Art
Frankfurt/M.
Niddastraße 84, 60329
tel +49 69 2445 0768
www.bernhardknaus-art.de

CHRISTIAN HAGEMANN
NOAH SHERWOOD
'Left to My Own Devices'
Photographs and sculpture
through 28 June

'SUMMER EXHIBITION:
DRAWING AND SCULPTURE'
Harald Kröner et al.
3 July–30 August

German Institutions

Bonner Kunstverein
Bonn
Hochstadenring 22, 53119
tel +49 228 69 39 36
www.bonner-kunstverein.de

CLAUDIA and JULIA MÜLLER
'Tut Tut Tut'
CHRISTOPH KELLER
'Beyond Kiosk'
Foyer:
PHILIPPE DECRAUZAT
Vorplatz:
JEPPE HEIN
through 1 June

Monika Sprüth Philomene Magers
Cologne
Wormser Straße 23, 50677
tel +49 221 38 04 15
www.spruethmagers.com

ROBERT ELFGEN
'Des bien ich'
through 26 July

Monika Sprüth Philomene Magers
Munich
Schellingstraße 48, 80799
tel +49 89 33 04 06 00
www.spruethmagers.com

AXEL KASSEBÖHMER
'Neue Arbeiten'
through 26 July

Staatliche Kunsthalle Baden-Baden
Baden-Baden
Lichtentaler Allee 8a, 76530
tel +49 7221 300 76-3
www.kunsthalle-baden-baden.de

NAIRY BAGHRAMIAN
through 6 July

STEPHEN PRINA
19 July–5 October

Kunstverein Braunschweig
Braunschweig
Lessingplatz 12, 38100
tel +49 531 49556
www.kunstverein-bs.de

Haus Salve Hospes:
YEHUDIT SASPORTAS
'Laboratory'
Cuboid:
JULIA HORSTMANN
'Zwischen den Wänden'
7 June–10 August

LISTINGS

GAK Gesellschaft für Aktuelle Kunst
Bremen
Terrhof 21, 28199
tel +49 421 500 896
www.gak-bremen.de

'FOS. MEMORY THEATRE TWIG'
1 June – 10 August

JOHN STEZAKER
30 August – 2 November

**MMK
Museum für Moderne Kunst**
Frankfurt/M.
Domstraße 10, 60311
tel +49 69 2123 0447
www.mmk-frankfurt.de

MIROSLAV TICHÝ
Photographs
BERNARD BUFFET
'Painter'
through 3 August

ANDREAS GURSKY
'Cocoonfrankfurt'
14 June – 3 August

Mannheimer Kunstverein
Mannheim
Augustaanlage 58, 68165
tel +49 62 140 2208
www.mannheimer-kunstverein.de

'ISLANDS AND GHETTOS'
In co-operation with Heidelberger
Kunstverein and Ernst-Bloch-Zentrum,
Ludwigshafen
6 June – 31 August

Kölnischer Kunstverein
Cologne
Die Brücke, Hahnenstraße 6, 50667
tel +49 22 121 70 21
www.koelnischerkunstverein.de

MARK LECKEY
'Resident'
Central Art Award 2008
through 8 June

MICHAEL KREBBER
21 June – 28 September

Schirn Kunsthalle Frankfurt
Frankfurt/M.
Römerberg, 60311
tel +49 69 299 88 20
www.schirn.de

MICHAEL SAILSTORFER '10 000 Steine'
TERENCE KOH 'Captain Buddha'
through 31 August

'TOTAL ENLIGHTENMENT:
MOSCOW CONCEPTUAL ART
1960 – 1990'
21 June – 14 September

Kunstverein München
Munich
Galeriestraße 4, 80539
tel +49 89 22 11 52
www.kunstverein-muenchen.de

'SOME NEIGHBOURS'
through 1 June
ALLORA & CALZADILLA
'Wake Up, Clamor, Sediments
Sentiments (Figures Of Speech)'
13 June – 13 July
Ludlow 38, New York
Kunstverein München | Goethe Institut
www.ludlow38.org:
ifau + JESKO FEZER
through 1 June

Museum Ludwig
Cologne
Heinrich-Böll-Platz, 50667
tel +49 221 2212 6165
www.museum-ludwig.de

'PAULA MODERSOHN-BECKER
AND THE EGYPTIAN MUMMY
PORTRAITS'
'PROGRESSIVE COLOGNE 1920 – 33
SEIWERT – HOERLE – ARNTZ'
through 15 June

MATTI BRAUN
'Özurfa'
through 31 August

Kunstverein in Hamburg
Hamburg
Klosterwall 23, 20095
tel +49 40 33 83 44
www.kunstverein.de

SHARON LOCKHART
through 15 June

Upper Floor:
BOJAN SARCEVIC
'Only After Dark'
Ground Floor:
'AUFTAKT'
5 July – 21 September

Kunsthalle Nürnberg
Nuremberg
Lorenzer Straße 32, 90402
tel +49 911 231 28 53
www.kunsthalle.nuernberg.de

BEATE GÜTSCHOW
'Ganz woanders'
through 15 June

'DAS GELÄNDE'
Winfried Baumann, Ross Birrell,
Claus Föttinger, Susanne Kriemann,
Jonathan Meese, Bernhard Prinz,
Jürgen Teller, Artur Zmijewski et al.
6 July – 31 August

Kunsthalle Düsseldorf
Dusseldorf
Grabbeplatz 4, 40213
tel +49 211 899 62 43
www.kunsthalle-duesseldorf.de

MEUSER
'The Woman Rides and the Horse Goes on
Foot' through 20 July
'PARKHAUS'
10 August – 21 September

KIT – Kunst im Tunnel
Mannesmannufer 1b, 40213
www.kunst-im-tunnel.de:
'VIDEO KOOP' through 27 July
'SPIEGELBILD' 16 August – 12 October

Kunstverein Hannover
Hanover
Sophienstraße 2, 30159
tel +49 511 32 45 94
www.kunstverein-hannover.de

ADRIAN PACI
through 15 June

'NORDLICHTER –
84. HERBSTAUSSTELLUNG'
28 June – 17 August

LEIGH BOWERY
30 August – 2 October

Edith Russ Site for Media Art
Oldenburg
Katharinenstraße 23, 26121
tel +49 441 235 32 08
www.edith-russ-haus.de

RAFAEL LOZANO-HEMMER
'Recorders'
7 June – 17 August

Frankfurter Kunstverein
Frankfurt/M.
Steinernes Haus am Römerberg
Markt 44, 60311
tel +49 69 219 31 40
www.fkv.de

'THE GREAT TRANSFORMATION –
ART AND TACTICAL MAGIC'
7 June – 7 September

SITE Santa Fe International Biennial
Frankfurter Kunstverein presents
Mandla Reuter
22 June – 26 October

Badischer Kunstverein
Karlsruhe
Waldstraße 3, 76133
tel +49 72 12 82 26
www.badischer-kunstverein.de

'ROM REPORT'
Dobliar, Girardet, Hertzsch & Page,
Holzfeind, Horowitz, Korpys & Löffler,
Neumeister, Nicolai, Schatz, Schmidt,
Scholz / Brinkmann
through 15 June
HEIKE BOLLIG
'On the Spot #3'
through 22 June
JUDITH HOPF
4 July – 7 September

Kunstmuseum Wolfsburg
Wolfsburg
Hollerplatz 1, 38440
tel +49 5361 266 90
www.kunstmuseum-wolfsburg.de

PHILIP TAAFFE
'The Life of Forms'
through 29 June

HEINRICH HEIDERSBERGER
'Return to the Point of Departure'
through 21 September

Netherlands

Paris

Annet Gelink Gallery
Amsterdam
Laurierstraat 187–189, 1016 PL
tel +31 20 330 20 66
www.annetgelink.com

DAVID MALJKOVIC
'Lost Memories From These Days'
In the Bakery:
DAVID MALJKOVIC and ROSA BARBA
through 28 June

Art Basel: Art Unlimited
Robert Suermondt
4–8 June

Galerie Diana Stigter
Amsterdam
Elandsstraat 90, 1016 SH
tel +31 20 624 23 61
www.dianastigter.nl

NICKY ZWAAN
In the Backspace:
SANG WOO KANG
through 28 June

Art Basel: Art Statements
Martha Colburn
4–8 June

Galerie Paul Andriesse
Amsterdam
Detroit Building, Withoedenveem 8, 1019 HE
tel +31 20 623 62 37
www.galeries.nl/andriesse

ANN LISLEGAARD
through 28 June

DWIGHT MARICA
5 July – 30 August

Art Basel
4–8 June

Juliètte Jongma
Amsterdam
New address:
Gerard Doustraat 128A, 1073 VX
tel +31 20 463 69 04
www.juliettejongma.com

'PIERROTING'
Donna Huddleston, Ursula Mayer,
Karen Sargsyan
**'WOOFF, WOOFF OR WHO KILLED
RICHARD WAGNER'** Theater 't Barre land
In collaboration with Karen Sargsyan and
Roald van Oosten
21 June – 26 July
Liste, Basel, 3–8 June
Tim Braden, Pablo Pijnappel

Torch
Amsterdam
Lauriergracht 94, 1016 RN
tel +31 20 626 02 84
www.torchgallery.com

TEUN HOCKS
New photographs, drawings, videos
through 28 June

The gallery is open by appointment only in
July and August.

Air de Paris
32, rue Louise Weiss, 75013
tel +33 1 44 23 02 77
www.airdeparis.com

STÉPHANE DAFFLON
'Up/Down'
THOMAS BAYRLE
'Un sacco di autostrada.../
Motorwaybags.../Voiture...Confiture'
through 26 July

Art Basel
4–8 June

Aschenbach & Hofland
Amsterdam
Bilderdijkstraat 165C, 1053 KP
tel +31 20 412 17 72
www.xs2art.com

JAN VAN DER PLOEG and THOM PUCKEY
through 21 June

Galerie Gabriel Rolt
Amsterdam
Elandsgracht 34, 1016 TW
tel +31 20 78 55 146
www.gabrielrolt.com

DOUGLAS WHITE
'Hartrot'
New installations
through 21 June

'SUMMERSHOW'
Group show of new work by gallery artists
28 June – 30 August

Volta, Basel
4–8 June

Martin van Zomeren
Amsterdam
Prinsengracht 276-hs, 1016 HJ
tel +31 20 420 81 29
www.gmvz.com

WILFREDO PRIETO
through 28 June

Liste, Basel
Wilfredo Prieto, Lucy Stein,
Alexandra Leykauf
3–8 June

Balice Hertling
65, rue Rébéval, 75019
tel +33 6 19 60 88 94
www.balicehertling.com

RETO PULFER
'Die Gunst Der Stunde
Die Kunst Der Wunde'
opening reception with performance
21 June, 6 – 9pm
continues through 19 July

Ellen de Bruijne Projects
Amsterdam
Rozengracht 207A, 1016 LZ
tel +31 20 530 49 94
www.edbprojects.nl

edb:
DARAGH REEVES
Dolores:
ZORAN TERZIC
through 28 June

SASKIA JANSSEN
'Summer Project'
5 – 12 July

Ronmandos Gallery
Amsterdam
Prinsengracht 282, 1016 HJ
tel +31 6 275 50 893
www.ronmandos.nl

DANIEL ARSHAM
Sculptures
HANS OP DE BEECK
Prints
through 28 June
Rotterdam
Rodenrijselaan 24, 3037 XE
+31 10 4677590:
RODERICK HIETBRINK through 21 June
Please contact the gallery for further
summer programme information.

Fons Welters
Amsterdam
Bloemstraat 140, 1016 LJ
tel +31 20 423 30 46
www.fonswelters.nl

Please contact the gallery for information.

galerie anne barrault
22, rue Saint-Claude, 75003
tel +33 1 44 78 91 67
www.galerieannebarrault.com

'MIDWEST'
Jeffrey Brown, Paul Hornschemeier,
Anders Nilsen
curated by Félicia Atkinson
21 June – 26 July

Volta, Basel
3 – 7 June

De Expeditie
Amsterdam
Leliegracht 47, 1016 GT
tel +31 20 620 47 58
www.de-expeditie.com

PIETERJAN GINCKELS
through 5 July

The gallery is open by appointment only
9 – 31 July and is closed in August.

Slewe Gallery
Amsterdam
Kerkstraat 105A, 1017 GD
tel +31 20 625 72 14
www.slewe.nl

MARTIN GERWERS
through 21 June

The gallery is open by appointment only in
July and August.

Zinger Presents
Amsterdam
Gerard Doustraat 134, 1073 VX
tel +31 62 493 90 47
www.zingerpresents.net

Please contact the gallery for information.

Cosmic Galerie
7 – 9, rue de l'Equerre, 75019
tel +33 1 42 71 72 73
www.cosmicgalerie.com

'THE OTHER WAY AROUND'
Benoît Broisat, Stefan Brüggemann,
James Hopkins, Gianni Motti,
Damien Roach, Jamie Shovlin
through 12 July

Liste, Basel
3–8 June

LISTINGS

Galerie Chantal Crousel
10, rue Charlot, 75003
tel +33 1 42 77 38 87
www.crousel.com

WADE GUYTON
through 14 June

REENA SPAULINGS
21 June – 2 August

Galerie Jérôme de Noirmont
36–38, avenue Matignon, 75008
tel +33 1 42 89 89 00
www.denoirmont.com

BETTINA RHEIMS
'Just Like a Woman'
A catalogue will be published
through 16 July

The gallery is open by appointment only
17 – 31 July and is closed in August.

Galerie Thaddaeus Ropac
7, rue Debelleyme, 75003
tel +33 1 42 72 99 00
www.ropac.net

ROBERT MAPPLETHORPE
'Lisa, Milton, Thomas & Ken'
ANTONY GORMLEY
'Works on Paper'
through 7 June

JULES DE BALINCOURT
Drawing Space:
'LANDSCOPE' Group show
Project Space:
JEON JOONHO
11 June – 26 July

Galerie Anne de Villepoix
43, rue de Montmorency, 75003
tel +33 1 42 78 32 24
www.annedevillepoix.com

KADER ATTIA
'Mythes et poésie du vide'
through 28 June

Galerie Marian Goodman
79, rue du Temple, 75003
tel +33 1 48 04 70 52
www.mariangoodman.com

GIUSEPPE PENONE
through 5 July

Galerie Nathalie Obadia
3, rue du Cloître Saint-Merri, 75004
tel +33 1 42 74 67 68
www.galerie-obadia.com

'UPSA DREAM'
Group show curated by Pascal Pinaud, with
John Armleder, Pascal Broccolichi, Noël
Dolla, Sandrine Flury, Philippe Gronon,
Bertrand Lavier, Stephane Magnin,
Emilie Maltaverne, Mathieu Mercier,
Pascal Pinaud, Ludovic Sauvage
through 12 July
Art Basel: Art Premiere, 4 – 8 June
Martin Barré, Jessica Stockholder
Art Basel: Art Unlimited, 4 – 8 June
Rina Banerjee

Galerie Patrick Seguin
20th Century Furniture &
Architecture
5, rue des Taillandiers, 75011
tel +33 1 47 00 32 35
www.patrickseguin.com

Permanent showroom:
20th century furniture and architecture by
PROUVÉ, PERRIAND, LE CORBUSIER,
ROYÈRE, MOUILLE, NOLL, JOUVE,
JEANNERET

Jousse Entreprise
24, rue Louise Weiss, 75013
tel +33 1 53 82 10 18
www.jousse-entreprise.com

ATELIER VAN LIESHOUT 'Slave City'
34, rue Louise Weiss, 75013:
JOEP VAN LIESHOUT
'Soft and Hard Edge Furniture 1989 – 90'
through 26 July

18, rue de Seine, 75006:
'MOBILIER D'ARCHITECTES DU MILIEU
DU XXÈME SIÈCLE'
Prouvé, Le Corbusier, Jeanneret, Jouve,
Matégot, Mouille, Noll, Perriand, Royère
Permanent exhibition

Galerie Orel Art
40, rue Quincampoix, 75004
tel +33 1 47 20 22 54
www.orelart.com

STEVEN J. SHANABROOK
'Devil's Necklace'
ANNOUCHKA BROCHET
'Extasy'
12 June – 26 July

The gallery is closed in August.

Moscow World Fine Art Fair
Booth 37
through 2 June

Suzanne Tarasième Paris
171, rue du Chevaleret, 75013
tel +33 1 45 86 02 02
www.suzanne-tarasieve.com

Please contact the gallery for information.

Yvon Lambert Paris
108, rue Vieille du Temple, 75003
tel +33 1 42 71 09 33
www.yvon-lambert.com

BETHAN HUWS
PAVEL BRAILA 'Wanted'
through 21 June
GROUP SHOW
27 June – 6 September
The Wall:
LORIS GREAUD
through July

Art Basel
Booth 2.1, R3
4 – 8 June

Galerie Emmanuel Perrotin
76, rue de Turenne and
10, impasse Saint-Claude, 75003
tel +33 1 42 16 79 79
www.galerieperrotin.com
AYA TAKANO 'Toward Eternity'
GUY LIMONE 'ça tourne!'
through 14 June
KEEGAN MCHARGUE
ERIC BENQUÉ
21 June – 26 July
Miami
194 NW 30th Street, 33127
tel 305 573 2130:
CARY KWOK, MARTIN OPPEL
through 26 July
Art Basel, Hall 2.1, Booth M4, 4 – 8 June

Galerie Daniel Templon
30, rue Beaubourg, 75003
tel +33 1 42 72 14 10
www.danieltemplon.com

JÖRG LOZEK
'Im Zimmer'
Impasse Beaubourg:
LARRY BELL
'Recent Works'
through 19 July

The gallery is closed in August.

Art Basel
Hall 2.0, Booth A3
4 – 8 June

Galerie Lelong
13, rue de Teheran, 75008
tel +33 1 45 63 13 19
www.galerie-lelong.com

SEAN SCULLY
'La surface peinte'
through 5 July

Art Basel
4 – 8 June

Galerie Almine Rech
19, rue de Saintonge, 75003
tel +33 1 45 83 71 90
www.galeriealminerech.com

UWE HENNEKEN
'Légion Troublée'
through 7 June

NATHANIEL RACKOWE
First Floor:
PADRAIG TIMONEY
AXEL GEIS
14 June – 19 July
Art Basel
Hall 2.1, Booth B5
4 – 8 June

Galerie Georges Philippe &
Nathalie Vallois
36, rue de Seine, 75006
tel +33 1 46 34 61 07
www.galerie-vallois.com

VINCENT LAMOUROUX
'Above'
Project Room:
ALAIN BUBLEX
'Nocturne'
through 20 June

SAVERIO LUCARIELLO
27 June – 1 September

Spain

Sweden

sala rekalde
Bilbao
Alameda de Recalde, 30, 48009
tel +34 94 406 87 55
www.salarekalde.bizkaia.net

'CALYPSO – ARTISTIC LEARNING PROCESSES'
Bizkaia Executive Council Grants for Artistic Creation, 2005 – 2006
through 22 June

ITZIAR OKARIZ
'Ghost Box'
'ERREAKZIOA – REACCIÓN'
10 July – 21 September

Galería Helga de Alvear
Madrid
Doctor Fourquet, 12, 28012
tel +34 91 468 05 06
www.helgadealvear.com

'EXTRAORDINARY RENDITION'
Elmgreen & Dragset, James Casebere, Alicia Framis, Santiago Sierra
through 19 July

The gallery is closed in August.

Galería Estrany-de la Mota
Barcelona
Passatge Mercader, 18, 08008
tel +34 93 215 70 51
www.estranydelamota.com

FRANCESC RUIZ
'BCN Eye Trip'
through 27 June

The gallery is closed in August.

Galería Oliva Arauna
Madrid
Barquillo, 29, 28004
tel +34 91 435 18 08
www.olivarauna.com

JORGE MOLDER
through 26 July

The gallery is closed in August.

Galería Soledad Lorenzo
Madrid
Orfila, 5, 28010
tel +34 91 308 28 87/88
www.soledadlorenzo.com

ROBERT LONGO
through 7 June

ÁNGEL MARCOS
12 June – 19 July

The gallery is closed in August.

Gävle Konstcentrum
Gävle
Kungsbäcksvägen 32, 801 31
tel +46 26 17 94 24
www.gavlekonstcentrum.se

'SAME SAME'
Sigurður Guðmundsson, Guðmundur Kristjánsson, Kristján Guðmundsson, Árni Guðmundsson
14 June – 28 August

Galería Joan Prats
Barcelona
Rambla de Catalunya, 54, 08007
tel +34 93 216 02 84
www.galeriajoanprats.com

JOSE MARIA SICILIA
June – August

galería elba benitez
Madrid
San Lorenzo, 11, 28004
tel +34 91 308 04 68
www.elbabenitez.com

'PAINTING (STILL)'
Raoul De Keyser, Bernard Frize, On Kawara, Jonathan Monk, Günter Umberg, Christopher Wool, Rèmy Zaugg
curated by Ignasi Aballi
June – July

The gallery is closed in August.

Galería Leyendecker
Santa Cruz de Tenerife
Rambla General Franco, 86, 38004
tel +34 922 280 053
www.leyendecker.net

JEREMY BLAKE
June – July

The gallery is closed in August.

Dunkers Kulturhus
Helsingborg
Kungsgatan 11, 252 21
tel +46 42 10 74 00
www.dunkerskulturhus.se

'NATURE OF MAN'
June 14 – 4 January

YNGVE RADBERG
'Case Closed'
27 June – 19 October

Galería Toni Tàpies
Barcelona
Consell de Cent, 282, 08007
tel +34 93 487 64 02
www.tonitapies.com

EDWARD BURTYNSKY
'New Quarries'
through 31 July

The gallery is closed in August.

Galería Pepe Cobo
Madrid
C/Fortuny, 39, 28010
tel +34 91 319 06 83
www.pepecobo.com

RINKO KAWAUCHI
through July

The gallery is closed in August.

Luis Adelantado Valencia
Valencia
C/Bonaire, 6, 46003
tel +34 96 351 01 79
www.luisadelantadovalencia.com

MIGUEL RAEL
Video, sculpture and painting
through 20 June

BAYROL JIMENEZ
Painting and drawing
23 June – 30 July

'X INTERNATIONAL CALL'
August – September

Lunds Konsthall
Lund
Mårtenstorget 3, 223 51
tel +46 46 35 52 95
www.lundskonsthall.se

CECILIA EDEFALK
'CECI'
through 24 August

Carreras Mugica
Bilbao
Henao, 10, 48009
tel +34 94 423 47 25
www.carrerasmugica.com

IGNACIO SÁEZ
6 June – 15 September

Galería Juana de Aizpuru
Madrid
Barquillo, 44, 28004
tel +34 91 308 36 20/+34 91 310 55 61
www.galeriajuanadeaizpuru.com

Please contact the gallery for information.

Elastic
Malmö
Ystadvägen 22/Bragegatan 15, 214 30
tel +46 70 656 43 19/+46 40 611 43 19
www.elasticgallery.com

MARIA HEDLUND
'The Whiteness Of The Whale, Part I, II & III'
through 14 June

Liste, Basel
3 – 8 June

The gallery is open by appointment only
15 June – 21 August.

Malmö Konsthall
Malmö
S:t Johannesgatan 7, Box 17127, 200 10
tel +46 40 34 12 93
www.konsthall.malmo.se

'THE HAMSTERWHEEL'
through 17 August

Magasin 3 Stockholm Konsthall
Stockholm
Stockholms Frihamn, 115 56
tel +46 8 5456 8040
www.magasin3.com

ANNIKA VON HAUSSWOLFF
'Ich bin die Ecke aller Räume'
FREDRIK SÖDERBERG &
CARL LARSSON
through 8 June

Switzerland

Galerie Guy Bärtschi
Geneva
3a, rue du Vieux-Billard, 1205
tel +41 22 310 00 13
www.bartschi.ch

MARINA ABRAMOVIC
'8 Lessons on Emptiness with a Happy End'
through 8 August

Art Basel: Art Unlimited
Fabrice Gygi 'Vigie'
Jointly presented with Galerie Chantal Crousel
4–8 June

The Nordic Watercolour Museum
Skärhamn
Nordiska Akvarellmuseet
Södra Hamnen 6, 471 32
tel +46 304 60 00 80
www.akvarellmuseet.org

'PACIFIC LIGHT – CALIFORNIA WATERCOLOUR REFRACTED 1908–2008'
through 7 September

Moderna Museet
Stockholm
Box 16382, 1 03 27
Visiting address: Skeppsholmen
tel +46 8 5195 5200
www.modernamuseet.se

'TIME & PLACE:
MILANO – TORINO 1958–1968'
through 7 September
'ECLIPSE – ART IN A DARK AGE'
through 24 August
The 1st at Moderna:
IVAN MOUDOV
through 21 September
JOSEPH KOSUTH
1 June through July

Kunsthalle Basel
Basel
Steinenberg 7, 4051
tel +41 61 206 99 00
www.kunsthallebasel.ch
ALEANA EGAN
'We sat down where we had sat before'
AHMET ÖĞÜT
'Mutual Issues, Inventive Acts'
through 8 June
ARMANDO ANDRADE TUDELA
GUIDO VAN DER WERVE
29 June – 7 September
'WORD EVENT'
Group show curated by Maxine Kopsa and
Roos Gortzak / Kunsthalle Basel
29 June – 31 August

BFAS Blondeau Fine Art Services
Geneva
5, rue de la Muse, 1205
tel +41 22 544 95 95
www.bfasblondeau.com

RAYMOND PETTIBON
'Punk Epocha:
70 Drawings from the Eighties'
through 19 July

Andréhn-Schiptjenko
Stockholm
Hudiksvallsgatan 8, 113 30
tel +46 8 612 00 75
www.andrehn-schiptjenko.com

UTA BARTH
'Sundial: New Work'
through 19 June

Galerie Nordenhake
Stockholm
Hudiksvallsgatan 8, 113 30
tel +46 8 21 18 92
www.nordenhake.com

SIROUS NAMAZI
through 20 June

ANN EDHOLM
28 August – 5 October

Kunsthaus Baselland
Muttenz/Basel
St. Jakob-Straße 170, 4132
tel +41 61 312 83 88
www.kunsthausbaselland.ch

'THE ETERNAL FLAME'
Eva Berendes, Michael Borremanns,
Steve van den Bosch, Philippe Decrauzat,
Friedrich Kunath, Fabian Marti, Kris Martin,
Edit Oderbolz, Florian Pumhösl,
Damien Roach, Hagar Schmidhalter,
Shirana Shahbazi, Claudia Wieser,
Jordan Wolfson
10 August – 5 October

MAMCO – Museum of Modern and Contemporary Art
Geneva
10, rue des Vieux-Grenadiers, 1205
tel +41 22 320 61 22
www.mamco.ch

'CYCLOPTICALLY'
Solo exhibitions by Christian Marclay and
Philippe Ramette
25 June – 21 September

Bonniers Konsthall
Stockholm
Torsgatan 19, 113 90
tel +46 8 736 42 48
www.bonnierskonsthall.se

'TELL A FRIEND'
through 8 June

Marabouparken Annex
Sundbyberg
Esplanaden 13, 172 68
tel +46 8 29 45 90
www.marabouparken.se

ERWIN WURM
'Spit In Someone's Soup'
through 31 August

Zentrum Paul Klee
Bern
Monument im Fruchtland 3, 3006
tel +41 31 359 01 01
www.zpk.org

'EAST OF EDEN: A GARDEN SHOW'
In Paul Klee's Enchanted Garden
through 31 August
'LOST PARADISE – THE ANGEL'S GAZE'
'ART PLAYGROUND – THE FRONT GARDEN'
through 26 October
'DRAGGED DOWN INTO LOWERCASE:
EXHIBITION OF THE
SOMMERAKADEMIE 2008'
6–17 August

Galerie Urs Meile Beijing – Lucerne
Lucerne
Rosenberghöhe 4, 6004
tel +41 41 420 33 18
www.galerieursmeile.com
SHU YONG 'Shu Yong – Bubbles'
through 5 July
Beijing
104, Caochangdi Cun, Cui Gezhuang
Xiang, Chaoyang District, 100015
tel +86 10 643 333 93:
NOT VITAL 'Tongue'
LI ZHANYANG 'Rent – Rent Collection Yard'
through 24 August
Art Basel, 4–8 June
Melbourne Art Fair, 30 July – 3 August

Index – The Swedish Contemporary Art Foundation
Stockholm
Kungsbro Strand 19, 112 26
tel +46 8 502 19 838
www.indexfoundation.se

SASKIA HOLMKVIST
through 8 June

The gallery is closed in July.

Bohusläns Museum Konsthallen
Uddevalla
Box 403, 451 19
tel +46 52 265 65 00
www.bohusmus.se

ANNA LING and ALEXANDER GUTKE
'Drawing a Line'
7 June – 7 September

Art & Public
Geneva
37, rue des Bains, 1205
tel +41 22 781 46 66
www.artpublic.ch

QIU XIAOFEI
'Pagoda of the Discarded'
through 28 June

Please contact the gallery for further
summer programme information.

Kunstmuseum St. Gallen
St. Gallen
Museumstraße 32, 9000
tel +41 71 242 06 71
www.kunstmuseumsg.ch

'TÀPIES, HARTUNG, UECKER, FÖRG'
From the donation of the Franz Larese and
Jürg Janett Foundation
'ARTIST'S PORTRAITS BY FRANZISKA
MESSNER-RAST'
through 15 June

DAVID CLAERBOUT 'After the Quiet'
through 31 August

'LADIES ONLY!' 28 June – 9 November

'Loose Associations' lecture (2002–ongoing). It's a slide talk which skips freely from 'desire lines' used in urban planning through 'trauma lines' painted on hospital floors to the Barbican building in London, Gander's auntie Deva, the design of institutional meeting rooms, fake Robin Day chairs, the Victoria and Albert Museum's collection of fakes, the famous photograph of Christine Keeler astride an Arne Jacobsen chair, Homer Simpson imitating Keeler's pose, the film made to accompany Bob Dylan's song 'Subterranean Homesick Blues' on its release in 1965, the work of Gillian Wearing, the NatWest Tower in London, aerial photos, blue heritage plaques, Sherlock Holmes, Inspector Morse, Morse code and so on. There is some art for which you need to know a whole back-story in order to understand it. Gander recognizes that some back-stories need art in order to understand them.

This made me think about the centrality of language in his work. Not just the spoken or written word, but body language, film language, design language, the languages of dress, work, travel, collaboration, making, thinking and talking about art. Gander is interested in how language conceals as much as it reveals. In an interview between the artist and Stuart Bailey, published in their collaborative book on Gander's work *Appendix* (2003), Bailey observes that when Gander commissioned the designer John Morgan to create a poster for the artist's lecture 'On Camouflage' in 2001, Gander and Morgan 'both independently spelt "camoflague" wrong throughout the project, so the word was camoflagued too'.[2] (The misspelling of the word in the transcript and its correct usage everywhere else in the interview makes the printed quote doubly perplexing. Or should that be 'camouflaged'?) Might it be interesting to begin this article by asking how, if Gander were to write it, he might use language as camouflage?

Alter egos and fictional characters populate Gander's work – David Lange, Abbé Faria, Marie Aurory, Spencer Anthony – a family of surrogates allowing him to avoid the issue of having a stylistic signature. Maybe the writer's name at the top of the article could be a pseudonym? Or what if the piece were delegated to a jobbing writer? Wasn't Gander's video *Ghostwriter Subtext (Notes on Speaking and Listening)* (2006), in which a professional ghostwriter interviews Hans Ulrich Obrist and Rem Koolhaas after their 24-hour interview marathon at London's Serpentine Gallery, all about scrambling critical authority?

Inasmuch as the article details objects and art works that, presumably, are not in the same room as the one in which you are reading, could Gander use the article as part of another work? After all, a monographic essay spins yarns that are not necessarily immediately verifiable. For example, it could be an inventory of works whose existence is dependent on their description in the text. And who is to say what the role of the accompanying images is? Gander's work is littered with clues, puzzles and mysteries inviting further investigation. Are these illustrations simply straightforward documentation or full of sneaky sub-plots and visual MacGuffins?

With the exception of this sentence, does the article contain the word 'mitim' – a palindromic word invented by Gander and designed to be inserted, uncommented on, into newspapers, magazines, crosswords or everyday speech, and meaning 'a mythical word newly introduced into history as if it had always been there'?

It occurred to me that the taxonomic list of questions could lend a Ganderesque quality to my introduction: nods to classic Conceptualism in the form of lists, diagrams, indexes and other frameworks for information crop up time and again in his work. Gander folds the authority of knowledge systems in on themselves, asking his audience to think about how, in the slippage between language, its presentation and that which it signifies, there lies an issue of trust – a subject central to 'Heralded as the New Black'. In *Your Life in Four Acts*

Although Ryan Gander employs the poker-faced formalism of Conceptual art, he uses it as a pane of precision-cut glass beneath which to press wildly allusive subject matter.

– *Forward* (2008) ordinary tourist maps are reworked and reproduced to include streets long since demolished. The work short-circuits the trust we need in maps in order for them to function but also serves as a record of how cities change. In making each map (of which there are so far five: London, Sheffield, Rotterdam, Amsterdam and Birmingham) Gander has noticed how many streets have disappeared beneath civic developments such as the South Bank Centre in London or the Bullring shopping complex in Birmingham, and how a city such as Amsterdam barely changes at all while Rotterdam is hardly recognizable from its older self. *Oxidized Silver on Paper* (2008) is a photographic contact sheet that, according to the accompanying wall caption, depicts 'fifteen frames of super black paint developed by the National Physical Laboratory, Teddington, Britain'. However, as the title suggests, a contact sheet is just silver oxide on paper, and shows absolute black to be mere shades of grey. We have to believe Gander's words, not his camera.

A similar game of trust is played in his series of 'Alchemy boxes' (2007–ongoing). *Alchemy box # 3* (*She*

Right:
A sheet of paper on which I was about to draw, as it slipped from my table and fell to the floor
2008
Dimensions variable
One hundred 15 cm crystal balls dispersed around the floor of the gallery spaces, in which there is a laser etched suspended image of a sheet of blank paper, on which I was about to draw, as it slipped from my table and fell to the floor.

Below:
Didactease Necklace
2006
Dimensions variable
A Tiffany's sterling silver coin edge circular pendant and chain, engraved with a Didactease emblem and a small asterism. Placed as if discarded on the floor of the gallery or worn by the gallerist / invigilator. The Didactease emblem uses mathematical symbols to produce the sentence 'There exists only one definition for everything, everywhere at any one time'. The work is in two parts, being accompanied by the poster Didactease Expanded, *2006 which is to be hung in the gallery with normal straight steel pins.*

spoke in images like some new language) (2008) is a wall-mounted unit constructed from one-way mirrored glass, to the same dimensions as Donald Judd's sculpture *Untitled – Blue and Yellow Painted Aluminium* (1989). (Gander has suggested that he chose the Judd because he thought it was so archetypically 'modern'-looking that he could almost imagine it being found in an illustrated children's storybook about art.[3]) Nearby, a text on the wall lists a large assortment of items that are supposedly inside the box: they include a book on body language, stolen from Shoreditch library, DVD sleeves for François Truffaut's film *Day for Night* (1973) and its original French-titled version *La Nuit américaine*, and a tube of 'Mystic Smoke from Finger Tips', a product that produces clouds of smoke at the click of a finger – more props for concealment. Recently Gander has begun to use the plinths that support other artists' work for his 'Alchemy boxes'. *Relic For A Living Man* (2008), exhibited in the Barbican Art Gallery's show 'Martian Museum of Terrestrial Art', uses the base of a Chris Burden vitrine to house its contents. Gander not only colonizes another artist's territory physically but invades it in other senses too; like

squatting tenants, his objects inhabit a physical space demarcated as having special market value, an outpost of land owned by a collector or commercial gallery. In a sense, the 'Alchemy boxes' are also about artistic intent and interpretation. The gesture of loading an object with unseen items says: 'Here is an object. I say it means these ten or 15 things. You may not be able to perceive them, but believe me, they're there.' Perhaps Gander's 'Alchemy boxes' suggest that the value of art exists only to be talked about. As Brian Eno once proposed in a conversation about whether value is intrinsic or merely conferred: 'Saying that cultural objects have value is like saying that telephones have conversations.'[4]

I wasn't entirely unhappy with Introduction Version Five, for it opened up a number of possible paths of thought. I nonetheless set it aside, since one of those paths led to the issue of appropriation, authorship and ownership, and thus a possible sixth option: writing about Gander using only examples of art works he has co-opted himself. I could have discussed *Enough To Start Over* (2006), for which Gander used a piece by Jonathan Monk, an artist whose work is built around having a

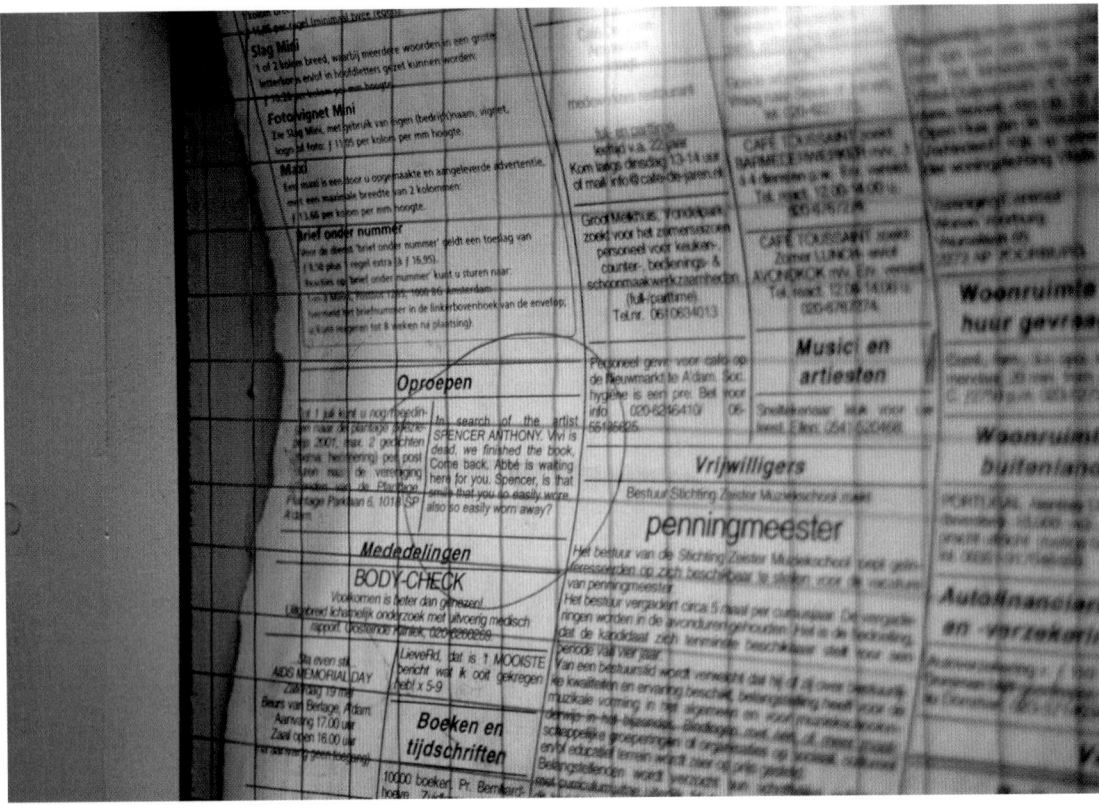

Body, design and film language are central to Gander's thinking; the language of dress, work, play and travel; of making and thinking about art.

magpie eye for art history. Monk's original consists of a passport photograph of himself as a teenager, pinned to the wall through the eyes with teardrop earrings. Gander bought the piece, removed the earrings and sent them to his mother. *Enough To Start Over* exists as a passport photograph of the artist's mother wearing the earrings, rewiring Monk's biography into Gander's own. Then in 'Heralded as the New Black' there is a work entitled *She walked ahead, leading him through a blizzard of characters* (2008), which appears to be an unpainted wall. The description of the work tells us it is a 'Newly plastered wall under which is a printed 2000 word text commissioned from a ghostwriter by the artist Mario Garcia Torres and paid for by Ryan Gander.' *I took my eyes off your hands too soon* (2007) features a pair of photographs. To the left is *Kiev MC Arsat PCS 4.5/55 mm Shift Lens, Focal Length: 55mm, Aperture scale: 4.5 to 22, Focusing Scale: 0.3 m (0.98 ft) to infinity, Minimum Focusing distance: 1.2 feet (0.5 meters), Field of view: 69 degrees (with shift) 84 degrees (with shift), Number of Elements: Nine elements in seven groups, Filter size: 72 mm, Weight: 2 lbs, Serial Number 0051, Douglas M. Parker Studio, Glendale, California, January 27, 2007* (2007), by the US artist Christopher Williams. To the right is a photograph taken by Gander of Williams' print, compacting layers of meaning onto the already loaded original. Balanced precariously high above a doorway is *The Learning Tree (When acorns fall into the wrong hands)* (2008), a 'fabricated Albers tea glass containing oil and a fabricated Michael Craig-Martin shelf from the work The Oak Tree, 1973': canonical design and Conceptual art repurposed as slapstick gag. As far as the introduction to my article went, all this could have provided rich pickings. In buying a Williams or Monk – that is, making

a clear economic transaction in order to own the works, rather than, say, using an existent reproduced image of them – does this change the rules of the appropriation game? The items are in one sense Gander's property, and thus it's up to him how he uses or abuses them. However, as Gander is an artist whose work seems so eager to pull others into its circle of conversation, I took *The Learning Tree …* as a warning that focusing on objects to the exclusion of the 'human interest' angle could result in a pratfall of the critic's own. So the seventh version swung right the other way.

'Oh my God: the invigilator! I can see a bloodstain, just above her knee. Is it from a nosebleed? Doesn't look like it. And she's still carrying on with her job! What a trooper. Well that's her pristine white Adidas tracksuit ruined. Are you OK? There's blood on your … no, hang on, it's red … thread … embroidered … in the shape of a bloodstain. Oh. And I suppose it's meant to be there, is it?' So my dramatization might have needed a little toning down, but this version addressed what the viewer's engagement might mean in today's slightly 'post-relational' art moment. Even without the bloodstain, the sight of gallery attendants clad head to toe in white tracksuits is going to put a spin on Gander's otherwise modest-looking work. An immediate reading of these modified track suits, *This Consequence* (2005), which are worn by gallery invigilators for 'Heralded as the New Black', is that they are like a clue or vital piece evidence discovered in a detective story. Pushing one's reading of the embroidered 'bloodstain' – oxymoronic in its deliberate articulation of chance or accident – leads to the darker question of how things we encounter in daily life can become normalized by familiarity or mass-manufacture. *This Consequence* is a projection of what could happen if a range of sportswear tailored with scars of violence subsequently became fashionable, ubiquitous and ultimately banal. (The work might take on an extra charge when exhibited at South London Gallery in Peckham, an area of London troubled by knife and gun crime.) Accessorizing *This Consequence* is the *Didactease Necklace* (2006), a silver Tiffany pendant also worn by one of the gallery invigilators, and which sports the 'Didactease logo': a graphically strong but scientifically shaggy assemblage of mathematical symbols which, when arranged in the correct order, should read: 'There is only one definition for everything, everywhere,

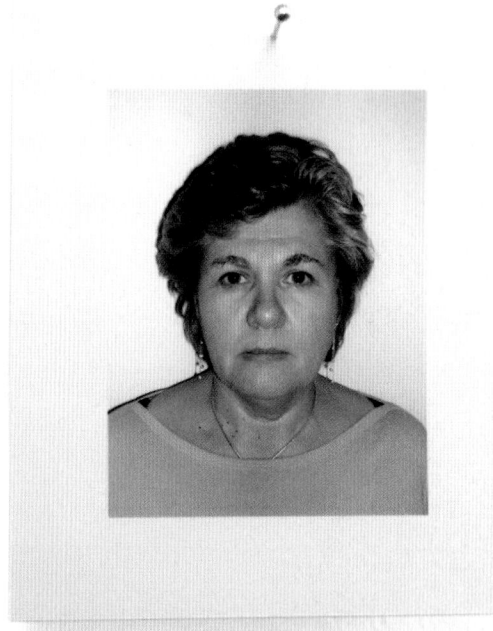

at any one time.' It was tacky name chains that inspired Gander to make the necklace: the faint ludicrousness of wearing your name – your definition – around your neck. The pseudo-profundity of the 'Didactease' statement (even its name punctures its authority) ill fits the logical language in which it is constructed, emphasizing its pidgin-science character. Mathematicians have told Gander that his arrangement of symbols doesn't actually form the intended statement.

I became anxious that Introduction Version Seven was focusing too much on audience experience. But conditions of spectatorship are fundamental to Gander's interest in the relationship between creativity and belief. He is currently developing an animated film entitled *As It Presents Itself*, which will feature six Wallace and Gromit-style claymation characters based on curator Matthew Higgs, the artist's mother, Frances Gander, the

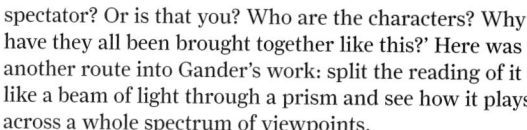

and Louis Lumière, and Morph – originally a claymation figure from the 1980s' British children's television art series *Take Hart*. (Another touchstone for Gander's work are the British television programmes of his childhood.) *As It Presents Itself* will be set in a theatre, where each character plays Scott Joplin's ragtime favourite 'The Entertainer' (1902) on the piano as though for an audition. A narrator's voice will ask questions such as 'Am I the

spectator? Or is that you? Who are the characters? Why have they all been brought together like this?' Here was another route into Gander's work: split the reading of it like a beam of light through a prism and see how it plays across a whole spectrum of viewpoints.

Despite their heavy ekphrasis, what were now eight alternative openings together seemed to refract Gander's work as though through a window made of irregular but tessellating glass shards. I thought of *A sheet of paper on which I was about to draw, as it slipped from my table and fell to the floor* (2008), which comprises 100 crystal balls, laser-etched to look as though a floating, blank piece of paper has been trapped in each one. Scattered throughout 'Heralded as the New Black', the spheres explicitly refer to closure of meaning and, in having to be tiptoed around in order to see the other works, serve as a constant reminder that there's never 'one

This is echoed in the appearance of Gander's fictional character David Lange in the video *Man on a Bridge (A Study of David Lange)* (2008). The scenario is simple: as a man crosses a bridge something just outside the camera frame catches his eye. He walks to the bridge parapet to peer over and, presumably, get a closer look. The film cuts. The action repeats. Gander asked the actor Roger Lloyd-Pack to play the part of Lange. Lloyd-Pack – a stalwart British actor famous for his hangdog expression as the character Trigger in the BBC television comedy series *Only Fools and Horses* (1981–2003) and for playing the role of Sherlock Holmes more times than anyone else – performs the action an astonishing 50 times, each with a slight variation of body language. Each of these interpretations could also be read as an out-take from the cutting-room floor, suggesting that somewhere there is a perfect take – or that perhaps there is no such thing as a 'right' version. Both *Man on a Bridge* and *A sheet of paper* ... may seem reliant on symbolism – the potential of a blank piece of paper, the bridge as a transition or link – but they essentially function on a structural level, in that their variation or multiplicity is itself an ode to possibility.

This seemed like a good place to begin.

Dan Fox is associate editor of frieze.

1 Brian Sholis, 'The Storyteller', to be published in the catalogue *Heralded as the New Black*, Ikon Gallery, Birmingham, 2008
2 Ryan Gander and Stuart Bailey, *Appendix*, Artimo, Amsterdam, 2003, p. 126
3 Conversation with the author, April 2008
4 Brian Eno, *A Year with Swollen Appendices*, Faber and Faber, London, 1996, p. 81

Switzerland

An ostensibly tidy, punctual and neutral country, and a global economic force, Switzerland here operates as an enigmatic representation of the often quite abstract social and political systems regulating our world.

Polly Staple discusses ways of seeing, including appropriation, power relations and reproduction – what is rendered both visible and invisible.

The image above shows an advertisement with the text overlaid on a mountain landscape:

GALERIE BRUNO BISCHOFBERGER
UTOQUAI 29, 8008 ZURICH SWITZERLAND
TEL 41 44 250 77 77 FAX 41 44 250 77 88
WWW.BRUNOBISCHOFBERGER.COM

Galerie Bruno Bischofberger advertisement

Advertisement
for Galerie Bruno
Bischofberger, Zurich,
published in *Artforum*
2007

1 Silvia Sokalski, PA to Bruno
Bischofberger, email correspondence
with the author, 16 February 2008

The image above is an advertisement for Galerie Bruno Bischofberger, Zurich on the back cover of *Artforum* magazine, a spot the gallery has booked since the mid-1980s.[1] The photographs are always of generic Swiss scenes: mountains and lakes, nuns and priests, farmers and cows, people gathering hay, making cheese or wearing traditional costumes and participating in festivals; they are largely rural and sometimes extremely odd: a close crop into, say, an image of a piece of bread or a laughing face blown up to fill the page.

These homely Swiss snapshots form a direct contrast to the roster of gallery artists listed across the image. Ordered according to business categories pertaining to their availability for purchase – 'In Exclusivity', 'Representing' and 'Works by' – the artists are only signalled by their last names: Tinguely and Sottsass, Clemente and Cucchi, along with a regular group of 1980s' American luminaries, such as Condo, Halley, Salle, Schnabel, Basquiat and Warhol.

These advertisements enigmatically circle the semantics that determine art-world consumer habits and viewing conditions. These images of Switzerland conform to a picturesque stereotype; the story they tell is, of course, a fiction of sorts: wealth and cultural logic masked by the minimal presentation of gallery information.

There is a collision of meaning here: what is being shown to us and what is actually being represented are two different things. This technique both animates and obscures, rendering abstract what is in fact an extremely precise system of value and information exchange, of public relations, art and commerce.

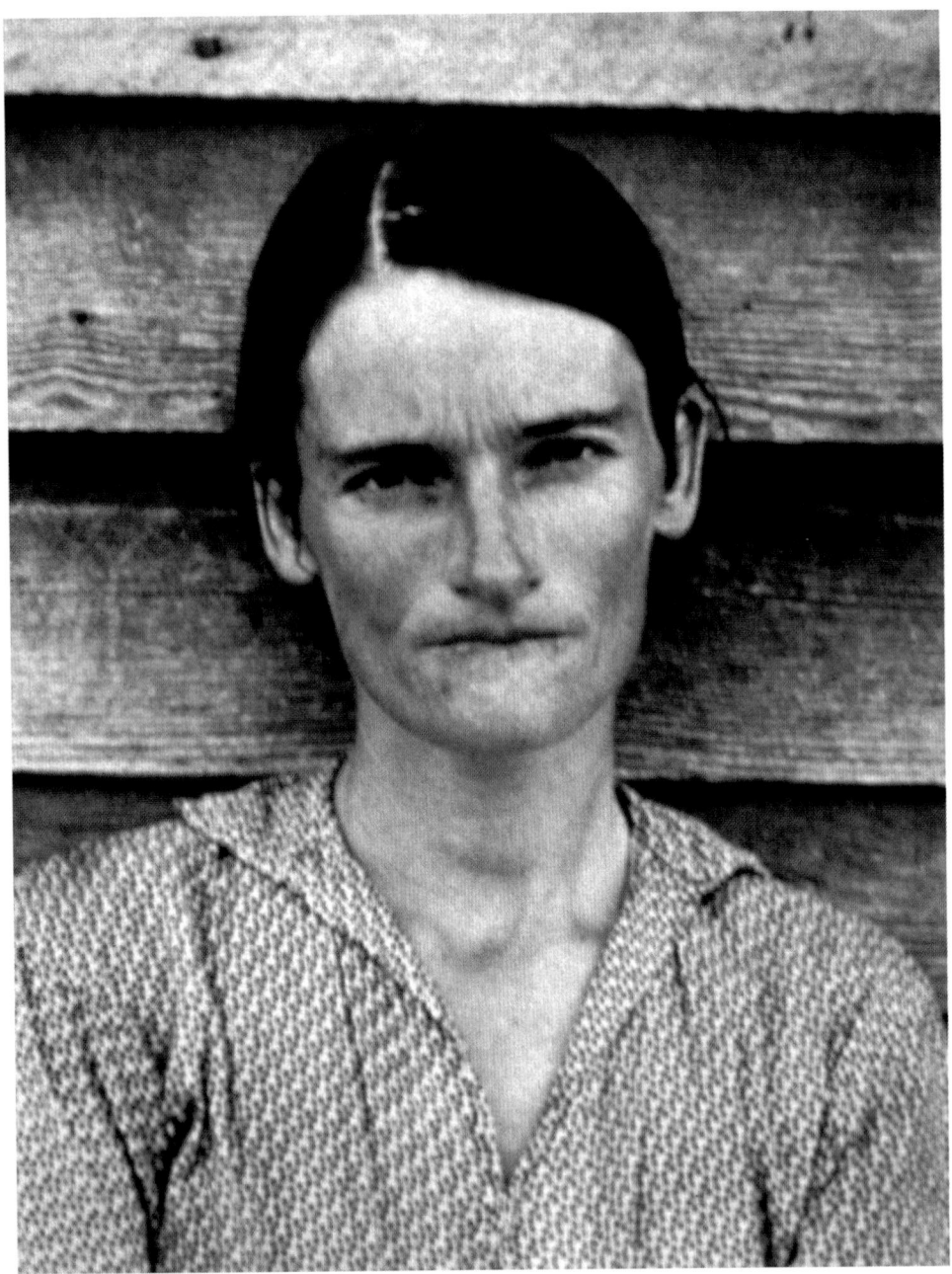

Sherrie Levine 'After Walker Evans' (1981)

Sherrie Levine's seminal work of appropriation 'After Walker Evans' (1981) consists of re-photographed bookplates from a Walker Evans exhibition catalogue. Evans' photographs of poor sharecroppers, taken in the 1930s for the USA's Farm Security Administration, are icons of pioneer photography. The impoverished interiors and stoic poses captured by Evans in such a minimal manner were subsequently fetishized for their perceived authenticity and beauty.

Levine's re-presentation of the Evans works as her own is an astute artistic strategy that questions not only the power relations inscribed in the action of the 'master' photographer Evans but also the subsequent art-historical canonization and market value of the original works. Property relations, patriarchal authority, authorship and originality are all brought under scrutiny.

Levine's gesture has a resilient potency in contemporary economic and artistic climates. The morality of appropriation, copyright law, the efficacy of recycling and a dialectical relationship to ownership – particularly bearing in mind the assimilation of Levine's work into the canon or the current ecstatic fêting in the museums and auction houses of the work of her direct contemporary Richard Prince – still begs various questions: what does it mean to own an image, how do we receive images and how do they accrue meaning?

Reproduced here in the pages of a magazine, without the physical scale and effect of the framed photograph, the image is still unsettling. The direct gaze and resilient aura of the woman in Evans' photograph are as biting as Levine's gesture of appropriation, the latter rendered invisible here but without a diminishing of the gesture's power.

To quote Levine: 'When I started doing this work, I wanted to make a picture which contradicted itself. I wanted to put a picture on top of a picture so that there are times when both pictures disappear and other times when they're both manifest; that vibration is basically what the work's about for me – that space in the middle where there's no picture.'[2]

Sherrie Levine
After Walker Evans #4
1981
Photograph
36×28 cm

2 Jeanne Siegel, 'After Sherrie Levine', *ARTS Magazine*, June 1985, pp. 141–4; reprinted in *Art Talk: The Early 80s*, ed. Jeanne Siegel, Da Capo Press, Inc., New York, 1988, p. 247

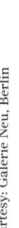

Sean Snyder *Korean Central News Agency, Pyongyand, DPRK* (2007)

Sean Snyder
Korean Central News Agency, Pyongyand, DPRK
(detail)
2007
Framed lightjet print
105×95 cm

Sean Snyder's selection and presentation of press images representing the North Korean leader Kim Jong Il are as precise a gesture as Levine's, although in this instance Snyder's work details a spillage of meaning. Kim Jong Il, if standing, is usually officially photographed from the waist up, a method that masks his diminutive stature. Here Snyder directs the viewer's attention downwards to Kim Jong Il's specially fabricated footwear, which is co-ordinated to his suit to hide the rather substantial platforms built into the shoes themselves. These images, assiduously sourced by the artist, reveal what is usually repressed. Kim Jong Il's vanity and power are often mythologized as both absurd and chilling. Snyder's simple picture-editing and rational grid arrangement emphasize the leader's elaborate image construction and stupid performance of power, but in doing so they also underscore that which is in turn vulnerable, banal and seemingly more 'real'.

Echoes of this spillage of meaning can be found in recent press images of Vladimir Putin with his shirt off – unbound by protocol here is a man with enormous self-regard and an identity built on aggressive power – and of Nicolas Sarkozy's shoe lifts, particularly when positioned next to Carla Bruni's elegant bare ankles in modest ballet flats. And then, in sharp contrast, the terrible blouson jackets of Saddam Hussein's executioners – terrifying because the lack of formal uniform signalled such violent chaos.

Alfred H. Barr Jr. looking at Alexander Calder's *Gibraltar* (1936) in 1967

This is an image taken in 1967 of Alfred H. Barr – the New York Museum of Modern Art's founding director – looking at an Alexander Calder sculpture, *Gibraltar* (1936).

The sculpture is an odd collection of objects positioned on a plinth: a lump of rock, a smooth shelf, what could be a ping-pong ball and two thin upright metal sticks, one supporting a lick of material, perhaps metal or stone. *Gibraltar* is a wonderful and absurd collision of weight and balance, form and content.

Barr confronts the strange shape with a thoughtful half-smile. He appears to be instructing the viewer how to look, searching for and directing meaning while simultaneously posing for the photograph. The sculpture resonates with all the totemic allure of a fetish. The photograph is a performative image of pedagogy and power. There is something both ancient and hilarious witnessed in this symbolic exchange.

Alfred H. Barr Jr., looking at Alexander Calder's *Gilbraltar* (1936)
1967

Cathy Wilkes *Non-Verbal* (2005)

Cathy Wilkes
Non-Verbal
(detail)
2005
Mixed media
Dimensions variable

3 Cathy Wilkes in reference to her installation *Our Misfortune* (2001), in conversation at a public event with the author, Cubitt Gallery, London, 20 January 2001

Cathy Wilkes' installation *Non-Verbal* (2005) consists of an arrangement of found and made objects including Maclaren prams, Sony televisions, salad bowls, a trough of petrol and partially clothed shop mannequins, their faces obscured by petite Expressionist paintings. Wilkes' immersive installations always have a palpable neurotic tension best described as conjuring a sense of arrested dynamic. The image here depicts a painting fixed to a mannequin's head: side-view, full-frontal. There is something brutal and obscene in Wilkes' confusion of sight lines. An exchange of social relations is made manifest, entailing some kind of refusal that is hard to read. The work appears grotesquely mannered, but the gesture is bluntly precise.

This jumping between linguistic registers is emphatic, pointing to either artifice or a heightened awareness. The jangling tone of the objects resonates; the scene has no clearly defined threshold, and, as such, it is experienced as an event.

The formal arrangement of Wilkes' installation has both the crispness and distance of a Social Realist photograph by Walker Evans or Dorothea Lange.[3] Wilkes' assemblage of objects conjures the psychological weirdness of experiencing the inanimate world – the stuff that surrounds us – and the present moment.

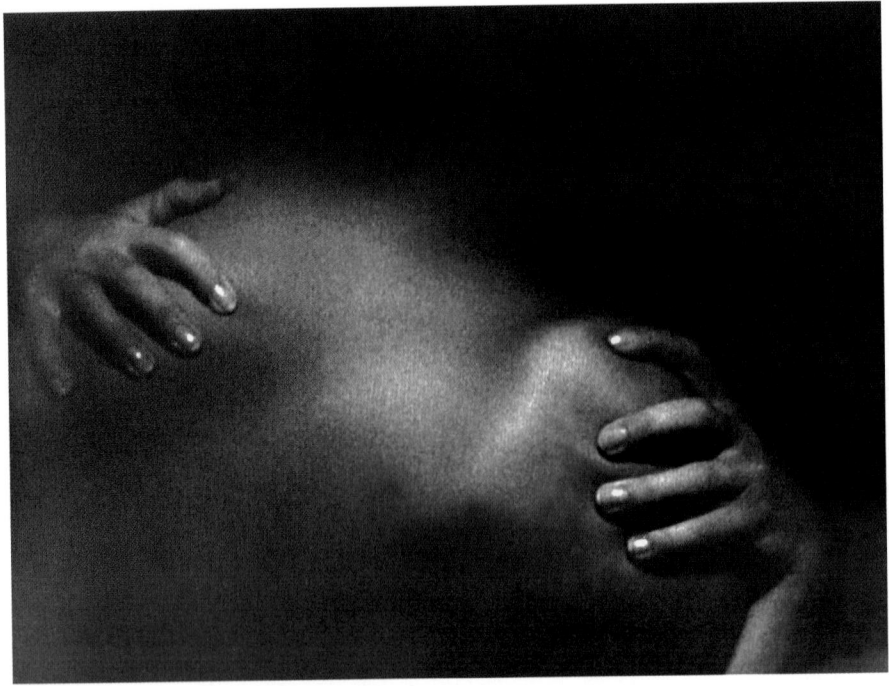

SCENARIO
Part 1
As the film opens, two pairs of bare shoulders appear, little by little. All we see are these shoulders – cut off from the body at the height of the head and hips – in an embrace, and as if drenched with ashes, rain, dew or sweat, whichever is preferred. The main thing is that we get the feeling that this dew, this perspiration, has been deposited by the atomic 'mushroom' as it moves away and evaporates. It should produce a violent, conflicting feeling of freshness and desire. The shoulders are of different colours, one dark, one light. Fusco's music accompanies this almost shocking embrace. The difference between the hands is also very marked. The woman's hand lies on the darker shoulder: 'lies' is perhaps not the word; 'grips' would be closer to it. A man's voice, flat and calm, as if reciting, says:
HE: You saw nothing in Hiroshima. Nothing.
To be used as often as desired. A woman's voice, also flat, muffled, monotonous, the voice of someone reciting, replies:
SHE: I saw everything. Everything.[4]

Alain Resnais *Hiroshima Mon Amour* (1959)

Alain Resnais' feature film *Hiroshima Mon Amour* (1959) is based on a screenplay by Marguerite Duras. The film is set in postwar Hiroshima, where a French actress, in the city to make a film about peace, embarks on an affair with a Japanese architect.

This simple narrative is a vehicle for an allegorical tale of love and desire set against the dynamic of history, the temporality of filmmaking and the difficulties of representation. Remembering is pictured here as a social responsibility, the personal is read through the political and the private act through public resonance. Resnais' use of a montage of narrative flashbacks, dissolve effect, documentary footage and a doubling motif of a film within a film was as innovative as his, and Duras', depiction of the postwar mixed-race romance and atomic subject matter.

The film still presented here is from the opening sequence of the couple embracing. The bodies fill the frame, putting the viewer immediately at an intimate relation to the narrative. The film then moves seamlessly back and forth from the couple to newsreel footage depicting the destruction and reconstruction of Hiroshima in the aftermath of the atomic bomb. The voice-over speaks of the denial and assertion of representation, of place and event – specifically of Hiroshima – creating a dissonance with the images so emphatically presented.

The film creates a tension that is tense-less – past, present and future are suspended in the lived moment. Hiroshima serves as both geographical site and enigmatic signifier.

To quote Duras from her screenplay synopsis: 'Their embrace – so banal, so commonplace – takes place in the one city of the world where it is hardest to imagine it: Hiroshima. Nothing is "given" at Hiroshima. Every gesture, every word, takes on an aura of meaning that transcends its literal meaning.'[5]

Alain Resnais
Hiroshima Mon Amour
1959
Film still

4 Marguerite Duras, original film script for *Hiroshima Mon Amour* (1959), directed by Alain Resnais, originally published as a picture book with text and accompanying images from the film in 1960 by Librairie Gallimard, Paris; 5th edn, Grove Press Inc., New York, 1961, p. 15
5 Ibid., p. 9

The explosions. Sometimes the smoke hides the crowd. Back to the beach.
Voice-over – Fausto Fawcett: (Brazilian radio personality and singer, resident of Copacabana)
If there is one place where ... mankind's Utopia exists ...
Copacabana must be that place.
Decadence in the poetical sense.
Copacabana's decadence is like a curtain ...
Protecting all that happens within.
Copacabana has no centre.
No ties to the golden youth ...
A sort of ...
Oasis ...
For all kinds ...
The explosions have finished. It is raining.
People walk over the drawings, the wave drawing.
There are lots of umbrellas, like an impromptu musical.
The crowd moves.
Voice-over – an anonymous fisherman from Copacabana:
Copacabana is wonderful.
It's a wonderful city.
Copacabana doesn't exist.[6]

Dominique Gonzalez-Foerster *Plages* (2001)

Dominique Gonzalez-
Foerster
Plages
(Beaches)
2001
Film still

Two films by Dominique Gonzalez-Foerster, *Rio de Janeiro* (2000) and *Plages* (Beaches, 2001), document life on Brazil's Copacabana beach. This still from *Plages* reveals the crowds occupying the beach and boardwalk on New Year's Eve. Shot from a building high above, the film gently sweeps over the scene. In the film notes Gonzalez-Foerster describes the camera as 'breathing in time with the waves'.[7] She could be describing the waves of sea, people or painted pattern of the boardwalk's paving stones. The camera circles through fireworks, smoke and explosions, and 'the atmosphere is at once volcanic, bellicose and festive'.[8]

6 Voice-over to Dominique Gonzalez-Foerster's film *Plages* (2001), published in *Dominique Gonzalez-Foerster: Films*, Collection Anna Sanders Films, co-published by Les presses du réel, Dijon, and Portikus, Frankfurt am Main, 2003, p. 42
7 Dominique Gonzalez-Foerster, screen notes accompanying text and image presentation of the film *Plages* (2001); ibid., p. 36
8 Ibid.
9 Elizabeth Fisher, 'Sodium Dreams', Bard College, Annandale-on-Hudson, NY, June–September 2003, http://tinyurl.com/5e7wa4
10 Voice-over, Dominique Gonzalez-Foerster, *Plages* (2001) op.cit.
11 Dominique Gonzalez-Foerster, 'Plans to Escape', *Flash Art*, November–December 2006, pp. 78–80

The work achieves a simple economy of filmmaking. Gonzalez-Foerster's films often utilize, to great melancholic effect, the indifferent gaze of a touristic register.[9] An attempt is made to define and locate Copacabana, but it is found to be a myth, a fiction and almost impossible to represent as a place.

As you watch the swarms of people on the beach, a selection of voice-overs – overlaid as though also in time with the waves, in rhythm with the moving images – recount memories of Copacabana, including a song, an architectural description and a teenage reminiscence. The stories embellish the images with personal narrative and Utopian aspiration. The last voice is that of a fisherman from Copacabana, who states: 'Copacabana does not exist.'[10]

Gonzalez-Foerster has said in relation to the invitation to make a project in Brazil and here with reference to Copacabana: 'I didn't want to build anything, and I only had visions of things that are either horizontal or go deep. I don't believe in any verticality. What I like in Rio or in Copacabana is that people are standing on the beach; they don't sleep or they are not lying [down]. It always looks like a giant meeting or opening and I wanted to go further with that feeling of the dynamic beach.'[11]

What Gonzalez-Foerster captures in *Plages* is a sense of continuous movement. There seems to be no beginning or end to the beach or to the film. What is relevant here is how the film represents a field of vision and signals a dispersal of looking.

Polly Staple is editor at large of frieze.

Photograph: Steve White

'Cellar Door (Once is
Always Twice)'
2008
Mixed media
Installation view at
Institute of Contemporary
Art, London

Doors of Perception

The multi-faceted
exhibitions of French
artist **Loris Gréaud**
reward leaps of faith
with wild flights of the
imagination
by Vivian Rehberg

Loris Gréaud's much lauded exhibition 'Silence Goes
More Quickly When Played Backwards', held at Le
Plateau/Frac-Ile-de France, Paris, in 2005, secured the
French artist's reputation as something of an art/science/
technology wunderkind, as fluent in the languages of
conceptualism as he is at navigating the complexity and
plurality of 'the post-medium condition'.[1] Those who
were present at the opening still wax rhapsodic about
the three-hour drum set played by artist/musician Gael
Angelis (also known as Man-Eater Orchestra), the energy
of which was converted into electricity to partially light
the show. Gréaud is not one to be outdone, even by
himself, so when Marc-Olivier Wahler, the director of the
Palais de Tokyo, invited him to mount his second major
solo show in Paris in just three years, he approached the
invitation as an experiment. He scheduled an appointment with a neurologist for an electroencephalogram
(EEG) and, once attached to the electrodes, got to thinking about his proposal, 'Cellar Door'. It turns out there
was a lot to mull over.

'Cellar Door', words J.R.R. Tolkien singled out for
their inherent beauty in his 1955 text 'English and Welsh',
would encompass the following: a television commercial/
internet teaser for Celador, flavourless button-shaped
gummy sweets sold in striped cellophane bags, whose
clever marketing slogan is 'A Taste of Illusion'; a libretto
entitled *Cellar Door: An Opera in Almost One Act*, written
by Raimundas Malašauskas and Aaron Schuster; and
said opera, for which the music was composed and con-
ducted by Thomas Roussel and performed by soprano
Marie Devellereau and the Radio France Philharmonic
Orchestra at the Palais de Tokyo (a further performance

is planned for a Paris theatre). It would also entail the conceptualization and creation of works intimately related to the libretto for two briefly overlapping exhibitions, 'Cellar Door', at the Palais de Tokyo in Paris and 'Cellar Door (Once is Always Twice)' at the Institute of Contemporary Arts in London.

Whereas the libretto, opera and exhibitions would provide the skeletal framework for the whole enterprise, its crux is the actual design and construction of Gréaud's studio out of modular prefab components, which is just getting underway outside Paris. As the off-stage protagonist of the opera, whose shadow is literally figured in both exhibitions, this future studio's omnipresence begs the question of its utility. Does Gréaud's emphasis on the studio as site of production – with all the symbolic and historical baggage that involves – amount to a retreat to an outdated notion of studio-based artistic creativity or a latent critique of post-studio art practice? Or does positing the studio as the spatially and temporally displaced origin of his work in fact enable him to relieve some of the pressures of an economy in which the exhibition over-determines an artist's mode of production and reception?

Unresolved questions, mysteries and apocryphal stories proliferate around Gréaud's art. He has tested viewers' capacities to suspend their disbelief by manufacturing the hypothetical scent of Mars (*Spirit*, 2005), making radiophonic attempts at teleportation (*Haunted Quantum #5*, 2005), fabricating walls out of air currents (*The Residents (2)*, 2005) and nano-sculptures invisible to the naked eye (*Why is a Raven Like a Writing Desk?*, 2006). The unverifiable nature of these works can nag at those who need assurances about the ontological status of art objects, but I rather appreciate the way they poke at the issue of lack situated at the heart of desire. *Frequency of an Image (M46 EDIT)* (2007), one of several works produced from the results of his EEG, arguably continues in this vein. This low-tech suspension lamp/sculpture consists of two bulbs in trim sockets hanging from cords attached to a vintage-style teardrop counterweight. The bulbs flicker like fireflies captured in glass jars to the frequency of Gréaud's brainwaves, supposedly translated from the printed recording of his EEG. If the most common illustration of a bright idea is a light bulb switching on, Gréaud's practice persistently stresses the fragile, evanescent nature of individual creative thinking, particularly through his customary collaborative and co-authorial working method, central to the production of all of the works mentioned above, by which he occupies the position of transceiver, tossing out ideas and letting others run with them and recuperating those that suit his purpose.

When 'Cellar Door' finally materialized at the Palais de Tokyo and the ICA, it seemed inconceivable that an object as modest as its precursor, *Frequency of an Image ...*, could ever be a gauge of the project's impressive scale and ambition. Gréaud mobilized the aforementioned contributors and the expertise of DGZ Research, the production company he runs with architects Marc Dölger and Damien Ziakovic, as well as a substantial number of other specialists and interlocutors. Granted the entire 43,000 square feet of the Palais de Tokyo's ground floor, he transformed the stripped interior of the 1937 building by organizing the space into chiaroscuro areas called 'bubbles', which either constituted works or contained them.

The conceptual *raison d'être* for these space bubbles is a vital episode in the *Cellar Door* libretto: 'Scene 4', in which black champagne bubbles fizz and pop while two main characters, Bucky Wonka (after Buckminster Fuller and Willy Wonka) and the Singer debate the philosophical implications of possibility and impossibility, while the 'music of multiplying rooms' plays all around.[2] Sound obscure? It somehow makes beautiful sense when you see the passage spatialized as a *mise-en-abyme* in the three quasi-identical black and white rooms Gréaud installed at the ICA, but perhaps only if you have read the libretto. There, behind successive high-speed automatic doors made out of black vinyl panels, the opera emits from low-hanging bulbous *Spore Speakers* (2008) that pulsate light and ooze tarry black resinous goo onto a geometric patterned carpet (*Nothing is True Everything is Permitted*, 2007). A sleek, glossy black elevation drawing of the future studio, rendered in 1:1 scale, emerges from the matte black wall, and neighbours a mirrored horizontal wall piece that reads *When people tell me I don't know how this story is going to end up I usually tell them: wait til the end and you will see yourself ...* (2008). I felt happy to oblige while sipping black champagne (another of Gréaud's inventions) served by male triplets at planned intervals during the opening reception.

Malašauskas and Schuster's imaginative and entertaining libretto, seemingly inspired by science fiction, children's tales, nonsense, surrealism, philosophy and hints of autobiography, is essential to understanding Gréaud's project. It recounts the artist's fantasy of a studio as a site of creative potential, metaphorized by the studio's quest for a door: 'This is the story of the Studio, a vast workshop distended in space and time [...] It is not so much a "Dream Factory" as a "Dreaming Factory", a production plant more stratospheric than Jack's beanstalk and more distorting than Alice's mirror, a place where cables climb the clouds and nanocircuits line the event horizon.'[3] In Paris, this dreaming factory could be accessed through a single black

All images courtesy: Yvon Lambert, Paris and New York, and the artist • Cellar Door photograph: Pierre Dumont

vinyl automatic door that whooshes up to uncover *La Bulle Studio* (The Studio Bubble, 2007–8), a glassed-in control room from which a technician was running the show, switching between an 'on' mode, during which all the works function, and a 'standby' mode, when only the opera drifts like Muzak through the dimly lit space via the same *Spore Speakers* found at the ICA. The identity of each bubble is indicated by a luminescent Perspex music stand that contains the corresponding passages of text from the libretto and sheet music from the score. After passing beneath *La Bulle Underworks* (The Underworks Bubble, 2007–8), a ceiling made from the cast of the earth after an underground fireworks explosion, one encounters *La Bulle Néon* (The Neon Bubble, 2008) a dazzling white neon sculpture of criss-crossing tubes representing the scrunched perspective lines of the Palais de Tokyo architecture, which is crammed into a room that emphasizes its monumentality. A bit further along, an inconspicuous rectangle cut into the wall reveals rows of empty red movie-theatre seats and a nebulous film Gréaud had shot (unbeknownst to his hired cameramen) on expired Super 16mm film stock he found in the basement of the Palais de Tokyo, once home to the Paris Cinémathèque and prestigious Fémis film school.

La Bulle Néon and *La Bulle Film Expiré* (The Expired Film Bubble, 2007–8) can be read as vestiges unearthed by Gréaud's conceptual and material archaeology of the exhibition site, without any obvious accompanying institutional critique, though the Palais de Tokyo floor plans crumpled into a massive neon ball may harbour some secrets. Similarly, it is tempting to read *La Bulle Plateau* (The Plateau Bubble, 2008) as an archaeology of the self, or at least of self-representation. In this series of rooms, which occupy roughly one-third of the space, Gréaud reinstalled his entire 2005 Plateau show backwards (does that make silence go more slowly?), and included its original brochures. The only new additions are hyperrealist paintings he commissioned of the destroyed photographs of the initial installation. It would be easy to let one's mind aimlessly wander through these different pockets of space–time, were it not for the harsh rat-a-tat-tat that signals the onset of a paintball war taking place in *La Bulle Merzball* (The Merzball Bubble, 2007–8), as players clad in militaristic gear take to this faceted, screened-in playing field modelled on Kurt Schwitters' *Merzbau*, or 'Cathedral of Erotic Misery' (1919–33), their guns loaded with pellets of International Klein Blue. On the opposite wall, facing this 'space of conflict and negotiation'[4], the elevation drawing of

Gréaud has created a hypothetical scent of Mars, attempted teleportation, fabricated walls out of air currents and made nano-sculptures invisible to the naked eye.

Opposite:
Loris Gréaud and DGZ Research
La Bulle Merzball
(The Merzball Bubble)
2008
Steel, synthetic fabric netting
Installation view from 'Cellar Door', Palais de Tokyo, Paris

Right:
La Bulle Plateau
(The Plateau Bubble)

Malašauskas and Schuster's opera libretto, seemingly inspired by science fiction, children's tales, nonsense, surrealism, philosophy and hints of autobiography, is essential to understanding Gréaud's project.

Opposite:
La Bulle Forêt de poudre
à canon
(The Gunpowder
Forest Bubble)
2008
Synthetic resin and
gunpowder
Installation view from
'Cellar Door', Palais de
Tokyo, Paris

Right:
Loris Gréaud and DGZ
Research
La Bulle Néon
(The Neon Bubble)
2008
Perspex and neon tubes
Installation view from
'Cellar Door', Palais de
Tokyo, Paris

Below:
End Extend
2006
Pyrotechnic installation
Dimensions variable

Gréaud's future studio, this time in reflective paint, fades in and out like a dream image as the black light trained on it shifts.

Gréaud claims his favourite exhibitions are the ones he has not seen, but has only heard about, and has repeatedly insisted that his exhibitions should not be perceived as ends in themselves.[5] Exhibitions, like images, matter only insofar as they produce unpredictable effects or serve as matrices for all sorts of creations, interpretations and failures. This may seem far-fetched, given the effort and expense this project entails, but Gréaud convincingly drives his point home in formal terms by integrating the possibility for the whole thing to go up in flames before our eyes. Extending into the furthest reaches of the Palais de Tokyo, a spooky devastated forest of bare sculpted trees (*La Bulle Forêt de poudre à canon*, The Gunpowder Forest Bubble, 2008) is lit by a mammoth inflatable moon, whose colour mutates from pure white to ominous red. Each tree is coated with a gunpowder mixture, and the woods are installed dangerously close to a vertical wall piece made from curved rows of fluorescent tubes filled with propane (*An Illusion of Explosion/Explosion of Illusion*, 2008). Tucked way in the back, Gréaud's film *Untitled (Dark Side)* (2006), housed in a gleaming white lacquered pod on four legs, plays for the empty space, and automatically switches off as soon as a visitor approaches.

There is an undeniable prankster-ish undertone to much of Gréaud's work, including his recent 'Vanishing References Portrait Series' (2007–8), painted with invisible ink, which pays homage to his numerous artistic heroes, including Marcel Duchamp and Buckminster Fuller. This playfully nihilistic attitude toward his predecessors grates on some of his critics. However, it would be an error to take his incessant flaunting of the possibility that an art work might not be just what you see, that it might fall to ruin, that it might not even exist, that it is inconclusive by nature, as anything but dead serious. Having absorbed and productively warped the once radical paradigmatic strategies of Conceptual art for undermining aesthetic autonomy, thwarting visuality and for dematerializing the object, Gréaud's work, exemplified by 'Cellar Door', embodies all of the messy contradictions entailed its spectacular rematerialization

(including his recourse to a return to the studio). In this day and age, when art and its producers have little hope of surviving outside the reach of the cultural industrial complex, Gréaud reminds us, and not without melancholic irony, that in order for them to keep us enchanted, we have to be willing to take a leap of faith.

Vivian Rehberg is Chair of Liberal Studies and teaches modern and contemporary art history at Parsons Paris School of Art & Design.

1 See Rosalind Krauss, *A Voyage on the North Sea: Art in the Age of the Post-Medium Condition*, Thames & Hudson, London and New York, 1999
2 Raimundas Malašauskas and Aaron Schuster, *Cellar Door: An Opera in Almost One Act*, JRP/Ringier, Zurich, 2008, p. 23
3 Ibid., pp. 23–8
4 Loris Gréaud interviewed by Marc-Olivier Wahler in *Palais* 05, Spring 2008, p. 69
5 Ibid., and in conversation with the artist on 23 April 2008

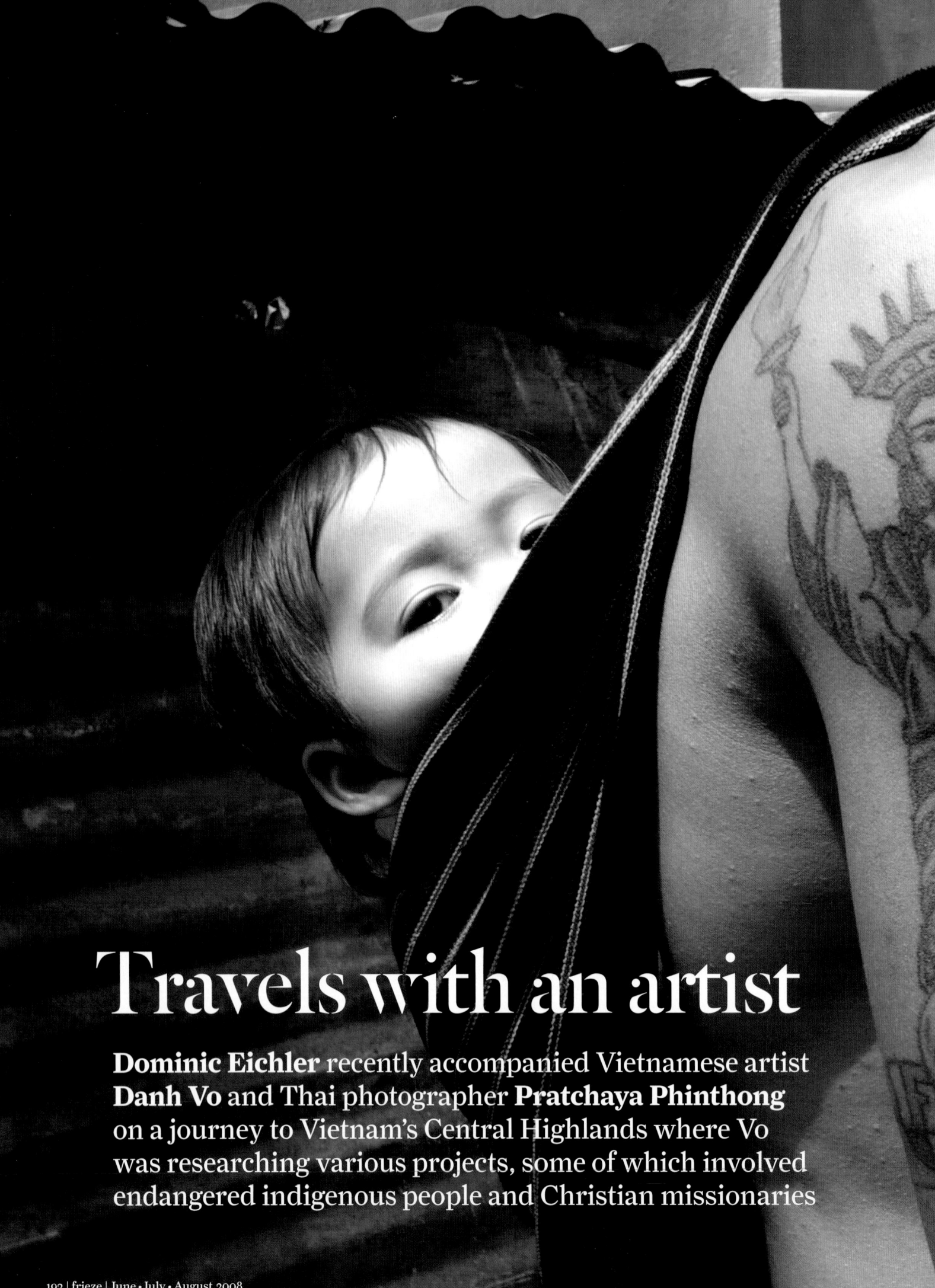

Travels with an artist

Dominic Eichler recently accompanied Vietnamese artist
Danh Vo and Thai photographer **Pratchaya Phinthong**
on a journey to Vietnam's Central Highlands where Vo
was researching various projects, some of which involved
endangered indigenous people and Christian missionaries

Buôn Kosir
2008
Dye destruction print
39×60 cm
Buôn Kosir is a village.
Its name translates as
'Village of the Kosir
spring'

A US army cot, salvaged from the Vietnam War, found in an Ede longhouse on the edge of the town of Buon Ma Thout.

Leaving the coastline far behind, Highway 14 crawls northwestwards out of the boom-town megalopolis of Vietnam's capital, Ho Chi Minh City. I'm perched in a hired silver Toyota van, an air-conditioned cocoon symptomatic of the affluence of what has been termed the country's economic 'new era'. Nonetheless, I'm reminded of the fragility of cocoons as the near-miss traffic around us obeys the basic rule of toot-first-look-later, to the tune of our silent driver's achingly sentimental Vietnamese synthetic pop. I realize that I've come halfway around the globe and don't really have any idea what my host, Vietnamese artist Danh Vo, has in store for me or our travelling companion, Thai artist and photographer Pratchaya Phinthong. All I know is that our trip to Vietnam's Central Highlands will have something to do with his research regarding various projects, which may or may not somehow become art, and that a number of them relate to his interaction with the endangered indigenous people and with Christian missionaries. But we also have 19th-century, coral-covered pirate swords and the funeral urn of an infant who never actually existed in our luggage. Danh wants me to be unprepared, perhaps so my

culture shock really takes effect. He wants me to feel out of place. And I do.

Out in the countryside, nearly all of the coveted roadside real estate is lined with box-shaped concrete houses painted bright pastels. Many of them belong to families from the north who resettled in successive waves during the aftermath of horrendous and protracted warfare: initially following the division of the country after the 1954 Geneva Accords ended the war between the colonial French Union forces and the Vietminh, and again after reunification in 1975 following the Vietnam War. It seems as though every other open-fronted dwelling also moonlights as a shop, selling anything from tyres wrapped in silver foil through plastic paraphernalia to beer and cigarettes. At dusk, their interiors, lit by televisions and fluorescent strip lighting, glow against the deeply repetitive landscape. This is not the Vietnam depicted in dewy neo-colonial films such as *Indochine* (1992) or *The Scent of the Green Papaya* (1993). Instead it would be perfect for an Asian Spaghetti Western, or a local drama set in the near future on this new frontier of globalization.

In the hills, coffee and rubber trees are the new settlers' flagpoles, although the colours

they fly have changed with the political climate. The Robusta coffee variety dominates, because it is comparatively easy to tend and fast-growing. It has a strong caffeine kick but little aroma, making it ideal for instant coffee. By the late 1990s, Vietnamese farmers had become one of the world's biggest suppliers of coffee, and the flood of their crops onto the market caused a devastating crash in its value. This disaster, which carried global repercussions, led some desperately impoverished growers to pull out their precious trees and plant maize instead. But although it is now farmed, this land was once a thick forest. A forester told Danh that, although the area had been subject to logging, bombing and the ravages of chemical defoliants such as Agent Orange, with which it was drenched during the Vietnam War, it was the land-hungry new settlers who were primarily responsible for the deforestation. It was also suggested to us that the European craze for Scandinavian furniture partly made from illegally traded tropical wood also took its toll.

There are now more than two million mostly poor but aspirant new Kinh settlers in the Central Highlands. (The Kinh are a principally coastal and river-delta people,

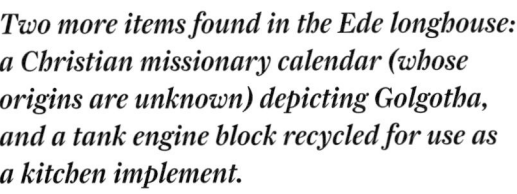

Two more items found in the Ede longhouse: a Christian missionary calendar (whose origins are unknown) depicting Golgotha, and a tank engine block recycled for use as a kitchen implement.

who constitute the majority of what we now consider the Vietnamese populace). For centuries, they had left the daunting, mist- and rainforest-covered mountains to the indigenous tribes known by the colonial French as the 'Montagnard' (hill people). These forest-dependent, subsistence-farming, self-sustaining communities were kept company only by their ancestral spirits, and a host of gods: the god of fierceness, for instance, and the god of the tree. Some kept elephants – now gone along with the forests that fed them. It wasn't the Montagnard who could be seen queuing on the roofs of embassies towards the end of the Vietnam War awaiting helicopter evacuation, even though some had been first allied and then later bombed and poisoned by the American-led forces. Considered as ethnic inferiors, they also had little to expect from the victorious North Vietnamese, since some of them had been their former enemies. Whatever the outcome of the war, they were destined to be the 'losers'. Outnumbered and surrounded on all sides, the indigenous hill people are slowly losing their way of life. Land is the currency on which the house of economy builds its foundations, and although land law reforms in 1993 meant

some indigenous individuals and families regained rights over their or their communities' traditional lands, those without the means to capitalize on those lands effectively often find themselves selling up to the Kinh settlers.

The regional capital of one province of the Central Highlands, Buon Ma Thout, is loud, alive and well. Here, you can have your face massaged and your hair dyed by ladies with long fingernails. We stay in the brand new business-class Hotel Eden. Its name is a poignant echo of the town's origins as the thriving village of the Ede, a matrilineal people whose numbers have dwindled to around 25,000, and the vestiges of which can be found on the outskirts of town. There is one street in Boun Ma Thout that cuts through a group of rotting, truncated longhouses constructed from massive, interlocking logs. Black pigs that know the road rules amble around and, in the gutter, illegal street gamblers dusted by passing motor scooters spend all day yelling at each other. At the far end of the street, past the trunk of a long-dead coconut palm, whose stability is threatened by the slightest breeze, is a narrow path. It's only about as wide as a pair of thin local hips, and abruptly plunges down a slope under

thick green foliage. Ten extraordinarily hospitable members of an extended multi-ethnic family, which Danh has befriended, show us the way. Loose steps have been dug into the red volcanic soil, although they are used far too often to last very long. We are told to stay on the path, as every open patch of ground to either side of it is filled with young green shoots in irregular rows that have been sown to be eaten, not trodden on by clumsy feet. Strolling down in single file, we hold out helping hands to each other and laugh when someone's flip-flops slip in the mud.

Now and then the daughters of the family unthinkingly pull leaves from bushes. One of them has a black-American soldier father unknown to her. Her uncle-in-law, whose ears stick out prominently, was fathered by a white-American soldier: a long-kept family secret. His now 75-year-old Ede mother buried his GI father's photograph in the forest, only unearthing it after the danger that her son might take advantage of a programme offering US citizenship to 'Amerasians' had passed. The family thinks I look like him, or like Rambo, or maybe both. Perhaps I do, but I'm a ridiculously pink, sun-burnt version. It's only about 30 years since people like

The saddle of the last missionary to use horses in the Central Highlands of Vietnam photographed on the floor of 'The Traditional Room', a museum in a seminary in Kontum documenting the history of Catholic missionary work in the region.

A polished French franc coin from the French Colonial period, which began in 1868 and ended in 1954.

me were the bomb- and chemical-dropping enemy: a fact that I'm conscious of as the locals become increasingly amused by my 'giant' size – I must weigh at least 15 stone or more, they think. While my trip is not as controversial as Jane Fonda's wartime visit to Hanoi, I still feel as though I am seen as something of a mammoth, fantastically rich exit visa. Otherness is a slippery membrane; ultimately, everybody is on the other side. Danh and his parents fled Vietnam on a boat in 1979 and were picked up by a Danish oil tanker. One of the war stories that his mother told him was that when she took the opportunity to see dead Viet Cong fighters displayed after the 1968 Tet Offensive, one of the bloodiest confrontations in what's known here as 'the American War', she was shocked to find that the corpses looked exactly like her.

The path delivers you to the top end of the valley where there is a large freshwater spring, encased in a brick and concrete block with metal spouts. Here, beneath the steady streaming water, women and girls come to wash. Our presence is an interruption, as if we have entered a bathroom without knocking. But it is also here that you get the first hint of the valley's idyllic meandering and the jolly, reliable stream navigating its base. Our two main guides are tough 31-year-old twin brothers from the Ede family, who would be hard to tell apart if it weren't for the fact they sport rival brands of fake designer baseball caps. After the Vietnam War, twins of both sexes were considered so precious that the government devised a special programme by which they were guaranteed sufficient food to sustain them. This life-assuring bargain

is preserved in their names, An and Toan, which were given to them at birth by the local communist authorities, and which when said together translate literally as 'sa-fety'. They think it's funny too. Elsewhere they would be cowboys, here they work for next to nothing watering coffee trees and carrying sacks. (One of their friends has a tattoo that wraps around his bicep – a version of the Statue of Liberty with a passing resemblance to Jesus. It cost him six US dollars.)

Toan tells us of the magic the valley once possessed. He shows us a pond in which the Ede believe that a stray chicken might be transformed into a fish. (Although everywhere there are signs of more insidious and tangible transformation in the form of property development and mounting, non-biodegradable trash.) Nearby I cut my toe and it immediately becomes infected, which they later interpret as a sign that I don't belong. They patch me up with chewed leaves and a banana-leaf string. (My agnostic German antiseptic also helps.) We eat under an ancient, solitary rainforest tree that can apparently read evil thoughts and trap dreams, and which someone once tried to burn down. We traverse prickly log bridges straddling two rock walls: remnants of the French colonists who once dammed the stream to make electricity for their plantations and labour camps, though not, of course, for the locals. When they went, the valley was eventually partly drained again and the villagers reclaimed their gardens and stripped the infrastructure of all of its saleable iron. But part of the old dam still creates an undertow as it plummets off one of the

largest remaining walls. It claims a life every year and is responsible for the turning of good magic into bad. Our guides are definitely not Catholics. One of their wives, a non-Ede Vietnamese, was for a while, but she gave it up.

It was this kind of belief that Bishop (Peter) Tran Thanh Chung, then still a zealous young Catholic priest, faced in the jungle while ministering to the indigenous people in the late 1950s and '60s. He was the last to ride horseback, ending a century of spiritual track-making by French-founded missions. The persistent, omnipresent Catholic Church has experience in grafting itself onto other, deep-rooted beliefs. The charitable work and education, and the crusade, continues anew today. A volunteer missionary couple from the USA – once high-ranking, highly paid engineers at Boeing with top secret clearance, who have given up everything to live in a seminary in Kontum – tell Danh of their admiration for the indigenous people's capacity and potential to believe; if only they could be persuaded to believe in the 'right' thing. A priest from Kontum thinks he may have found the very saddle used by Bishop Peter, although no one can be certain. Finally, after much ado and a lengthy deal-making process, aided by amiable, beer-drinking, indigenous nuns, god's saddle descends on loan from the mountains once again, headed this time on a new trip into the contemporary art world as part of an installation in a performance art exhibition Danh is planning. I realize our trip is the performance and that the saddle is only its symbolic subject.

Out here, though, the art world feels like it's on another planet as Toan jokes that he finds our safari camera harder to operate than catching and skinning a live cobra. (Danh, who has seen him bait one of the deadly snakes with a chicken, which they consumed after it had been killed by the snakebite, assures us he's speaking from experience.) Eventually we arrive at a cave veiled by a waterfall, which once served as a shelter during aerial bombardments in the 1970s. In the damp semi-dark we are shown rocks bearing markings in memorial of those who died here. The cave was once massive, but sometime back its roof collapsed. Its interior can no longer be penetrated: we face an impasse. Eventually we turn back to the valley, with its path, gardens and troubled beauty. We have been welcome here, but I ask myself how much my presence is symptomatic of a long chain of destructive, if perhaps inevitable, change. And I find myself glad that the cave has sealed itself off and that no words I might write or pictures we could take can ever divulge all of its secrets.

Some of the artefacts, images and documents gathered on our trip are about to find themselves, or have already ended up, in the incongruous context of galleries and international art exhibitions, including the Yokohama Triennale 2008, Manifesta 7 and in a Statements booth at Art Basel. A typical characteristic of Danh's practice is that he remains open minded about the final form his works and installations will take until the last minute before a show opens. For instance, his 2007 solo exhibition 'Untitled', at the Brandenburgischer Kunstverein in Potsdam, featured handmade blankets with wartime helicopters woven into them, casually folded and piled next to a door without further explanation or even being designated as a work. His research-oriented art is not the kind of issue-fed conceptualism that you are meant to 'get' or solve even while it raises questions relating to the construction of identity and the legacy of colonialism and war. Rather it exists in the relations and negotiations between people and authorities of all kinds, as well as in the multiple contradictory and revealing projections of his viewing public. The critically deconstructed or fragmented information his work offers always points to the telling fictions in all presumed facts and to that which is unresolved or unknown.

Dominic Eichler is a contributing editor of frieze. *This piece was partly written on a night train to Hanoi in collaboration with the Berlin-based artist Danh Vo whose friendships, research and work is the basis of its content. The accompanying photographs were taken by Pratchaya Phinthong for Danh Vo and selected by the artist to accompany this piece.*

⊗ Find out more at frieze.com

Two diamond shapes cut into the wall of the longhouse serve as a chimney.

The Rose Gardens
(display: II) (III)
2007
Lambda print
152×122 cm

Still Life

American writer **A.M. Homes** talks to British
artist **Sarah Jones** about photography, film,
memory, roses, psychoanalysis, women and hair

A.M. Homes: I first 'met' Sarah Jones, when I visited the exhibition 'Another Girl, Another Planet' at New York's Lawrence Rubin Greenberg Van Doren Gallery in New York, in 1999. Her photographs were rich with colour, and psychological tension, and fixated upon hair, identity and home. I met Sarah several years later at an artists' colony in upstate New York and we became friends, e-pals, chatting across continents and around the world, about our work and what it means to be a woman and an artist, and how we would like first and foremost to be known simply as artists. She is deeply serious, sees life with a Technicolor, X-ray vision all her own. I'm fascinated talking with her and hearing about what catches her eye or draws her in. We talked for hours – here is part of our conversation.

A.M. Homes In some ways your photographs are like musical compositions. There is a sense of time suspended and time stretching out in your photographs, which is kind of magical.

Sarah Jones I think the sense of something being at once frozen yet able to expand is quite musical. In early photographic portraits, people were literally clamped to chairs in order to remain motionless for long exposures. Photography allows us to scrutinize something; like putting a glass dish over a specimen to look more closely at it. I'm really interested in what can be expressed with the most limited of means or well chosen vocabulary. My background in dance influences me too. During my recent fellowship at the National Media Museum (in Bradford, UK), I was looking at the stereoscopic photographs; I'm interested in the slight shifts from one image to the next. It made me think of how the lens sees the world. I started photographing my new work in a municipal rose garden, from the front and back. I wanted one to be the mirror of the other and to be able to 'measure' what I saw or imagined. The photographs revealed how distance from camera to subject to viewer can affect the image, how actual space related to photographic space and how light defines this. There was a feeling of being able to grab hold of a subject and it slipping away. Perhaps photography allows us to daydream; reverie is where time seems to stretch out.

AMH Do you compose or conceptualize, for lack of a better word, in language, images or colours?

SJ I often start by taking snapshots, sketches, and see what they might suggest or I think of the books I've read recently or films I've seen, or something I remember. My work is built on the idea of a world that has its own rules, its own fiction. I have particular ideas that I want to explore; at the moment they concern the notion of mirroring, both as an act of photographing something and as a term related to psychoanalysis, to how we might behave with one another, or how also we might view an image, a portrait. Jean Cocteau's *Orphée* (1950) influenced my thinking here also – a parallel imagined world. When you look closely at one subject – like the roses or the couch or an analyst's office – something can suddenly fall into place. It's how a choreographer might construct a dance, or a composer might compose music; taking one gesture as a motif to build upon. It's a similar thing for me with photography, constructing an image out of something that's already there. Later, there may be a fine-tuning of sentences or nuances; the lighting and the composition are very specific in my work.

AMH When you end up with one image, are there others that are slight variations?

SJ Yes, but I use the one work that suggests how to go forward.

AMH Do you ever go back and reshoot?

SJ Yes, but sometimes it's not possible. You might return the next day to a park and the trees have been felled! We're all familiar with the idea of photography freezing something. I was remembering, as a child, seeing how long I could hold my breath for, and in a sense that's both to freeze the world and also perhaps to freeze yourself within the world. I think that's what I do with my photographs.

AMH When you're a child, your world changes so much more quickly than it does when you're an adult.

SJ My little girl was telling me that sometimes, as she is trying to fall asleep, everything in her head seems to be moving at a fast speed, all her thoughts, collections of images, whilst around her, in the physical world, things seem to be in slow motion. It made me think how there's often so much to take in, to make sense of, and I think people use photography to try to isolate a moment or an experience.

AMH To control something until you're able to really go back and process it or look at it, or understand what it is.

SJ Yes. I was looking at one of the rose prints this morning and thinking about the effect of the lighting I have used. The light falls on the foreground, on the first couple of planes, which makes the subject feel as though it's been pushed to the surface of the photographic space, isolating the subject; it reminds me of pressed flowers. I remember finding some in a second-hand novel once. When you open the page, you've got that double-take – something picked, a totem, up against language, fiction. It made me think about the photograph as a keepsake, the way that pressed flowers are.

AMH How did you become a photographer?

SJ My first degree was in art and dance. I painted a lot, sometimes transcribing photographs; I didn't enjoy the theatre world as I like working alone, so I ended up in the darkroom. I like photography's limitations. I'm interested in the very specific language of the photograph, how it relates to experience, to the real, the everyday.

AMH What kind of dance were you interested in?

S*J*   Contemporary.

AMH Do you still have that interest?

S*J*   I go and see it, but I've lost any fantasy about dancing again.

AMH Could you ever see yourself doing some sort of performance-based work?

S*J*   Not presently.

AMH Why not?

S*J*   I'm interested in perhaps moving to film but I always come back to the still. There's so much more I want to explore with that.

AMH I think that in a lot of your images there's a real sense of gesture.

S*J*   I was interested in dancers and choreographers who use everyday gestures in their work, which was a relatively new thing when I was studying; choreographers like Pina Bausch. The group of girls I started photographing when I was at Goldsmiths doing an MA from 1994–6 (the 'Francis Place'/ 'Mulberry Lodge' series) use gestures that are quite naturalistic but also there's a sense of awkwardness; the locations effect our reading of them. There's a sense of the uncanny in those rooms and the figures are both comfortable and ill at ease. They're at a point of change; their adolescence.

AMH Very often in your work there is a sense of difference or loss.

S*J*   Photography is always associated historically with the idea of the death of the moment, or the lost moment, but it's odd because a photograph is also a permanent document of a lost moment.

AMH How important is memory in your work?

S*J*   Memory always slips away from us; each time you go back to it, it has changed, perhaps our relationship with that memory may have altered. A psychiatrist I met at Bellevue Hospital Center in New York was talking about the layout of her therapy rooms. I'd never seen rooms like this before. They didn't seem institutional. They were stripped back, but she'd hung cloth on the walls, introduced plaster casts of Greek columns, benches and paintings, an electric organ in one room. Everything was well-worn, like a stage set made from discarded objects. She described how the people that she sees have been in and out of institutions for many years, and their memories are sometimes completely locked down, and if they were to arrive in an institution that looked like every other institution, nothing would ever change. So she hopes that in using these rooms as props something might be opened or unlocked. It made me think about memory, about the way it can unlock something. It's the same with the couches. In a sense they're very straightforward photographs, but you don't always see the actual couch; it's the idea of a couch, which refers to other couches in other places. Perhaps this is the effect of the formal compositional structure that I use in

Above:
Analyst (Couch) (I)
2007
Lambda print
122×122 cm

Below:
Arrangement (Analyst) (I)
2007
Lambda print
61×61 cm

Opposite:
Consulting Room (I)
1995
C-type print
150×150 cm

photographing them, the flatness of the space. It allows for a different kind of interaction.

AMH What is your interest in psychoanalysis and couches?

S*J*   The first psychoanalyst's couch I photographed was over ten years ago, when I was doing my MA. It came from my response to the theory I was being taught. I was interested in what would happen if you pictured the place where psychoanalysis was carried out, and where people might re-live experience in order to loosen the grip their past has on them. I was interested in what relationship the image of the couch might have to this. All of the early couches I photographed are at the British Institute of Psychoanalysis. The head of the institute was fascinating. He spoke about how patients in the room often imagine the presence of a third person, and he suggested that the camera could be like this third eye; an onlooker, an audience. This then unfolded a whole way of photographing the couches, which developed into photographing the girls and the roses and the trees, and my relationship to photography.

AMH There's such a huge difference between theory and what happens on the analyst's couch. Do you think you'll finish with the couch at some point?

S*J*   I've started a new series that includes an image of a red couch, which signals a departure in that I've titled it *Analyst (Couch) (I)* (2007) whereas the other photographs are titled as rooms, such as *Consulting Room (Couch) (I to XXI)*. The word analyst might refer to a protagonist, or a re-telling. Also colour is more important. I recently made a group of photographs titled 'Colony (Couch)' of beds in respective studios at Yaddo Artists, Colony. These refer obliquely to the analyst couches too. An analyst's room to me is like a mystery with certain codes and signals; there are certain conventions made manifest. I think that one of the reasons I've been interested in photographing them is because of the sense of ritual and place.

AMH In a funny way, because it's ritualized and mythologized, what goes on is an ethereal, psychic thing you can't even see.

S*J*   A curator, Jeremy Lewison, asked me to photograph his mother's couch. She was an analyst and had recently died; it was very strange being in her space. It was like a memorial to her but was soon to be dismantled, as they were selling the house. I suddenly was aware of the great weight of the photograph being the only thing that would remain of that room. It took me a long time to make something I felt was in some way meaningful, given the context. The work became about the light in the room, how it fell on the couch.

AMH I remember, when my grandmother died, I photographed everything in her house. She used to sit on her couch all day, and where she sat, the carpet had worn away. It was the strangest thing. This woman has lived in a place for a very long time, and then suddenly she doesn't return.

SJ Some of the couches that I photograph are well lived-in; they may just be couches, but their history is revealed very quickly in the imprint of the bodies of the people who have lain on them.

AMH How do analysts feel about their couches? What is their relationship to their own couch? Are they aware of it?

SJ Before I came to New York I was given lots of email addresses of analysts and I asked them to describe their couch, their rooms, the lighting and very particular details. When I arrived to photograph the rooms, though, they looked very different from how I had imagined them. The couches were often sagging and worn, bearing testament to the analyst having practised for many years. I became interested in the idea of still life through talking to analysts; and have been making some new work around this; the arrangement of objects in the rooms, the possible narratives and associations.

AMH It's interesting to me when people have been in practice for a long time and you walk into the waiting room, and it's full of books from 1967.

SJ Apparently any change in an analyst's room can be disruptive for the patient. One analyst told me that many of his patients would know immediately if something had disappeared or been moved.

AMH I wonder what most patients look at while they're talking?

SJ I made a number of photographs of the ceiling; I wanted to photograph what a patient might see whilst lying on the couch, and the light on it at certain times of day. I was also thinking about what Sigmund Freud says about analysis, about a 'talking out' of the body; lying on the couch facilitating this.

AMH Where did the blue you use so much come from?

SJ It's like the pleasure of certain colours, perhaps, or how they have been used historically – blue to indicate the Sublime, or distance in Renaissance painting. William Gass' book *On Being Blue: A Philosophical Inquiry* (1976) has influenced me. A recent work around the colour blue is titled *Cove (virtual film studio) (I)* (2007). The location is an infinity cove painted in chroma-key blue, normally used to map on

Photography allows us to scrutinize something; like putting a glass dish over a specimen to look more closely at it.

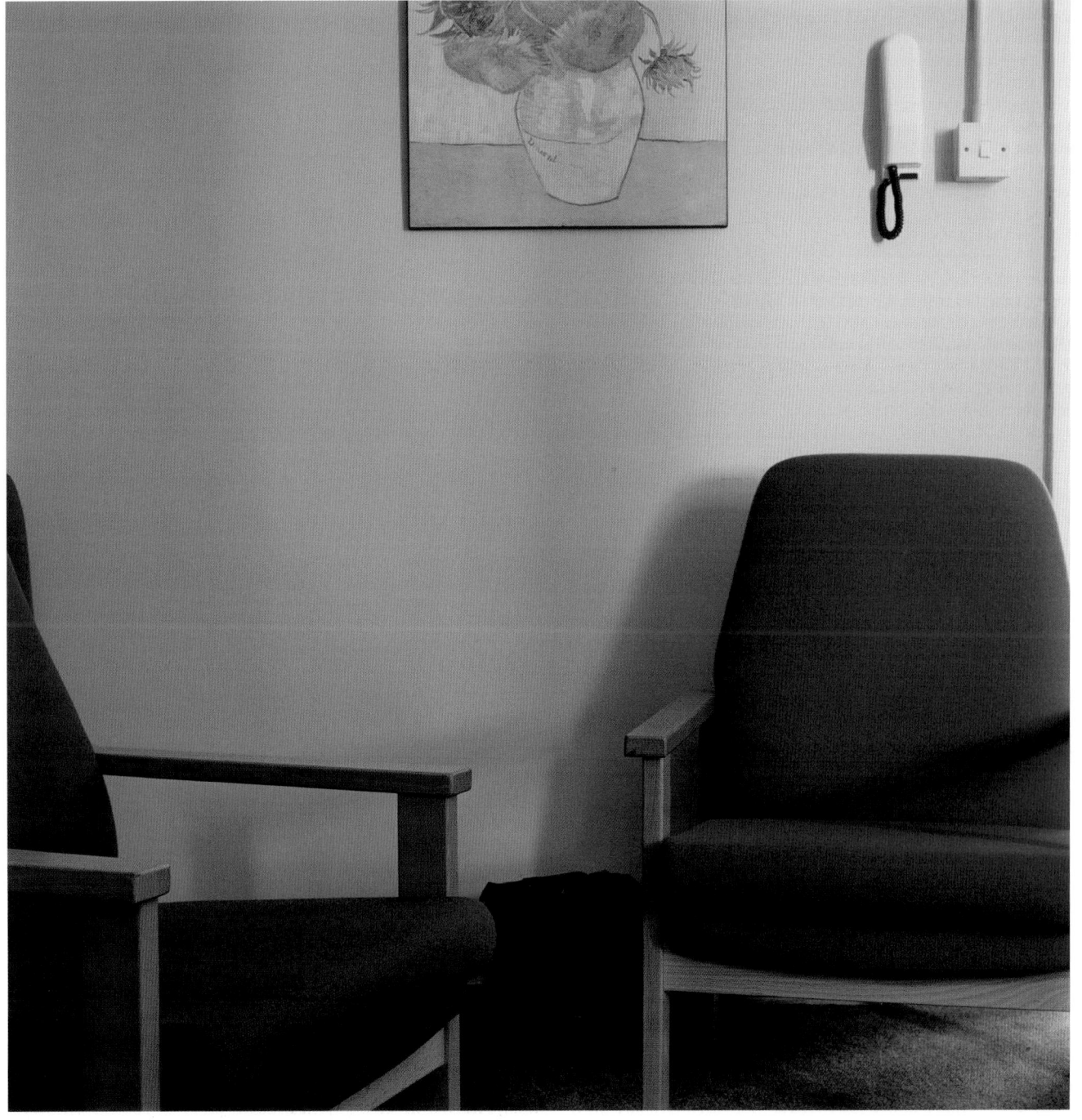

locations after filming, but in photographing it something else happens, and it becomes about the surface of the walls and the layers of painting. As a location it refers to the idea of illusion or allusion. I'm interested in the surface of the photograph in relationship to this.

AMH Are there things that you think about that are relevant to understanding your work?

SJ My practice stretches over a long time, and the images are very much part of an ongoing exploration. So much of my work is about the portraits. Even if there isn't literally a figure, it's referred to, in the couches, the marks on the wall or how the viewer might experience the rose garden images. I'm really interested in the small shifts that happen from picture to picture.

AMH I find it harder to track small shifts, but I think it's very rare to see something only once in the course of a career.

SJ You're dealing with the image but also trying to find something in it that might convey a feeling or a concept; something you're trying to understand or have yet to articulate. In my latest show my work continues to be about formal concerns such as measuring, photographic space and systems, light, and about pleasure, more than it's ever been. I realize also, for all of that, the work is a little uneasy, has an unsettling effect, but I'm not entirely sure why. There is perhaps a gap between the document and meaning: a separation.

AMH I think there's a mysterious underplay in your photographs. They're never just an image of a thing. They're the thing plus something we can't possess or really articulate.

SJ I wonder if it's partly to do with the layering that goes on in the image. Although flowers have been used for centuries in art, I'm interested in what you can add to them as a subject. The roses are quite ordinary, they're in a park near my studio. I photographed them during the day but allude to the night, because of the way that they are lit, the way they have been recorded on film.

AMH How do you do that?

SJ I shoot with big studio lights, brightly exposing the flowers so that the background falls away, so any context or specific location disappears. I love that, bringing the subject right to the foreground.

AMH What kind of camera are you using?

SJ A 5 x 4, large-format camera.

AMH What's your film stock of choice?

SJ I've spent ages trying to find the right film, the right range, contrast and density. I used to work with one type of film stock that is no longer made, which completely devastated me. I had to move up to 5 x 4 format for the same luminosity and sharpness.

AMH I'm not conscious of how a choice of a lens or format effects what I'm seeing, and yet it does so profoundly.

SJ Absolutely, and working with the large-format camera is so different; you have to tilt your idea of the world to take photographs with a large format, so already your subject's on its head.

AMH How do you decide what the appropriate size of the images is?

SJ I want my work to be in some way a surrogate for the actual; often the scale of the image relates to life size. My work is both documentary and imagined. If you have a measurement system, then perhaps you're able to equate certain things.

AMH What is the system?

SJ I photograph things front-on with as little direction or intervention as possible; it's about stripping everything right back, in a Beckett-like way. If you strip language as far back as you can,

The Living Room (Curtain) (I)
2003
C-type print
150×150 cm

strangely, there's often more of it. I want to reveal the workings or truth of something, and that's the starting-point. I think this is built into the history of photography, which is very much about social context, order and cataloguing – how, also, it was put to use in institutions.

AMH The history of photographic portraiture is intense but brief, unlike painting.

SJ With the 'Actor' series in 1995 I was trying to unravel what a photographic portrait is, so I titled the portraits 'actor'. It was a way of describing my relationship to photography in our lives. I offered the actors six gestures, drawn from a Piero della Francesca painting. When I was in art school, photography was seen as a liberator; painters no longer had to paint figuratively, because photography's promise was that it could describe the world truthfully. In contemporary practice we're now examining photography's relationship to the notion of the real.

AMH Do you think the camera has a sense of perception that's different to that of the photographer? That it betrays you?

SJ Often it does things that I hadn't realized it would do.

AMH Are there times you're surprised or caught off-guard by what appears that you hadn't conceptualized?

SJ Yes. As with the roses, they look so different in a photograph; perhaps it's like holding an object up to the light, turning it in your hand, to attempt to know it better?

AMH It's interesting, the idea that when you make the image, when you look at it, it could turn out to violate the rules relating to what it was and what you thought you were doing.

SJ You think you know something, then it moves out of the illusion

Cove (virtual film studio) (I)
2007
Lambda print
122×122 cm

The Park (II)
2002
C type print
130×170 cm

Hair has a resonance in the places where I take photographs – the edges of urban parks, or areas that are unkempt. Long hair is like nature gone slightly mad.

of the space into a photographic, cinematic space. We've learnt different ways of seeing through photography and cinema.

AMH Can you talk more about the role of narrative in your work?

SJ   I'm interested in how a narrative is constructed, even within very formal structures, and in carrying motifs across works. I think photography leaves this gap where the viewer can bring their own narrative and experience to the image.

AMH What is it about hair that interests you?

SJ I recently met a woman on the street who had long hair piled up on top of her head like a nest, and it reminded me of my new roses, which are visceral, spindly and beautiful, in bloom but slightly diseased. Hair has a resonance in the locations in which I put the people who I photograph – the edges of urban parks, or places that are unkempt – so there's a relationship to the location and figure as an allegory; hair as nature gone slightly mad.

AMH What is the power of long hair?

SJ It's been associated in art history with death, mortality and sexuality, but having extremely long hair in the face of the speed of modern life could be seen as an affectation.

AMH What work by other artists do you revisit?

SJ There's work that I revisit a lot, in the same way that I do with my own work. I'm both reassured and slightly uneasy when I look at something again. I was looking at some Edward Stieglitz photographs, and the way that he photographs the landscape, the light in his pictures, is fantastic. I often return to Diane Arbus' work. I've looked at Lee Friedlander too quite a lot recently. He photographed

the rose gardens at Yaddo. It's interesting how different artists look at the same place and get something very different from it.

AMH What other kinds of things do you look at?

SJ One of Edward Hopper's last paintings, *Sunlight in an Empty Room* (1963), has influenced my work recently and I've been looking at Gustav Klimt again. The Mark Rothko room, now at Tate Modern, is really important to me. His paintings are so powerful. When my father died, a long time ago, I spent a lot of time in that room.

AMH We have one too, in the National Gallery of Art in Washington. I spent forever sitting there.

SJ It's extraordinary, limiting your palette to such an extent, painting and repainting the same formal structure – and yet his paintings are so powerful. Complex and moving. How did he do that?

AMH It is what it is, and it's not what it is; it's something more.

A.M. Homes is the author of numerous books, including her memoir, The Mistress's Daughter *(2007) and the novel* This Book Will Save Your Life *(2006). She writes frequently on art and collaborated with photographer Bill Owens on his new book* Bill Owens, *published by Damiani Press (2008).*

Sarah Jones lives in London. Her work is included in 'Street & Studio: An Urban History of Photography' at Tate Modern until 31 August, and 'The Society of London Ladies', a group exhibition at Dispari & Dispari in Reggio Emilia in Italy until 24 June, 2008. She has also recently been awarded The Meredith. S. Moody Photography Residency at the Yaddo Artists' Colony in Saratoga Springs, New York.

Susan Philipsz

Songs as memorials; the presence of the
past in empty spaces *by Jonathan Griffin*

Opposite:
Follow Me
2006
Four channel sound
installation
Installation view at
CGAC, Santiago de
Compostela
2008

Below left:
*There is Nothing Left
Here*
2006
Sound installation
Installation view at
CGAC, Santiago de
Compostela
2008

Below right:
The Internationale
1999
Sound installation
Installation view at the
Biennale of Sydney
2008

When, exactly, did folk music die? I don't mean the genre that occupies the section on record shop shelves between country and blues: I mean the custom of passing songs down through generations and augmenting, recombining and misremembering them through repetition. In Britain, at least, some say its death coincided with the Industrial Revolution or the time when gramophones became affordable for most households. Or perhaps, as the artist Susan Philipsz might suggest, it never actually died: it simply became more complicated, the lineage of a song becoming entangled over time in a thicket of different ownerships, contexts and media.

Philipsz' art works, which frequently consist of nothing more than an empty gallery and a recording of the artist herself singing, rely heavily on such intricate histories. Take the traditional Irish ballad 'The Lass of Aughrim', for instance, which the artist appropriated for her installation *The Dead* (2000). The song, which describes the seduction, rejection and death of a young girl, plays a pivotal role in James Joyce's short story 'The Dead' (1914), reminding Gretta Conroy of the tragic death of her childhood sweetheart. It was later used in John Huston's film of Joyce's story, released in 1987, shortly after the director's own death, and more recently in Pat Murphy's biopic *Nora* (2000), where it is performed by Ewan McGregor, who plays Joyce. It would probably only complicate matters to mention that the title of the ballad also refers to the site of the bloodiest battle ever fought on Irish soil.

So the song, while functioning as a memorial to something lost, is nevertheless very much alive, a half-full vessel that is topped up each time it is reframed by new contexts and references. It provides a temporal paradox that

is central to Philipsz' work: that which is past, or absent, used as a device to return the viewer to the present. In *The Dead* the artist sings 'The Lass of Aughrim' a cappella, as she does most of the cover versions that feature in her sound installations. The listener, sitting in a darkened auditorium, becomes hyper-sensitized to the sound of the artist's breath and the occasional snatch of noise from beyond the studio. Her voice is unpolished but not off-key; she does not seem to be performing the song so much as reciting it to herself. This sense of interiority, of a refusal of the normal relationship between the audience and the performer, is awakened further when the spectator notices flecks of white appearing on the auditorium's screen. A 35mm projector is in fact playing pure black film, which as time passes and the film deteriorates, is populated by an increasing number of white marks. A reference to the blanket of snow that falls 'all over Ireland' at the end of Huston's film, this device is also Philipsz' analogy for the relationship between entropy and growth, the ongoing moment in which the obliteration of the past meets the emergence of the future.

For the exhibition 'Stay with Me' at Malmö Konsthall in 2005 Philipsz recorded herself singing three songs that are in different ways pleas for the past to persist into the future and, as the show's title suggests, for the listener not to abandon the singer. 'Watch with Me' (1972) by Joe Wise, 'Nothing Lasts Forever' (1997) by Echo and the Bunnymen and 'Pyramid Song' (2001) by Radiohead are themselves all fragments from the recent history of popular culture, but in Philipsz' voice they take root in the here and now. The emptiness of the white spaces in which they are heard produces in the viewer an increased awareness of their surroundings. When Philipsz uses objects such as organ pipes or the rims of glasses to make sounds, the architecture itself seems to breathe, and its emptiness becomes as full of potential as it is devoid of the past.

Often Philipsz installs her work in unexpected corners of the public realm: under a bridge during 2007's Sculpture Projects Muenster; in the Shrine of the Nymphs near the base of the Acropolis at the 2006 Athens Biennial; in a hillside shelter for the forthcoming Folkestone Triennial; or piped through the speakers of a Tesco supermarket to unsuspecting shoppers. With *Follow Me* (2006) she has haunted cemeteries in Berlin and Santiago de Compostela with an overlaid and repeating recording of the Yardbirds' 1966 psychedelic hit 'Happenings Ten Years Time Ago'. Despite each work's specific and elaborate points of reference and the reliance on the communal pool of familiarity on which the songs draw, the experience of the listener is deeply solitary. It is nothing like the confident singalong of the crowd at a popular band's concert and everything like the overheard noise of a radio from a next-door flat. This allows Philipsz to handle overtly political subject matter with a delicacy that would otherwise be nearly impossible to achieve. In *The Internationale* (1999), which she has sited in various locations, including an underpass in Ljubljana and an abandoned turbine hall for the Biennale of Sydney, she performs the left-wing anthem as something like a lullaby or an elegy, which emanates from overlooked spaces like a scent on the breeze. It is said that sound never truly disappears; its energy just dissipates into a continuous and inaudible hum in the world around it.

Klara Lidén

Anarchic urbanism;
pigeons, song and dance
by Sam Thorne

Below left:
Elda för kråkorna
**(Heating for
Crows)**
(detail)
2008
Mixed media
Installation view

Below right:
Bodies of Society
2006
DVD still

Opposite:
Paralysed
2003
DVD still

For *Elda för kråkorna* (Heating for Crows, 2008) the young Swedish artist Klara Lidén did little more than shrink half of Reena Spaulings' dilapidated Lower East Side space down to a tight, blank-walled corridor that led to a tiny room furnished with a sofa. Once seated, eyes accustomed to the dim lighting, the viewer became aware of the faint sound of scratching, uncomfortably close. The walled-off space had been given over to local pigeons, which scrabbled for food in the area surrounding the darkened alcove. As though designed with the express intention of slyly tripping up close readers of Brian O'Doherty, *Elda för kråkorna* made the white cube seem uncomfortably permeable, the viewer all too aware of the big, dirty city that lay beyond the gallery walls.

Over the past five years Lidén had made a number of improvised constructions and videoed performances that offer basic propositions for ways of living, all of which run sharply counter to the norm. These have included renovating a bunker-like space on the banks of the Spree in Berlin, where she is based, and offering it to whoever cared to stay, setting up an underground postal service that operated briefly in Stockholm, and pasting blank paper over advertising hoardings in Copenhagen. Recalling what Guy Debord famously called 'anarchic urbanism', Lidén's feral actions, although robust, languish towards the bottom of the city's food chain, supported by the DIY practicality of squat-living.

'Heating for crows' is a common Swedish expression implying a waste of energy, and the architectural interventions that Lidén has made (with zero construction costs) for gallery shows are economically built from scavenged resources. For her first solo exhibition at Reena Spaulings in New York, Lidén constructed a loft space from discarded cardboard boxes and piping (*Benign*, 2004), while in *Do Not Cross the Line Blues* (2006) a bunk was fashioned from police barriers and woven fabric. In both of these cramped, elevated refuges Lidén cut short any participatory reverie by showing documentation of the gritty surrounding area where the materials were sourced.

Lidén's spiky videos, few of which run to more than four minutes, are all attuned to how routines can be performed and disrupted. Although in *Ohyra* (2007) Lidén actually beats herself up for not being able to perform standard domestic tasks ('Scheisse, I'm so fucking bad at washing dishes', she shouts), these performances are tightly managed exercises in taking account of one's own actions rather than losing control. In *Bodies of Society* (2006) Lidén paces back and forth across a small bare room in her Stockholm apartment, a bicycle propped at one end. She seems at ease, despite holding a long metal rod. Lidén taps the bike provocatively, as though to test how it sounds – perhaps, even, to check what it is. As the vocal on the woozy backing track comes in – 'I don't want to talk about it / I don't wanna talk about it', delivered with the ennui of a 1990s' slacker rock dirge – she begins to club the bike methodically to pieces, while remaining all the time eerily calm.

As with *Unheimlich Maneuver* (2007), for which Lidén – echoing Lucas Samaras' 1963 exhibition at the Pace Gallery in New York – moved the contents of her apartment into Stockholm's Moderna Museet, these videos are equally entranced and disgusted with the sheer quantity of stuff that anyone can accumulate. In *550 Jamaica Avenue* (2004) the camera roams around an abandoned Brooklyn apartment that Lidén discovered upstairs from her own while staying in New York. She is glimpsed through a doorway, lodged between mounds of trinkets and old photographs, doggedly pedalling on a rattling exercise bike. Later, seated at a piano, Lidén plays a solemn and artless elegy – perhaps for whoever once lived in the apartment – in which the screamed finale sounds something like: 'Ich brauche mein space' ('I need my space'). Like Bruce Nauman in his video *Violin Tuned D.E.A.D* (1968), Lidén – topless and asexual – turns away from the camera for the duration of the performance. In other videos she is roughly or else androgynously dressed, this sustained ambiguity skipping the more programmatic demonstrations of femininity's performativity, never insisting on the importance of sexual difference.

Her much-admired video *Paralysed* (2003) is accompanied by a garbled song of the same name from 1968 by The Legendary Stardust Cowboy, an unhinged Texan now remembered, if at all, for providing David Bowie with half of his Ziggy Stardust moniker. On a sparsely filled Stockholm commuter train Lidén dances, earnestly and ineptly, up and down the carriage, quickly shedding a hooded military jacket and jeans to reveal a pink slip and shorts. She rolls on the floor, flips clumsily over seats and pirouettes with the enthusiasm of a child at a party. The impassioned performance quickly tests what happens when the unspoken rules of public behaviour are ignored, and the answer is – depressingly or enlighteningly – nothing. While so much recent politicized art favours defensive reticence over actual engagement, Lidén's small but fiercely intense gestures retain a stranglehold on individual agency.

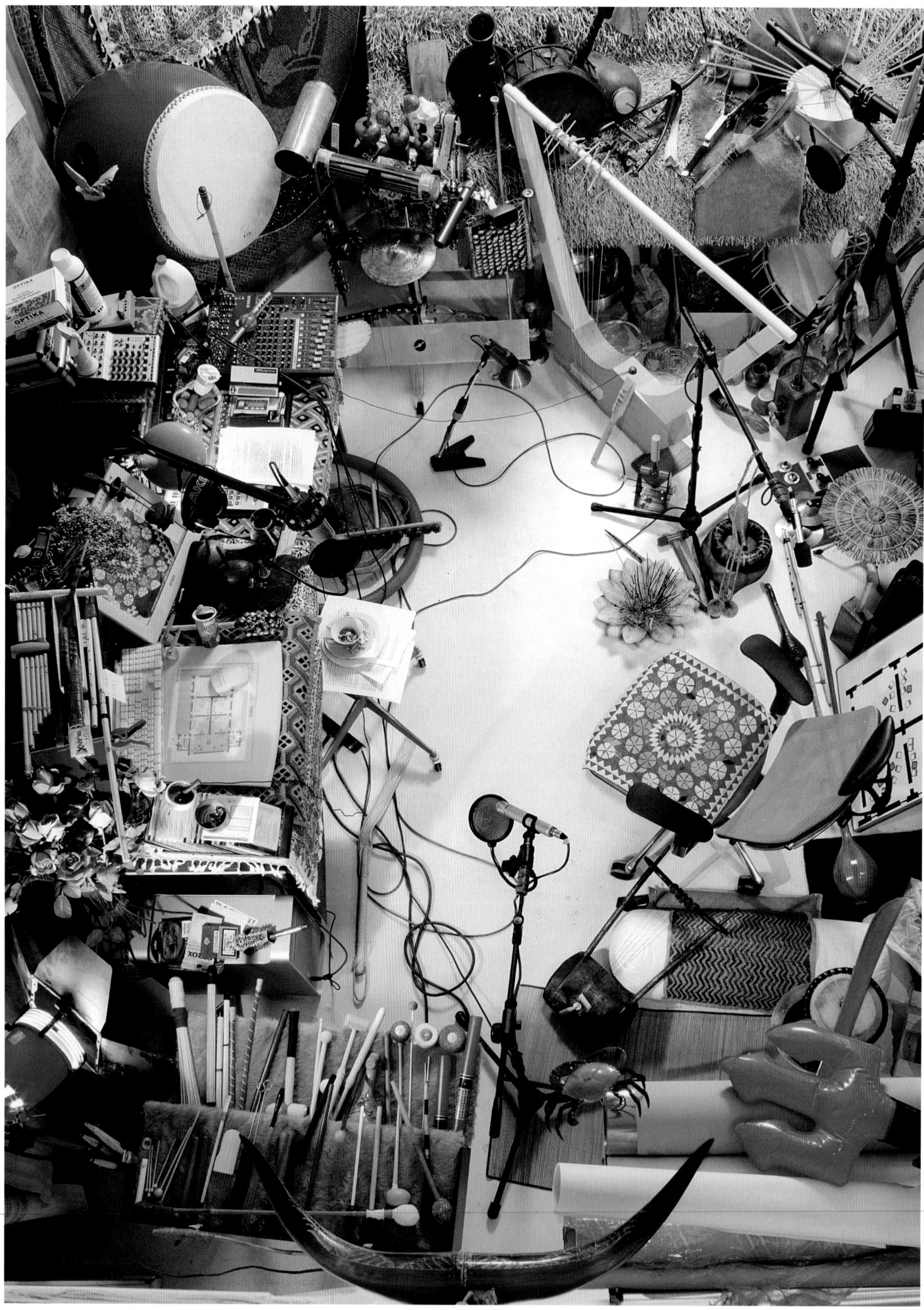

Roberto Cuoghi

Metamorphosis and 'life-sharing'; decadent humour and demon kings
by Luca Cerizza

Opposite:
'Šuillakku'
2008
Mixed media
Production photograph

Below left:
Il Coccodeista
1997
Mixed media on tracing paper
25×20 cm

Below middle:
The Goodgriefies
2000
DVD still

Below right:
Pazuzu
2008
Epoxy, varnish, fibreglass, polystyrene, steel
595×296×250 cm

To radically simplify the diversity of forms and appearances Roberto Cuoghi's art takes, we could identify a common denominator in the concept of metamorphosis. The idea of constant transformation and change, the hybridization of forms and identities, is a recurrent theme in the work of this Milan-based artist.

In some of his early projects, Cuoghi subjected his body to a variety of metamorphic processes, testing his physical capacities in a rather extreme fashion. While still a student at Milan's Brera Art Academy, for instance, Cuoghi wore a pair of Schmidt-Pechan prisms – which rotate whatever is viewed through them by 180 degrees – mounted onto welders' goggles for five consecutive days (*Il Coccodeista*, 1997). The glasses provided Cuoghi with a completely distorted vision of the world, obliging him to completely redefine his sense of sight and orientation. The project generated a video, a series of drawn self-portraits and a number of bitterly ironic, occasionally melancholic, short poems that related his experience of these exceptional circumstances, including the effects of the medicines he took to ease the pain provoked by the prisms. The resultant drawings and poems were accordingly executed in an elementary style and resembled the creations of a small child.

In 1998, at the age of 25, Cuoghi embarked on another radical first-hand experience. In an attempt to reverse the natural progression of time, he assumed the appearance of his father who, shortly after, became seriously ill. Cuoghi gained six and a half stone, dyed his hair white, grew a long beard, and dressed and acted like his father. Within a few weeks, the artist had transformed himself into an old man: the numbers had been inverted, time accelerated. Neither a performance nor a disguise, Cuoghi maintained his new persona for several years, in an ambiguous struggle between fiction and reality. Although it generated

no further art works, news of Cuoghi's attempt to 'life-share', to duplicate and consequently prolong another existence, spread by word of mouth until it passed into art-world lore. Cuoghi's imitation survived the original, but his body paid a high inheritance tax: when his father passed away, the artist started to reverse the premature aging, but the stress to which he had subjected himself over the years rendered the process extremely slow and painful, even necessitating some surgical operations.

In an attempt to move away from employing his body directly in his art, Cuoghi represented himself as a cartoon in a number of works. In the video animation *The Goodgriefies* (2000), for example, he portrayed himself as an old man wearing dark glasses and as a fat Indian divinity, a hybrid creature among other monstrous bodies, created by combining characters from classic cartoons such as *Loony Tunes* and *Peanuts* with those from more recent series such as *The Simpsons* and *South Park*, producing a parade of grotesque-yet-comical figures. Cuoghi subsequently completed a number of darker and more disturbing paintings. Executed employing an exquisite, painstaking technique, in which multiple layers of glass and various materials are superimposed onto one another to create a range of disquieting images – from evil smiling creatures to unreadable geographical maps – the works evoke an Odilon Redon dream gone bad.

In Cuoghi's world, hybridization exists at every level, between past and present, nature and technology, highbrow and popular culture. By revealing the level of adulteration and corruption hidden in any given form or story, his work questions identity, authority and authorship, origin and originality, in a world increasingly influenced by the forces of globalization and digitalization. Although it is tinged with a dark, almost decadent humour, Cuoghi's art alludes to the fact that we are living in a time in which

every residual concept of purity is redundant: the mythical era of Babel revisited.

It therefore comes as no surprise that Cuoghi's latest project, 'Šuillakku' (2008), which recently opened at the Castello di Rivoli Contemporary Art Museum in Turin, focuses on Assyro-Babylonian history and mythology. After an extended period of research involving historians, archaeologists, ethno-musicologists, linguists and industrial designers, Cuoghi produced a sculpture and a sound installation. Located on the museum's monumental staircase, the sculpture, which is over five meters tall, is an enlargement of a tiny bronze statue from the Louvre of the Assyrian deity Pazuzu, king of the demons of the wind. Following the principle that evil drives evil away, Pazuzu was frequently invoked as protector, and has a millenary history of reincarnations that in recent times has extended to *The Exorcist* (1971) and the video for 'Rock It' (2004) by Gorillaz. Inside the museum, rooms resonated with the myriad voices of Cuoghi's overwhelming sound installation. The artist researched and reconstructed a number of ancient musical instruments, which he then used to accompany himself singing a lamentation from around 612 BC invoking the protection of the Assyrian gods.

The symbolic relevance of Cuoghi's project becomes clearer when we consider that the lamentation dates from a time when one of the world's first great empires was under threat from neighbouring populations. In *Une brève histoire de l'avenir* (A Brief History of the Future, 2006), Jacques Attali predicted that the global domination of the American empire will end about 20 years from now; Cuoghi speaks in a more metaphorical fashion about our fear of the unknown and about a world gone wrong. The road to Babylon is paved with anguish, despair and death.

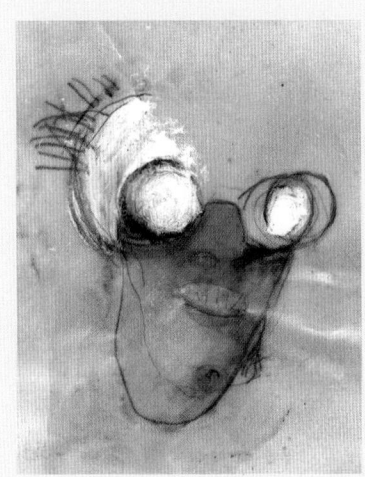

Javier Téllez

Invisible populations; animals, sight, translation and interpretation

by Steven Stern

Below left:
One Flew over the Void (Balla perdida)
2005
DVD still

Below right:
El león de Caracas (The Lion of Caracas)
2002
DVD still

Opposite:
Letter on the Blind, For the Use of Those Who See
2007
Film still

A warm tyre, a vulture's wing without feathers, a plastic wall, curtains from a mansion: these are descriptions offered by the subjects of Javier Téllez' latest film, six blind people confronting a four-ton metaphor. *Letter on the Blind, for the Use of Those Who See* (2007) realizes the famous parable, documenting an encounter between a group of blind New Yorkers and an Indian elephant. Yet the work is not so much an allegory as a drama of local perceptions. The five men and one woman sit on chairs in the centre of an empty, derelict Brooklyn public swimming-pool and, one by one, come forward to meet the animal. They share on-the-spot impressions and, in a voice-over, offer commentary on their separate histories. The stately pace of the film, keyed to the participants' careful movements, creates a heightened, ritual feel. Shot in intense, high-contrast black and white, almost entirely in close-up, the elephant becomes less a recognizable form than a tactile expanse, its craggy hide frequently filling the entire screen. Like the Denis Diderot (1749) essay from which it takes its title, Téllez' film commissioned by Creative Time, is an exercise in translation between the senses, an experiment in synaesthesia.

It's a quixotic project, this attempt to visualize the unseen, but an apt one for the Venezuela-born, New York-based Téllez. Over the past decade he has worked with 'invisible' populations: the disabled, the poor and those institutionalized for metal illness. That the concept of 'working with' is linguistically – and politically – ambiguous is precisely the point. These marginal communities are, essentially, Téllez' medium. At the same time his film, video and installation-based pieces grow out of and encompass extended collaborative work with his subjects. He walks a tricky, often unsettling line. He flirts with – and

yet avoids – the twin perils of exploitation and do-gooder-ism, deriving ethics and aesthetics from the situation in which he finds himself.

If it's possible to be born into such a role, Téllez' autobiography would qualify him. The son of two psychiatrists, he grew up tagging along to the institution his father supervised. At a yearly festival there were beauty contests: doctors and patients would, for a day, exchange uniforms. Such carnivalesque reversals remain a powerful trope in Téllez' work. *One Flew over the Void (Balla perdida)* (2005) – created for inSite, a biennial event straddling the Mexico/US border – is literally a carnival. With residents of a Mexican mental institution the artist developed a public spectacle – part circus, part protest march – around the theme of borders, literal and metaphorical. The rally culminated in a professional human cannonball being shot over the fence dividing Tijuana and San Diego.

Bizarrely resonant images such as this, simultaneously absurd and heady with reference, form the core of Téllez' projects. In the video *El león de Caracas* (The Lion of Caracas, 2002), a stuffed and mounted lion makes its way down the vertiginous steps of a hillside Caracas shanty town, borne by four uniformed police officers. The lion, symbol of the Venezuelan capital, here takes the place of a Holy Week saint, while the procession also recalls the all too common ritual of police carrying a corpse out of the *ranchitos*. As giggling children rush forward to touch the immobile animal, the cops shuffle awkwardly in the background, all enlisted in a strange portrait of power and powerlessness. For *You Are Here* (2002) Téllez presented patients of an appallingly medieval Venezuelan mental institution with an enormous inflatable ball, a super-sized version of a stuffed cat toy. Rolling it through the labyrinthine corridors and out into the courtyard, they somehow spontaneously conspire (after many harrowing minutes of the blackest of slapstick comedy) to push the huge

object over the wall, effecting its escape.

La Passion de Jeanne d'Arc (Rozelle Hospital) (The Passion of Joan of Arc, Rozelle Hospital, 2004) offers a more elaborate intervention. Téllez spent a month in workshops with a group of 12 women at an institution in Sydney. After viewing the Carl Dreyer film *La Passion de Jeanne d'Arc* (1928) the patients wrote new intertitles. Unsurprisingly, they reconceived it as the story of 'JDA', committed for believing she was Joan of Arc, 'suffering from grandiose visions and auditory hallucinations'. Presented as a two-channel piece, the revamped silent film is accompanied by a series of intimate interviews with the co-creators. One woman conducts a dialogue with a marionette therapist, perfectly ventriloquizing the language of the professional mental health worker; another reads journal entries detailing her electroshock treatments. A young woman offers a giddy monologue of her institutionalization, while explaining her knowledge of Morse code through a past life memory. Suddenly, she breaks into song, a moving hymn proclaiming her resistance to rules and bureaucracy.

In the words of British psychologist Adam Phillips, madness 'is defined, so to speak, by what it elicits in others'. And it is precisely through definition that the so-called mad are contained, administered and treated, in ways that are more or less useful, more or less humane. Téllez' work manages to escape this logic: it is designed to elicit a response while circumventing the structure of definition altogether. He offers nothing as positivist as a 'position' on mental illness, and certainly nothing in the way of a cure. Rather, his odd and compelling spectacles embrace the irrational as a method of translation pressed to its limits. They are a series of letters on the mad, for the use of those who think themselves sane.

Time and Space

The sculptures of Polish artist **Monika Sosnowska**
respond to architecture, memory and emotion
by Kirsty Bell

This page and inset:
Untitled
2005
Wood, lacquer
Installation views at
Galerie Gisela Capitain,
Cologne

A steel skeleton of a housing block – the type that, concrete-clad, took over the Polish landscape in fleets during the 1960s under communism – is crushed and squeezed into another symbolic Polish building: the country's pavilion in the Giardini at the Venice Biennale, a 1930s' symbol of national prestige. The violent force involved in twisting and crushing these huge beams of steel to fit inside the considerably lower structure of the pavilion, is strangely unapparent in the work, however, which seems instead to serenely inhabit its new home, a three-dimensional line drawing in space. Like a tree impeded from growing naturally and forced to adapt and twist its branches, it moulds itself within the confines of its habitat. The forcing together of these two obsolete forms of architecture becomes, then, an exercise in adaptability and conformity; a metaphor for the many lives forced to adjust to the social requirements of an antisocial architecture.

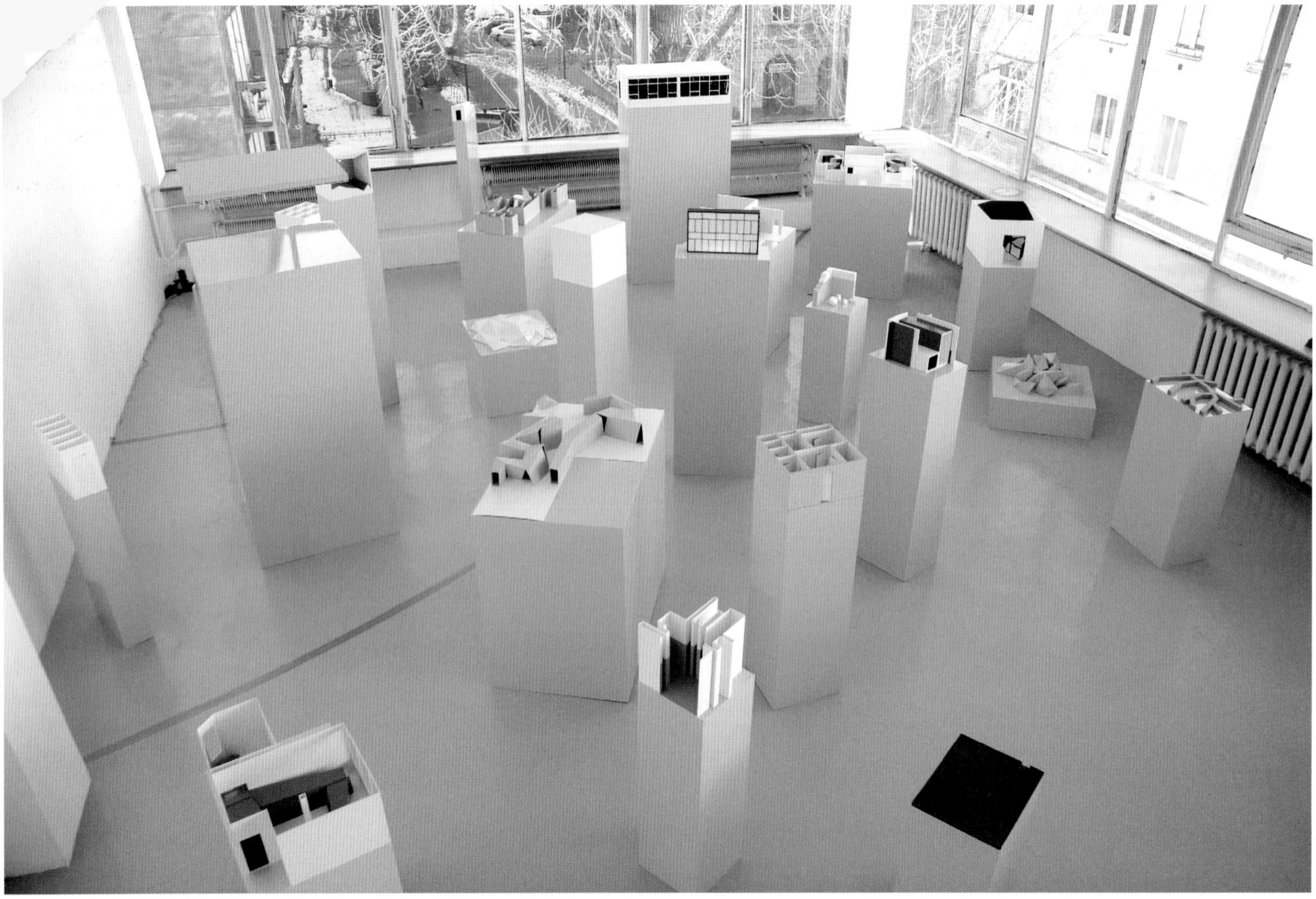

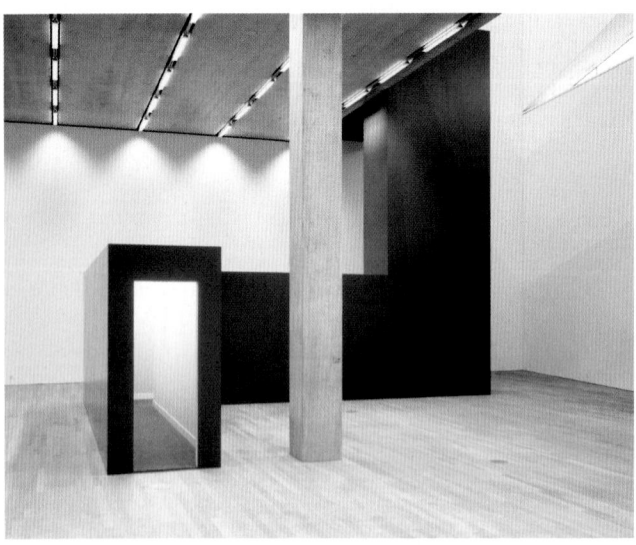

'Display'
2005
Mixed media
Installation view
at Foksal Gallery
Foundation, Warsaw

Corridor
2003
Mixed media
Installation view at
Schaulager, Basel, 2008

Though it is the skeleton of a life-sized building, it looks like a model, albeit a very large one, as its title, *1:1* (2007), corroborates. The piece raises an ambiguity central to many of Monika Sosnowska's works: to what extent should they be considered in architectural terms, and to what extent as sculpture? Is there a line that separates the functionality of one from the formalism of the other? Can the characteristics of one infect those of the other? Sosnowska has described her works as having a parasitical relationship to the architecture they inhabit. Usually determinedly site-specific, they borrow some of their site's characteristics (the doorway, the room, the walls of a corridor) but then abandon them to indulge their own perversely formal nature. Like Bruce Nauman's corridor works, they become what Paul Schimmel termed 'environments of controlled response';[1] works in which, as Nauman put it, 'somebody else would have the same experience instead of just having to watch me have that experience'.[2] In Nauman's case, the corridors evolved from props in his studios (the first one was built for the video *Walk with Contrapposto*, 1968) and relate to performance and the study of movement and perception in different types of space. For Sosnowka, however, these works engage the associative emotional triggers of architecture and a subjective psychological involvement with space. Her architectonic environments employ the decorative vocabulary of various institutions, from the dull green paint halfway up the walls in *Corridor* (2003) to the hospital-bright white walls and strip lighting of the looping labyrinthine corridor that invaded the whole of Kunstmuseum Liechtenstein (*Loop*, 2007). Though her works often draw on the communist brand of institutionalism she experienced growing up in 1970s' Poland, its vocabulary is generic enough to have a wide appeal. She engages not just a perceptual here-and-now, but an individual response to interior space based on memory and emotion.

However, Sosnowska's careful staging of illusion and disillusionment prevents her installations from simply being theatrical set pieces. While the clinical corridors of *Loop* insert an abstract space into a museum through which the audience can take an otherworldly tour, the illusion is fractured at the point where the outside of the corridor construction is suddenly visible, cutting through a gallery room at the end of the loop. From the reverse, the structure is all provisional plasterboard and metal framing, completely without psychological content or allusion. It appears in a gallery together with a small group of figurative paintings, chosen by Sosnowska from the museum collection. So we

Corridor courtesy: kurimanzutto, Mexico City; photograph: Tom Bisig • Display courtesy: Foksal Galery Foundation, Warsaw

To what extent should these structures be considered in architectural terms, and to what extent as sculpture?

Above:
Untitled
2008
Metal
c. 15×5×2 cm

Below:
1:1
2007
Steel
Installation view at the Polish Pavilion, 52nd Venice Biennale

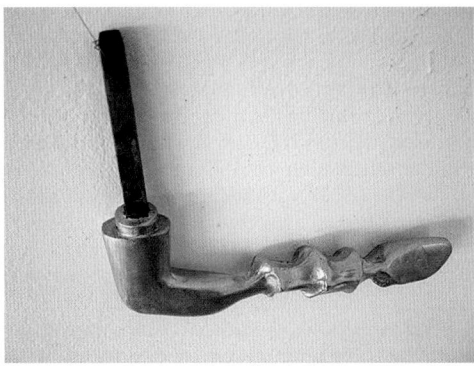

are encouraged here to read the structure in purely sculptural terms, as an object whose dimensionality contrasts with the paintings' flatness and the illusional depth they propose. The use-function and emotional engagement involved in an interior appreciation of the installation contrasts with this newly distanced exterior view. The interiority of architecture and exteriority of sculpture are revealed to be back to back, but separated by a gulf of alienation.

In his well-known study *The Poetics of Space* (1958), Gaston Bachelard observes that: 'Outside and inside form a dialectic of division, the obvious geometry of which blinds us as soon as we bring it into play in metaphorical dimensions. It has the sharpness of the dialectics of yes and no, which decides everything.'[3] Bachelard goes on to explain how this duality becomes inflicted with the notion of alienation, so that 'simple geometrical opposition becomes tinged with aggressivity. Formal opposition is incapable of remaining calm.' The intensity of Sosnowska's works is built on exactly this notion of an aggressive intervention into cool formal dialetics.

The emotional complexity of such an apparently simple dualism as inside/outside, extends to scale with the problematic notion: big or small. Robert Morris describes scale as the crucial element that affects the apprehension of sculptural objects: 'The size range of useless three-dimensional things is a continuum between the monument and the ornament.'[4] Scale is always related to the constant of the body, and an increase in scale brings with it a change in perception from a private, intimate appreciation 'essentially closed, spaceless, compressed and exclusive'[5], to a more public and physical appreciation: 'Things on a monumental scale [...] include more terms necessary for their apprehension than objects smaller than the body, namely, the literal space in which they exist and the kinaesthetic demands placed upon the body.' Sosnowska engages both these aspects of scale explicitly in a work such as *Untitled* (2005). Installed in Galerie Gisela Capitain, Cologne, a door-like aperture invited viewers to enter a black room-like structure that gradually diminished in size until they could no longer pass through, and were obliged to crouch, squat, kneel. The wide-open room morphed into the narrow tail of a shiny black beast: spaceless, compressed and exclusive. Scale is impressed on the participator in bluntly physical and experiential, as well as psychological, terms.

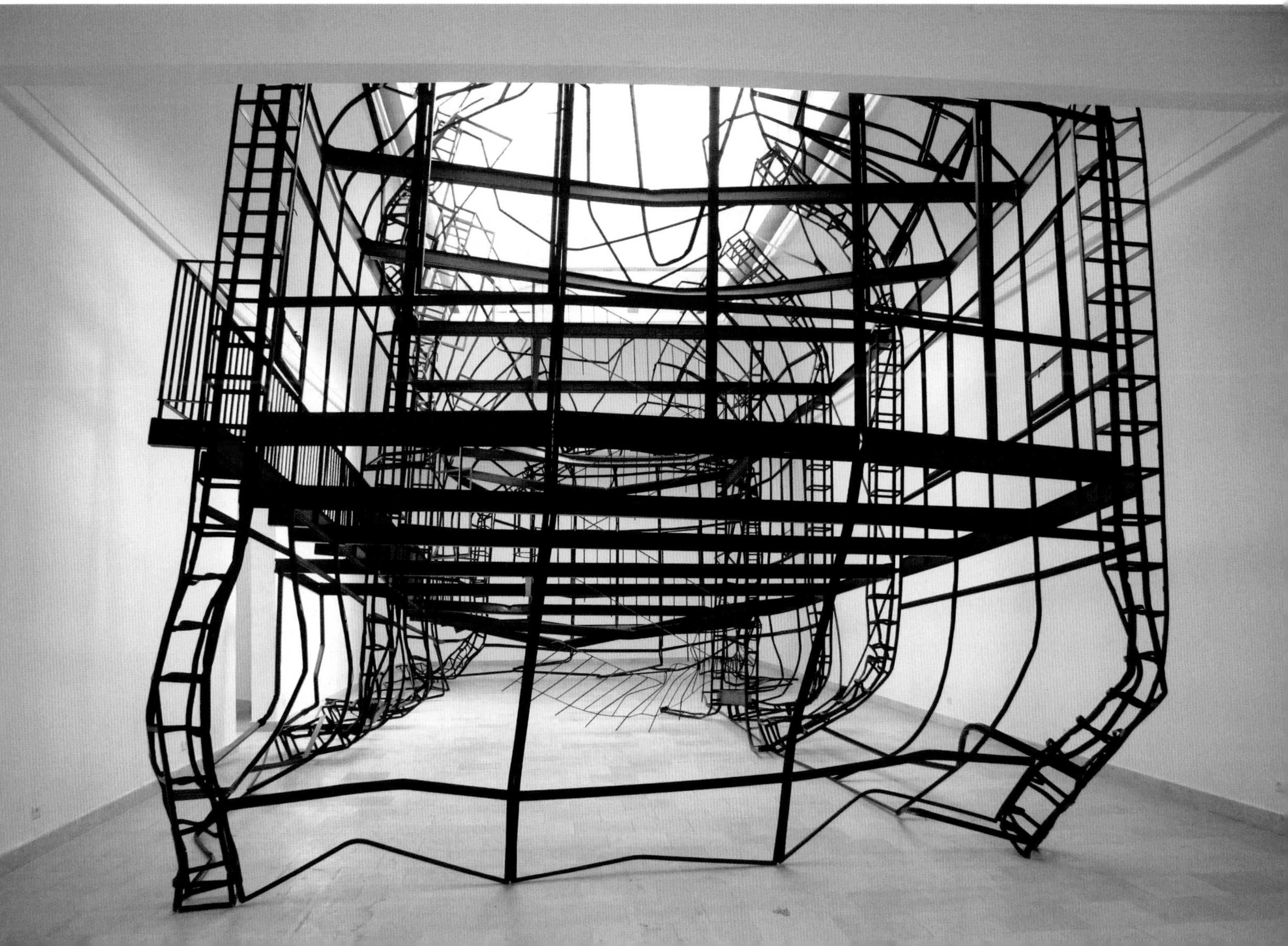

1:1 courtesy: Foksal Gallery Foundation, Warsaw; Galerie Gisela Capitain, Cologne; kurimanzutto, Mexico City and The Modern Institute/Toby Webster Ltd., Glasgow, and the artist • Untitled courtesy: Foksal Foundation for Contemporary Art, Warsaw

For Sosnowska, illusion is a quality of space, shown in all its variety in 'Display', an exhibition at the Foksal Gallery Foundation in Warsaw in 2005, where she showed a collection of models of previously completed projects. While models are always the starting point for her large-scale projects, here they formed a virtual city of absurd architectural possibilities. With the large-scale installations reduced to Lilliputian size, visitors were able to observe them from a great height, as mathematical conundrums, spatial impossibilities, variations on the idea of space and architecture in a playful, material sense. As Robert Smithson noted: 'It is well to remember that the seemingly topsy-turvy world revealed by Lewis Carroll did spring from a well ordered mathematical mind.'[6] Sosnowska's models suggest the Utopian brainstorming that led to the disasters of social housing projects, as much as Vladimir Tatlin-esque constructivist sculptures. These works engage the 'privateness' of appreciation their small scale allows, while also asserting an idea of the 'public-ness' that their large-scale realization calls for.

For her current exhibition at the Schaulager in Basel, Sosnowska looks again at the question of scale, but does so through a change in the scale of her works' architectural surroundings, rather than of the works themselves. This is the first time she has shown existing pieces together outside of the original sites that determined their formal specifics, but she addresses this problem by relating them all to their new site, explicitly in terms of scale. In the vast lower gallery of this Herzog & de Meuron-built exhibition and art storage space, from which all the dividing walls have been removed, Sosnowska's works appear like blown-up versions of the models in 'Display'. They are no longer site-specific installations, however, but objects that have shrunk relative to the size of the room in which they now find themselves: they are full-size models, all replicated on a scale of 1:1 – a fact recalled by the title of the show. Extracted from the confines of their original sites, these convoluted structures can now be seen from without in all their dimensionality. Their experiential element is sidelined as the illusions they conjure are revealed from the

Above:
Untitled
2006
Steel and enamel paint
Installation view at
Schaulager, Basel, 2008

As Robert Smithson noted: 'It is well to remember that the seemingly topsy-turvy world revealed by Lewis Carroll did spring from a well ordered mathematical mind.'

Right:
Corridor
2006/8
MDF, carpet, fluorescent lights
Installation view at
Schaulager, Basel, 2008

Left:
Concrete Ball
2008
Concrete and steel
Installation view at
Schaulager, Basel, 2008

start. Rather, we look at them as sculptures: their tendency towards the architectural is overshadowed by their arrangement as separate objects in a larger space – from the hulking but modest steel skeleton of *1:1*, squeezed in to fit under the ceiling here, to the landscape of tiny Tom Thumb houses lodged inside a paper bag (*Untitled*, 2003). Bachelard, again, puts it succinctly when he writes: 'Everything, even size, is a human value [...the] miniature can accumulate size. It is vast in its own way.'[7]

This curtain-lifting on the illusionistic nature of many of Sosnowska's works coincides with a shift in focus in her art from spatial illusion – which is narrative, time-based and experiential – to material illusionism, a confounding of expectations to do with the nature of materials. This is the case with the housing block skeleton of *1:1*, where its heavy steel frame assumed a lightness and flexibility completely at odds with the physical facts of its material. Or with the white cubic room that, door ajar and jammed between two exterior walls of the Sprengel Museum in Hanover, looked as if it had just dropped from the sky and got stuck there (*Untitled*, 2006); its crumpled walls seemingly formed from paper, but in fact made out of steel.

These transubstantiations have the effect of transforming the way we view Sosnowska's work, from a psycho-spatial experience to an anthropo-architectural one, in which solid matter can behave in an emotional, uncontrollable fashion. Such is the case with the banisters she made for the Foksal Gallery Foundation, as one stray railing defies the expectations of strict uniformity by running willy-nilly down the stairwell (*Hand Rail*, 2006). The Minimalist insistence on a physical appreciation of objects with regard to their materials is flipped by Sosnowska's suggestion of a psychological component to materials or their use-forms. The associations implied by earlier installations have, in recent works, transferred to the materials themselves, which seem to have taken on the memories of the institutional architecture they manifest. They run wild; they bend under the strain of expectations to conform; they are tired and floppy or crushed by the demands of the institution. In a tiny work in the Schaulager, a door handle is imprinted with the indentations of the hand that has squeezed it open and closed countless times (*Untitled*, 2008). At the other end of the scale is a huge concrete ball embedded with steel frames and trusses, with one stray rod flailing out of it like an expressive arm (*Concrete Ball*, 2008). It appears like a wrecking ball that has absorbed the remnants of the building it was knocking down; the act of destruction has turned into a creative moment, and documents its own production. Architecture intertwines with individual psyche, and seems to imply that we leave an imprint on buildings as much as architecture imprints on us.

In the catalogue for Sosnowska's exhibition at the Polish Pavilion in Venice, Tomasz Fudala wrote: 'One can read into the architecture of the period all of the ailments of communist reality.'[8] Likewise, the current architectural landscape in Poland can be read as the culmination of attempts by the post-communist population to adjust to its current reality. While some of the antisocial housing structures have been knocked down, many more have been modified with cosmetic measures: a bright new cladding, a fresh coat of paint on a dull grey façade. These obsolescent architectural styles are still a reality for many, and Sosnowska addresses the catalogue of ailments they bring with them in her sculptures, as materials that either conform against their nature or resist their expected functions. A concrete public fountain bubbles up filthy water as if from the ailing bowels of the national bedrock (*Dirty Fountain*, 2006), while the ceiling in a corridor drips steadily into a puddle on the floor (*The Fountain*, 2006). Decay, decline and ruin become as omnipresent as skirting boards or stairwells. They are inevitable. In Smithsonesque terms, the ruin becomes the monument itself, but Sosnowska builds her ruins from scratch, hybrid Modernist-futuro follies for a post-Utopian era.

Kirsty Bell is a writer living in Berlin.

Ⓢ Find out more at frieze.com

1 Paul Schimmel, *Bruce Nauman*, ed. Joan Simon, Walker Art Center, Minneapolis, and Wiese Verlag, Basel, 1994, p. 77
2 op. cit. p. 78
3 Gaston Bachelard, *The Poetics of Space*, Beacon Press, Boston, 1969, p. 211
4 Robert Morris, 'Notes on Sculpture, Part 2' *Artforum*, vol. 5, no. 2, October 1966
5 ibid.
6 Robert Smithson, *Robert Smithson: The Collected Writings*, ed. Jack Flam, University of California Press, Berkeley, 1996, p. 21
7 op. cit. p. 215
8 Tomasz Fudala, 'A Dream of Prefabricated Houses' in *Monika Sosnowska*, Polish Pavilion, 52nd International Art Exhibition, Venice, Zacheta National Gallery of Art, Warsaw, 2007, p. 32

Loop
2007
Mixed media
Installation view
at Kunstmuseum
Liechtenstein, Vaduz

I was running late, which is easy to do here. My taxi was stopped by a police officer, and the driver, depressed about the ticket, couldn't find the building. His old Russian Lada coughed its way about the pitted streets of Nuevo Vedado until I decided to try my luck on foot. I stopped the first person I came across. He asked me whom I was looking for. 'Roberto Gottardi,' I told him, 'the architect'. 'Ah,' he nodded, 'Señor Gottardi.' He led me to an old, Soviet-style apartment building of stained concrete and pointed up. 'Fifth floor,' he said.

The first half of this story takes place in Havana, in the actual city, with its actual skies, actual poinciana trees and salt-air decay. The second half takes place in another, less stubbornly material Havana, in the Havana of fantasy and nostalgia – which is to say, in Miami. You'll have to find the other halves in the spaces between these two. But for now, Havana, a city that, perhaps more than most, wears its past atop its present – like a baggy suit, like a paste diamond, like a lousy marriage, like the silence that follows a fit of laughter, like a headache, like a suit that's much too tight.

I was sweating by the time Gottardi came to the door – no elevator, tropical heat – but his apartment was as cool as a cave. He had an air-conditioner, which denotes relative prosperity in Cuba, and what little sunlight passed through the window was tamed by

in Havana in January 1959. Like many European leftists, he was enthralled by Cuba's revolution. In Caracas he had met a Cuban architect named Ricardo Porro, a young radical who had fled Fulgencio Batista's government. Porro returned to Havana and invited Gottardi and another Italian architect, Vittorio Garatti, to join him. Their talents were sorely needed, as half of the island's architects had left. A new nation was to be built, and not only that. Cuba intended to construct, in Che Guevara's words, a 'new man'.

Gottardi arrived in December 1960. The following month, as legend has it, Castro and Guevara played a round of golf on what had until recently been the manicured greens of the Havana Country Club, a few miles west of the capital. The society they envisioned had no place for country clubs, so the two revolutionaries agreed to build an art school. Culture would be no longer a commodity hoarded by the wealthy but the birthright of the people. It would begin here, where the rich had played, created by the children of the poor.

Castro assigned the project to Porro, who brought on Gottardi and Garatti. None of the architects had any experience with such scale, but then, Gottardi pointed out with eyebrows raised, 'the revolution meant that anything was possible'.

Above:
Roofscape of the School of Plastic Arts
1965

Opposite:
Aerial view of the School of Modern Dance
1965

Havana and its doubles

Novelist Ben Ehrenreich explores the history of Cuba's National Art schools – a tale that reflects the hopes and failures of a revolution

a pane of green glass. The walls were lined with paintings and books. A folding partition broke the room in half, concealing an unmade bed and a wooden scale model of Gottardi's latest design for the School of Dramatic Arts.

Gottardi – a fit, energetic man of 77 with a white handlebar moustache – welcomed me inside. He and his wife, the actress and dancer Luz María Collazo, have lived in the same small apartment for 30 years. 'In Cuba', he said with a smile, 'we don't have a choice.'

But there was nothing like self-pity in the old architect's voice, and no trace of bitterness. He was more excited than he'd been in years. After decades of abandonment and nearly eight years of delays, construction was finally set to resume on the National Art Schools. In his old age Gottardi may see the grandest dream of his youth made real; only a certain wary calm tempered his enthusiasm. He told me the story of the art schools, which is at the same time the story of the Cuban revolution, of its saddest failures and its most ebullient hopes. Born and educated in Venice, Gottardi was working in Caracas when Fidel Castro's victory march arrived

The schools would be located on five campuses, and Gottardi would design the School of Dramatic Arts. Aside from a few basic directives, the architects were given complete creative licence. 'The euphoria of that time', he told me, 'is difficult to describe'. But 47 years later it still lit his eyes and lifted the timbre of his voice.

They worked night and day. Gottardi described the process as being like an intoxication, a euphoric spell that he couldn't quite shake off. Musicians and dancers practised on the lawns as masons worked around them. Everyone lent a hand. The project was not merely inspired by revolutionary ideals – it embodied them. The buildings themselves were extraordinary, departing equally from the chilly Modernism that had dominated the architecture of the time and from the colonial Neo-Classicism that had preceded it. Porro designed the School of Modern Dance as an explosive complex of interconnected, fragmentary vaults. His School of Plastic Arts turned to Cuba's African roots – a surreally erotic sub-Saharan village recast in brick among the palms. The

All images courtesy: John A. Loomis • Photographs this page and opposite: Paolo Gasparini

Photograph: Paolo Gasparini

**Aerial view of the
School of Plastic Arts**
1965

**The School of Plastic Arts
turned to Cuba's African
roots – a surreally erotic
sub-Saharan village recast in
brick among the palms.**

cupolas of Garatti's School of Ballet curved
through a ravine and his School of Music
wound like a lizard's tail tracing the banks of
the river that limned the old club.

Gottardi's School of Drama, a complex
of airy classrooms surrounding a central
amphitheatre, strived to recreate the intimacy
and spontaneity of urban space. Brick-walled
corridors curved like alleys in a North African medina. Sight lines were intentionally
obscured, 'so that you wouldn't know what's
coming', Gottardi said. 'Like life.'

On 26 July 1965, though they were far from
complete, the National Art Schools were officially declared open. But their inauguration
was also a death sentence; construction would
never resume.

A lot had changed in four years. Porro's conviction, expressed years later to the architecture scholar John A. Loomis, that 'architecture
must add a poetic dimension to everyday life',
no longer fitted the prevailing ideology. Castro
began to lean towards a Soviet model. The art
schools' ecstatic organicism suddenly reeked
of heresy. Their design, possessed as it was by
revolution, was accused of being 'insufficiently
revolutionary'. Gottardi repeated the phrase
with a tired shrug.

In the end only Porro's buildings were sub-
stantially completed; Garatti's music school
was not even half done. Although most of the
classrooms were finished, the theatre at the
centre of Gottardi's drama school would never
be built. Its winding corridors converged on
empty space. The metaphors are impossible to
resist: as the years passed, Castro's revolution
grew more stultified, and the art schools lan-
guished. Roots and vines ate at the mortar and

cracked the terracotta tiles. Looters took what
they could. The revolution's bright dream was
pilfered and abandoned.

Porro left Cuba for Paris in 1966. Garatti was
briefly gaoled in 1974, accused of espionage. He
returned to Italy. Gottardi stayed on. He has
remained humbly faithful to the revolution,
although it has not always repaid his loyalty
with kindness. 'He was marginalized,' one
acquaintance of Gottardi's later told me. 'He
won't talk about it, but it really broke his spirit
for a little while.'

Not long after the publication in 1999 of
Revolution of Forms, Loomis' monograph about
the art schools, Castro attended a conference on Cuban architecture. One architect
present bravely reminded the President of
the art schools' shameful state. Two days later
Gottardi, Porro and Garatti were informed
that construction would resume – the schools
would finally be finished. The three architects
'were like schoolboys', Loomis recalled. They
were 'bouncing off the walls'.

Workers began cleaning the site, uprooting
plants to forestall further decay. A guard was
posted to discourage looters, but nothing else
happened for years. The art schools made the
World Monuments Fund's list of the world's
most endangered treasures in 2000 and in
2002. They had been nominated in 1996, along
with the Taj Mahal and Angkor Wat, but no
one in the Cuban government was willing to
sign off on the application, and the nomination
was dropped.

In recent months the momentum had
picked up again. 'Next week we will finally
break ground.' He was still waiting for his
plans to be approved, Gottardi said, clearing

the books from his desk. The officials supervising the project had wanted to proceed as though nothing had changed, but the architect had refused. We lifted the wooden maquette from its place behind the partition and laid it out on the corner of the desk. His new design was harsher and less organic than the original. Angled metal roofs would replace the vaulted brickwork. It was also more flexible – the roofs could be adjusted by hand to accommodate the movement of the sun. 'I am not the same man I was when I was 30,' Gottardi observed with a smile that was at once sad and triumphant. 'And Cuba is not the same country.'

.

The second half of this story is set in another Havana – not the city of two million inhabitants in which I met Gottardi, but a place more ethereal, more blurred, and perhaps even more decayed by age. This half is set in Havana as it is remembered and as it is imagined. It takes place, therefore, in the Miami suburb of Kendall, in a drab, stucco subdivision of low-slung townhouses, ample parking, leaning palms. 'This is not a city,' the architect Nicolás Quintana told me, dismissing the world outside his home with an impatient wave of his bandaged arm.

Quintana, who is 82, has not been back to Cuba since 8 January 1960. He had just been released from hospital – he had fallen a few days earlier, and the back of his head was still bandaged, as were both of his wrists. He was unable to stand, and remained seated for the length of our conversation, swivelling about his office on the castors of his chair. His injuries did not appear to have depleted him. 'My foundations are weak, but my roof doesn't leak – yet,' he joked with good cheer that was only slightly forced.

An air-conditioner hummed somewhere. The room was bright, its walls lined with glossy colour photos of Quintana's grandchildren, a faded diploma from the University of Havana, several framed architectural drawings – a hotel in Rio de Janeiro, the master plan for the Cuban beach city of Varadero, the National Bank building in Havana.

A few months before he left Cuba for good, Quintana met Guevara. Quintana had been commissioned to design a new National Bank, and the raffish *guerrillero* had been appointed as the bank's president. He had his boots off, Quintana remembered, and his toes protruded from the holes in his socks. He asked Quintana if he was a petit bourgeois. Quintana answered that he was not. 'Then you're a revolutionary', Guevara said. Quintana demurred. 'Look, Comandante', he responded, 'the man who tends my storerooms is a bourgeois. I am a *gran* bourgeois.'

Quintana was the son of one of the most successful builders in Cuba. He was also part of a generation of young architects (including Porro) determined to throw off the shackles of Beaux-Arts convention in favour of a distinctly Cuban brand of Modernism. 'We formed a bloc in everything and against everything,' Porro would later write of his friendship with Quintana and Frank Martínez, another of their classmates. 'We were three Quixotes ready to organize a crusade against the infidels. We

Roofscape of the School of Music
1963

Entrance of the School of Modern Dance
1965

School of Modern Dance photograph: Paolo Gasparini · Roofscape photograph: Mayito

The School of Ballet during construction, with the shower room enclosure on the left and the scaffolded dance pavilion on the right
1961

Interior view of the Dance Pavilion, School of Modern Dance
1965

were the most revolutionary, the most surprising.' Despite their political differences and the distance between them, Quintana still phones Porro, he told me, 'every time I have a chance'. (Quintana spoke admiringly of the National Art Schools, although he saw them not as an abandoned beginning but as an end, 'the swan song of Cuban Modernism' after which 'Cuban architecture as a movement was totally destroyed'.)

While still students, Quintana and Porro symbolized their break with the canon by staging a public burning of the texts of Giacomo Barozzi da Vignola in the plaza at the University of Havana. 'The thing got out of control', Quintana laughed, slightly embarrassed at the memory. He spent three days in gaol. 'My father didn't want to get me out.' Quintana *père* had, after all, designed the Beaux-Arts building in which the School of Architecture was housed.

Quintana's progressivism did not end with aesthetics. In 1958 he passed topographical maps of the Escambray mountains, where Guevara was still fighting, to Castro's 26th of July Movement. 'I wasn't supporting the Movement', he clarified. 'I was supporting getting rid of Batista. You could call it a mistake.' Within a year the architect had joined a group of professionals who were clandestinely conspiring against the new socialist government. Guevara found him out. At their final meeting he gave the architect three choices: exile, prison or the firing squad.

Quintana fled to Caracas, taking with him his family, his art collection, his books and his cars. He arrived one year before Gottardi made the opposite migration. The National Bank was never built as he'd designed it. In fact, in the end it was constructed not as a bank but as the towering Hermanos Ameijeiras Hospital, which became a symbol of Cuba's greatest revolutionary pride, its healthcare system. Quintana disowned the building, which he has called 'a faithful physical representation of the concept ofthe absurd'.

In Venezuela, Quintana raced Porsches for a while. He moved to Puerto Rico, then back to Caracas before settling in Miami, which he called 'the cemetery of the elephants'. He laid out the master plans for several Latin American cities, designed hotels, condominiums, a sports arena. But it was his latest project that he referred to as 'the most sweeping and cherished of my entire life'. Called 'Havana and Its Landscapes: A City towards the Future', it was at the same time an attempt, Quintana told me, to re-conquer the past. 'They have stolen history from us,' he said.

The assumption behind the project was the same one that had fuelled Miami politics for a generation: at some point Castro would die, the market would triumph, the exiles would be free to return. (Never mind that Castro had already ceded power and that his government appeared more stable than ever: these were articles of faith.) Investors would step in to rebuild Havana, or so the credo went, and Quintana's project was meant to provide a template for the new city that would emerge.

So for the past three years, with the help of his students at Florida International University and substantial funding from the American housing giants Century and Lennar Homes (to American investors Cuba is a vast blank slate, an untapped market conveniently close to home; when the rush starts, no one wants to be left behind) Quintana has been revisiting the city of his birth – without, of course, setting foot on the island. His plans are ambitious: he would like to see the city return to its population density in 1959, which means that overcrowded sections of the old downtown would have to be emptied and rebuilt. The most dilapidated buildings would be replaced with parks. Satellite imaging has made things easier. 'We can identify the buildings that are in bad shape without actually going there,' Quintana enthused. 'We can tell how many people are living in the buildings.'

Quintana whirled over to the computer and with a few clicks of the mouse opened a 3-D animation of the 'satellite cities' he envisioned for Havana's periphery: clusters of sleek, interconnected towers bridged by pedestrian walkways. Instead of suburban shopping centres, Quintana planned 'urban activity centres' that would combine housing, office space and entertainment. 'A new thing will emerge.' The city would be reoriented towards its now-industrial bay. Port facilities would be relocated to Mariel, about 40 kilometres west of the capital. Shopping centres would overlook the water. 'The Bay of Havana will become the most important tourist bay in the Americas.'

The architect was about to turn his attention to the Malecón, the city's seafront boulevard. Aided by satellite images and digital photos sent by friends in Cuba, his students would construct a 12-foot model – one of

Dance Pavilion photograph: Paolo Gasparini • School of Ballet photograph: Michelena

**Aerial view of the
School of Ballet**
1965

28 maquettes they planned to build replicating every single building along the Malecón's miles-long expanse. Among them, inevitably, would be Quintana's Hermanos Ameijeiras Hospital. Ironically, it was the Cuban government's infrastructural neglect, which Quintana decried at every opportunity, that made his project possible. Physically, at least, Havana had remained largely unchanged. In one paper Quintana referred to it not as a living city but as 'the archive of our history that speaks to us of the past'.

And – more irony – his greatest concern was not the ongoing decay caused by salt, humidity and time but the more active assaults of capitalism. 'If massive investment comes into Havana, it could simply turn into something else', Quintana worried. And that something else, the sort of subdivided overdevelopment that has transformed the American landscape over the last few decades (with the eager assistance of Quintana's corporate sponsors), was anathema to the architect's mid-century Modernist vision of urbanism. He has called suburbanization 'anti-Cuban ... anti-historic, anti-economic, antisocial and absolutely stupid'. Only Havana, he told me, 'hasn't been lost yet'.

Before I left Quintana, I asked him whether it was discouraging that his plans remained in the realm of the imaginary. 'The guy will die,'

he answered with a shrug, referring, of course, to Castro. But Quintana is one year older than the former Cuban president. I asked him if he expected to see the changes he had been waiting for since 1960. He didn't hesitate. 'I don't think it will take more than two more years.'

Gottardi and Quintana met once, it turns out, a few years ago, on Gottardi's last visit to the USA. (The Bush administration has since made cultural exchange visas nearly impossible for Cubans to obtain.) Gottardi went to Miami, and the two architects spent a day together. They got along quite well, it seems. Quintana remembered the day fondly. 'We think differently about politics,' he said. 'That's all.'

I emailed Gottardi to ask him what he remembered of the meeting. He didn't write back, but I didn't worry too much about it. Internet communication is difficult in Cuba and tightly controlled. Months after I left Havana, though, I heard through a friend that he was doing well, and busy. He was still waiting to hear if his plans had been approved. Construction had not yet begun.

Ben Ehrenreich's novel The Suitors *is published by Harcourt (2006). He lives in Los Angeles.*

Fidel Castro and Che Guevara played a round of golf in the former Havana Country Club. The society they envisioned had no place for country clubs, so they agreed instead to build an art school on the site.

Back

Flow

Studio Museum of Harlem, New York, USA

Entering 'Flow', the Studio Museum's latest survey exhibition dedicated to emerging artists from Africa under the age of forty, you pass a map of the world. Placed adjacent to a substantial wall text, the map is overlaid with a graphic that records what Paul Gilroy once described as the 'patterns of flow and itinerancy that characterize outer-national adventure and cross-cultural creativity'. In simpler terms, the graphic records the 'where from' and 'where now' of the show's 20 artists, four of whom still live on the continent, while the rest live and work beyond Africa's 'salt borders', to borrow from Wole Soyinka.

Neatly executed, the map/graphic ably illustrates the show's conceptual premiss. Not only does it suggest the complex 'ecologies of belonging', as Gilroy phrases it in his landmark book *The Black Atlantic* (1993), but it also reveals 'the opposition between geography and genealogy'. The net result is an expansive, evolutionary statement about contemporary

Otobong Nkanga
Alterscape Stories:
Spilling Waste
(detail)
2006
C-type prints
Diptych, 1×1 m each

African art, one that necessarily acknowledges 'the multiple ways people, resources, cultures and ideas move', to quote the exhibition's curator, Christine Y. Kim. Fittingly, the ideological lobbying ends here.

Installed across two floors, 'Flow' introduces itself with a set of fences used in horse jumping. While Mounir Fatmi's *Obstacles* (2007) don't exactly trip you up, the curatorial intention is clear: these objects, painted in bright stripes, are meant to interrupt the viewer's flow from outside in. The implied metaphor – of impasse and arrest – although achingly self-conscious, is easy to grasp, which may explain why Simon Njami used the work to introduce the final, Johannesburg version of his sprawling group exhibition 'Africa Remix', which, despite extensive travelling, never made it to the USA.

'Flow' includes four artists spotlighted by 'Africa Remix': Fatmi, Moshekwa Langa, Otobong Nkanga and Michele Magema. The South African-born Langa's work is thoughtfully hung near the entrance – thoughtful because Langa has long worked with free-association maps, which range from cryptic diagrams and quasi-cartographic renderings to allusive visual taxonomies. Unfortunately the selection here isn't always very good, with Langa's three works offering poor rehearsals of earlier ideas and moods.

Like Langa, Nkanga lives between Amsterdam and Paris and also works across a range of media. In *Alterscape Stories: Spilling Waste* and *Uprooting the Past* (both 2006), a photographic diptych and triptych, the artist looms, silhouetted and god-like, over a mountainous diorama, its bare rocky topography and spare urbanism echoing scenes from Nkanga's birthplace in northern Nigeria. Similar to *Stripped Bare* (2003), an investigative series of photographs shown in 'Africa Remix', depicting single homesteads in lush vegetation, Nkanga's performative photography is less captivating, though, than her acrylic, ink and watercolour works on paper (five of which are shown), that state her interests in architecture and topography with greater poise.

For a show with continental ambitions it is unsurprising that 'Flow' the narrative threads are often strained. Paradoxically, this – and the speculative conversations it prompts – is also the show's strength. One such exchange happens between the Nigerian Olalekan B.

Jeyifous, whose architectural models are more Buckminster Fuller than Bodys Isek Kingelez, and the Eritrean Dawit L. Petros, in whose photograph a handful of snow is offered as a mountain. Installed in close proximity on the mezzanine level, the two Brooklyn residents proffer imaginative possibilities.

A similar reliance on imagination marks the portraiture. Eschewing physiognomy, Thierry Fontaine hides his face behind shells, cracked mirrored glass and a wet mask of white clay. The Réunion-born photographer's refusal to be fixed by the lens recalls Morocco's Hicham Benohoud, whose *Version Soft* (2003) series of portraits, shown in 'Africa Remix', similarly masked subjectivity with surreal props. In a similar vein, Grace Ndiritu's slow building but fun DVD projection *The Nightingale* (2003) shows the London-based artist manically wrapping and rewrapping her head to a pop soundtrack by Baaba Maal. By contrast, Mustafa Maluka's sitters are visible and distinct. His large-scale acrylic and oil portraits of hipsters, however, teeter on the edge of kitsch. (Perhaps this is where they find their momentum.) Kehinde Wiley is an obvious reference, as is late Andy Warhol, whose rudimentary technique Maluka's generic archive echoes.

Given the revisionist agenda underpinning the display of contemporary African art in the decades since 'Primitivism in 20th-Century Art' (1984) and 'Magiciens de la Terre' (Magicians of the Earth, 1989), 'Flow' cannot claim to be groundbreaking. In this sense the show functions like the auxiliary of the sanitation trucks that flash past Latifa Echakhch's motionless camera as it records the mop-up activities following a street demonstration in Marseille. The frenzied action having passed, it is now time to tidy up, consolidate and take stock. 'Flow' achieves this admirably, without hectoring or fuss.

Sean O'Toole

Mustafa Maluka
I'm not going anywhere, this is home
2006
Acrylic and oil on canvas
183×133 cm

Cristina Lucas
Rousseau y Sophie
2007
DVD still

Montehermoso Cultural Centre, Vitoria-Gasteiz, Spain

A day in my life: on the morning of a recent trip to Spain to visit 'The Furious Gaze' – a show considering 'feminism as a source of knowledge that is vital for understanding the world we live in' – I receive an invitation to a show in the UK that includes one woman out of 15 artists, yet it's not a show about masculinity: it's about 'play', something the curators have obviously decided women artists know nothing about. On the plane I read that the Spanish Prime Minister, José Luis Rodríguez Zapatero has received a mixed reaction to Spain's first female-majority cabinet; I also read that the Office for National Statistics has announced that women in their 40s in Britain earn 20 percent less per hour than their male counterparts. When I land in Bilbao, I pop into the Guggenheim to see 'Art in the USA: Three Hundred Years of Innovation', a survey of 'the art of a nation struggling to define itself during the first centuries of its existence', curated by Thomas Krens, Susan Davidson, Elizabeth Kennedy and Nancy Mowll Mathews. It is, apparently, the most significant display of American art ever seen in Spain. Although there are around 200 often brilliant works on display, only five women artists are represented, despite the fact that the show declares itself 'a composite picture of the American experience – its myths, dreams, ordeals and vulnerabilities'. *Composite*? Rarely have I witnessed such a breathtaking gulf between curatorial intention and actuality. I mean, *come on*!

All of which is a lengthy way of explaining why, before I had even seen it, I welcomed the premise of 'The Furious Gaze', whose co-curators – Xabier Arakistain, Director of the Montehermoso Cultural Centre, and Maura Reilly, Curator of the Elizabeth A. Sackler Center for Feminist Art at the Brooklyn Museum in New York – see feminism 'as an essential framework for investigating visual works that deal with situations of inequality experienced by women'. The show takes its title from a term coined by the Spanish philosopher Amelia Valcárcel. In her text *La Política de las mujeres* (The Politics of Women, 1996) she describes the situation of women who, having reached their 30s assuming that discrimination against women is a thing of the past, have their expectations shattered by the realization of a glass ceilings in the workplace. To accompany 'The Furious Gaze' Arakistain also programmed the 'Contraseñas/Passwords' project, inviting 12 Spanish and international curators and theorists to 'document the many lines of criticism and artistic creation based on feminist viewpoints that have been developed in an audiovisual format since the 1960s'.

'The Furious Gaze' included work by 20 women artists from Afghanistan, Australia, Ireland, Italy, Japan, the Netherlands, Spain, Sweden, the UK and the USA who are around the age of those in Valcárcel's study – that's to say, in their 30s and 40s. Although most of these artists use gender and sexuality as their starting-point, their work is wildly divergent. Highlights included: Andrea Bowers' installation of a video and posters (the latter made especially for this exhibition), *Letters to an Army of Three* (2005/8), which records 30 men and women reading letters sent to 1960s' abortion rights activists; the Afghan artist Lida Abdul's video of the artist washing an Afghan rug with an ice-block; Italian artist Lara Favaretto's photograph of men holding up a donkey (*Mondo alla Rovescia*, The World Back-to-Front, 2002), and her mysterious installation *Prima* (2005), which comprised five air canisters

The Furious Gaze

and childrens' party whistles; and the Japanese artist Yurie Nagashima's deadpan photograph of a heavily pregnant woman giving the viewer an adamant finger – an unambiguous response to Nobuyoshi Araki's hugely popular photographs of Japanese women in bondage. Humour bubbled near the surface of many of the works, including the Australian artist Tracey Moffat's hilarious video collage of moments from classic films exploring relationships between men and women, *Love* (2003), and the US artist Kathe Burkhart's super-camp series of paintings 'Liz Taylor' (2002). I kept returning to two slapstick videos by the Spanish artist Cristina Lucas: *Rousseau y Sophie* (2007) is her response to Jean-Jacques Rousseau's theories about women as expounded in his book *Emile: or, On Education* (1762), in which the French philosopher wrote of men and women: 'One ought to be active and strong, the other passive and weak [...] it follows that woman is made specially to please man.' Lucas' riposte? To film women and children banging, laughing at, mocking and thumbing their noses at Rousseau's statue in a park in Madrid to the accompaniment of a brass band. Opposite this video was *Tú también puedes caminar* (You Can Walk Too, 2006) Lucas' retort to the passage in Virginia Woolf's essay *A Room of One's Own* (1929) in which Woolf quotes the words of a prominent music critic: 'Of Mlle. Germaine Tailleferre one can only repeat Dr Johnson's dictum [...] "Sir, a woman's composing is like a dog's walking on his hind legs. It is not done well, but you are surprised to find it done at all."' Lucas' film shows a series of remarkable dogs, walking on their hind legs, much to the merriment of bystanders.

Arakistain has made it clear that while this is the first major show he has curated at this extraordinary space, he intends feminism to continue to be integral to future exhibitions at the centre. This is as it should be: women represented fairly not as the exception but as a matter of course. Despite evidence to the contrary, it shouldn't be that difficult.

Jennifer Higgie

Lara Favaretto
Mondo alla Rovescia
(The World Back-to-Front)
2002
Photograph
180×240 cm

Bas Jan Ader
Primary Time
1974
Video still

The Museum of Modern Art, New York, USA

When I started learning about the art of the 1960s, about ten years ago, the period seemed book-ended by two texts: Clement Greenberg's *After Abstract Expressionism* (1962), which accounted for the importance of colour in the paintings of Barnett Newman and Mark Rothko, and Lucy Lippard's *Six Years* (1972), which chronicled the work of countless Conceptual artists. Colour seemed anathema to the latter group, who, one initially supposed, banished it from their work. But once one took a closer look at Lippard's artists, it became clear that almost all of them were interested in colour – just not in the way that had been important to their predecessors. Colour instead was interesting as a ready-made material, as a product of new industries and technologies. Colour was something to be not so much mixed on the palette as found on cars and clothing or in domestic interiors. Curator Ann Temkin's 'Color Chart' examines at this alternative approach to colour, concentrating on the 1960s but looking back to Marcel Duchamp (the colour swatches in *Tu'm*, 1918) and forward too.

The first few galleries were the strongest parts of the show: it was wonderful to see *Tu'm*

and Robert Rauschenberg's *Rebus* (1955) in one glance and clever too, to have Frank Stella's six-part suite of paintings from 1962 (once owned by Andy Warhol) brought together with a set of Warhol's six smallish *Marilyns* (1962), a chromatic juxtaposition that did much to undermine any residual claims that posit a complete separation between Minimalism and Pop.

One of the show's strongest arguments was to indicate how colour became a battlefield on which younger artists confronted their elders. The ways in which they fought revealed much about their sensibilities. Bas Jan Ader's arrangements of flowers in Piet Mondrian's colours (*Primary Time*, 1974) was a tender skirmish, and a witty one (all those green stalks would have infuriated the Dutchman). By contrast Richard Serra fought Joseph Albers (his former teacher) more aggressively. In *Color-Aid* (1970-1), shown as a video but which makes better sense as a film, Serra let the camera frame be filled with a single colour. From time to time his finger intrudes into the frame to remove the colour, which we realize is a sheet of card in a stack of the kind that Albers used to teach with. As each sheet is removed, we begin to concentrate less on the papers' colours than on Serra's fingers. As they press down, blood

Color Chart

drains out, turning them from pink to yellow, but the dirt under his nails is pretty constant. Serra thus exchanges the colour combinations that the cards might provide with the real colour of the body.

'Color Chart' also revealed how the most seemingly ordered and anti-subjective approaches to colour generated unexpected affects. Blinky Palermo bought off-the-shelf cloth and simply stitched lengths together, but the straightforwardness of this process belies the optical play generated where a blue meets a red in *Untitled* (1969). Alighiero Boetti had square panels coated with industrial paint whose brand names he then attached to the panels, using letters made of painted cork. For all that this seemed to be about doubling (the work presents both a colour and its name), brand names such as 'Oro Longchamp' don't just identify the colour: they set our thoughts on metals and racecourses. This vaguely humorous operation was picked up by John Baldessari and especially Bruce Nauman, whose photocopy of a colour chart replaced its colour with a range of greys that have since turned to browns.

It was a surprise that Temkin decided not to include the work of Brazilians working so intently with colour at this time. Even if they did not use colour charts, the 'rules' of her exhibition seemed flexible enough to have included, for instance, Lygia Pape's *Wheel of Delights* (1968), a circle of bowls of unpredictably flavoured coloured water. Such quibbles aside, the historical parts of the show made significant arguments that will surely alter the way this period is understood. The latter sections were more problematic (around a third of the space was devoted to work of the last 15 years). It was certainly important to indicate the ways in which more recent artists have addressed colour and race together, but some of the works did little to demonstrate really new thinking about colour. Thankfully, the show closed with a piece whose quirky humour matched its experimental intelligence. In 2000 Christopher Williams attempted to record the brand colours of Agfa, Kodak and Fuji by using film and developing materials produced by each company to photograph a dishwasher stacked with plates whose colours corresponded to the companies' logos. (For Kodak the plates are mainly yellow with some red.) This investigation into the connection between commerce and colour picked up a strand from the earlier part of the show, but Williams was also able to point to a moment of failure: Agfa's products cannot, he realized, accurately reproduce the company's own brand colours, which come out too red. If many artists in the show seemed to celebrate the new colours of an industrial world, by pointing to this tiniest discrepancy between a brand's image and its product, Williams laid the confidence of capital to question.

Mark Godfrey

Richard Bell
Australian Art It's an Aboriginal Thing
2006
Synthetic polymer paint on canvas
240×360 cm

National Gallery of Australia, Canberra

As Indigenous art continues to grow in popularity in Australia and abroad, new art centres are established in communities and new artists emerge, it now seems a good moment to take stock of its recent developments. In this respect 'Culture Warriors: National Indigenous Art Triennial '07' is an appropriate vehicle for such reflection.

This inaugural show was scheduled to coincide with the 25th anniversary of the opening of the National Gallery of Australia (NGA) to the public. At its inception in October 1982 the first gallery featured masterworks from each of the collection areas: from Gianbattista Tiepolo to Fred Williams, from Buddhist sculpture to New Guinea figures and Mayan ceramics. At the entrance to the room, however, hung bark paintings by George Garrawun and Jimmy Njiminjuma, to announce the fact that the artistic traditions unique to this country have their place within the great art traditions of the world.

Six years later, on the occasion of the bicentenary of European settlement in Australia, the NGA acquired the monumental installation *The Aboriginal Memorial* (1988), by artists from central Arnhem Land. The memorial celebrates cultural survival, but its power lies in its anticipation of a transition on the national scale - from an unjust society to an equitable one. By 1991 the gallery had replaced the Postmodernist hang in the first room of the building - a clear statement of the NGA's attitude to the significance of Indigenous art in the modern era. The exhibition, then, is a timely landmark in the NGA's history.

The intention is to invite different curators to direct each triennial: for this one the 30 artists in the show were selected by Brenda L. Croft (Senior Curator of Indigenous Art at the NGA), and each artist is represented by work from the last three years. The title, 'Culture Warriors', reflects the place of Indigenous artists in current debates about Australian history and questions of identity, colonization, cultural dispossession and social diaspora, and their opposites: cultural affirmation, continuity and the reclamation of history. Last year also marked the 40th anniversary of the federal referendum, which, *inter alia*, counted Indigenous people as citizens of Australia. As Croft notes in the introduction to the catalogue, 21 of the artists in the exhibition were at one time not listed as Australians.

The show opens with Danie Mellor's installation *The Contrivance of a Vintage Wonderland* (2007), which re-orientates evolutionist paradigms within past museological practice where Aboriginal people were classified among the flora and fauna of the country. Dennis Nona's life-size bronzes of ancestral dugong and a crocodile, together with Vernon Ah Kee's text piece *not an animal or a plant* (2006), set the broader themes of the exhibition.

The first rooms focus on modern developments of ancient traditions. Jean Baptiste Apuatimi's bold gestural canvases of conventional Tiwi

Culture Warriors

body-painting designs find resonance in the audaciously chromatic landscapes of Maringka Baker and Jan Billycan, who, despite their advanced age, only started exhibiting in the public domain in recent years, although their work is evidence of decades of experience in making art in ceremonial, and hence, private circumstances. More recognizable styles of desert painting can be seen in Doreen Reid Nakamarra's exquisitely vibrant canvases.

The work of Gulumbu Yunupingu and John Mawurndjul (Njiminjuma's younger brother) take the tradition of painting on bark to new heights, exploring conventional clan designs and iconography to create sensory images that can only be described as contemporary breakthroughs in this ancient tradition of painting. Both produce images of light, respectively the sparkle of the constellations and the sunlight reflecting off the surface of bodies of water: visual metaphors for the ancestral energies that vivify the universe.

The inventive sculptures of Yawkyawk ancestral woman/fish beings made from natural fibres and dyes by Anniebell Marrngamarrnga from West Arnhem Land take the art of weaving, commonly practised by women, in new directions in terms of scope and scale. Possum-skin cloaks, a type of decorated clothing once common in the south-eastern part of the continent, form the canvas for pictorial narratives in Treahna Hamm's work.

Identity, history and the spaces between black and white societies are potent themes for several artists in the show. Julie Dowling's evocative depictions of resistance to cultural and environmental oppression are juxtaposed with Christopher Pease's reinterpretations of colonialist images, which belie benign representations of settlement. The dignity of the individual, so often negated in history, is celebrated in the drawings of Kee and the photographs of Ricky Maynard. Judy Watson's luscious surfaces of pigment washed into canvas embody emotion as they relate stories of oppression and personal histories. Watson's series of etchings based on her grandmother's official permit to marry a white person, 'under the act' (2007), is a major statement on colonization.

From the subtlety of Watson's paintings the exhibition moves towards a brash climax in the provocative political and social commentaries of Gordon Hookey and Richard Bell. Hookey's is an art of protest, based on poster art and comic books, rendered in a visual argot at once confronting and humorous. The exhibition ends with Bell's critique of the domination of the modern Western tradition in Australian art, as symbolized by the Roy Lichtenstein parody in *Big Brush Stroke* (2005) and Jackson Pollock-like drips in *Australian Art It's an Aboriginal Thing* (2006). The latter work, in turn, neatly poses the question of identity in Australian art. Bell's satirical video *Uz vs Them* (2006) finally sets the arena of debate in a boxing ring – as befits a warrior.

Wally Caruana

Maureen Paley, London, UK

Jemima in Her Bedroom (2007) wasn't the same painting on second viewing. Her head had swung up, transforming the subject from downcast to upright; her arm had moved; a hat, asymmetrical and tilted, had vanished; and the bed had shifted position. To fix the image's mutable co-ordinates I'd had to see four more of Maaike Schoorel's radically bleached-out canvases: literally, my retinas required adapting to a world of whites, within which pallid, smudgy-looking but deceptively precise hints of figuration gather momentum over time.

Schoorel's aesthetic feels, at first, like a formal gambit. How far can one reduce the visual chassis to nothingness, it asks, and still maintain some kind of directed conveyance? This show, the artist's second at the gallery and entirely composed of female nudes, almost seemed designed to test this in real time, offering different points along

a scale of legibility. *Emma-Louise from Above* (2008) dissolves in shifty vectors, a miasma of ambiguity about position: one assumes foreshortening and begins to arrange anatomic cues accordingly but remains locked out of the depicted space. *Katherine* (2008) is, by contrast, a model of communicative clarity and relatively unequivocal marking, conjuring in delicate wisps of brownblack, pale pink, aqua and yellows a recumbent figure, darkest around the eyes, whose stare locks calmly and guilelessly onto ours. Hoary notions of the gaze are reanimated, then complicated: we're looking at someone whom, to some degree, we feel we have built.

But additionally *Katherine* is an opticalcognitive paradox, in that while we are making her appear she seems to be disappearing into memory: there is, in fact, a tipping point in that no sooner is she composed than she seems to be retreating again, not visibly but within a

Maaike Schoorel
Emma-Louise from Above
2008
Oil on canvas
145×110 cm

Maaike Schoorel

conceptual schema that seems to underlie these canvases. For to reduce the human figure as far as Schoorel does (the models are all friends of hers – she works from her own photographs of them) is to become entangled, willingly or not, in some kind of unwieldy poetic discourse about loss, transience, finitude etc.: a cloud of Sebaldian ennui that is frankly distracting. One has the sense that there *was* more there (indeed, in technical terms Schoorel must work this way), and that it has been attenuated; and it's difficult not to see this in somewhat metaphorical terms. One tends to want to keep thinking about the paintings' possible parameters, because otherwise, once they have performed their neat conjuring trick – first there is no mountain, then there is – one can feel dissatisfied with them and cast about for purpose.

Back to the content, then: it's notable that Schoorel, here and elsewhere, practises a sort of wilfully anaemic update on Intimism. She blows life – or creates the conditions for life to be blown – into figures who are, essentially, caught in the midst of not doing much. *Monica in Her Living Room* (2008) is more active than anyone else: seen side-on, long hair cascading down, she appears to be actually walking, whereas Katherine, Jemima and Emma-Louise are lying down or sitting. The lounge she's in is a dream space, just a set of prompts and blurry contours with which the determined eye composes. These are paintings of activity pared right back, effected in a style that is itself a reduction to near-stillness. As such, in a manner not dissimilar to the recent school of improvised music that surrounds isolated notes with oceans of silence, they're tacitly opposed to a world of noise, excess, stimuli, figuring it in its absence. So there is a cultural politics at work here, but one whose overtly binary quality again doesn't take it very far: not least because it's an argument for the compensatory contemplative that's been latently advanced within art for decades.

That aside, and even if it makes them easier to be impressed by than to like, Schoorel has a bunch of smart rapprochements at work in these paintings. They marry the you-finish-the-artwork logic of Modernism with the ostensible fixity of figurative painting; they chart a peculiar ontological space between the monochrome and the figure; they cleverly reanimate a somewhat hoary school of portraiture as a consensually acceptable parading of ghosts. But still one ends up feeling that the most interesting work is that which doesn't resolve into some kind of implicit argumentation or strategy. For all its smoky vexations, *Emma-Louise from Above* ended up being the painting I kept going back to. Although I could feel it at work on me, I didn't know quite where the image was, and Schoorel didn't seem to want to tell me that, or, indeed, anything else. This looked from the outset like a show with a lot of room to manoeuvre in it; but, lastingly at least, here was the only place I really found it.
Martin Herbert

Andreas Lutz and Anders
Guggisberg
Tasmanian Devil
2007
Mixed media on canvas
160×240 cm

Aargauer Kunsthaus, Aarau, Switzerland

In this exhibition entitled 'Leben im Riff' (Life on the Reef) by Swiss artist duo Andres Lutz and Anders Guggisberg, the work on show created a strong suggestion of something having gone completely out of control. The duo's first survey exhibition in the ten years they have been working together featured key works in new, precisely choreographed constellations – modelled on the grand bourgeois home, with an emphasis on the study, the library and the living room – which contested the cosiness and orderliness of Western domesticity, our educated middle-class penchant for smart art and comforting nature.

The first room was the study: behind a central desk hung a huge painting (a ghostly scene of faces and masks, painted in a faux-Expressionist manner), lining the walls were large shelves filled with sculpted birds. The elements were almost those of a normal study, yet things were strangely out of kilter: the desk looked too rough-hewn and a huge mound of earth welled up behind it (*Le Bureau*, The Office, 2003); the birds – crudely fashioned from plaster or wood – were half scorched and far too numerous (*Die Pilger*, The Pilgrims, 2006); and what appeared to be an air-conditioning unit was overgrown with Irish moss. At first glance, the next room seemed to pursue this theme of nature getting the upper hand: wood chips on the floor, spades and rakes against the wall, more birds, partition walls made from bare planks used as notice boards. But the nature in evidence was less that of the great outdoors than the back garden. The adjacent room continued the theme, but offered a further twist on it. Reminiscent of a natural history museum, birds of prey stood about on crates with their wings spread wide, which created an uncanny, morbid atmosphere.

Lutz & Guggisberg's *Bibliothek* (Library, 1999–2008) functioned as a veritable bulwark of a sentiment pervading the entire exhibition – the bourgeois yearning for nature. The work includes a collection of fictitious books with titles such as *Der Buchfink* (The Chaffinch),

and landscapes painted in the style of the Old Masters. Our preoccupation with perfecting and ordering culture proceeds, it implies, at the expense of nature, which we now only tolerate in tamed, romanticized or trivialized form. But Lutz & Guggisberg's charred and headless birds, with gaping holes instead of necks, will not be driven away, even if they are just crudely cobbled together, rotting away on racks and crates.

Ich sah die Wahrheit (I Saw the Truth, 2005) explores how the clarity and structure of Modernism was instituted at the cost of repressing its dark and the monstrous side. On a mirrored tabletop stands a small sculpture assembled out of delicate twigs and sticks, its giant shadows playing a magical game on the wall behind. In formal terms, the work is reminiscent of the kinetic sculptures and architectural models of classical Modernism, but its fragility and artisanal air also recall handcrafted toys. The title is ironic: although it appears to deconstruct the ideologies of establishing truth, for Lutz & Guggisberg there is no clear truth, and everything they present us with has a dark side as well as a light one. Their deconstructions are not fiercely intellectual, but playful in a child-like manner, staging a kind of mania that refuses to be pinned down.

The high point of the show was undoubtedly *Floss* (Raft, 2008), a sloping wooden floor on which perched sofas, wall racks, knick-knacks, side tables and rolls of toilet paper; a dilapidated, chaotic living room that is never going to see better days. Gallery-goers were allowed to enter this stage-like scenario of things coated in plaster, including a sort of icing-sugar-coated cake that was actually formed more like a piece of shit. The room was a hive of activity, filled with small wooden figures pushing rakes about or pulling strings to manoeuvre objects, so busy that they didn't notice the threat of chaos and collapse all around them.

This exhibition presented a climax of Lutz & Guggisberg's stratagem to reveal the ominous lack of moderation that underpins our culture of order and cleanliness: the atmosphere was impressive, the aesthetic precise and densely wrought. The only question is how much more mileage the two artists can get out of their pet hate: middle-class culture. For much of what they stage with such verve is appropriated from an outmoded, stuffy way of life with which vivacious partygoers, agile managers and the global art audience can no longer identify. But perhaps this is precisely the point, at least in the case of *Floss*: the idea that this good old enemy, the all-mod-cons bourgeois way of life, is finally in danger of going irrevocably off the rails.
Yvonne Volkart
Translated by Nicholas Grindell

Lutz & Guggisberg

Barbican Art Gallery, London, UK

Curated by Francesco Manacorda and Lydia Yee, and featuring works by over 100 artists from the 1960s to today, 'Martian Museum of Terrestrial Art' turned on the conceit that a band of extraterrestrial anthropologists have travelled to Earth to investigate the phenomenon of 'contemporary art' and have subsequently presented their findings to their fellow Martians in the form of an exhibition, to which we earthlings have access through unnamed means. According to Manacorda and Yee's fictional schema, the civilization of the Red Planet has 'developed without the domain of art or aesthetics', leading the curators' alien avatars to interpret the art works they've collected as nothing more than artefacts, which they've displayed in one of four categories according to their perceived use value: Ritual, Communication, Kinship and Descent, and Magic and Belief.

Despite the sci-fi sheen provided by the runic font in graphic designer Sara de Bondt's 'bi-lingual' signage, this museum was, with its cabinets of objects grouped by formal similarity, a deliberately High Victorian affair. Throughout the exhibition signal pieces were accompanied by explanatory texts, which combined deliberately point-missing empirical description, mock bewilderment, cod authority and art-historical in-jokes. Thus, the folded tarp that covered Chris Burden as he lay in LA's La Cienega Boulevard for his performance Deadman (1972) was identified as having 'protective properties', although 'it did not, however, prevent him from being arrested', and Piero Manzoni's Artist's Shit (1961) was described as pointing 'towards the unaccountably high price of art on Earth today'. Different people will, of course, have different appetites for this

kind of material, but for me its repetition did it few favours, transforming something that was at first flush funny into something that felt increasingly forced and even (against, I'm sure, the curator's wishes) a little self-satisfied. To some degree this is a problem of scale. When Jorge Luis Borges wrote, in 1966, of a fictional Chinese encyclopaedia entitled the Celestial Emporium of Benevolent Knowledge, in which animals were divided into 14 categories, including 'embalmed ones', 'mermaids' and 'those that tremble as if they were mad', a paragraph was sufficient for him to make his point about the absurdities inherent in any taxonomic system. By contrast, the blockbusting 'Martian Museum of Terrestrial Art' provided the viewer with the whole voluminous encyclopaedia, index and all.

Manacorda and Yee deserve credit for staging a show of such off-beat curatorial ambition in a usually mainstream British venue, as they also do for assembling a group of works that, even outside the framework they imposed on them, provided much for the viewer to be excited about – space constraints do not permit even a cursory snapshot, but some highlights included Jeffrey Vallance's Cultural Ties (1979), in which the artist mailed neckties to world leaders, Matthew Day Jackson's nightmare-catching mobile Hung, Drawn & Quartered II (Treeson) (2008) and Nancy Grossman's gimp-mask-like Head (1968). However, the exhibition remained problematic, not least because the fiction it turned on meant that any given work it contained could conceivably be substituted for another, and because that fiction felt so unsteady on its feet. So close were the 'Martians' it evoked to 19th-century ethnographers in the Augustus Pitt Rivers mould that the only thing that felt truly alien about

them was that their society, despite having clear analogues of human language, natural and social sciences, architecture and even curatorial practice, somewhat illogically had nothing that might be compared to art – even the most chauvinistic Victorian, after all, admitted some vague commonality between the Western canon and objects and images produced elsewhere. As such, Manacorda and Yee's aliens failed to convince either as a satire on what are anyway long-discredited anthropological models or as a picture of the truly 'other'. (A more interesting, or at least more consistent, fiction might have involved, say, an alien curator blasting the 'barbarism' of our blue planet on the grounds that we have yet to discover how to make art in four dimensions.)

And yet the exhibition's most significant cause for concern was the way in which it modelled its public, or publics. A small number of visitors to this big institution may be relied on to get its every arch gag, but what of the others? I'm pretty sure that it wasn't the curators' intent to cast them as bug-eyed aliens, goggling dumbly at the material culture of an (art) world they will never understand, but it's hard to see how the 'Martian Museum of Terrestrial Art' did not do this. While contemporary art stands at a distance from many people's lives, this is a distance measured not in parsecs but (interest in the form notwithstanding) usually by the very earthbound stuff of where you were born, how much money your parents earned and what kind of education you received. As innovative at times as genuinely thought-provoking Manacorda and Yee's show was, somewhere along the line their control over the analogies they employed ran away with them, and an unbidden conservatism breached the curatorial airlock.
Tom Morton

'Martian Museum of Terrestrial Art'
2008
Exhibition view

Martian Museum of Terrestrial Art

Galeria Vermelho, São Paulo, Brazil

Senha, carta, arte, nulo, pátria and *obra* ('password', 'letter', 'art', 'null', 'fatherland' and 'work') were some of the 30 words Carla Zaccagnini fashioned from old folded-up beer labels for her exhibition 'Bifurcações e Encruzilhadas' (Junctions and Intersections). Like components in some larger game, the folded-up pieces belonging to the series 'Correspondência' (Letters, 2007-8) reflect a recurring strategy adopted by this Brazil-based Argentinian artist, in which she creates a kind of lens through which situations and objects can be seen in terms of both their similarities and their differences.

This is the case in *Sobre la igualdad y las diferencias II: a casa ao lado* (On Sameness and Differences II: The House Next Door, 2005), carried out in partnership with the archaeologists Liesbet Sablon and Sofie Geelen. Originally created for the 'Cité-Action' exhibition in Assenede, Belgium, in 2006, the installation brought together artefacts discovered in two abandoned houses located on the same street and classified according to archaeological criteria. The objects found in the houses – pens, teacups, towels, dresses – had their typological kinships reinforced by the support of a specially designed piece of furniture by Leonardo Padilha. However, although the objects are practically the same, their styles and details of use and wear differ, revealing that while the habits and accoutrements of domesticity are similar from one house to another, they are never identical. This somewhat obvious point would be a lacklustre

conclusion were it not for Zaccagnini's ability to turn the exhibition into a challenge to the viewer, enabling one to leave the show with the desire to use her lens out in the real world, folding up beer labels to find messages hidden in the banal or searching for congruencies between disparate things around us.

This may explain why some of the works on show were less fully developed formally, since their essential feature is the idea behind their creation rather than the object or image. Such is the case in the series 'Sobre la igualdad y las diferencias: casas gemelas' (On Sameness and Differences: Twin Houses, 2005). Here Zaccagnini, who will take part in the 28th São Paulo Biennial in October, presents photographs of houses in Havana, Cuba, constructed with identical structural designs, in sets of two to six buildings, which over time and through the gradual alterations and actions of residents have evolved in entirely different directions. Yet the pictures are often taken from different angles, sometimes with residents appearing or cars passing by or parked outside, resisting the strictly documentary approach found in the classic images of Bernd and Hilla Becher and their counterparts.

In Zaccagnini's work the registration comes from a quick snapshot, aiming not at photography *per se* but rather at generating discussion. The same is also true of 'Todas las descripciones son comparativas: grandes felinos' (All Descriptions Are Comparative: Large Cats, 2007-8), a series of drawings copied from the pages of an encyclopaedia of animals. Since each copy is handmade,

Carla Zaccagnini
Sobre la igualdad y las diferencias II: a casa ao lado
(On Sameness and Differences II: The House Next Door)
2005
Mixed media
Installation view

the pages of the encyclopaedia are transformed into something obviously subjective, irregular and non-authoritative, again reinforcing the idea that concept and process trump formal results. This clumsy-looking activity is echoed in *Kleuren, knippen en opplakken a/b* (Colouring, Cutting and Gluing a/b), (2006-8), composed of two pairs of popular Belgian colouring books with the same printed pictures but filled in by different people with the same pens. Here the artist stimulates the development of distinction, as she does with the Cuban houses, appealing to a process that can only lead to highly divergent outcomes.

Even within such a Conceptual body of work, it is surprising how Zaccagnini occupied the entire gallery (including the exterior walls) with a work that was the only one that did not produce an object: *Uma e três casas (projeção)* (One and Three Houses (Projection]) and its counterpart *Uma e três casas (prospecção)* (One and Three Houses [Prospecting], 2008). In the former, the artist redesigned the windows and doors of the three adjacent houses that the architect Paulo Mendes da Rocha co-joined to create the new expanded space of Galeria Vermelho. In the latter, with the help of restorers, the artist removed multiple layers of paint on the rear wall by means of archaeological 'prospecting', revealing its physical history. In this work, as in the dry game-playing evident in other pieces in the show, the artist achieved a visual synthesis, providing a conceptual lens for perceiving a world that is sometimes beyond our sight.
Fabio Cypriano

Carla Zaccagnini

Compton Verney, Warwickshire, UK

'C ... O ... N ... Ceiling? ... Concealing!' The girl's voice is strained, as though pressing to convey urgent meaning but struggling to decipher the letters of a text that she is reading. In the large, dark room the recording of her voice is crisp and close, and we can hear every exasperated breath, every 'hmmm' and 'hah', as she pores over the unseen script. Her perplexity over the text may well reflect the viewer's puzzlement at a sequence of colour slides that accompany her monologue in James Coleman's installation *I N I T I A L S* (1993-4). Shot in what seems to be a hospital but could almost be a theatre's green room, the photographs depict a cast of six figures in a series of tense but ambiguous relationships that allude variously to medical procedures and to performance in front of an audience or camera. While the girl falters letter by letter and word by word through a passage that occasionally opens to reveal moments of clarity ('Did a shadow pass? It passed, but a moment ago.'), so too does the viewer's understanding of the projected images wax and wane over the work's 21 minutes.

Coleman is an artist whose international standing over the past four decades (he has participated in every documenta since 1987 and is represented by three major commercial galleries) is somewhat at odds with his relative unfamiliarity to a contemporary audience in the UK. His film *Retake with Evidence* (2007), a grandly installed and even more grandly orated quasi-Shakespearean soliloquy delivered by Harvey Keitel, left many visitors to documenta 12 perplexed and frustrated by the lack of contextual information. Coleman is an artist who expects much of his audience; he insists on the willing participation of the viewer in attempting to unravel meaning where there are often only thickening layers of complication and uncertainty beneath the surface. It is a game that, understandably, not everyone is prepared to play.

This gruff stance can occasionally border on the antagonistic. An untitled video installation, dated 1998-2002, accompanied *I N I T I A L S* in an adjacent gallery. While the slides of the latter almost filled the entirety of one wall, the video was projected far smaller, reminiscent in size and position of a painting as opposed to the immersive scale of cinema. The image appeared to depict ice floes floating in deep black water, filmed from an aeroplane or satellite. The work constantly seemed to be on the point of resolving itself, for despite the stillness of the image, there seemed to be slight changes in the fading shades of grey around the white forms, as though the ice was melting or accreting before our eyes. These changes were so gradual, however, that it was only when compared with the memory of the image a few minutes previously that a difference could be detected – motion slowed down to the point of invisibility, thought replacing ocularity, and doubt elbowing its way into the viewer's perception. 'Did a shadow pass? It passed, but a moment ago.'

Back in the neighbouring gallery, the indistinct narrative of *I N I T I A L S* alternately developed and dissolved in a similar way. The opening shot of stacked hospital beds (the only image not featuring people) is double-exposed, but slowly resolves into a singular viewpoint. An androgynous male figure carefully applies make-up to the face of a man in a Byronic white shirt and waistcoat. A woman stands behind a table on which she is folding or unfolding white fabric. In the background we occasionally see what looks like medical equipment. Another woman pauses pensively, holding what looks like architectural plans. In another shot she carries a bucket and plastering tools, and we notice the freshly plastered-over cracks in the duck-egg blue walls.

While the scenes draw attention to the construction of their own artifice, there is a simultaneous sense of psychological tension that is somehow independent of the situations being enacted, a technique that draws heavily on Bertolt Brecht's theory of the *Verfremdungseffekt*, the distancing or alienation effect. The actors (for this is what they clearly are) seem as internally removed from us, and from each other, as the narrator's voice seems close. At times the girl's voice seems to address them rather than the viewer: 'Why do you gaze, one upon the other?' No answer, of course, is forthcoming.

In a nearby gallery an exhibition of paintings and sculptures by Alberto Giacometti provided an unexpected complement to Coleman's work. Giacometti's dissolving (or rather emerging) figures, which often seem to describe the process of the artist's apprehension of his subjects rather than their outward appearance, share Coleman's sensitivity to the untrustworthiness of representation. Something Giacometti once said could equally be applied to the work of Coleman: 'One continues knowing that the closer one gets to the model, the more it withdraws.'

Jonathan Griffin

James Coleman
INITIALS
(detail)
1993-4
Slide projection and audio recording
Dimensions variable

James Coleman

Cherry and Martin, Los Angeles, USA

It Is What It Is (The Old In and Out) (2008) consists of two replica Donald Judd tables cast in rich bronze that double as pedestals for two seated sculptures that perch – compact and aloof – atop their respective Minimalist plinths. Derived from Pre-Columbian Moche ceramics, these therianthropic figures, replete with antlers, formal headwear and ceremonial garb, are cheeky and elegant. Further scrutiny reveals that their hands are forming (somewhat surreptitiously) the 'in and out' sign that alludes almost universally to sexual intercourse – a moderately racy anachronism that cuts the reserved, ceremonial character of the bronze figures and dilutes the stoic formalism of the Juddian tables. Completing this web of dissonant references is the lurking knowledge that the subtitle, *The Old In and Out*, refers back to the phrase made famous by the pronouncements and misdeeds of Malcolm McDowell and his band of goons in Stanley Kubrick's adaptation of Anthony Burgess' ultraviolent novel *A Clockwork Orange* (1962).

It Is What It Is (The Old In and Out), like much of Mabry's work, flirts wilfully with facile humour, infantile puns and poor taste, shrewdly courting the predictable charge that the artist's sculptures and drawings objectify and exploit ethnographic artefacts and in doing so purposefully rouse the petty, pseudo-political controversies that routinely build and dissipate in the world of contemporary art. One might even suggest that Mabry's propensity for baiting – and perhaps exposing – high-minded liberal politics is a medium in and of itself, providing the infra-logic for his work. In this sense his practice emerges directly from a loosely knit contingent of like-minded LA-based multi-media artists such as Paul McCarthy (Mabry's teacher at UCLA), Mike Kelley and the late Jason Rhoades, who have all demonstrated a healthy investment in pranks, scatological humour and self-conscious political incorrectness, and have an equivalent aptitude for provoking revulsion as well as adventurous, socially grounded critical thought. Although after repeated exposure Mabry's preferred strategy of combining popular culture references, ethnographic imagery, formalist conventions and punning, often sexual, titles becomes rather predictable, the particular juxtapositions he offers are often nuanced and suggestive.

A comprehensive grasp of Mabry's imagery and referents demands considerable time investment on the part of the viewer. In fact, in order to evaluate the consonances and dissonances that play between the elements that compose his work, once must mimic the cultural archaeology undertaken by the artist to conceive and produce it. Like *It Is What It Is (The Old In and Out)*, *Taboo-boo* (2007) combines a specific reference to canonical Minimalism with a no less overt but calculatingly less specific allusion to so-called ethnographic sculpture. Here the Minimalist tradition is represented by the West Coast sculptor

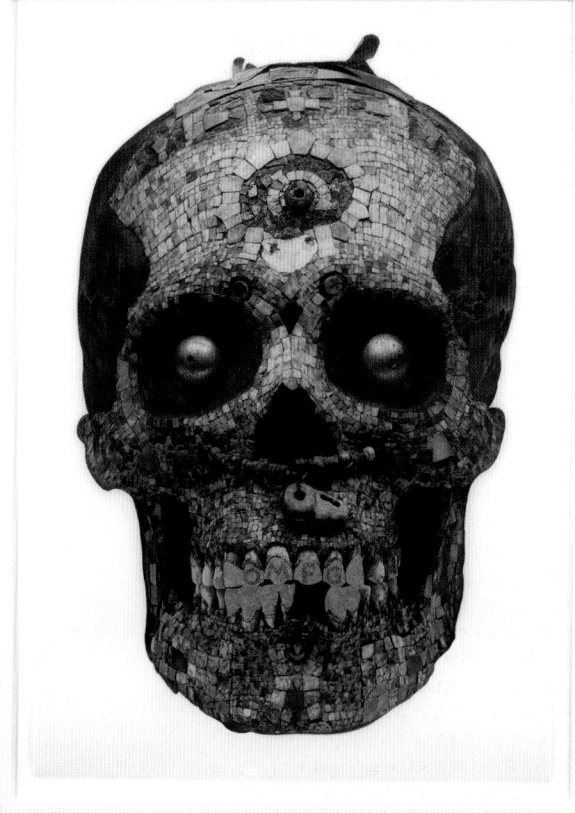

Nathan Mabry
Mosaic Skull (OMFG)
2008
Coloured pencil and
Swarovski crystals on
Mylar
130×94 cm

John McCracken, renowned for constructing monolithic fibreglass and plywood armatures coated with 20 to 30 coats of a single colour to yield a highly reflective, lustrous surface that registers even minute changes in the surrounding environment. Mabry apes McCracken's heavily autographic style of object-making, using bronze and glossy black car paint, but he elaborates on this spare composition with two bronze Snafu figures cast from wood originals, placed vertically head to head against the austere, McCracken-like plank. The uncanny compositional harmony achieved in the work implies but, significantly, does not actually establish a deeper relationship between the two traditions that collide in the sculpture. The relationship remains obdurately formal, even superficial, inviting the critically minded viewer to adopt one of two opposite (and obvious) positions: the first is that Mabry's work levels the playing field and argues for the formal integrity of anonymously produced sub-Saharan ritual objects and, concomitantly, undermines the importance we assign to individuality, innovation and autographic expression in the Western tradition; the second is that the implication of mere formal parity robs the Snafu sculptures of their cultural resonance, reducing them to decorative integers in an essentially Western, market-minded strategy. Mabry does not resolve this opposition or even adopt an obvious position; he simply makes

this time-honoured dialectic, and the attendant critical discourse surrounding it, the subject and effect of his work.

The most arresting and suggestive work in the show is a drawing executed in coloured pencil on Mylar that side-steps this rather laboured dispute through its sheer physical presence. Entitled *Mosaic Skull (OMFG)* (2008), the work is an imposing 130 x 94 cms and is a precise rendering of a Mexican Mixtec ceremonial skull opulently studded with jade and turquoise tiles. The obligatory popular culture flourish occurs in the form of a 'grill' composed of Swarovski crystals spelling out 'OMFG' ('Oh My Fucking God'). Sacred and irreverently profane, camp and straightforwardly beautiful, *Mosaic Skull …* is a drawing with sculptural presence that exists as a fastidious record of Mixtec extravagance and as a canny riff on contemporary modes of profligate self-adornment. Unlike much of Mabry's production to date, *Mosaic Skull …* does not lean on the gaudy formal/conceptual currency of juxtaposing autographic Western Minimalist conventions with anonymous, non-Western ritual sculpture. Instead, this drawing seamlessly integrates the most contemporary of pop cultural motifs with grand Mexican Mixtec imagery to present two divergent expressions of a shared set of socio-cultural values that span many hundreds of years.
Christopher Bedford

Nathan Mabry

Limoncello, London, UK

To misquote Ecclesiastes, 'The sun also rises, the sun goes down […] All art is meaningless and a striving after wind.' Vanessa Billy's *Suns Neither Rise Nor Set* (2008) comprises two convex glass discs that looked over her small exhibition 'Flexible Values', creating a new horizon on which these twin celestial bodies were halted. *Glow*

(2008) was simply a layer of yellow pastel dusted over a section of the gallery's white windowsill, but it radiated with the light of these new suns and bathed the show with subdued rays.

The spirit of Arte Povera has lately been reinvigorated, and Billy's transient, mute poetry displayed, with its simple materials, an affinity with the earlier movement but also a further sense of dramatic irony. The two-part *Fluids*

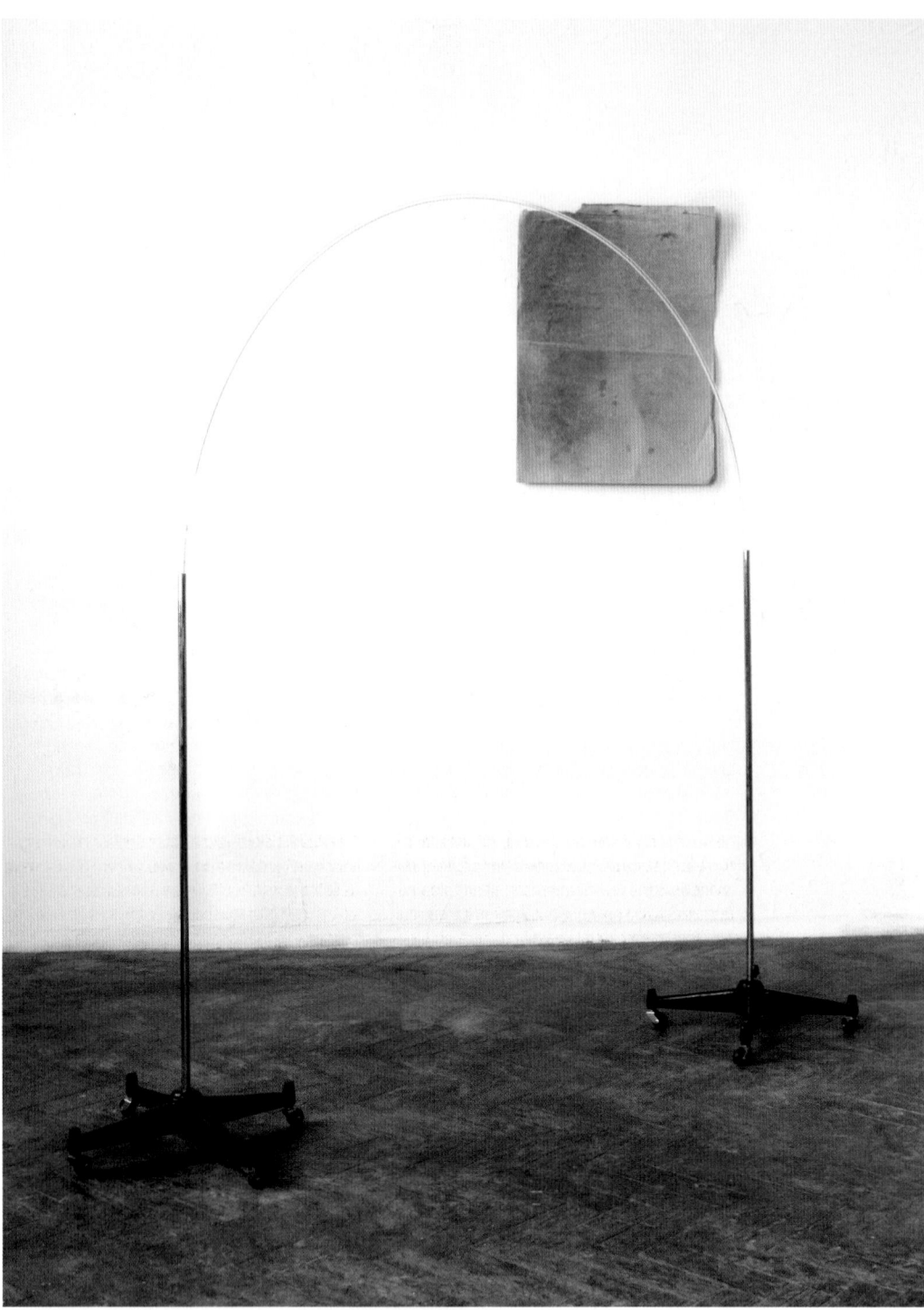

Vanessa Billy
Fluids
2008
Steel, acrylic and pastel
on paper
Dimensions variable

(2008) was a diminutive fountain-like entrance to what seemed to be a faded carnival; a thin stream of clear plastic arched between two steel green bases, set askew from its accompanying poster, which showed a spectrum of blue, purple and pink merged and diffused like colours refracted underwater. The sand from *Dry Stamina* (2008) was spread underneath, a wedge of sand that filled the step between the gallery's two levels but had dispersed with time. At the rear the dozen red plastic misshapen arches of *Support Brackets* (2008) acted like a two-dimensional theatrical backdrop to a distant flock of seagulls. 'Flexible Values' set the spirit of Arte Povera loose in the faded grandiosity and elusive romanticism of a desolate seaside town, as though the artist's collection of objects were the shorthand sketches of an abandoned proposal for Robert Smithson to design a Butlins holiday resort.

Similar in tone to the work of the Mexican artist Gabriel Kuri, each of Billy's works casually maintains a discrete presence with a self-conscious sense of weight. As though they were theatrical props, Billy is fully aware of their temporary metaphorical value, setting us the task of casting about for connections before they are flung into the bin or washed into the sea. Hints of transformation began to emerge from the balance of materials used that suggested traditional methods of industrial conversion: sand and glass, paper and wood. In *Supporters* (2007), a low plywood plinth held up a sanded piece of cedar that resembled a smooth, sea-worn pebble, the wood's age rings transformed into geological stripes. Billy quietly proposes a new elemental ecology in the weathered progression that flowed from the larger stone of *Supporters* to the smaller particles of *Dry Stamina* and on to the melted sand of *Suns Neither Rise* …. A similar metamorphosis took place in *Four Times Weathered* (2007), two square concrete blocks topped by a slight pyramid, each face holding a small, bunched-up tissue. The withered tissues seemed to bear marks of the pastels used in *Fluids*, ritually laid like seashells set out to dry, taking on evocative shapes in their cast-off abstraction; one of them even resembled a seahorse.

Billy set the gallery as a frontier for an encounter that shapes our environment, like the seafront. And like holiday resorts, galleries gather around this frontier, imbued with idealism and decorated with promises of escape. 'Flexible Values' set out a new stall along this coast, the 'land' of the exhibition shaped and transformed by a visual erosion, the artist's deftly curated negative spaces between the works evoking an invisible sea of meanings in which the artist is happy to let us swim. But don't expect a lifesaver: Billy's seafront shares an escapism that can only lead back to ourselves. She readily acknowledges the futility of this striving after wind and revels in its physical sensations, letting explicit answers dance elusively on the constantly receding horizon.
Chris Fite-Wassilak

Vanessa Billy

Johann König, Berlin, Germany

Manfred Kuttner's history has something fable-like about it: in the early 1960s in Dusseldorf, he and three other young artists – Gerhard Richter, Sigmar Polke and Konrad Lueg (later known as Konrad Fischer) – form a group and show together several times. But by the end of 1964, Kuttner was sidelined; his more abstract approach no longer fits with the 'New Realist' work of the other three. With a wife and small children to support, he gives up art in favour of an advertising job and a stable wage. After his final exhibition in Rene Block's Berlin gallery in 1965, his paintings languish in the cellar of his house in the Rhineland.

It is almost impossible to view Kuttner's works, pulled out and dusted off (and in some cases restored) 40 years later, outside of this prism of mythologizing history. They have a kind of instant credibility given his close association with Richter, Polke and Lueg. But there is something about their slapdash Op-art effects and embrace of feverish neon colours that renders them still startling. The eight neon abstract paintings exhibited here share some of the systematic patterning of Victor Vasarely or Bridget Riley, but they have none of the taut perfectionism on which his Op art contemporaries depended for their hallucinatory effects. A kind of handmade carelessness and experimental air frees them from illusionism to investigative instead approaches to process and materials.

In *Achterbahn* (Roller Coaster, 1964), for instance, rows of blue circles line up against a red background; in each circle is a pink square, centrally placed, in some rows upright, in others turning, rolling over. The effect is giddying: the circles seem to jiggle in various directions, like rows of cogs or the rattling wheels of roller coaster coaches. Attempts to trace any coherent system, however, are foiled by blue drips that trespass onto the pink squares, or uneven white gaps around them, while areas that should surely be red are left untouched. Although close up it bears a certain similarity to a child's potato-print painting, its thrilling and unexpected vibrancy when seen from a short distance clarifies why his work was initially christened 'kinetic' art. Another painting *Tombola* (1962) racks up a barrage of patterning in complementary colours to similar dizzying effect, the breaks in its pattern alluding to the slippages, coincidences, juxtapositions and velocity of daily life. Attempts at ordering seem forever skewered by the introduction of another experiment, an accident, a 'what if'.

This relation of abstraction's attempt at ordering to reality's confusion was spelt out more clearly in a selection of Kuttner's ink on paper drawings from 1962. *Matratze* (Mattress) is a linear arrangement of diagonal lozenges, looping script and circles that loosely represent the springs of a mattress. An 8mm film (*A–Z*, 1963) develops this abstractionist take on reality further: a fast edit of still shots pictures the journey from

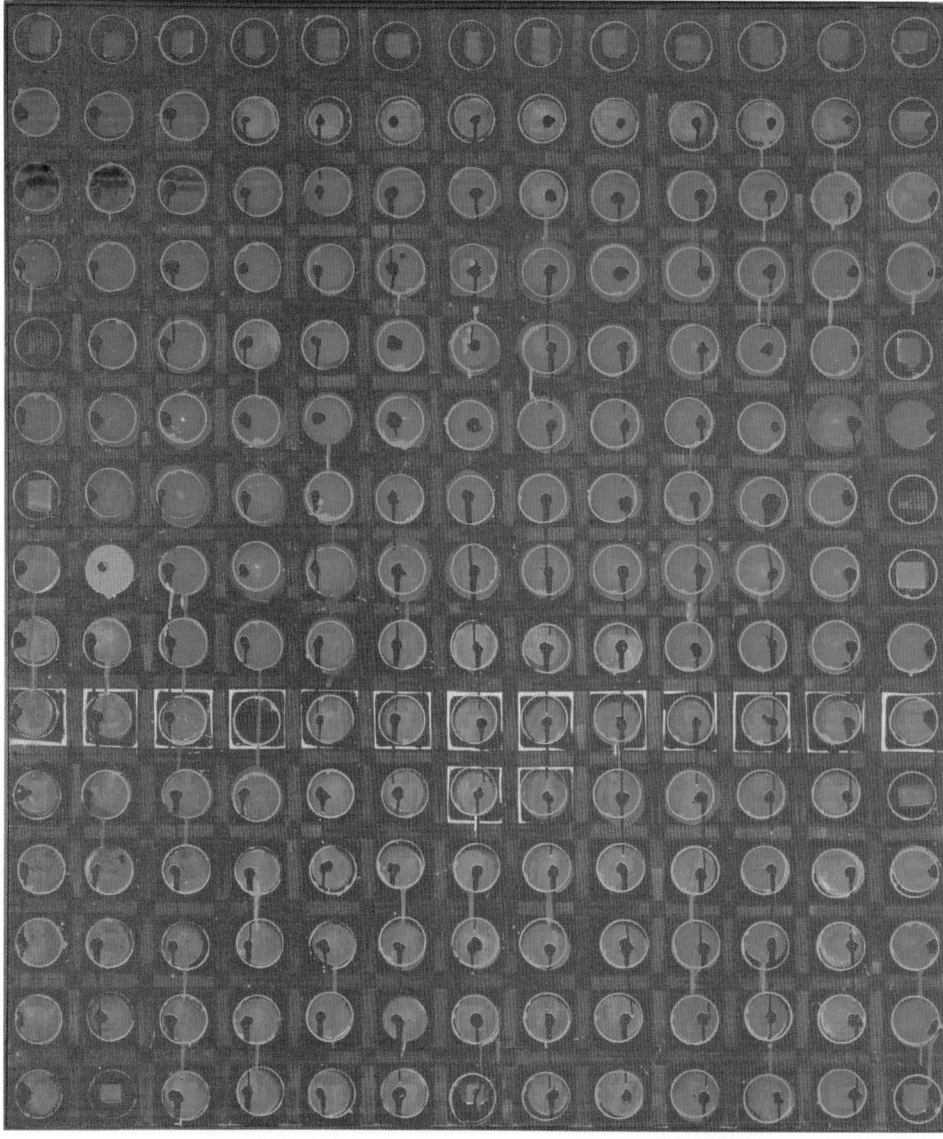

Manfred Kuttner
Tombola
1962
Tempera and fluorescent paint on canvas
151×131 cm

his apartment through the streets of Dusseldorf to his studio, focusing on crowds of people, shop windows, signage. Intermittently, hand coloured frames blinking red or yellow appear, introducing a hallucinogenic atmosphere into the relentless flow and thrum of the everyday. Also included in the exhibition were three earlier, transitional works: canvases whose dense grey surfaces of layered patterning have little to distinguish them. The discovery and interest in the material qualities of a newly patented fluorescent paint was clearly a turning point for Kuttner, spawning not only the vibrant paintings here but also several dada-esque objects such as a chair coated in fluorescent pink and balanced on four metal pins so that, initially, it seems to hover slightly (*Heiliger Stuhl*, Holy Chair, 1962/2006).

The real strength of Kuttner's work, however, lies in his abstract paintings, which share qualities with those of many younger contemporary artists;

Thomas Scheibitz and Anselm Reyle are obvious examples (Kuttner's work was shown with theirs at Tate Modern in 2007). Reyle in particular shares a concern with the alienating properties of fluorescent paint and a fascination with the effect of drips or paint-can imprints on geometric abstraction. But artists such as Udomsak Krisanamis also spring to mind, whose process of abstraction is all-encompassing, absorbing whatever is around it, while remaining free to daydream or peter out.

Kuttner had just three productive years as an artist before he gave up at the age of 28. This is a very limited field to mine, and it is hard not to conjecture where his work might have gone had he continued, particularly since he died last year at the age of 70. But it is nonetheless instructive and rewarding to have the opportunity of seeing these long-hidden alternatives to the New Realism or Op art perfectionism of Kuttner's generation.
Kirsty Bell

Manfred Kuttner

Museo del Barrio, New York, USA

In his essay 'Commitment' (1962) the German philosopher Theodor Adorno affirmed the importance of politically committed works of art, using the example of Bertolt Brecht's plays to argue that commitment itself becomes a force of aesthetic production. Brecht may be a European antecedent, and therefore technically an incorrect predecessor of 'Art≠Vida: Actions by Artists of the Americas, 1960–2000', but he is also its stealthy pioneer, whose vicious combination of melodrama and social outrage haunts so many of the works that inhabit this recent exhibition of postwar Latin American cultural production.

Organized by Deborah Cullen, 'Art≠Vida' was the first survey of performance art of Latin America, including over 100 artists and collectives working in the US, Puerto Rico, the Dominican Republic, Cuba, Mexico and other countries in Central and South America. Ambitious in scale, the exhibition was a revisionist survey on a par with Paul Schimmel's pioneering performance art exhibition 'Out of Actions: Between Performance and the Object' at the Museum of Contemporary Art, Los Angeles, in 1994. Or it would have been, if it had the same sort of institutional heft, donor base and budget. As it was, the size and budget of 'Art≠Vida' were closer to 'Body and the East', a survey of Eastern European performance art organized by the Museum of Modern Art in Ljubljana that should have found an institutional partner in New York but didn't, and was instead lovingly sponsored by the alternative space Exit Art in 2001, and which consisted almost entirely of photo-based documentation.

The ephemeral nature of performance is the *raison d'être* for viewing often copious quantities of documentation – the magazine and news clippings, artists' statements and manifestos, photographic records and occasional snippets of grainy film and video footage or sound recordings. And there was some fantastic footage in 'Arte≠Vida': video documentation by the Santiago-based CADA (Art Actions Collective); Victor Grippo's large panoramic photos of *Traditional Rural Oven for Baking Bread* (1972), a performance in which the artist, questioning traditional notions of artistic labour and visibility, baked and gave away fresh bread in a Buenos Aires plaza until the police dismantled the operation; and Nao Bustamante's performance *Indigurrito* (1992) at a now defunct alternative theatre in San Francisco, a hilarious, sexualized *faux* Catholic ritual of salvation for 500 years of white male sin.

But it was the lack of objects in this survey that proved most troubling: there were some – Lygia Clark's do-it-yourself Möbius strip and Tunga's comb, filled with an obscene cascade of blond hair – but what about the heavy wooden apparatus of Papo Colo's extraordinary *Superman 51* (1977) performance? The work is an endurance piece, in which the artist ran at full speed for ten straight minutes along the empty West Side Highway in Manhattan, dragging behind him a netted armature of 51 wooden beams.

It is an ironic, poignant work, referencing the futility of Puerto Rico's bid for official recognition as the 51st state in the United States. In an exhibition with hundreds of black and white photographs Colo's epic performance got lost. In the absence of video documentation the object itself would have enriched the viewing experience, showing at first hand how cumbersome such a 'superman cape' would actually be. The same goes for Cildo Meireles' *The Sermon on the Mount: Let There Be Light* (1979), a cube built of 126,000 Fiat Lux matchboxes, installed on a sandpaper-covered floor, that was once heavily guarded owing to the high potential for fire hazard. While re-creating the piece might have violated stringent fire codes, even a small table-top model would have been a welcome addition: anything to spice up its reductive representation via three tiny black and white photos.

In a tumultuous era of military dictatorships and state-sanctioned kidnapping, disappearance and murder, much of the work here was explicitly political, part of what the playwright and literary critic Ariel Dorfman has called 'the testimonial genre': that is, visceral social critique that bears witness to the many brutalities and repressions. Some of these works are fairly well known, such as Marta Minujin's large-scale, ephemeral public sculptures, for example *Panettone Obelisk* (1979) or *The Parthenon of Books/Homage to Democracy* (1983). Others, such as those by the Chilean Diamela Eltit, who is well known as an experimental novelist but initially made Gina Pane-like self-mutilation works, are included but not explored in depth. Overall, the categories of organization – always semi-ambiguous in large group shows – follow a rough chronology leading from the late 1960s into the explosion of now classic works made by Americans in the 1990s: a candy piece by Félix González-Torres, Daniel Martinez' *I Can't Imagine Ever Wanting To Be White* museum tags for the 1993 Whitney Biennial, Coco Fusco and Guillermo Gómez-Peña's extended performance *Year of the White Bear: Two Undiscovered Amerindians Visit the West* (1992–4). This creates a rather false chronology in the show's own historical path, as though people stopped doing interesting things in other countries and only recently started doing them in the US, rather than the multiplicity of everything happening all at once.

Jenni Sorkin

Nao Bustamante
Rosa Does Joan
1992
Video still

Art≠Vida

Various venues, Glasgow, UK

Glasgow International (known as 'Gi') is an inclusive biennial – but how can that possibly work? The art map is spattered with meta-phorical bloodstains from skirmishes between curatorial paratroopers and local partisans. Cu-rated by Francis McKee, who understands this town well enough not to foist any overarching curatorial overview on it, the festival's theme, 'Public/Private', is, in effect, a non-theme – basically a support opportunity for everyone in the city (galleries, artists and curators) to do twice as much as usual, with everything open-ing at the same time and with equal billing. It's hard to imagine other biennial organizers putting such trust in the local art scene.

And yet it worked. Rather than a big thematic central show, there were many solo or small group exhibitions in a variety of venues: big museums, small galleries and temporary spaces. Jim Lambie once again displayed his talent for spectacle by transforming the Glas-gow Museum of Modern Art into a trinket box with a light peppering of implacably decorative objects on an Op-art black and white floor while Jonathan Monk's work at Tramway was a cool echo of Lambie – he gold-leafed the re-sidual tramlines that traverse the gallery's vast space; and Adel Abdessemed had his first solo show in the UK in Douglas Gordon's house, part of which has been turned into a gallery by new commissioning agency The Common Guild.

Along the Saltmarket, among the pawn-shops and new Polish cafés, Katri Walker and Dani Marti showed seven videos in a space that retains features of shop-front and office. It was blacked out and painted black; you could stand in one room and see the video in the next through internal windows. Marti's meditation on opinionated men in the Australian outback was compelling, as was Walker's scrutiny of one Mexican man's faith in God. The function room of The State pub on Holland Street comes from a different era (Guinness £1.80 a pint!). In this

Alasdair Gray
Credit Panel (Film Sequence With Liz Lockhead)
1972
Pencil, biro, oil, watercolour and acrylic on paper
106×127 cm

Dani Marti
Still Under
2008
DVD still

wood-panelled, low-ceilinged cellar, artists known collectively as A. Vermin added to the accumulated pub jumble, enhancing old pho-tos, aluminium-plating objects and painting supine figures beneath the bar. They picked up on the more disconcerting aspects of the place and emphasized them. Kalup Linzy's R & B drag act was an opening weekend highlight at a temporary space created by the artist-run collaboration Washington Garcia to showcase the New York artist's soapy video vignettes and tidy gouaches.

At the Centre for Contemporary Arts Catherine Yass' *High Wire* (2008) – co-commis-sioned by Artangel and Gi – comprised of four large projections of French high-wire artist Didier Pasquette attempting to walk across a thin wire stretched between the top of three 1960s' tower blocks in Red Road, north Glasgow. He fails to complete the crossing and retreats in the face of high winds – a failure that, in a sense, liberates the work.

Alasdair Gray is a touchstone for the Glasgow art scene, partly because his big-gest and best novel, *Lanark* (1981), seems to contain everything today's artists might strive for. He is represented here by a show at Sorcha Dallas' gallery of work from the 1970s – a group of paintings that look like coloured-in drawings, intended as a backdrop

for a television drama. Gray's illustrative style, like his writing, is singular and unambiguous. Dallas builds on the cross-generational picture in a thoughtful show 'run run' co-curated with artist Alex Frost at the Collins Gallery of 13 art-ists. The brief – an analysis of the relationship between art, science and digital technology – was sufficiently elastic to include both a John Latham book and plaster work from 1964 and a couple of Rob Churm's recent extravagantly meticulous pen and ink drawings.

Equally attentive to detail is Calum Stirling's solo show 'Rostra Plaza' at the Mitchell Library – five miniature worlds on wooden turntables, each with an array of tiny cameras trained on it. The turntables move in-termittently, and the images from the cameras are projected on a big screen, combined in an ever-changing montage that recalls a past vision of what the present might look like. At Transmission, Melanie Gilligan's show 'Prison for Objects' attempted to dissect the trans-formative forces behind everything everyone else seemed to be doing.

I once co-curated a show of artists in Manchester for 'anyone who's any good'. There were 11 artists in it, and they weren't all good. In Glasgow, McKee has pulled off a top-notch biennial with a similar premise.
Martin Vincent

Glasgow International

Culturgest, Lisbon, Portugal

Confronting the work of Portuguese artist Ricardo Jacinto might initially call to mind Robert Smithson's pet Pascalism: 'Nature is an infinite sphere, whose centre is everywhere and whose circumference is nowhere.' However, in the case of Jacinto, the reverse occurs: his highly structured work has no centre, nothing to grab onto, but it is nonetheless rich in rhizomatic activity. Trained as a visual artist, a musician and an architect, Jacinto enlists all of his skills and interests to produce modest yet disorienting *Gesamtkunstwerke*. The artist's first major survey, entitled 'Earworm' – which the wall text describes as 'a song, or part of a song, that gets stuck in your head and goes on and on and on' – was comprised of a selection of works that dated from 1999 to the present, and included ongoing projects, complimented by the staging of another

of Jacinto's projects, 'Les Voisins' in Culturgest's northern outpost in Porto. The notion of the earworm played out through the survey in the repetition and meme-like persistence of certain motifs, making the exhibition a complex affair in which works mingled to form a nervously dynamic and obliquely networking whole.

One of the earlier works in the show, *O (de Eco a Narciso)* [O (from Echo to Narcissus), 1999], is a sculptural installation that consists of a microphone hung by a chord, swiftly rotating in a broad circle above three peripherally placed modes of self-replication: a round mirror; a closed-circuit video camera and television screen; and a speaker, which was registered through brief, violent blips of feedback. With the auto-erotic self-involvement true to its mythological title, this tautology didn't seem to need a viewer to fulfil its own desires; in fact, the swinging microphone made the work hard to access. The

difficulty of focusing on any given aspect of its parts, and the impossibility of ignoring such a kinetic, clangorous entity, set up a repulsion-attraction scenario that resisted resolution.

The multi-part installation *L3 D23 R-3* (2007) was more physically spread out and varied in its themes and components. *L3 D23 R-3* refers to a subterranean coordinate in Portugal's Panasqueira mine, one of the largest tungsten mines in the world. The work comprised three sculptural installations, a wall painting, music, a drawing and a wall text. Each of the sculptural installations suggested the perceptual experience of being in the mine. For instance, *Mine* was a 1:1,000 scale maquette of the mine's galleries, made of wood, two-way mirrors and a strobe light placed at head height. The reflection of the blinking light upon the mirrors created a *mise-en-abyme* of the space, vastly extending it. Meanwhile a speeded-up recording of the artist practising Johann Sebastian Bach's *Cello Suites* (1717-23) was broadcast throughout the space. Its antic tempo corresponded to the pace of the strobe light, while a wall painting of a black striation, which wrapped around the majority of the exhibition, doubled as the literal contour of Bach's score and the negative representation of a white quartz seam as seen along the walls of the mine. Bach's mathematical modes of composition were here juxtaposed with the systematic parcelling and dismantling of earth – both capable of multiplying indefinitely. Combined with the strobe lights, music and numerous physical parts, the work successfully overwhelmed the senses.

A collaborative project *Parque* (Park, 2001-ongoing), consisted of a performance involving musicians, architecture, Dan Graham-esque two-way mirrors and the audience, in which the spectator is simultaneously surrounded by the work and displaced by its two way mirrors. *Parque* is typical of Jacinto's *oeuvre*, which solicits, divides and privileges the viewer's attention in sometimes conflicting ways through different modes of perception (aural, visual and even spatial). To complicate matters, most of Jacinto's work, albeit thoughtfully composed, is constructed ad hoc (and liable to evolve and become more complex from presentation to presentation): facture plays a decidedly secondary role. And while the work is process-based in so far as it often reveals its own process in the disunity of its parts, it is not about process per se. So you can't hang your hat on either of those interpretive standbys. What Jacinto's art requires is an almost total reconfiguration of how one looks, and the verbs one uses to do it (hearing, sensing, feeling – in one white, laboratory-like room containing three maquettes of different projects, the temperature was significantly lowered – in addition to seeing). As trite as it might sound, this work didn't make much sense until I intellectually and physically 'abandoned' myself to it. Only then did my body start looking for me.
Chris Sharp

Ricardo Jacinto
The Cones
(detail)
2008
Mixed media
150×140×243 cm

Ricardo Jacinto

Friedrich Petzel Gallery, New York, USA

The silvery black and white panorama of Sugar Loaf Mountain and Guanabara Bay, a gleaming ocean and the lights of Rio de Janeiro's high-rises, has the dreamlike aura of an old postcard. Another image floats above this scene: a photograph of an envelope addressed to the Friedrich Petzel Gallery, with a return address that consists simply of the names of three artists – Gabriel Lester, Jean-Pascal Flavien and Ducha. This was the evocative poster/invitation for 'Micro-Nation CAPACETE,' a sampling of art works, ephemera and documentation exhibited to mark the ten-year anniversary of the Rio-based curatorial collective Capacete Entertainment. Its goal of using the city as an interdisciplinary laboratory for examining and documenting aesthetic, political and social processes in Brazil may sound daunting, but the Capacete 'micro-nation' has produced exuberant Conceptual work that would be unimaginable elsewhere.

Conceived by local and international artists, critics and curators (in her catalogue essay Teresa Riccardi speculates that participants now number over 1,000), Capacete projects often take the form of interventions that transform or reveal aspects of the urban environment, although some are executed elsewhere in Brazil or South America. The impresario is Helmut Batista, who founded Capacete Entertainment (first named Espaço P and Espaço Purplex) in July 1998 in an apartment in the Flamengo neighbourhood of Rio. *Capacete* means 'helmet', a cryptic moniker until one learns that it was inspired by a character in Jim Jarmusch's *Night on Earth* (1991) – an immigrant New York cab driver named Helmut who is persistently called Helmet. This allusion carries a whiff of playful punning absurdity but also emphasizes the importance of fluid and subjective experience. As Riccardi writes, Capacete '[moves] around the area, trying to catch the essence of the ways its artists produce their work'. While forging a relationship with the art market on its own terms, it has pursued an array of strategies to reach a diverse audience, including residency programmes, travelling projects, a quarterly newspaper published until 2004, catalogues, a mobile office at the 2002 São Paulo Biennial and Capacete Cinema; it also collaborates with festivals and institutions.

For this exhibition Batista focused on works with a performative element. Greeting visitors – much as the statue welcomes tourists to Rio – was a photograph by Ducha of Rio's famous *Christ the Redeemer* bathed in crimson light. Closer examination revealed figures at the statue's base. In 2004 Ducha, who has completed multiple projects for Capacete, climbed Corcovado Mountain in order to place red filters over the white spotlights illuminating the revered monument, a slyly suggestive intervention that reached a metropolis-wide audience, until authorities stepped in and removed the gels. 'I feel

'Micro-Nation CAPACETE'
2008
Installation view

myself as inside a drawing,' Batista remarks in the catalogue of this and other Ducha projects, which have included spending two weeks in a cave in Sugar Loaf Mountain and creating a sailing club in Guanabara Bay.

Red signals another alchemical transformation in Flavien's three drawings in vermilion crayon depicting scenes, at once futuristic and antediluvian, of dinosaurs alongside a geometric architectural structure in a tropical setting. Under the auspices of Capacete, Flavien constructed the building in the drawing, titled *Viewer* (2007) – with four boxlike 'heads' that allow light to penetrate – on a cliff in a rural area about 45 minutes' drive outside Rio. The show included a model (he originally planned to make only a small version with transparent objects, which one could peer at and through, housed in the openings), along with video footage of the structure shot from a distance and of a bag of red dye, accompanied by an anxious drone recalling sci-fi soundtracks. In an interview with Batista published in the catalogue Flavien remarks: 'It sounded interesting at one point to put together

the word architecture and the word science-fiction. Is there such a thing already? What is it to make a science-fiction building?'

Lester's colour photographs of Peruvian petrol stations, published in a book titled *Sixty-two Gasoline Stations along a Stretch of the Pan American Highway*, grapple with time as well, and to a similarly mysterious effect – the structures feel outside of time, while their design ranges from dated to contemporary. Lester calls the series 'a timeless roadside present, where impressions of the past are received by the future'. The title, of course, pays tribute to the petrol stations Ed Ruscha shot along Route 66 in 1962, of which Lester was unaware when he began the project. His other contribution to the show, *A Man of Action Returns* (2006), is a film that he shot high in the Andes in Super-8 and transferred to DVD. Amid dancing black and white grains he materializes like a ghost, gestures dramatically and pantomimes pulling a rabbit out of a hat. Behind him the mountains seem to tremble.

Kristin M. Jones

Micro-Nation CAPACETE

Estratos

PAC Murcia (Proyecto Arte Contemporáneo / Contemporary Art Project), various venues, Murcia, Spain

You can glean everything you need to know about a place – or so the wisecrack goes – on the drive from the airport to the hotel. This seemingly reductive suggestion on the journey into Murcia provided an unexpectedly instructive overture to 'Estratos' ('strata' in Spanish), the first of this compact city's Proyecto Arte Contemporáneo / Contemporary Art Project ('PAC's) – what promise to be lean biennials in all but name. From a terminal that was brimming with Brummies and other Brits who had arrived from a rash of low-cost flight destinations, past the several dozen monstrous new golf resort-towns which draw them here near the Costa Cálida, the impression was that this Spanish region is just the latest to undergo a rapid leisure property invasion. Yet, set against curator Nicolas Bourriaud's context for 'Estratos' as a lateral consideration of contemporary archeology, the invasive 'golfing' of the landscape surrounding Murcia seems like just the most recent in a layer of civilisations. Perhaps future excavations of 18-holed ruins will portray them as baffling sacrificial structures?

I cannot imagine Robert Smithson would have ever taken to the fairways, but such spurious unearthing would doubtless have amused him – or at least his sardonic 'ruinologist' act of *Hotel Palenque* (1969–72). Though Smithson's art was visibly nowhere in this 21-artist multi-venue art project (the loan of *Hotel Palenque* apparently fell through), his influence was simultaneously everywhere throughout the two main 'keynote'

exhibition displays, as well the several satellite venues and public spaces throughout the city. Cyprien Gaillard's practice is haunted by Smithson's legacy – no more so conspicuously than in *The Smithsons* (2005), a crepuscular video of housing developments along the New Jersey riverfront. Also hosted in the Espacio AV venue, exquisite work by Ilana Halperin spun out from a study of the Icelandic island of Eldfeld – a volcanic accretion that was 'born' in 1973, the year of the artist's birth, and Smithson's death. Through a series of graphite drawings, charts, photographs, mineral sculptures, a publication and a screening of a 1970s' documentary by the 'Global Volcanism Programme', Halperin interwove narratives of eruption and Smithson-coincidence with the history of both herself and the Icelanders whose houses have been buried by lava. Sited in a former church, Allan McCollum's *The Dog From Pompei* (1991) – 45 contorted plaster sculptures made from a 'mould' formed during the 1st-century eruption of Vesuvius – similarly resulted from spectacular geological sculpting. Nearby it was artists themselves that were about to be buried, as the intrepid (or foolhardy) Abraham Poincheval & Laurent Tixador prepared to spend almost a month holed-up together in two conjoined cargo containers underneath a roadside verge.

The city Archeology Museum hosted a new project by Mark Dion – both the venue and the artist were surely shoo-in choices. Dion had replicated a cell, graffiti and all, from the city's prison alongside facsimile toothbrush-weapons and other improvised inmate tools. Among the other newly commissioned elements of the project –

Joachim Koester
Tarantism
2007
Film still

Paulina Olowska
Accidental Collages
2004
Screen prints
99×74 cm each

only five of the artists in total – Marjetica Potrc had perhaps responded most directly to the social context. She channeled her production financing into *A Farm in Murcia: Rainwater Harvesting* (2008), allowing an agricultural facility located outside the city (the site itself was closed to visits) to capture rainfall. Judging by the sign that read '*Agua Para Todos*' (water for all) on the Casa Constitucional in Murcia's historical centre, Potrc's modest act intervened into a fractious civil-resource war.

Several contributions provided an indispensably oblique take on the archeological tenor of 'Estratos'. Paulina Olowska's *Accidental Collages* (2004) and Joachim Koester's film *Tarantism* (2007), for example, dealt respectively with remnants of cultural evidence concerning the artist's own unresolved projects and the convulsive dance known as the Taranta. Yet three similarly more tangential selections that seemed promising in principal – Keith Tyson, Paul Noble and Verne Dawson – were betrayed by a rather mean choice of work. Elsewhere, while Eve Sussman's slick film *The Rape of The Sabine Women* (2005) strained for its vaunted epic dimension, Lara Almarcegui's *Rubble Mountain, Murcia* (2008) – a seven-storey school building converted into the huge mound of demolition debris which sat between narrow city streets – seemed almost effortless.

Angered by his fellow artist's critical writings, Donald Judd once distributed badges which protested 'Smithson is not my spokesman'. Though Smithson would doubtless be suspicious of the contrasting impulse of Bourriaud's 'cultural confinement' (as the former once labelled curating) of his legacy in the formal gallery displays part of 'Estratos' – he would surely have felt ruinously at home with Almarcegui's anti-monument to the processing of our cultural inheritances.
Max Andrews

Peer, London, UK

The first steps into a solo career after achieving success as part of a group are never easy, yet this is the situation that Milly Thompson faces in her exhibition at Peer. Thompson was part of the prominent art collective BANK, which in the 1990s staged a series of exhibitions that pilloried the contemporary art scene. Members dropped out slowly over the years until the group finally broke up in 2005, by which time Thompson had been part of BANK for 15 years. It is thus inevitable that the group casts a long shadow over her new endeavours, but happily she brings those experiences into her latest work.

For its subject matter this show continues to draw on the machinations of the art world, and particularly on what it means to be an artist in today's commercially driven market. Two of the works focus on Thompson herself: she performs a subtle dance between revealing fears of mediocrity or failure and critiquing the art world's over-interest in such personal disclosures. This is most prevalent in *Opera* (all works 2008), a text piece contained in a short book that visitors are encouraged to keep. BANK was renowned for its witty use of wordplay, both in its exhibition titles and in works created by the group, and this dexterity is evident in *Opera*, where Thompson explores the art-world preoccupation with the question-and-answer artist interview.

The piece begins conventionally enough. Thompson and an anonymous interviewer discuss BANK, and particularly the success and sense of

belonging that came with being part of the group: 'We really cracked it. We were the beautiful people. It was great.' Proceedings, though, suddenly take an unexpected turn, and new voices – of other artists and writers – appear scattered throughout the conversation. These are woven into the text rather than presented as simple quotations (although their origin is revealed in footnotes), and serve to disrupt the intimate flow of the interview while simultaneously hiding Thompson within it. Thompson uses the pseudo-interview to critique both the self-conscious nature of interviews and the way they are used to explain art works to an audience. In alerting us to this game-playing, though, questions of authenticity arise, which are, of course, also tackled by Thompson in the interview.

In the photographic work *La danse de l'amour et de la haine de soi* (The dance of self-love and self-hate, 2005) Thompson is on her own. She remains both present yet hidden – quite literally – by appearing in the centre of the work but shrouded almost completely beneath a blanket, slumped and dejected as though overwhelmed by the work at hand. Despite this, the studio in which she is placed is strangely impersonal. With its empty champagne bottle and coffee jug, and its walls strewn with source photographs and drawings, it fulfils all expectations of the 'artist's studio' while revealing little.

A series of drawings, of figures sketched alone but grouped as though at some kind of dinner

party, is similarly hard to penetrate. The figures are disengaged from the audience – avoiding eye contact and presented with their mouths either covered or simply erased. More observational analysis is encouraged in a video work, *Basking in the melodrama of my own self-consciousness*, which reveals a middle-aged woman sitting alone in an outdoor café. Her dress and demeanour signify that she is wealthy, but we are left to speculate idly on her importance to Thompson, with few clues, although in the interview she is explained as signifying a terror of ageing and loneliness. Edited into the video are stock images of hand-crafted pottery and footage of expressive dance, all of which appear hopelessly unfashionable in the glare of a white cube space.

By contrast, a series of brightly coloured Modernist sculptures that round off the exhibition are confident. While the materials used are basic – they are constructed from the humble balsa wood – neatly undercutting any slickness, the works are subtitled 'a curator's friend', teasingly acknowledging the sculptures' easy, fashionable style.

Self-consciousness runs throughout the works here, yet with Thompson's gently humorous and insightful touch they never become self-indulgent. Thompson reveals a multitude of opinions and ideas on the contemporary art world while never clarifying where her own sentiments lie, alluding to the performance that is inherent in being an artist and to the genuine anxieties that such role-playing entails.

Eliza Williams

Milly Thompson
La danse de l'amour et de la haine de soi
(The dance of self-love and self-hate)
2005
Inkjet print
54×78 cm

Milly Thompson

Pauline Boudry
& Renate Lorenz
Normal Work
2007
DVD still

Les Complices, Zurich, Switzerland

The 19th-century British diarist Arthur Munby was fond of working women, especially when heavy physical labour had given them a pronounced masculine appearance. On his extensive travels around Britain, he took photographic portraits of many such women. Munby explored his preferences not only in these private sociological studies, but also in a sadomasochist love affair with his maidservant Hannah Cullwick, whom he secretly married after a 20-year relationship in 1873. In her free time, Cullwick, sometimes accompanied by Munby, would visit photographic studios to pose as a labourer, a black slave or a bourgeois lady.

While researching the representation of gender roles, Berlin-based artists Renate Lorenz and Pauline Boudry happened upon an archive of images and writings by this 19th century couple, from which they adopted a number of motifs to form the basis of their Zurich show. A room devoted to the 'Cullwick and Munby Collection' presented some of the original images in a museum-like setting; with selected framed works documenting this historical attempt to broach the boundaries of gender and status via staged photography.

For Cullwick, slipping into the part of the exotic Other while continuing to embody a number of roles in her working and private life doesn't seem to have been a problem. In spite of her altered social status after marrying Munby, Cullwick insisted on continuing to work for him and on being paid

a wage for doing so. In today's terms, Cullwick's hobby of staging photographic scenes and her way of life, both departing from what would have been generally accepted gender roles, could be described as queer. At the same time, taken together, the diaries and photographic material she left behind vividly conjure up the working conditions of a Victorian domestic servant. In one image, her dirty hands push up the short sleeves of her dress further still, revealing her muscular arms to the photographer. The leather strap she wears around her wrist, her 'slave band' as she called it, symbolizes her role in the relationship with Munby.

A century and a half later, Boudry and Lorenz's 13-minute colour DVD *Normal Work* (2007) invites viewers to a public rehearsal of Cullwick's staged scenarios. The projection is framed by theatre curtains. Against a series of backdrops, including a Romantic landscape and a 19th-century bourgeois salon, an actor (credited as Werner Hirsch, though it remains unclear whether this in turn might be the pseudonym of a drag performer) recreates four of Cullwick's poses, directed from off-screen by a clearly audible female voice. As he constantly checks his posture in a mirror and varies the identity of his figure, there are brief pauses and strange uncertainties in his performance. From the comfort of the 'auditorium', viewers are able to follow the laborious rehearsals and ultimate control required to create these still images: a serving girl in Victorian dress steps in front of a landscape; she slowly pushes up the sleeve of her smock, showing off her

well-developed muscles; looking proudly into the camera, she smiles contentedly. Visibly marked by the way she earns her living, the maid presents her body to the camera as attractive, desirable, almost auto-erotic.

Ultimately, the uncertain relationship between the mirror, the director and the performer prevents the latter from becoming a mere object of historical scenery and costumes. Instead, by choosing to film a portrayal of a rehearsal, Boudry and Lorenz force a constant repositioning of the characters in relation to wage labour, sexuality and social role, successfully linking the visual fantasies of a historical worker with the working process of contemporary artistic production. As the film starts, the performer walks across the set in modern street clothes and personally puts the finishing touches to various details on a woodland backdrop. In the second scene, he re-enacts a historical performance against this background, while in the third, an S&M photograph (Del LaGrace Volcano's *Daddy Boy Dykes*, 1991) suddenly appears in its place. In the final scene, he – still in the attire of a Victorian woman – starts to speak of the various other jobs he will have to do in the coming weeks to finance his participation in Boudry and Lorenz's film project. Speaking in English with a strong German accent, he explains that he actually has a master's degree, and earns his living as a part-time university lecturer, assistant librarian and furniture packer.

Burkhard Meltzer
Translated by Nicholas Grindell

Pauline Boudry
& Renate Lorenz

John Connelly Presents, New York, USA

Little compares to the shock of seeing the skeletal images of Jorge Zontal and Felix Partz in 'Negative Thoughts', AA Bronson's breathtaking exhibition of 2001. The men were Bronson's partners in the Conceptual media-based art collective General Idea, and the photos, taken in 1994, capture the ravaging effects of AIDS: Zontal just months before he died; Partz just hours after his death. These images stand among the most disarming encounters with mortality made during that decade and are a rare testimonial to life and death. 'Negative Thoughts', a breakthrough show for Bronson as a solo artist, was also a raw self-portrait in which he publicly shared his grief for his lost friends and partners, as well as for the passing of an artistic identity and experiment – General Idea – that had defined his professional career.

Intimate experience and introspection continue to characterize Bronson's artistic practice, which has shifted away from reflective memoriam and towards spirited living. Although he has lost his collaborative moniker, Bronson continues to make work with others, and 'AA Bronson's School for Young Shamans' shared his experience as an elder statesman who learns significantly from the younger queer artists he is helping to guide.

The exhibition was divided into two sections. In the main gallery were works by Bronson spanning 40 years, and although many of the pieces on view were self-portraits, none evinced a fixed identity of the artist. Witness the mesmerizing 'Mirror Sequence' series (1969–70), in which Bronson photographs his own fractured reflection; *Evidence of Body Binding* (1970), which caught disembodied sections of his own flesh tied taut with string; costumed portraits shot by Zontal in

the mid-1970s; or the recent *Self-portrait, August 2, 2007* (2007), a colour photograph in which the artist's naked body is captured in the reflection of a silver orb that sits amid the detritus of his office desk. The suggestion is that Bronson's 'self' is an amalgamation of the circumstance and people that surround him – an impression that is strengthened by the inclusion of printed ephemera from his archives that reference trauma (newspapers from John F. Kennedy's assassination) and transgression (assorted folios dealing with sexually 'aberrant' behaviour).

Bronson describes his General Idea years as a time in which the group eclipsed the individual, and this exhibition suggests that he still locates himself in reference to those he holds most dear. By including a billboard-size picture of his lover Mark cradling his premature daughter Anna, or self-portraits by Zontal, Bronson continues to define identity in part through shared experience. In this respect the 'young shamans' he enlisted are a similarly clubby group, and the onslaught of art work that occupied the side gallery and comprised the show's second half was rife with insider references. The focal point was a shrine-like tent, *Cabine* (2008), by Bronson and Scott Treleaven, around which densely hung drawings, photographs and films competed for space. *Cabine* was the site of an opening night performance in which a nude Michael Dudeck sat perfectly still while holding a fish. After the fact the canopied *cabana* felt over-theatrical, as did item idem's armour-like coat made of gold Louis Vuitton bags and dedicated to the original shaman-artist Joseph Beuys. Elsewhere, spirituality and sexuality collided in interesting ways. In Christophe Chemin's film *The Gold Room* (2004) the artist's constant jumping, often in the nude, turns into a levitation through

AA Bronson
Self-Portrait, August 2, 2007
2007
Glycee print
76×61 cm

the spaces of an apartment, and J.X. Williams' assorted brooms, paddles and measuring sticks, resting against the strewn floor, straddle folk religion and flagellation.

Curator Bill Arnheim describes Bronson's practice as the 'interweaving of tantalizing pleasures and profound trauma', themes that resonate throughout the younger men's work. Particularly impressive was Naufus Ramirez-Figueroa's *Masturbating in the Fatherland* (2007), a provocative film in which scenes of the artist masturbating with a carrot are intercut with footage of his musician father singing a Guatemalan folk-song. Pride and enjoyment are evident in both scenarios, colliding brilliantly. Also excellent was Bronson and Terence Koh's collaboration *The painter looks through to the other side of the hole/In search of the White Knave* (2004/2007), a life-size replica of twinned toilet stalls joined by a glory hole. Koh's side was covered in cut-out photocopies of gay pornography, while Bronson's pristine white space offered the lingering visitor an untitled artist's book filled with pictures of spread rectums downloaded from the Internet.

The painter ... resonated on multiple levels, from the fetishes of architecture, design and gallery installation to the evolving sites of illicit sex from public rest-rooms to the Internet and beyond. It also invited physical and emotional engagement, underscoring the latent performative nature of much of the work here. Inside the stall, I felt acutely aware of my outsider status as a straight woman, but I also felt privileged to bear witness to a vital dialogue Bronson created among a sub-set of the young gay art community. As with his portraits of Zontal and Partz, he continues to be a 'survivor' who helps viewers and 'young shamans' alike to continue to turn towards life.

Katie Sonnenborn

'AA Bronson's School For Young Shamans'
2008
Exhibition view

AA Bronson's School for Young Shamans

Joonsung Bae's *The Costume of Painter Kiss AP2/2* (2007), a lenticular image that, when viewed from one angle showed a brooding Caravaggio-esque figure smooching a silk-gowned maiden and from another showed the maiden *sans* clothes, while Debbie Han's science fiction-y digital light-jet print *Walking Three Graces* (2007) transformed Antonio Canova's sculpture from 1814-17 into something between the replicants of Ridley Scott's *Blade Runner* (1982) and John Wyndham's *Midwich Cuckoos* (1957). And yet among the disparate works in Lee's show, commonalities now and then emerged. Mee-kyoung Shin's beautiful pots carved from pearly soap were echoed by the lunar *Vessel* (2005) in Bohnchang Koo's digitalized print, and the pale luminescence – a cathode ray penumbra – that emanated from both pieces also suffused Daesoo Kim's large-format photograph *Bamboo Field* (2003), as though moonbeams had soaked into the crop's woolly fronds. Close by this grouping, a flat screen showed Paik's *Beuys and Shaman* (1999), a documentary video of a memorial rite (all anointed fedoras and smouldering sage) that the artist performed four years after the death of his friend Joseph Beuys. I was reminded of the pair's shared interest in the moon, something Paik described in the title of a 1965 piece as 'the oldest TV'.

Like most Europeans, my knowledge of the history of postwar Korean art is pretty skimpy, and it would be reckless of me to pass comment on whether Lee's show provided a representative survey. In the end, though, this was perhaps not her point. By appropriating Paik's zappy way with his material, she pointed to fresh modes of negotiating two nearly exhausted exhibition genres – those based on nationality and those based on influence. Good Morning not to Paik's familiar work, then, but to the way in which it is beginning to inform curatorial practice.

Tom Morton

Korean Cultural Centre, London, UK

On New Year's Day 1984 the Korean video art pioneer Nam June Paik broadcast his telethon-like work *Good Morning Mr. Orwell* from a series of satellite-linked television studios in New York, West Germany, South Korea and Paris' Pompidou Centre, to an estimated audience of some 25 million people. Comprising live and pre-recorded material, its highlights included Merce Cunningham dancing with his own delayed image, John Cage producing music by trilling a feather across the needles of a cactus, and British synth-pop trio the Thompson Twins performing their drive-time classic 'Hold Me Now' (1983). Plagued with technical problems as the piece was (each studio was forced by faltering satellite links into a series of local improvisations), it remained for Paik an effective rebuttal of Orwellian prophecy. In the artist's 1984 television was not a lens through which an oppressive state might pry into its citizens' most private moments, but rather the enabler of a sunny sort of globalization, in which geographically and culturally distant viewers might gather together to watch what was in effect an avant-garde precursor of 1985's Live Aid – an event in which, oddly enough, the Thompson Twins also participated.

Staged at London's newly opened Korean Cultural Centre (KCC) and featuring work by Paik and 24 other Korean artists born between the late 1930s and the early 1980s, 'Good Morning Mr. Nam June Paik' embraced the enthusiastic, day-break

spirit of the 1984 broadcast. Significantly, the exhibition was largely unconcerned with Paik's influence on Korean art – Young Kyun Lim's video *Nam June Paik's Wink* (2003), in which a still image of the artist peering out of a screen-less TV set now and then flutters a single set of eyelashes, was perhaps the only piece here that would be inconceivable without his example. But if artistic disciples were in short supply, Paik's channel-hopping method of ordering and reordering visual information – exemplified by his seminal and widely known video *Global Groove* (1973), the centrepiece of the KCC show – was employed by curator Jiyoon Lee to bring together a group of works that were as varied in their preoccupations and tone as the collective contents of the TV listings.

A click of the metaphorical remote, and the bourgeois comedy of Waljong Lee's paper frieze of poppies, canaries and irate golfers *Jeju Median Way* (2007) gave way to the melodrama of Jonghak Kim's tense, mustardy, Van Gogh-like canvas *Landscape of Sorak Mountain* (1988). Another click, and the rolling news of Atta Kim's impressive photographs of Korea's demilitarized zone – images whose eight-hour exposure time reveals not movement but an eerie, entrenched stillness – was replaced by the (home from) home improvement of Goldsmiths' alumnus Youngin Hong's digital collages, which re-imagine London's grey skyline as a fecund habitat for gigantic birds, butterflies and blooming flowers. Bodice-ripping historical drama was provided by

Atta Kim
ON AIR Project
2003
Chromogenic print
188×248 cm

Young Kyun Lim
Nam June Paik's Wink
2003
Video still

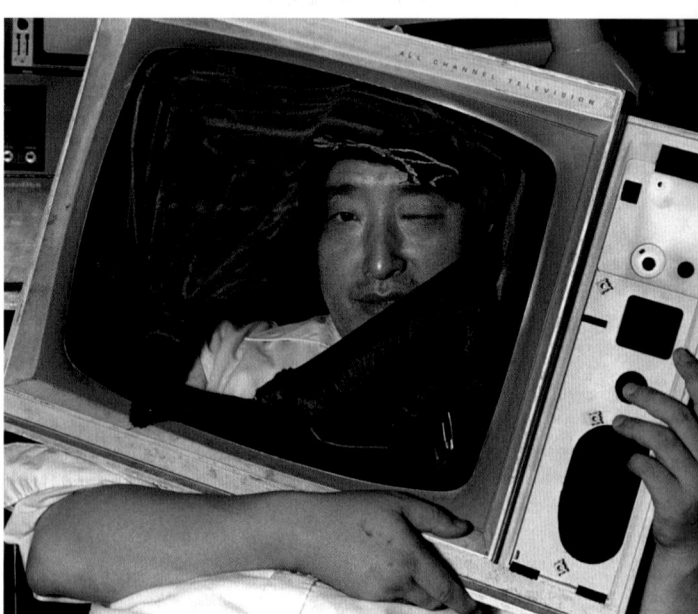

Good Morning
Mr. Nam June Paik

Galleria Francesca Kaufmann, Milan, Italy

Modernist architects often called for customised building based on the manual combination of parts to be replaced by mass production. Alison and Peter Smithson, for example, responded to this debate with their *The House of the Future* (1956), which was to be assembled from various parts, rather like a car, and which would only have become financially viable when produced in very large numbers. At the same time, however, the likes of John McHale and Eduardo Paolozzi were creating Pop art collages; hand-made using specially imported American magazines. In art, then, supposedly retrograde techniques – the direct assembly of materials from different contexts – were the subject of ongoing experimentation, as has always been the case with the avant-garde.

In architecture today, mass customization and rapid prototyping represent attempts to resolve the conflict between unique features and mass production at a high technological level. In art, on the other hand, collage is currently being rediscovered as a modest, manual form of expression that is considered particularly well-suited to the times – one need only think of recent exhibitions such as 'Collage: The Unmonumental Picture' at the New Museum in New York. More in keeping with the format of a gallery show, 'Cohabitation: 13 Artists and Collage', which consisted mainly of new works plus a small number of earlier examples tracing the development of collage since the 1960s, was less concerned with claims to emblematic status for the medium. Most of the featured artists had no previous links with the gallery and some were exhibiting in Italy for the first time. In a direct sense, the title 'Cohabitation' refers to the coexistence of disparate elements in a collage; on a broader level, it also refers to human and architectural bodies.

Looking at the works by Linder and John Stezaker, one is struck at first by a feeling of déjà vu, a memory of earlier phases in their careers, both artists having been 'rediscovered' in recent times. With astonishing insistence, Stezaker continues to work with two images per collage. The three pieces on show, *Marriage (Film Portrait Collage) L / LI / LII* (2008), function like optical puzzles: at first glance, the two conjoined faces hardly fit together; then they suddenly seem perfectly to complement and comment on each other. (Goshka Macuga's works *Angel of Anarchy I / II / III*, 2008, are highly elegant hybrids similar to Stezaker's, also working with just two elements, in this case blending movie beauties with trees.) Linder's untitled pieces from 2007 are tougher and more homogeneous than her earlier works. Perhaps the most striking difference to the work of her predecessors from the Independent Group is the more subtle joining of parts, creating combinations with absurd psychological and sexual connotations – disproportionately large rose blossoms covering women's eyes, heads or legs – that seem plausible.

Cohabitation

The work of architect and designer Carlo Mollino (1905–73) not only blurs the borders between artistic genres, but also breaks down the distinction between a project and its realization. Having initially photographed architecture himself, Mollino later collaborated with other photographers. Especially in his work with Riccardo Moncalvo (who recently passed away at the age of 93), this partnership was a symbiotic one. In fact, when Moncalvo started to work on his own on commissions by Mollino, he still did so very much in the latter's spirit. His photomontage of Mollino's design for Turin's Theatre Royal (*Fotomontaggio del Teatro Regio di Torino*, c. 1965) is a prime example. The image is constructed of four carefully matched layers: a photograph of a model of Mollino's planned project is spliced into an image of the surrounding buildings; the background is a dramatic sky; the broad but deserted streets are animated by a single female passer-by and a Pininfarina sports car parked in front of the theatre – both somewhat surprisingly depicted in colour against the black and white background. Together with a tiny arcade that has been added to the townscape, receding into infinity in a crazy

John Stezaker
Marriage (Film Portrait Collage) L
2008
Collage
27×18 cm

perspective, these insertions open up new, unspecified, latently erotic horizons of meaning.

The show – which, in addition to those already mentioned, included works by Candice Breitz, Maggie Cardelus, Lorna Macintyre, David Maljkovic, Lecia Dole-Recio, Frances Stark, Nicole Wermers and Pae White – raised issues of collection and selection; both in terms of the curatorial choices of works on display, and in relation to the genre of collage, which is dependent on these factors. In collage, the disparate elements must fit together, at least graphically, and this calls for a range of options. To this end, Stezaker purchased a comprehensive collection of photographic material from the film industry; others, such as Moncalvo, painstakingly assembled their own archives of backgrounds, figures, etc., by taking each photograph themselves. Perhaps this marks the continuing relevance of collage: the way it mixes not only different techniques and references, but also otherwise distinct roles, thus rendering production and collection visibly interdependent.

Frank Boehm
Translated by Nicholas Grindell

Galerie Barbara Weiss, Berlin, Germany

Maria Eichhorn's work can come across like the person at a dinner party who, regardless of the attendant social balancing acts and middle-class nodding, says something in a loud, strong, dry voice; something that has been bugging her. It might seem inappropriate in the moment, but there is nearly always a point to what she says. In her most recent solo exhibition, this was once again the case, but to really drive the issues home, Eichhorn also used the device of rhetorical reiteration: the show consisted entirely of works previously made for unrelated, far-flung occasions and contexts since 2001. Was the show intended to invoke artistic introspection? Or was it simply the case that the works deserved another airing for her hometown audience? Whatever the rationale, an interesting thing happened as a result: the traditional flow of ideas and works from the hot-house of an established commercial gallery to the outside world and its plethora of institutions and biennials was reversed.

Take *von 12,37 bis 36,08 = 24,94 von 100%* (From 12,37 to 36,08 = 24,94 from 100%, 2007), produced for the Steirischer Herbst festival in Graz, which consists of a bookshop display table in the form of a Venus symbol, and the artist's thick publication listing all of the festival's female participants, from the event's inception in 1968 until 2007. The percentages referred to in the title indicate, respectively, the ratio of women participants in the first and last years, and the average percentage overall. Whatever one may think of gender quotas, the facts give weight to the idea that, even in what's considered to be one of the

most progressive contexts for contemporary art, the most basic feminist goals of equal representation for women have not been achieved. Eichhorn employed women from 'feminist backgrounds' to work at her bookshop and they received the proceeds from the sales. In its gallery incarnation, the women weren't present however, and viewers couldn't touch the displayed books, although copies could be purchased from the gallery desk. This seemed a strange move, removing the relational aspect and turning the work into a formal, information-orientated piece. The table made of plywood looked good, as did the books lined up with incredible precision like dominos, a marching band or a chorus line. But somehow, coming to the table for a good chat would have also been nice.

Joint Account No. 1711601, Bank of Fukuoka, Yahata Branch 411 (2001) compounded this sense that the works on display had the status of after-the-fact evidence. This project was originally conceived and realized for the duration of the first Yokohama Triennial. Eichhorn arranged for her production budget to be deposited into an open-access bank account, which literally anyone could make deposits into or withdrawals from at will. Of course, you had to know about it, for instance by taking an information sheet displayed in Yokohama. The work, as explained in an extensive dossier accompanying this new exhibition that gives the background to all of the works, was intended to demonstrate 'the idea of people acting for the common good, with each participant being equally responsible'. In the show, the piece was reduced to a savings account passbook lying in a brick-sized hole cut into the gallery wall,

Maria Eichhorn
von 12,37 bis 36,08 = 24,94 von 100 %
(From 12,37 to 36,08 = 24,94 from 100%)
2007
Wood, steel, linoleum, Perspex, books
180×400×200 cm

behind glass. Perhaps, by implication, the Utopian moment the work created is also now unreachable.

The best work in the exhibition concerned censorship and the arbitrary exercising of power. *Prohibited Imports* (2003), the only piece made originally for a gallery setting, consists of a wood-framed glass vitrine filled with books. On top of these volumes lie two copies of Robert Mapplethorpe's 1992 monograph opened at the same page. One of these twin photographs of *Patrice, N.Y.C.* (1977), depicting a man's groin, was defaced with sandpaper by Japanese censors to remove part of the penis. Eichhorn had posted all of the books contained in the vitrine to a Japanese address knowing that they might be subject to censorship. The other books, which included Douglas Crimp's *AIDS: Cultural Analysis / Cultural Activism* (1988) and a biography of Jodie Foster – presumably included in the selection not necessarily to court the censor but to make a point about queer intertexuality, and the power of words versus image and a queer intertexuality–, were left unscathed. Oddly, the anonymous censor's careful handiwork has something appealing about it; the mark looks like a white cloud hovering over the image, rather than inscribed on it. It is this that gives the work a strange, personalized extra layer of subtlety.

Eichhorn's hard-nosed and enduring critique of art institutions, and of financial, legal and administrative frameworks, is testimony to the fact that, even when she repeats herself firmly, the art-world powers that be will still keep inviting her to participate in their events, and that, while she won't necessarily have an easy time, they definitely need to be exposed to voices like hers.
Dominic Eichler

Maria Eichhorn

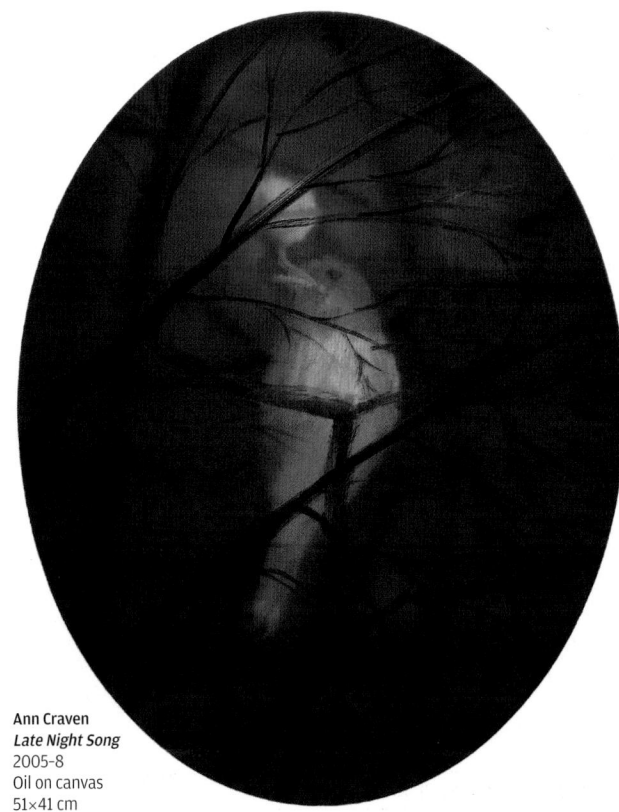

Knoedler Gallery, New York, USA

Ann Craven uses conceptual precepts to guide her paintings. Beginning with clichéd, stock subject matter such as birds, deer, moons and flowers, she neutralizes her storybook content through continual variations and repetitions, shifting the conversation about her work into a theoretical frame that considers the body as a whole, rather than its individual parts. For example, in 2002 and 2004 Craven staged two identical exhibitions at the Gasser & Grunert Gallery, New York, which differed only in the size of the works on view; another time she hung simultaneous installations of a series of 400 moons: the originals were shown in New York, while 400 brand new copies were placed on view in Cincinnati.

Such stratagems eliminate any sense of individuality or preciousness within Craven's work, and the wry, cerebral installations urge viewers to approach the paintings as interchangeable objects. This trajectory continued last summer, when Craven exhibited a group of palette paintings made from off-strokes and paint pools alongside stacks of cardboard boxes in which the 400 moon copies sat, hermetically sealed.

At Knoedler, the esteemed uptown gallery more closely associated with the Frick Collection than, say, the New Museum, Craven's skill as a painter was celebrated. Working wet on wet, her deft brushstrokes have gained surety with every year, and in the new paintings rigidity and precision have been replaced by looser brushstrokes, washes of colour and a softer, more expressive touch. The installation consisted of two themes (birds and moons), which are subjects that have occupied Craven for over a decade. Six expertly

rendered new bird paintings hung in the front gallery. Of particular note were *Wasn't Sorry Calla Lily #1* and *#2* (2008), mirror-image paintings in which the birds are seen beginning to dissolve into the background. Also wonderful is *Bold as Love* (2008), in which a bird sits in front of a vortex of pinks and violets that dominate the canvas and draw the viewer in. Girlish colours for seemingly girlish subjects, the paintings invoke the *grande dame* Georgia O'Keeffe in palette, subject, form and forcefulness. Arthur Dove, another American Modernist, also comes to mind with his unnerving, powerful and sometimes terrifying natural abstractions. Birds are generic and somewhat pedantic subjects, and Craven has used them *ad nauseam* as a vehicle to develop her own visual language. Here, as they veer towards abstraction, she seems to be on the brink of something new.

In the main gallery 94 moon paintings progressively wrapped around the room in a horizontal band. The works date from 1995, when Craven began sneaking outdoors to capture the moon in its various guises, and the project has grown compulsively since then (on a good night she will make as many as ten paintings). In them the sky ranges in colour from midnight blue to jet black, creating space for a yellow sliver, a lipstick smudge, a white smear or an amber orb. Around the room the moon dips and rises, waxes and wanes, slides behind clouds and peeks out from trees, a veritable skyscape that marks the passage of time.

Halfway through the installation Craven decided the moons needed to rise up further, and the entire series shifted in register by nearly three feet, from 153 to 234 centimetres above

Ann Craven
Late Night Song
2005–8
Oil on canvas
51×41 cm

Anna Craven
Below Left: *Wasn't Sorry Calla Lily #2*
Below Right: *Wasn't Sorry, Calla Lily #1*
2008
Oil on canvas
Each 152×122 cm

the floor. This was the first time she has rehung midway through a show, and the impact was striking, particularly in this multi-levelled and refined exhibition space. It made the installation feel alive and transitory, much like the moons themselves, which hover between a sketch and a painting. Measuring 36 centimetres square, they felt portable, conveying a sense of immediacy, even haste. Much like John Marin's five-minute landscapes of the rugged Maine coast, they are complete but not completed.

What, then, to make of these paintings, which hover between conceptual idiom and beautiful object? Installed in groups or series, the sheer volume of works triggers a debate about the conventions of both painting and exhibitions. Yet taken as individual entities, the conceptual framework recedes into the object's history, and once you move beyond the naive subject matter it is possible to luxuriate in her deft sense of colour and assured touch. That this is so readily possible is a constant surprise, for logic suggests that this type of straightforward, representational painting would short-circuit rather than open out. However, by reworking, re-presenting and returning to the same stock subject matter, Craven is building a corpus that engages the most pressing issues of today's art world, including questions of consumption, collection, authenticity, value and skill. It is a curiously compelling project, and this latest manifestation suggests that there is still far to go.
Katie Sonnenborn

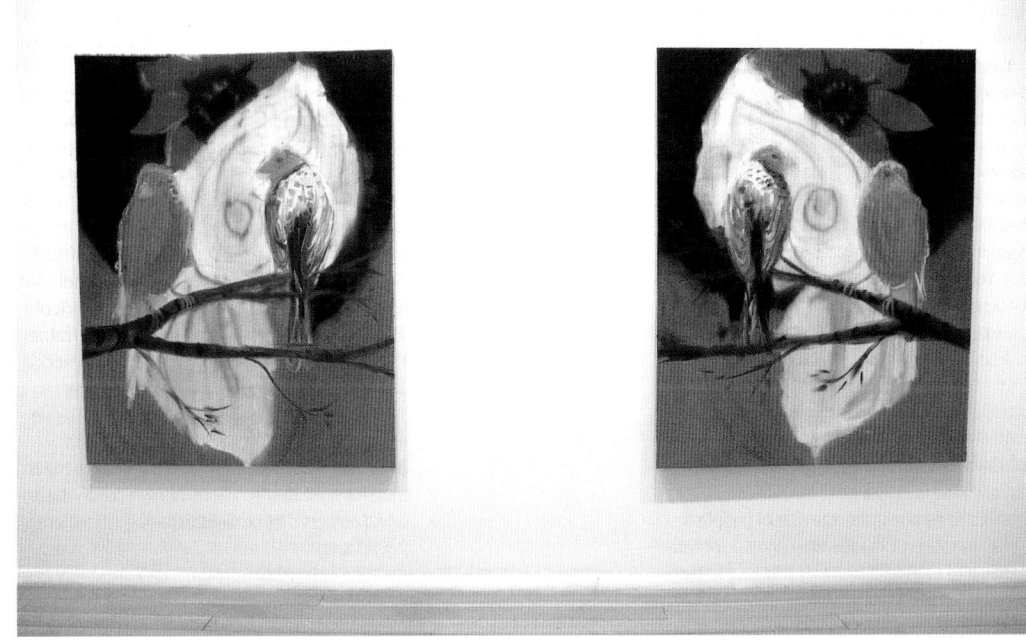

Ann Craven

Tomas Saraceno
Galaxies Forming along Filaments, Like Droplets along the Strands of a Spider's Web
2008
Elastic rope
Installation view

Tanya Bonakdar Gallery, New York, USA

The startling news that the universe is structured like a sponge was revealed when astronomers discovered that galaxies cluster into filaments and wall-like sheets, leaving huge voids of nearly empty space. In his dramatic installation *Galaxies Forming along Filaments, Like Droplets along the Strands of a Spider's Web* (2008) Tomas Saraceno applied another analogy inspired by that finding: the comparison between our 'spongy' universe and a complex spider web in which groups of stars and other matter are strung like shining beads of water along invisible strands. Saraceno, a former architect known for following in the tradition of other maverick designers who have developed provocatively inventive projects with the goal of changing human behaviour and living conditions – such as Buckminster Fuller, Archigram and the Ant Farm group – also has a knack for presenting his conceptual projects in ways that capture the imagination.

Along with a Fuller-esque collapsing of the micro- and macro-cosmic, the idea of energy spanning vast expanses of time came into play. Sitting near a window in the entryway was *Planet Earth, 500 Million Years (Working Title)* (2008), a vaguely planetary agglomeration of eye-like solar-powered lamps that gathered energy from both the sun and the artificial interior lighting to illuminate the gallery at night. Next was the show-stopping *Galaxies Forming along Filaments …*, a lacy, bulbous shape formed of, and suspended from, interwoven elastic rope that stretched to the floor, walls and ceiling – picture an almost

mystically delicate celestial loofah. (It also resembled a human brain's neuronal network, another smaller structure to which the universe has been compared.) The room was flooded with light, and that stark brilliance combined with the unevenly spaced, perspective-demolishing, radiating strands of elastic was initially disorienting. To pass through the main ground-floor gallery in which the piece was installed to reach other works in a smaller room behind it, one had to choose a path and duck under or step over the ropes in the way. Bumping into one meant sending shivers throughout the skeletal cosmological web, but clumsiness worked to the viewer's advantage, providing this surrogate universe with a sense of tangible interconnectedness and mutability.

If this spiky web was somewhat menacing and other-worldly, it was also poetic, an adjective that has often been applied to Saraceno's buoyant creations and one that Fuller (who saw Albert Einstein as a great poet) embraced. The importance of playful, intuitive experimentation to his project was made even clearer in a selection of photographs and smaller sculptural works. These tied the giant web to such projects as *Air-Port-City* (2002-ongoing) a vision for cell-like airborne cities – Saraceno has compared it to a flying airport – that can separate and come together like clouds or nomadic tribes, erasing political, social, cultural and military boundaries. The title of *Flying Garden/Air-Port-City/12SW* (2007), a cluster of PVC balloons joined with elastic rope and fabric webbing, relates to another aspect of *Air-Port-City*, its incorporation of rootless plants, native to Africa and South America,

that take in all their nourishment through their leaves. *Hydrogen Cloud Explosion (Working Title)* (2008), a Perspex geometrical structure housing another network of black elastic – an enclosed, miniature variation on the installation in the first room – suggests an elegant, ship-in-a-bottle-style model of galaxies in the throes of birth. And in *Air-Port-City Cloud Classification* (2008) white-paper dodecahedrons arranged on the floor hinted at how the cloud-like platforms might join together, while they also called to mind the ancient equation between this topological form and the universe, as well as another astonishing recent scientific theory: that the universe may, in fact, be shaped like a dodecahedron.

Does it matter whether Saraceno's proposals are practical? Unlike many technology-besotted art works generated in the early part of this century, which flirted with a creepily decadent disregard for real-life implications, his futuristic visions are, for the most part unobtrusive, idealistic and likely to inspire other outside-the-box thinkers. But there is also something undeniably sad about his overarching awareness of the need to escape what Fuller – who hoped that we would be able to head off the current global-warming crisis by deploying technological innovations to tap renewable energy sources – lovingly called 'Spaceship Earth'. Saraceno's own brand of optimism can be as contagious as his creations are visionary and thought-provoking, and perhaps it's not too late for such architect-poets to save us. At the same time his radiant webs, bubbles and clouds are a reminder of darker, perhaps intractable realities.
Kristin M. Jones

Tomas Saraceno

Galleria S.A.L.E.S, Rome, Italy

A stout cavalier straddles a parade horse, his head bowed slightly to survey his troops in promenade. In the fresco he created for Florence Cathedral, Paolo Uccello painted Sir John Hawkwood and his horse in one-point perspective, on the same level with the viewer, but depicted the cenotaph on which the mercenary and his horse stand in three-point perspective, viewed from below. The multiple vanishing points upset the hierarchy between the subject and the object, disorienting the viewer and the viewed: the equestrian statue is indeed monumentalized on the impressive cenotaph, but Uccello's perspectival play pulls the viewer up alongside the cavalier.

In Shahryar Nashat's recent exhibition, 'Placed High for Dramatic Impact', two idealized plinths on flat, coloured backgrounds – *Disappointed Pedestal (Red)* and *Disappointed Pedestal (Green)* (both 2008) – are also portrayed as though viewed from below, but they lie empty, commemorating only their own forms. The artist employs a similar strategy in a black marble sculpture of a plinth resting on another plinth. The work, entitled *Downscaled and Overthrown* (2008), is the show's centrepiece, though it is displayed in a back room like a treasured relic. The marble sculpture rests on a tall pedestal built from medium-density fibreboard, the rough surface of which accentuates the gleaming polish of the rich rock: while the synthetic, processed MDF recalls the tangible truths of everyday experience, the dark marble radiates the glow of an ideal like Aristotle's 'phantasma' that distant image of an idea that appears in foggy flashes in the mind before a thought is articulated. In Nashat's double plinth, the 'downscaled' pedestals memorialize the absent, overthrown symbols of power that once proudly announced their dominance. Thus, the stage deposes the staged, and – to quote the title of a 2004 Kunstmuseum Solothurn exhibition featuring Nashat – succeeds in 'overthrowing the king in his own mind'.

Taken from Russian novelist Andrei Bely's masterpiece, *Petersburg (*1913), about a son's plot to assassinate his Tsarist official father, this quote asserts that power can only be overturned by first feigning submission, then sneaking up to the throne and taking a swift kick at one of its weak, rotted legs. The best instant to strike is when the powerful are caught offguard: when bodyweight shifts as an ankle turns or in a moment of repose when one foot bears the body's entire physical mass. As if to illustrate these subtle points of weakness, Nashat truncates downloaded images of classical, virile, bronze figures at the shins and the calves (*Foot-Height Abridged Hercules in Repose* and *Calf-Height Abridged Satyre*, both 2008). Two larger inkjet prints, *The Calf of Adrian Hermanides* (2008) and *The Foot of Adrian Hermanides* (2008), also 'abridged' but considerably less monumental, are photographs Nashat took of an artist colleague. In the first, a bare leg lies limp, thrown upon the seat of a stool and turned to show its calf; in the second, a naked foot is planted flat on a cardboard

Shahryar Nashat
*The Foot of Adrian
Hermanides*
2008
Inkjet print
119×84 cm

box, its toes tensed and contracted. Nashat offers these oft-overlooked points of tension, vital to a figureís stability, to a desirous and fetishizing gaze.

When a regime falls, the monuments to its figureheads are broken off at the ankles and toppled from their pedestals. Suddenly, all points of reference are lost. The displaced desperately seek a new ruler who can assure them a defined place in the world. Who is the subject and who is the object in this exchange? In Nashat's video *Modern Body Comedy* (2006), two men act out these questions in a choreographed performance in which a pair of shoes and socks, a false moustache and a broken chair are the props for their power games. When one man kneels to lace the other's shoes, his gesture seems obsequious; yet it could also be an expression of dominance,

as he has, in effect, immobilized his partner. The film ends with the two actors on the floor in a confused embrace, somewhere between tickling and wrestling.

Like Uccello's fresco, Nashat's work sends tremors through the ground between the subject and the object. Human existence, Nashat seems to say, is a constant struggle for dominance, played out not just between the self and the other, but also schizophrenically between the self and itself. Nashat's work dismisses the dominant/subordinate dichotomy, demonstrating that such concepts are illusions conjured to reorder the muddled superimposition of roles, identities and meanings we encounter in daily life.
Emily Verla Bovino

Shahryar Nashat

Tariq Alvi
Matter to Matter
2008
Collaged magazines
Dimensions variable

bandaged woman, who observes Killian and Bellamy from an undefined distance, Bellamy writes: 'When they finally reach him, Tariq tells them about an image he found on the web of two teen boys with their heads in nooses. "They were hanged", he says, "because they were gay." "Who hung them?" Dodie asks. "The entire community."'

That stark image appeared as one element of a mixed-media collage titled *The Importance of Hanging* (2008), suspended beneath a lavender transparency gel and surrounded by prices cut out from sales circulars. The image of the two young Muslims was at the centre of the picture, their masked executioners half-visible as they placed nooses around the boys' necks. ('In later images the hanged boys are swinging,' the bandaged lady reminds us, 'their blindfolds have been pulled down and their hands are bound behind their backs.') The elegance of the picture's visual form belied its blunt iconographic message. Or did it? Alvi's collage lacked the elemental clarity of John Heartfield's designs for *Arbeiter-Ilustrierte-Zeitung* or Martha Rosler's series 'Bringing the War Back Home: House Beautiful' (1967–72); instead we were offered sickening conflations. Consumer value is commensurate with the 'cost' of life; execution becomes mere 'image', immersed in a field of radical reductions – the abstraction and flattening that Karl Marx argues are inherent to value as bare number. To 'think' this picture was to enter a vortex and never return.

Matter to Matter and *QX International* (both 2008) presented a diptych of sorts. Mounted on one wall was a single framed issue of *QX Magazine International*, 'a guide to the gay scene in London'. Across the room was a second copy of the same magazine, torn into tiny shreds and then reconstituted into clusters of roughly uniform colour. Attached directly to the gallery wall, they created a constellation of disconnected masses, fragments of text and severed plots of flesh emerging from monochrome asteroids.

The first impression was that Alvi had acted out a calm and meticulous rage against the magazine – its bare consumerism, its presentation of eroticized bodies and social occasions as impoverished opportunities to buy and sell. Yet severed from their original context, the rainbow clusters referred ambiguously back to the Utopian *Map of San Francisco*. And perhaps further back as well, to Hélio Oiticica's 'body of colour', Ellsworth Kelly's *Spectrum Colours Arranged by Chance* (1951) and Piet Mondrian's 'new plastic expressions'. From comminuted elements of gay pop life were made to emerge, to borrow the words of Alvi's London gallerist, Martin McGeown, 'particles of pictorial energy, bits of broken language, fragments of speech, invented words, a new language, freshly minted'. Haunted by those boys, their image, the appalling price they paid for who they were, Alvi's 'new life' remains inchoate, pure potentiality, but to his credit still tactile, still polymorphous – still present. You can't walk away from love.

Julian Myers

2nd Floor Projects, San Francisco, USA

Made in 1996, Tariq Alvi's *Map of San Francisco* transformed a conventional print map of the city into a saturated profusion of primary colours – a kaleidoscopic pattern evoking both Modernist colour grids and the 'gay flag' designed by Gilbert Baker in 1978. The affectionately disfigured map longed for San Francisco from a distant remove, as a faraway Utopia of sexual freedom and polymorphous perversity – Alvi had recently graduated from the Jan van Eyck Academie in Maastricht and was then living in the Netherlands. A meditation on sexuality, consumerism, value, disease and disability, his 2005 presentation at the CCA Wattis Institute for Contemporary Art, San Francisco, took a darker tone. Called 'Super-Pride and Super-Prejudice', the exhibition again invoked the rainbow flag, but this time as a piece

of disconcerting queer kitsch – a massive T-shirt with rainbow letters spelling out 'I ♥ Super-HIV' and a wheelchair covered in cut-outs from gay pornography suspended upside down from the ceiling.

Mounted at 2nd Floor Projects – an apartment gallery located in the Mission and run by the artist Margaret Tedesco – this latest show, titled 'Hanging Matters', was a sort of homecoming for the artist. It marked his engagement with the writers Kevin Killian and Dodie Bellamy, to whom Alvi had dedicated two works in the show, folded and framed white handkerchiefs: one for each (*Two Hankies*, 2005). Killian's was marked with a stylized horse-head, Bellamy's with the bust of a woman covered, except for her closed eyes and closed lips, with bandages. For the exhibition Bellamy produced a mesmerizing and self-reflexive text titled, after Alvi's gift, *The Bandaged Lady*. In one passage she recounts a phone conversation with Alvi about an image of a hanging. In the voice of the

Tariq Alvi

Institute of Contemporary Art, Philadelphia, USA

Some contemporary art exhibitions benefit from a simple, constrained premise, and 'The Puppet Show' was clearly one of them. No real confusion about what lies ahead as your mind scrolls through all the numerous puppet projects that you have seen over time. Curated by Ingrid Schaffner, senior curator of the Institute of Contemporary Art, Philadelphia, and Carin Kuoni, Director of the Vera List Center for Art and Politics, this quirky show explored the puppet as proxy, prosthetic, alibi and childhood bugbear.

Entering the exhibition, one traversed a theatrical 'backstage' wooden construction designed by Terence Gower, where Andy Warhol's hand puppets of Spiro Agnew and Richard Nixon greeted visitors and introduced the rest of the puppet community, a smattering of which was displayed on shelves behind chicken wire. I couldn't help but recall the terrifying delight that Punch and Judy shows provoke, with their rancorous childhood conflicts and traumas played out in cloth, wood and lots of stuffing. I was suddenly immersed in a world of small and large creatures alike (ants, monsters, large-lipped children, rickety Victorian crones, a dangling ostrich). One small video screen played Lotte Reiniger's animation *Prince Achmed* (1926), while another showed the band Japanther playing in their marionette collaboration with Dan Graham and Tony Oursler, *Don't Trust Anyone over Thirty* (2004).

Clearly puppets come with a certain creepiness factor. Indeed, the creepy and the contemporary have been friends for a long time. The introductory wall text cited Alfred Jarry's staging of *Ubu Roi* in 1896 as a signature moment, when a puppet for grown-ups danced around a Parisian

theatre uttering the popular expletive '*merde!*' Yes, excrement and childhood: no wonder Sigmund Freud found puppets so compelling. In much contemporary art the puppet continues to appear as surrogate, joker, childhood spectre and physical and psychological prosthetic.

In the main gallery space was Dennis Oppenheim's *Theme for a Major Hit* (1974), a kinetic sculpture of five marionettes tapping their feet and rattling the floor in a percussive cacophony as their heads jiggled to the pulsing rhythm of the controlling strings being lifted and lowered by gears high above. Elsewhere, more sculptural works were on display, including examples by Anne Chu, Annette Messager, Kiki Smith, Louise Bourgeois, Maurizio Cattelan and Nayland Blake. Chu's clunky geological *Landscape Marionette II* (2003) was mesmerizing, as were Messager's suspended pencil-pierced pillows in *Faire Parade* (1995). Mike Kelley's sculpture *Gussied Up* (1992) – furniture with children's clothes adorning bedposts and table legs – made particularly evident the curious corporeal confusion that puppets and dummies elicit and express as stand-ins for our own perplexing body-images.

The curators were clearly amenable to teasing out the sculptural and performative implications that puppetry and slapstick buffoonery provide, bringing a diverse range of contemporary artists into dialogue with one other. Many criss-crossing themes about behaviour and volition thus emerged, ranging from the hypnotized performances of Matt Mullican to Bruce Nauman's *Violent Incident (Man/Woman Segment)* (1986), which

Guy Ben Ner
Elia: A Story of an Ostrich Chick
2003
Production photograph

Christian Jankowski
Puppet Conference
2003
DVD still

recasts gender relationships as a series of sadomasochistic gestures. It became clear that, among its many uses, the puppet frequently serves in art as a surrogate for artistic frustration and self-reflection. Paul McCarthy's video *Painter* (1995) depicts an obsessive artist visited by collectors who, equipped with oversized noses, grovel to sniff his proffered butt. In 2005 Rirkrit Tiravanija and Philippe Parreno produced marionette *doppelgängers* of themselves and of Liam Gillick and Hans Ulrich Obrist that were available for conferences. The video shows their diminutive selves discussing Obrist's book of interviews. Although narcissistic, self-referential and a tad cloying, one can't help but feel that these projects emerged out of the basic condition of helplessness and programmed behaviour.

Christian Jankowski's *Puppet Conference* (2003) also defied certain expectations, re-enacting the conference atmosphere we all know and sometimes dread with a myriad of plushy muppet-like panel participants such as Lamb Chop, Grover and the bow-tied Fozzie Bear. Instead of opting for easy art-world satire, Jankowski inserted himself into the action as moderator and host, asking the attending puppets to describe their 'work' and indulge in a little soul-searching. Although seemingly pat and ready-made, 'The Puppet Show' proved surprisingly fresh and deeply enjoyable, suggesting multiple meanings for the proliferation of all these pint-sized proxies and surrogates, and tugging at the strings of our collective imagination.

Nato Thompson

The Puppet Show

Claes Oldenburg standing next to *Lipstick (Ascending) on Caterpillar Tracks* 1969 Installation view, Yale University, Connecticut, USA

If you could live with only one piece of art, what would it be?
If I'm choosing, then the most expensive and compact piece we can find.

Tom Burr

What images keep you company in the space where you work?
I try to keep a relatively good self-image nearby. I also like pictures of people I know or people I wish I knew.

What was the first piece of art that really mattered to you?
The first piece of art that captivated me was Claes Oldenburg's *Lipstick (Ascending) on Caterpillar Tracks* (1969/1974), which was built and installed in a corner of the Yale University campus when I was young. I think the original version was sort of an *ad hoc* structure, painted plywood, and was assembled by Oldenburg and students as a form of protest against the Vietnam War and as a platform for public speakers. It was a large red cosmetic phallus mounted on top of the bulky base of an army tank. I think later it was redone in Cor-Ten steel and placed somewhere else on the campus as a more permanent monument. I think I saw both versions, but I may be making that up. I liked what it looked like, then and now, and I liked the idea of the two versions: the original bound up in theatrical action and the later one built to withstand the elements and time, becoming sedate and settled like the buildings around it. I always thought the second should have ivy growing over it.

What film has most influenced you?
Rainer Werner Fassbinder's *Querelle* (1982).

What is your favourite title of an art work?
I like my own titles. I just did a piece called *Bent, Bandaged, Beat up, Beat up again, and Bewildered* (2008), which I find myself repeating in my head. Or two other recent pieces I did: *Pants* and *Black Pants* (both 2008). Yesterday I went to see Isa

Genzken's show at Hauser & Wirth in London, 'Ground Zero', and I liked all her titles. *White Horses* (2008), for instance, I think is good. *Hotel Tools* (2008) is wonderful. I did a large group of collages last summer to mark the passing of August, or to slow it down, and I just had two of them framed for the White Columns benefit in May. I call them *Horse Shit, Diptych*.

What do you wish you knew?
Like many people, I wish I knew how to play the piano.

What should change?
Certain government policies, the rising cost of living, the omnipresence of religion, bad fashion, back pain. Things like that.

What could you imagine doing if you didn't do what you do?
I can imagine doing lots of things. I'm drawn to people who seem to have a more fractured and fragmented professional life than I do, who wear many hats. This is some sort of ideal for me, but it's elusive at the same time. There is a singularity of purpose that is required of artists these days in order to get things done. Maybe it was always the case.

What music are you listening to?
I'm not listening to any music right now. Just an abnormally loud hum coming from my laptop, which worries me, and some traffic in the distance. I'm in a hotel at the moment, so I am also listening for the sound of my room service breakfast coming down the hall.

What are you reading?
The books on the floor of my hotel room include *Conspicuous Consumption* (1899) by Thorstein

Veblen – I haven't read it yet, just thumbed through it. The back covers declares: 'With its wry portrayal of a shallow, materialistic "leisure class" obsessed by clothes, cars, consumer goods and climbing the social ladder, this withering satire on modern capitalism is as pertinent today as when it was written over a century ago.' There is also a copy of *Walter Benjamin's Archive* (2007), the catalogue from the 'Duchamp, Man Ray, Picabia' exhibition at Tate Modern and a copy of *New York* magazine.

What do you like the look of?
I like the look of my breakfast, which finally just arrived.

What is art for?
I think there might be some clues in the Oldenburg experience I mentioned, and the schizophrenic logic of that *Lipstick ...* piece, if you consider it a two-step process or two parts of the same thing. The first *Lipstick ...* embodied a social energy born of necessity, like a politically charged barn-raising. The second version became an enduring but complacent, solid and mute monument. This reminds me again of Genzken's exhibition, particularly the upstairs space of the gallery called the American Room. Her 'Ground Zero' proposal suggested spaces or buildings that had a social purpose (a sexy disco and a hospital, among several others), places that had public access and functions other than office towers and different from monuments.

Tom Burr lives in New York. He will be exhibiting new work at Stuart Shave/Modern Art, London, in the spring of 2009.